I0015751

Practical Ansible

Learn how to automate infrastructure, manage configuration, and deploy applications

James Freeman
Fabio Alessandro Locati
Daniel Oh

BIRMINGHAM—MUMBAI

Practical Ansible

Copyright © 2023 Packt Publishing

All rights reserved. No part of this book may be reproduced, stored in a retrieval system, or transmitted in any form or by any means, without the prior written permission of the publisher, except in the case of brief quotations embedded in critical articles or reviews.

Every effort has been made in the preparation of this book to ensure the accuracy of the information presented. However, the information contained in this book is sold without warranty, either express or implied. Neither the authors, nor Packt Publishing or its dealers and distributors, will be held liable for any damages caused or alleged to have been caused directly or indirectly by this book.

Packt Publishing has endeavored to provide trademark information about all of the companies and products mentioned in this book by the appropriate use of capitals. However, Packt Publishing cannot guarantee the accuracy of this information.

Group Product Manager: Preet Ahuja

Publishing Product Manager: Preet Ahuja

Book Project Managers: Aryaa Joshi & Ashwini Gowda

Senior Editor: Romy Dias

Technical Editor: Rajat Sharma

Copy Editor: Safis Editing

Proofreader: Safis Editing

Indexer: Hemangini Bari

Production Designer: Joshua Misquitta

DevRel Marketing Coordinator: Rohan Dhobal

First published: June 2020
Second edition: September 2023
Production reference: 1300823

Published by Packt Publishing Ltd.
Grosvenor House
11 St Paul's Square
Birmingham
B3 1RB, UK.

ISBN 978-1-80512-997-4

www.packtpub.com

In memory of my grandfather Ray, who always demonstrated the power of calm and joy in situations where many would succumb to stress.

– James Freeman

To everyone that sees automation and simplification as something to pursue.

– Fabio Alessandro Locati

To my son, Justin, and daughter, Jennie, for their continued support, patience, and encouragement throughout the long process of writing this book.

– Daniel Oh

Contributors

About the authors

James Freeman is an accomplished IT professional with over 25 years' experience in the technology industry. He has more than a decade of first-hand experience in solving real-world enterprise problems in production environments using Ansible, open source, and AWS. As part of this work, he frequently introduces Ansible as a new technology to businesses and CTOs for the first time. In addition, he has co-authored five books and one video training course on Ansible, facilitated bespoke Ansible workshops and training sessions, and presented at both international conferences and meetups on Ansible.

I would like to thank Raminta Rimkute and Nicki Chartrand for their constant belief and support, for seeing something in me, and for believing that I'm capable of more than I ever thought possible.

Fabio Alessandro Locati – commonly known as *Fale* – is an EMEA associate principal solutions architect at Red Hat, a public speaker, an author, and an open source contributor. His primary areas of expertise are Linux, automation, security, and cloud technologies. Fale has more than 15 years of working experience in IT, with many of them spent consulting for various organizations, including dozens of Fortune 500 companies. Fale has written *Learning Ansible 2.7*, *Learning Ansible 2*, and *OpenStack Cloud Security*, and has been part of the review process of multiple books.

I would like to thank the many people that, during my life, have motivated me to learn more, and that helped me in the process of writing this book.

Daniel Oh is a Java Champion and senior principal developer advocate at Red Hat. He works to evangelize building cloud-native microservices and serverless functions with cloud-native runtimes to developers. He also continues to contribute to various open source cloud projects and ecosystems as a **Cloud Native Computing Foundation** (**CNCF**) ambassador to accelerate hybrid cloud platform adoption in a variety of enterprises. Daniel also speaks at technical seminars, workshops, and meetups to elaborate on new emerging technologies for enterprise developers, SREs, platform engineers, and DevOps teams.

*I would like to first and foremost thank my loving and patient wife and kids for their continued support, patience, and encouragement throughout the long process of writing this book. Thanks also to the **subject-matter experts** (SMEs) in the Ansible community project for their continuous contribution with their practical code – obviously critical references for this book.*

About the reviewers

Werner Dijkerman is a freelance-platform, Kubernetes (certified), and Dev(Sec)Ops engineer. He's currently focused on, and working with, cloud-native solutions and tools, including AWS, Ansible, Kubernetes, and Terraform. He also focuses on infrastructure as code and monitoring the correct "thing," with tools such as Zabbix, Prometheus, and the ELK stack. He has a passion for automating everything and avoiding doing anything that resembles manual work. He is an active reader of comics, self-care/psychology, and IT-related books, where he is a technical reviewer of various books about DevOps, CI/CD, and Kubernetes.

Rewanth Tammana is a security ninja, open source contributor, AWS community builder, and full-time freelancer. Previously, he was a senior security architect at the National Bank of Dubai. He is passionate about DevSecOps, the cloud, and container security, and he has contributed over 17,000 lines of code to Nmap and holds industry certifications such as CKS and CKA.

Rewanth presents at security conferences such as Black Hat, DEF CON, HITB, CRESTCon, and PHDays. Rewanth was recognized as a Bugcrowd MVP researcher in 2018, having identified vulnerabilities in various organizations. He has published an IEEE research paper on an offensive attack in machine learning and security, and he was selected for the prestigious Google Summer of Code.

Table of Contents

3

Defining Your Inventory   77

4

Playbooks and Roles   103

Part 2: Expanding the Capabilities of Ansible

5

6

7

8

Coding Best Practices   235

9

Advanced Ansible Topics   259

Part 3:Using Ansible in an Enterprise

10

11

12

Troubleshooting and Testing Strategies   339

13

Getting Started with Ansible Automation Controller   355

14

Execution Environments   373

Assessments   385

Index   389

Other Books You May Enjoy   396

Preface

Welcome to *Practical Ansible – Second Edition*, your guide to going from being a beginner to a proficient Ansible automation engineer in the space of a few chapters. This book will provide you with the knowledge and skills required to perform your very first installation and automation tasks with Ansible and take you on a journey from simple one-line automation commands that perform single tasks all the way through to writing your own complex custom code to extend the functionality of Ansible, and even automate cloud and container infrastructures. Throughout the book, practical examples will be given for you to not just read about Ansible automation but also actually try it out for yourself and understand how the code works. You will then be well placed to automate your infrastructure with Ansible in a manner that is scalable, repeatable, and reliable.

Who this book is for

This book is for anyone who has IT tasks they want to automate, from mundane day-to-day housekeeping tasks to complex infrastructure-as-code-based deployments. It is intended to appeal to anyone with prior experience with Linux-based environments who wants to get up to speed quickly with Ansible automation and to a wide range of individuals, whether system administrators, DevOps engineers, or architects looking at overall automation strategy. It will even serve hobbyists well. Basic proficiency in Linux system administration and maintenance tasks is assumed; however, no previous Ansible or automation experience is required.

What this book covers

Chapter 1, Getting Started with Ansible, provides the steps you need for your very first installation of Ansible, and explains how to get up and running with this powerful form of automation.

Chapter 2, Understanding the Fundamentals of Ansible, explores the Ansible framework, gives you a sound understanding of the fundamentals of the Ansible language, and explains how to work with the various command-line tools that it comprises.

Chapter 3, Defining Your Inventory, gives you details about the Ansible inventory, its purpose, and how to create your own inventories and work with them. It also explores the differences between static and dynamic inventories, and when to leverage each type.

Chapter 4, Playbooks and Roles, provides you with an in-depth look at creating your own automation code in Ansible in the form of playbooks, and how to enable effective reuse of that code through roles.

Chapter 5, Creating and Consuming Modules, teaches you about Ansible modules and their purpose, and then provides you with the steps required to write your own module, and even to submit it to the Ansible project for inclusion.

Chapter 6, Creating and Consuming Collections, explores Ansible Collections, covering their design, intention, and why they are essential to the future of Ansible. We then proceed to guide you through the creation and consumption of your own collection to give you first-hand experience.

Chapter 7, Creating and Consuming Plugins, explains the purpose of Ansible plugins, and covers the various types of plugins that Ansible uses. It then explains how to write your own plugins, and explains how to submit your code to the Ansible project.

Chapter 8, Coding Best Practices, provides an in-depth look at the best practices that you should adhere to while writing Ansible automation code to ensure that your solutions are manageable, easy to maintain, and easy to scale.

Chapter 9, Advanced Ansible Topics, explores some of the more advanced Ansible options and language directives, which are valuable in a scenario such as performing a roll-out to a highly available cluster. It also explains how to work with jump hosts to automate tasks on secure networks, and how to encrypt your variable data at rest.

Chapter 10, Network Automation with Ansible, provides a detailed look at the importance of network automation, explains why Ansible is especially well suited to this task, and takes you through practical examples of how to connect to a variety of network devices with Ansible.

Chapter 11, Container and Cloud Management, explores the manner in which Ansible supports working with both cloud and container platforms and teaches you how to build containers with Ansible, along with methods to deploy infrastructure as code in a cloud environment using Ansible.

Chapter 12, Troubleshooting and Testing Strategies, teaches you how to test and debug your Ansible code, and gives you robust strategies to handle errors and unexpected failures both with playbooks and the agentless connections on which Ansible relies.

Chapter 13, Getting Started with Ansible Automation Controller, provides an introduction to Ansible Automation Controller and its upstream open source counterpart, AWX, demonstrating how this powerful tool provides a valuable complement to Ansible, especially in large, multi-user environments such as enterprises.

Chapter 14, Execution Environment, provides an introduction to Execution Environments, demonstrating how to create them, how to share them, and how to use them both on the command line and within Ansible Automation Controller.

To get the most out of this book

All the chapters of this book assume you have access to at least one Linux machine running a relatively recent Linux distribution. All examples in this book were tested on Fedora 38 and Ubuntu Server 22.04, but should work on just about any other mainstream distribution. You will require Ansible 2.15 installed on at least one test machine too – the installation steps will be covered in the very first chapter. Later versions of Ansible should also work, though there may be some subtle differences, and you should refer to the release notes and porting guide for newer Ansible versions. The final two chapters also take you through the installation of AWX, but this assumes a Linux server with Ansible installed. Most of the examples demonstrate automation across more than one host, and, if you have more Linux hosts available, you will be able to get more out of the examples; however, they can be scaled up or down as you require. Having more hosts is not mandatory, but enables you to get more out of the book.

Software/hardware covered in the book	Operating system requirements
At least one Linux server (a virtual or physical machine).	Fedora 38 or Ubuntu Server 22.04, though other mainstream distributions (including newer versions of these operating systems) should work.
Ansible 8.0	As above.
AWX release 22.4.0 or later	As above.

If you are using the digital version of this book, we advise you to type the code yourself or access the code from the book's GitHub repository (a link is available in the next section). Doing so will help you avoid any potential errors related to the copying and pasting of code.

Download the example code files

You can download the example code files for this book from GitHub at `https://github.com/PacktPublishing/Practical-Ansible-Second-Edition`. If there's an update to the code, it will be updated in the GitHub repository.

We also have other code bundles from our rich catalog of books and videos available at `https://github.com/PacktPublishing/`. Check them out!

Conventions used

There are a number of text conventions used throughout this book.

`Code in text`: Indicates code words in text, database table names, folder names, filenames, file extensions, pathnames, dummy URLs, user input, and Twitter handles. Here is an example: "The first is called `ansible-core`, and this contains the Ansible runtime code (such as the `ansible-playbook` command, which we'll see in use later), as well as some built-in functionality that is core to all playbooks and roles."

A block of code is set as follows:

```
tasks:
- name: Install/Update to the latest of Apache Web Server
  ansible.builtin.apt:
    name: apache2
    state: latest
```

When we wish to draw your attention to a particular part of a code block, the relevant lines or items are set in bold:

```
handlers:
- name: Restart the Apache Web Server
  ansible.builtin.service:
    name: apache2
    state: restarted
```

Any command-line input or output is written as follows:

```
$ python3 --version
Python 3.10.6
```

Bold: Indicates a new term, an important word, or words that you see onscreen. For instance, words in menus or dialog boxes appear in **bold**. Here is an example: "Select **System info** from the **Administration** panel."

> **Tips or important notes**
> Appear like this.

Get in touch

Feedback from our readers is always welcome.

General feedback: If you have questions about any aspect of this book, email us at customercare@ packtpub.com and mention the book title in the subject of your message.

Errata: Although we have taken every care to ensure the accuracy of our content, mistakes do happen. If you have found a mistake in this book, we would be grateful if you would report this to us. Please visit www.packtpub.com/support/errata and fill in the form.

Piracy: If you come across any illegal copies of our works in any form on the internet, we would be grateful if you would provide us with the location address or website name. Please contact us at copyright@packt.com with a link to the material.

If you are interested in becoming an author: If there is a topic that you have expertise in and you are interested in either writing or contributing to a book, please visit authors.packtpub.com.

Share your thoughts

Once you've read *Practical Ansible - Second Edition*, we'd love to hear your thoughts! Scan the QR code below to go straight to the Amazon review page for this book and share your feedback.

https://packt.link/r/180512997X

Your review is important to us and the tech community and will help us make sure we're delivering excellent quality content.

Download a free PDF copy of this book

Thanks for purchasing this book!

Do you like to read on the go but are unable to carry your print books everywhere?

Is your eBook purchase not compatible with the device of your choice?

Don't worry, now with every Packt book you get a DRM-free PDF version of that book at no cost.

Read anywhere, any place, on any device. Search, copy, and paste code from your favorite technical books directly into your application.

The perks don't stop there, you can get exclusive access to discounts, newsletters, and great free content in your inbox daily

Follow these simple steps to get the benefits:

1. Scan the QR code or visit the link below

https://packt.link/free-ebook/9781805129974

2. Submit your proof of purchase

3. That's it! We'll send your free PDF and other benefits to your email directly

Part 1: Learning the Fundamentals of Ansible

In this section, we will take a look at the very fundamentals of Ansible. We will start with the process of installing Ansible and then we will get to grips with the fundamentals, including the basics of the language and ad-hoc commands. We will then explore Ansible inventories, before looking at writing our very first playbooks and roles to complete multi-stage automation tasks.

This section contains the following chapters:

- *Chapter 1, Getting Started with Ansible*
- *Chapter 2, Understanding the Fundamentals of Ansible*
- *Chapter 3, Defining Your Inventory*
- *Chapter 4, Playbooks and Roles*

1

Getting Started with Ansible

Ansible enables you to easily deploy applications and systems consistently and repeatably using native communication protocols such as SSH and WinRM. As a result, Ansible is agentless and so requires nothing to be installed on the managed systems (except for Python, which, these days, is present on most systems). As a result, it enables you to build a simple yet robust automation platform for your environment.

Ansible is straightforward to install and also comes packaged for many modern systems. Its architecture is serverless as well as agentless, so it has a minimal footprint. You can choose to run it from a central server or your own laptop—the choice is entirely yours. You can manage anything from a single host to hundreds of thousands of remote hosts from one Ansible control machine. All remote machines can be managed by Ansible, and with sufficient playbooks created, you may never have to log in to any of these machines individually again.

In this chapter, we will begin to teach you practical skills to cover the very fundamentals of Ansible, starting with how to install Ansible on a wide variety of operating systems. We will then look at how to configure Windows hosts to enable them to be managed with Ansible automation, before delving in greater depth into how Ansible connects to its target hosts. We'll then look at node requirements and how to validate your Ansible installation, before finally looking at how to obtain and run the very latest Ansible source code if you wish to either contribute to its development or gain access to the very latest features.

In this chapter, we will cover the following topics:

- Installing and configuring Ansible

- Getting to know your Ansible installation

- Managed node requirements

Technical requirements

Ansible has a fairly minimal set of system requirements—as such, you should find that if you have a machine (either a laptop, a server, or a **virtual machine** (**VM**)) that is capable of running Python, then you will be able to run Ansible on it. Later in this chapter, we will demonstrate the installation methods for Ansible on a variety of operating systems—it is hence left to you to decide which operating systems are right for you.

The one exception to the preceding statement is Microsoft Windows—although there are Python environments available for Windows, there is as yet no native build of Ansible for Windows. Readers running more recent versions of Windows will be able to install Ansible using **Windows Subsystem for Linux** (henceforth, **WSL**) by following the procedures outlined later for their chosen WSL environment (for example, if you install Ubuntu on WSL, you should simply follow the instructions given in this chapter for installing Ansible on Ubuntu).

Installing and configuring Ansible

Ansible is written in Python and, as such, can be run on a wide range of systems. This includes the most popular flavors of Linux, FreeBSD, and macOS. The one exception to this is Windows, where though native Python distributions exist, there is as yet no native Ansible build. As a result, your best option at the time of writing is to install Ansible under WSL, proceeding as if you were running on a native Linux host.

Once you have established the system on which you wish to run Ansible, the installation process is normally simple. In the following sections, we will discuss how to install Ansible on a wide range of different systems so that most readers should be able to get up and running with Ansible in a matter of minutes.

Understanding Ansible version numbers

When the previous edition of this book was published, Ansible followed a relatively simple version numbering scheme. All releases of Ansible included all the modules, plugins, and other code accepted into the Ansible release (which was version 2.9 in the previous edition of this book).

This worked well for many years but also created a problem for the maintainers of Ansible—as its popularity and adoption grew, the number of modules (the lifeblood of Ansible, which perform the actual automation tasks you will run) numbered in the thousands. Releasing these with the core Ansible software meant that if a bug was discovered in a module, or perhaps a new release with new features was available, then there had to be a new release of Ansible before end users could take advantage of this. Not only did this slow down releases of new module code, but it also created a significant workload for the Ansible maintainers.

As a direct result of this, Ansible was split into two separate packages. The first is called `ansible-core`, and this contains just the Ansible runtime code (such as the `ansible-playbook` command, which we'll see in use later), as well as some built-in functionality that is core to all playbooks and roles. The `ansible-core` package follows the *classic* Ansible versioning scheme, and so where the previous release of this book was written around Ansible 2.9, this version of the book will be based around `ansible-core` 2.15.

All the modules and plugins that provided the functionality present in the 2.9 release (the last release before the package split was implemented) are contained in the **Ansible community package** release. This follows semantic versioning, meaning that, as the current release at the time of writing is 8.0, the next major release will be 9.0.

To enable this separate management of `ansible-core` and modules, plugins, and the like, an implementation called **collections** was created. Collections are individually bundled sets of modules, plugins, and roles intended for a specific purpose; we'll be learning all about these in detail in *Chapter 6, Creating and Consuming Collections*, so don't worry if this all seems a bit daunting—it will all become clear later in the book.

Each release of the Ansible community package is dependent on a specific version of the `ansible-core` package, and the 8.0 release we will use in this book depends upon `ansible-core` version 2.15. You can find the change log and other details about the 8.0 release here: `https://github.com/ansible-community/ansible-build-data/blob/8.0.0/8/CHANGELOG-v8.rst#v8-0-0`.

The beauty of this separation of code lies in this: let's say you want to create a playbook or role based around new functionality in a module; you can install an updated collection containing the module without updating your entire Ansible installation (or, indeed, waiting for the next release, as you would have had to until after version 2.9 was released).

With this information in hand, we'll proceed to explore the specifics of installing Ansible on a variety of systems, but it's important to discuss this upfront as if you've had exposure to any of the 2.x releases of Ansible, the new versioning scheme will look rather different.

If you'd like to read more details on the rationale behind the new versioning scheme, release cadence, and how it works, the official Ansible documentation here has more details: `https://docs.ansible.com/ansible/latest/reference_appendices/release_and_maintenance.html`.

Installing Ansible on Linux and FreeBSD

The release cycle for Ansible is usually about six months, and during this short release cycle, there are normally many changes, from minor bug fixes to major ones, new features, and even sometimes fundamental changes to the language. At the end of each release cycle, you would expect to see a new version of the Ansible community package (for example, 8.0), and a corresponding release of the `ansible-core` package (for example, 2.15). While there are native packages still built for many operating systems, your mileage will vary as to how up to date these are, and the recommended way to install Ansible is now to use the PIP package manager for Python.

There will, of course, be exceptions to this. For example, if you are using a commercial Linux distribution such as **Red Hat Enterprise Linux (RHEL)**, especially to perform workflows supported by your operating system vendor, then you should make sure you use the packages provided by that vendor. They will invariably also provide instructions on how to install Ansible.

This does bring with it a separate challenge. When Ansible was installed using your native package manager such as yum, dnf, or apt, it would be updated along with your system. When using PIP, you will need to ensure that you update Ansible separately (we will show you how shortly).

Talking of upgrades, most playbooks that were created under the 2.x releases of Ansible will still work today, and you will often find that updating does not specifically cause any issues. However, it is strongly recommended that you read the porting notes for each release to ensure your code remains functional as you intended it. As such, an Ansible upgrade should be a planned activity, and it is almost certainly not desirable to patch Ansible in line with your operating system. In short, the move away from native operating system packages to PIP package management is unlikely to cause you any issues, and may even prove beneficial.

Suppose you want to install Ansible on a node—the following procedure should work on any version of Linux or FreeBSD provided the required version of Python is available:

1. Check that Python is installed on your intended node—henceforth, we will refer to this as the **control node**, as it will be the one automating (controlling) tasks on other **managed nodes**, on which Ansible does not need to be installed. You can check whether Python is installed and on your PATH using a command such as this:

    ```
    $ python3 --version
    Python 3.10.6
    ```

    Here, you can see that Python 3.10.6 is installed. The minimum requirement for Ansible 8.0 is Python 3.9, so in this instance, we are good to proceed. However, if you find that Python is not present, please refer to the documentation for your operating system for guidance on how to install it.

Tip

Depending upon your system, Python may be run using a command such as python, python3, or python3.10—again, please refer to the documentation for your operating system to learn more. Ansible will work in any of these cases, but it is important to understand how to run Python on your system to complete the rest of this process. Here, we will assume that Python is executed using the python3 command.

---

2. Once you know that Python is installed, the next step is to ensure that the PIP package manager is installed. A successful query of this should look something like this:

```
$ python3 -m pip -V
pip 22.0.2 from /usr/lib/python3/dist-packages/pip (python 3.10)
```

You may see output such as this:

```
$ python3 -m pip -V
/usr/bin/python3: No module named pip
```

In such cases, you will need to install PIP. You can do this by running the following command:

```
$ curl https://bootstrap.pypa.io/get-pip.py -o get-pip.py
$ python3 get-pip.py --user
```

Most operating systems will also have a native package for installing PIP—for example, on Ubuntu, you can install PIP using this command:

```
$ apt install python3-pip
```

How you install PIP doesn't matter—as long as it's installed, you can proceed to the next step.

3. With these steps completed, all that is left is to install Ansible. Now, this might seem like a bit of a departure from the previous ways of installing Ansible, where operating-system-native packages were available for most major operating systems. Yet the beauty of using PIP is that once you've learned how to install and manage Ansible on one system, the method is exactly the same on all others, regardless of whether you are using Fedora, Ubuntu, FreeBSD, Debian, or Gentoo.

    In fact, even if you're using Linux under WSL, the installation method is exactly the same once you've got WSL up and running. The simplest and easiest way to complete your Ansible install is to run the following command:

```
$ python3 -m pip install --user ansible
```

The output should look something like this:

```
jamesf@controlnode:~$ python3 -m pip install --user ansibl
e
Collecting ansible
  Downloading ansible-8.1.0-py3-none-any.whl (44.8 MB)
                               44.8/44.8 MB 6.6 MB/s eta 0:00:00
Collecting ansible-core~=2.15.1
  Downloading ansible_core-2.15.1-py3-none-any.whl (2.2 MB
)
                               2.2/2.2 MB 2.9 MB/s eta 0:00:00
Requirement already satisfied: resolvelib<1.1.0,>=0.5.3 in
 /usr/local/lib/python3.10/dist-packages (from ansible-cor
e~=2.15.1->ansible) (1.0.1)
Requirement already satisfied: cryptography in /usr/lib/py
thon3/dist-packages (from ansible-core~=2.15.1->ansible) (
3.4.8)
Requirement already satisfied: PyYAML>=5.1 in /usr/lib/pyt
hon3/dist-packages (from ansible-core~=2.15.1->ansible) (5
.4.1)
Requirement already satisfied: jinja2>=3.0.0 in /usr/lib/p
ython3/dist-packages (from ansible-core~=2.15.1->ansible)
(3.0.3)
Requirement already satisfied: packaging in /usr/local/lib
/python3.10/dist-packages (from ansible-core~=2.15.1->ansi
ble) (23.1)
Installing collected packages: ansible-core, ansible
  WARNING: The scripts ansible, ansible-config, ansible-co
nnection, ansible-console, ansible-doc, ansible-galaxy, an
sible-inventory, ansible-playbook, ansible-pull and ansibl
e-vault are installed in '/home/jamesf/.local/bin' which i
s not on PATH.
  Consider adding this directory to PATH or, if you prefer
 to suppress this warning, use --no-warn-script-location.
  WARNING: The script ansible-community is installed in '/
home/jamesf/.local/bin' which is not on PATH.
  Consider adding this directory to PATH or, if you prefer
 to suppress this warning, use --no-warn-script-location.
Successfully installed ansible-8.1.0 ansible-core-2.15.1
```

Figure 1.1 – Installing Ansible using PIP on Linux

From the output here, you can see that this command has successfully installed Ansible 8.0.0, along with its dependent package, `ansible-core` 2.15.0—these are the latest versions available at the time of writing.

Also, you will note that Ansible has been installed in /home/james/.local/bin, which is not on the system path, so you won't be able to run commands such as `ansible-playbook` without either updating the path or specifying the full path.

Thus, if you want to run the `ansible-playbook` command, you could run it as follows:

```
$ /home/$USER/.local/bin/ansible-playbook
```

Alternatively, you could update your path, and then you can run the command without needing to specify the full path, as follows:

```
$ export PATH=$PATH:/home/$USER/.local/bin
$ ansible-playbook --version
ansible-playbook [core 2.15.0]
...
```

Of course, this process is only installing Ansible for the current user. This will often be sufficient for most scenarios, but there might be times when you have multiple developers accessing the same control node, and in this case, you would want them all to access one centrally installed copy of Ansible—otherwise, one developer might have version 6.2.0 and another 8.0.0, and your development processes would be inconsistent.

If you want to install Ansible for everyone, you should follow the preceding process up to *step 2* to ensure that PIP is installed. Then, proceed as follows:

1. Install Ansible as the root user by running the following command:

    ```
    $ sudo python3 -m pip install ansible
    ```

2. Now, you will find that Ansible is installed centrally—on my Ubuntu Server 22.04 test system, I see the following results after running this command:

    ```
    $ which ansible-playbook
    /usr/bin/ansible-playbook
    $ ansible-playbook --version
    ansible-playbook [core 2.15.0]
    ...
    ```

PIP has more tricks up its sleeve, however, and we're going to show you another one now—specifying your installation version.

So far, we've just been specifying the ansible package for installation. This works great if you always want the latest and greatest version, but what if, for reasons of development or consistency, you want to install a specific version?

First of all, suppose that you want to install Ansible 6.2.0 because you need to test or develop against that version. You could do this by altering your install command as follows:

```
$ python3 -m pip install --user ansible==6.2.0
```

This will install version 6.2.0 (and the corresponding version of ansible-core, which in this example is 2.13.8) in your local user directory, and if you watch the installation process closely, you'll see that it uninstalls any version you have already installed, even if it's newer. Proceed with caution if this isn't what you want.

> **Tip**
>
> You can, of course, add a `==6.2.0` suffix to any of the installation commands we've given previously to specify the version to be installed. You can also change `6.2.0` to any valid version number. You can explore the available versions by browsing to the following URL: `https://pypi.org/project/ansible/#history`.

Any time you want to upgrade your installed Ansible version (when it has been installed using PIP), you can simply add the `--upgrade` flag to the installation command, as in the following example:

```
$ python3 -m pip install --user --upgrade ansible
```

This example command will install the very latest version, as we have not explicitly set one otherwise.

If you ever need to remove Ansible from your system for any reason, PIP can also handle this—for example, you could run this command to remove the version of Ansible and `ansible-core` that you installed (note that you must specify both—dependencies are not automatically removed):

```
$ python3 -m pip uninstall ansible ansible-core
```

Once you've mastered these commands, you will be set to install, maintain, and uninstall Ansible on all your control nodes.

Working with virtual environments

Another incredibly useful and powerful feature of Python is **virtual environments** (henceforth **venvs**). Venvs are small isolated Python environments that are separate from both the system install of Python (and its libraries) and all other virtual environments. This is incredibly useful for Ansible development. For example, let's say that you have a set of playbooks and roles that you developed under Ansible 2.7.18, and these have all been tested and known to work well. You want to upgrade to Ansible 8.0.0, but you can't take the risk of the existing code being inoperable in case you have to use it.

With venvs, you can have an isolated Ansible 2.7.18 and an isolated Ansible 8.0.0 environment on the same machine, and you can switch between them at will. To get started, follow the process provided next:

1. To start with, you will need to make sure you have both an operable Python environment and PIP, as described earlier in this chapter. Once these are in place, proceed to *step 2*. If you are going back to a version of Ansible as old as 2.7.18, you'll also need to ensure it supports the Python version you are using. My Python environment on Ubuntu Server 22.04 is version 3.10, which is not supported by Ansible 2.7.18. As a result, I'll install Python 2.7, like so:

    ```
    $ sudo apt install python2 python-pip
    ```

2. Ensure that you have the Python module called `venv` installed—this can be installed using PIP, and while most operating systems have a native package for it, Ubuntu Server 22.04 only has it for Python 3. Thus, I installed it with the following command:

    ```
    $ sudo pip2 install virtualenv
    ```

3. You're now ready to create your first venv—let's create one for Ansible 2.7.18:

    ```
    $ python2 -m virtualenv ansible-2.7.18
    ```

4. This will create a venv under the current directory containing the minimum set of files for an operating Python 2 environment. Now, we'll activate the environment (without this step, you will still be using the system Python environment):

    ```
    $ . ./ansible-2.7.18/bin/activate
    (ansible-2.7.18) $
    ```

5. Note how your prompt changes to include the name of the venv when you run this command. Now, you can install Ansible using PIP as before, being sure to specify the version (note the `--user` flag is not required in a venv):

    ```
    (ansible-2.7.18) $ python -m pip install ansible==2.7.18
    ```

6. You'll see Ansible installed via PIP in the usual way. Now, you should be able to query the version of Ansible installed, as follows:

    ```
    (ansible-2.7.18) $ ansible-playbook --version
    ansible-playbook 2.7.18
    ...
    ```

7. That's it—we have Ansible 2.7.18 working in its own Python environment, all isolated from the system and other environments. Now, we can repeat the process for Ansible 8.0.0. You will doubtless have received warnings that Python 2.7 is deprecated during this process (this is to be expected), so we definitely want to use our system-installed version of Python 3.10 for the later version of Ansible. As such, we first want to deactivate our venv so that we can revert to the system-installed Python libraries. Here's how we can do that:

    ```
    (ansible-2.7.18) $ deactivate
    $
    ```

8. Note how your prompt returns to normal, demonstrating that the venv is no longer active. As before, we need to ensure we have the Python venv library installed—however, there is a native package for it, so we can simply install it using this command:

    ```
    $ sudo apt install python3-venv
    ```

9. Now, you can create a Python 3 venv for Ansible 8.0.0 and activate it using the following commands:

```
$  python3 -m venv ansible-8.0.0
$  . ./ansible-8.0.0/bin/activate
(ansible-8.0.0) $
```

10. You can now install Ansible via PIP in the same manner as before:

```
(ansible-8.0.0) $ python3 -m pip install ansible
...
(ansible-8.0.0) $  ansible-playbook --version
ansible-playbook [core 2.15.0]
...
```

11. That's all that is required! You can now switch between your **venvs** at will, simply using the `deactivate` command first, and then using the appropriate `activate` command as demonstrated previously.

In this example, we've used completely different versions of Python and Ansible, yet they remain isolated from each other on the system. As such, you can safely use the older version to run your playbooks while you test your updated code on the newer version. This is quite an extreme example, and you almost certainly won't need to go back to Python 2.7 and Ansible 2.7.18, but it does demonstrate how nicely you can create completely separate Python environments for your development and testing work without needing multiple systems.

Installing from GitHub

It has always been possible to run the very latest development version of Ansible from GitHub, and this is as true today as it has always been. However, there is now one important caveat. If you have done this previously (on releases of Ansible from the 2.x series or earlier, on which the previous edition of this book was based), then you would be working with the complete install of Ansible, including all the modules you might want to use. Since the introduction of collections, you will now only be checking out the code for `ansible-core` when you do this. As such, if you want to test code including module calls, you will need to install or manage collections to go alongside your `ansible-core` setup.

We will explore the management of collections in *Chapter 6*, *Creating and Consuming Collections*, so we won't specifically explore this here—however, for completeness, we will show you how to install `ansible-core` development releases from code.

To do this, follow these steps:

1. Check that you have PIP installed—if you don't, please take a look at how we did this earlier in the chapter. Once you have this (and, by inference, a working Python 3 environment), you can move forward to the next step.

2. Clone the Ansible GitHub repository, like so:

```
$ git clone https://github.com/ansible/ansible.git
$ cd ansible
```

3. Ensure you have all development requirements installed using PIP:

```
$ pip install -r requirements.txt
```

4. Now, source the `hacking` environment setup—this will set your shell up so that you can access the development version of Ansible you just cloned. You will need to do this every time you open a new shell or reconnect to your development host so that the setup is transient, which is normally perfect for development work:

```
$ source ./hacking/env-setup
```

5. You should now be able to use all the usual Ansible commands from this development release, such as `ansible`, `ansible-playbook`, and `ansible-galaxy`.

> **Note**
>
> On Linux distributions such as Ubuntu 22.04, the default Python installation is Python 3, and the binary used to execute it is named `python3`. This won't work on the development install of Ansible, which expects the Python binary to be called `python`. You can fix this on Ubuntu 22.04 by installing a special meta package. To do so, run this command: `sudo apt install python-is-python3`. Or, you could just create a symbolic link from `python3` to `python` by running the following command: `sudo ln -s /usr/bin/python3 /usr/bin/python`.

6. When you run the `env-setup` script, Ansible runs from the source code checkout, and the default inventory file is `/etc/ansible/hosts`, which will not have been created by your code checkout; however, you can optionally specify an inventory file wherever you want on your machine (see *How to build your inventory*, `https://docs.ansible.com/ansible/latest/inventory_guide/intro_inventory.html#inventory-basics-formats-hosts-and-groups`, for more details). The following command provides an example of how you might do this, but obviously, your filename and contents are almost certainly going to vary:

```
$ echo "app01.example.org" > ~/my_ansible_inventory
$ export ANSIBLE_INVENTORY=~/my_ansible_inventory
```

This demonstrates another powerful way to configure Ansible—environment variables. The `ANSIBLE_INVENTORY` variable is used to tell Ansible where to look for its inventory file by default—this is normally `/etc/ansible/hosts`, but in the preceding example, we are changing this to the `my_ansible_inventory` file in our home directory.

> **Tip**
>
> You can learn about the various Ansible configuration variables here: `https://docs.ansible.com/ansible/latest/reference_appendices/config.html#environment-variables`.

7. Once you have completed these steps, you can run Ansible exactly as we have discussed throughout this chapter. The `env-setup` script alters your `PATH` variable so that you don't need to specify the location where you checked out the Ansible repository. By way of example, if you set up your inventory using the environment variable as demonstrated previously, and have cloned the Ansible source and run the `env-setup` script, you could run the ad hoc `ansible.builtin.ping` command that we are now familiar with, as follows:

```
$ ansible all -m ansible.builtin.ping
[WARNING]: You are running the development version of Ansible.
You should only run Ansible from "devel" if you are modifying
the Ansible engine,
or trying out features under development. This is a rapidly
changing source of code and can become unstable at any point.
app01.example.org | SUCCESS => {
    "ansible_facts": {
        "discovered_interpreter_python": "/usr/bin/python3"
    },
    "changed": false,
    "ping": "pong"
}
```

With this in place, you can now work with the development branch of Ansible just as you would if you had installed it by any other means.

8. Of course, the Ansible source tree is constantly changing, and it is unlikely you would just want to stick with the copy you cloned. When the time comes to update it, you don't need to clone a new copy; you can simply update your existing working copy using the following commands:

```
$ git pull -rebase
$ git submodule update --init --recursive
```

This concludes our look at installing Ansible on Linux—now that we've done that, we'll look at some of the specifics of installing Ansible on macOS.

Installing Ansible on macOS

In this section, you will learn how to install Ansible on macOS. The easiest installation method is to use Homebrew, but you could also use the Python package manager (PIP). The procedure for installation with PIP is the same as for Linux, so we won't go over that again here.

Instead, let's get started with the Homebrew installation method, which is probably your fastest and easiest approach on macOS.

If you don't already have Homebrew installed on macOS, you can easily install it, as detailed here:

1. Normally, the two commands shown here are all that is required to install Homebrew on macOS:

    ```
    $ xcode-select –install
    $ /bin/bash -c "$(curl -fsSL https://raw.githubusercontent.com/
    Homebrew/install/HEAD/install.sh)"
    ```

    If you have already installed the Xcode command-line tools for another purpose, you might see the following error message:

    ```
    xcode-select: error: command line tools are already installed,
    use "Software Update" in System Settings to install updates
    ```

    You may want to open the **Software Update** setting from **System Settings** on macOS and check whether updates to the Xcode command-line tools are required, but as long as they are installed, your Homebrew installation should proceed smoothly.

2. If you wish to confirm that your installation of Homebrew was successful, you can run the following command, which will warn you about any potential issues with your install—for example, the following output is warning us that, although Homebrew is installed successfully, it is not in our PATH, and so we may not be able to run any executables without specifying their absolute path:

    ```
    $ brew doctor
    Please note that these warnings are just used to help the
    Homebrew maintainers
    with debugging if you file an issue. If everything you use
    Homebrew for is
    working fine: please don't worry or file an issue; just ignore
    this. Thanks!
    Warning: Homebrew's sbin was not found in your PATH but you have
    installed
    formulae that put executables in /opt/homebrew/sbin.
    Consider setting the PATH for example like so
      echo 'export PATH="/opt/homebrew/sbin:$PATH"' >> ~/.bash_
    profile
    ```

3. Also, check that Python 3 is installed; you can either use the version installed with macOS (normally found in /usr/bin/python3—this should be the case with almost all modern installations of macOS) or you can install a newer version via Homebrew by running the following command:

    ```
    $ brew install python3
    …
    ```

```
$ which python3
/opt/homebrew/bin/python3
$ python3 --version
Python 3.11.3
```

With this completed, you can now proceed to install Ansible.

4. To install Ansible via Homebrew, run the following command:

```
$ brew install ansible
```

5. Now that you have installed Ansible using your preferred method, you can run the `ansible` command as before, and if all has gone according to plan, you will see output similar to the following:

```
$ ansible --version
ansible [core 2.15.0]
  config file = None
  configured module search path = ['/Users/james/.ansible/
plugins/modules', '/usr/share/ansible/plugins/modules']
  ansible python module location = /opt/homebrew/Cellar/
ansible/8.0.0/libexec/lib/python3.11/site-packages/ansible
  ansible collection location = /Users/james/.ansible/
collections:/usr/share/ansible/collections
  executable location = /opt/homebrew/bin/ansible
  python version = 3.11.3 (main, Apr  7 2023, 20:13:31)
[Clang 14.0.0 (clang-1400.0.29.202)] (/opt/homebrew/Cellar/
ansible/8.0.0/libexec/bin/python3.11)
  jinja version = 3.1.2
  libyaml = True
```

6. You can upgrade Ansible easily using the `brew` command, as follows:

```
$ brew upgrade ansible
```

Now that you have learned the steps to install Ansible on macOS, let's see how to configure a Windows host for automation with Ansible.

Configuring Windows hosts for Ansible

As discussed earlier, there is no direct installation method for Ansible on Windows—simply, it is recommended that, where available, you install WSL and install Ansible as if you were running Linux natively, using the processes outlined earlier in this chapter.

Despite this limitation, however, Ansible is not limited to managing just Linux- and BSD-based systems—it is capable of the agentless management of Windows hosts using the native WinRM protocol, with modules and raw commands making use of PowerShell, which is available in every modern Windows installation. In this section, you will learn how to configure Windows to enable task automation with Ansible.

Here are some examples of what Ansible is capable of when automating Windows hosts:

- Gathering facts about remote hosts
- Installing and uninstalling Windows features
- Managing and querying Windows services
- Managing user accounts and a list of users
- Managing packages using Chocolatey (a software repository and accompanying management tool for Windows)
- Performing Windows updates
- Fetching multiple files from a remote machine to the Windows host
- Executing raw PowerShell commands and scripts on target hosts

Ansible allows you to automate tasks on Windows machines by connecting with either a local user or a domain user. You can run actions as an administrator using the Windows `runas` support, just as with the `sudo` command on Linux distributions.

Also, as Ansible is **open source software (OSS)**, it is easy to extend its functionality by creating your own modules in PowerShell or even sending raw PowerShell commands. For example, an InfoSec team could manage filesystem **access control lists (ACLs)**, configure Windows Firewall, and manage hostnames and domain membership with ease, using a mix of native Ansible modules and, where necessary, raw commands.

The Windows host must meet the following requirements for the Ansible control machine to communicate with it:

- Ansible attempts to support all Windows versions that are under either current or extended support from Microsoft, including desktop platforms such as Windows 8.1, 10, and 11, along with server operating systems, including Windows Server 2012 (and R2), 2016, 2019, and 2022.
- You will also need to install PowerShell 3.0 or later and at least .NET 4.0 on your Windows host.
- You will need to create and activate a WinRM listener, which is described in detail later. For security reasons, this is not enabled by default.

Let's look in more detail at how to prepare a Windows host to be automated by Ansible:

1. With regard to prerequisites, you have to make sure PowerShell 3.0 and .NET Framework 4.0 are installed on Windows machines. On many modern Windows versions, you will find these are already in place, but if you're still using an older version of PowerShell or .NET Framework, you will need to upgrade them. You are free to perform this manually, or the following PowerShell

script can handle it automatically for you. You will observe that this script is not from the official Ansible repository—however, the owner is a maintainer and reviewer of the official Ansible repository. Nonetheless, whenever downloading scripts, it is good practice to review the source code and ensure that it is aligned with your security protocols and requirements:

```
[Net.ServicePointManager]::SecurityProtocol = [Net.
SecurityProtocolType]::Tls12
$url = "https://raw.githubusercontent.com/jborean93/ansible-
windows/master/scripts/Upgrade-PowerShell.ps1"
$file = "$env:temp\Upgrade-PowerShell.ps1"
$username = "Administrator"
$password = "Password"

(New-Object -TypeName System.Net.WebClient).DownloadFile($url,
$file)
Set-ExecutionPolicy -ExecutionPolicy Unrestricted -Force

&$file -Version 5.1 -Username $username -Password $password
-Verbose
```

This script works by examining the programs that need to be installed (such as .NET Framework 4.5.2) and the required PowerShell version (we have specified 5.1 on the last line of the preceding code snippet—valid values for this are 3.0, 4.0, or 5.1. We also specify an account with administrator privileges, so be sure to set the $username and $password variables appropriately for your system. If a valid username and password are set, and a reboot is required after the script finishes, it will automatically restart and log on at reboot so that no more action is required, and the script will continue until the PowerShell version matches the target version.

It is important to note that if the credentials are set to enable automatic reboots, they are also stored in plaintext in the registry, so it's important to check that they have been cleared out after the script run. The following snippet of PowerShell will achieve this, and it is recommended you run it after the script as a matter of routine to ensure your credentials do not get leaked:

```
$reg_winlogon_path = "HKLM:\Software\Microsoft\Windows NT\
CurrentVersion\Winlogon"
Set-ItemProperty -Path $reg_winlogon_path -Name AutoAdminLogon
-Value 0
Remove-ItemProperty -Path $reg_winlogon_path -Name
DefaultUserName -ErrorAction SilentlyContinue
Remove-ItemProperty -Path $reg_winlogon_path -Name
DefaultPassword -ErrorAction SilentlyContinue
```

If the username and password parameters aren't set, the script will ask the user to reboot and log in manually if necessary, and the next time the user logs in, the script will continue at the point where it was interrupted. The process continues until the host meets the requirements for Ansible automation.

Once you have completed the script run, you should set the execution policy back to a more secure value. For Windows servers, this would be achieved using this PowerShell command:

```
Set-ExecutionPolicy -ExecutionPolicy RemoteSigned -Force
```

On Windows clients (for example, Windows 10 or Windows 11), this would be achieved via the following command:

```
Set-ExecutionPolicy -ExecutionPolicy Restricted -Force
```

These are the default settings for the aforementioned operating systems, but if you want to check the execution policy setting prior to performing any of the script runs, you can query it before running your scripts with the following command:

```
Get-ExecutionPolicy
```

Once you have the required version of PowerShell and the .NET Framework installed, you can move on to the next step.

2. When PowerShell has been upgraded to at least version 3.0, the next step will be to configure the WinRM service so that Ansible can connect to it. WinRM service configuration defines how Ansible can interface with the Windows hosts, including the listener port and protocol.

   If you have never set up a WinRM listener before, you have three options to do this, as follows:

   - Firstly, you can use `winrm quickconfig` for HTTP and `winrm quickconfig -transport:https` for HTTPS. This is the simplest method to use when you need to run outside of the domain environment and just create a simple listener. This process has the advantage of opening the required port in the Windows Firewall and automatically starting the WinRM service.

> **Note**
>
> More recent versions of Windows (for example, Windows Server 2022) will only let you run `winrm quickconfig -transport:https` if you already have a **Secure Sockets Layer** (**SSL**) certificate installed on your node that matches its hostname and is not self-signed. If this is not the case in your environment, the simplest approach is actually to use the PowerShell commands given next.

   - If you are running in a domain environment, I strongly recommend using **group policy objects** (**GPOs**) because if the host is the domain member, then the configuration is done automatically without user input. There are many documented procedures for doing this available, but as this is a very Windows domain-centric task, it is beyond the scope of this book.

   - Finally, you can create a listener with a specific configuration by running the following PowerShell commands with administrative privileges:

```
$selector_set = @{
    Address = "*"
```

```
     Transport = "HTTPS"
}
$value_set = @{
    CertificateThumbprint =
"2c8951160e63b33593e7bbc3a22414a5ab259717"
}


New-WSManInstance -ResourceURI "winrm/config/Listener"
-SelectorSet $selector_set -ValueSet $value_set
```

The preceding `CertificateThumbprint` value should match the thumbprint of a valid SSL certificate that you previously created or imported into the Windows Certificate Store. Note that if you use this method to configure your WinRM listener, the Windows Firewall is not automatically configured. You can configure it appropriately to listen on port 5986 (HTTPS) using a PowerShell command such as the following:

```
New-NetFirewallRule -DisplayName 'WinRM over HTTPS' -Profile
'Any' -Direction Inbound -Action Allow -Protocol TCP -LocalPort
5986
```

In this simple example, we will perform basic authentication against a Windows host—this will only work with local accounts (not domain accounts) but is a quick and easy way to get acquainted with Windows automation. When you are ready to start experimenting with Kerberos authentication, the Ansible documentation provides a valuable reference for you to work from: https://docs. ansible.com/ansible/latest/os_guide/windows_winrm.html.

In the meantime, it is important to note that basic authentication isn't enabled by default on Windows hosts. To enable it, run the following PowerShell command:

```
Set-Item -Path "WSMan:\localhost\Service\Auth\Basic" -Value $true
```

If you are running in PowerShell v3.0, you might face an issue with the WinRM service that limits the amount of memory available. This is a known bug, and a hotfix is available to resolve it. An example process (written in PowerShell) to apply this hotfix is given here:

```
[Net.ServicePointManager]::SecurityProtocol = [Net.
SecurityProtocolType]::Tls12
$url = "https://raw.githubusercontent.com/jborean93/ansible-windows/
master/scripts/Install-WMF3Hotfix.ps1"
$file = "$env:temp\Install-WMF3Hotfix.ps1"

(New-Object -TypeName System.Net.WebClient).DownloadFile($url, $file)
powershell.exe -ExecutionPolicy ByPass -File $file -Verbose
```

Configuring WinRM listeners can be a complex task, so it is important to be able to check the results of your configuration process. The following command (which can be run from Command Prompt) will display the current WinRM listener configuration:

```
winrm enumerate winrm/config/Listener
```

If all goes well, you should have output similar to this:

```
Listener
    Address = *
    Transport = HTTP
    Port = 5985
    Hostname
    Enabled = true
    URLPrefix = wsman
    CertificateThumbprint
    ListeningOn = 10.0.50.100, 127.0.0.1, ::1,
fe80::460:ba22:fac4:71ff%5

Listener
    Address = *
    Transport = HTTPS
    Port = 5986
    Hostname
    Enabled = true
    URLPrefix = wsman
    CertificateThumbprint = 2c8951160e63b33593e7bbc3a22414a5ab259717
    ListeningOn = 10.0.50.100, 127.0.0.1, ::1,
fe80::460:ba22:fac4:71ff%5
```

According to the preceding output, two listeners are active—one to listen on port 5985 over HTTP and the other to listen on port 5986 over HTTPS, providing greater security. By way of additional explanation, the following parameters are also displayed in the preceding output:

- Transport: This should be set to either HTTP or HTTPS, though it is strongly recommended that you use the HTTPS listener to ensure your automation commands are not subject to snooping or manipulation.

- Port: This is the port on which the listener operates, by default 5985 for HTTP or 5986 for HTTPS.

- URLPrefix: This is the URL prefix to communicate with—by default, wsman. If you change it, you must set the ansible_winrm_path host on your Ansible control host to the same value.

- CertificateThumbprint: If running on an HTTPS listener, this is the certificate thumbprint of the Windows Certificate Store used by the connection.

If you need to debug any connection issues after setting up your WinRM listener, you may find the following commands valuable as they perform WinRM-based connections between Windows hosts without Ansible—hence, you can use them to distinguish whether an issue you might be experiencing is related to your Ansible host or whether there is an issue with the WinRM listener itself:

```
# test out HTTP
winrs -r:http://<server address>:5985/wsman -u:Username -p:Password
ipconfig

# test out HTTPS (will fail if the cert is not verifiable)
winrs -r:https://<server address>:5986/wsman -u:Username -p:Password
-ssl ipconfig

# test out HTTPS, ignoring certificate verification
$username = "Username"
$password = ConvertTo-SecureString -String "Password" -AsPlainText
-Force
$cred = New-Object -TypeName System.Management.Automation.PSCredential
-ArgumentList $username, $password

$session_option = New-PSSessionOption -SkipCACheck -SkipCNCheck
-SkipRevocationCheck
Invoke-Command -ComputerName <server address> -UseSSL -ScriptBlock {
ipconfig } -Credential $cred -SessionOption $session_option
```

If one of the preceding commands fails, you should investigate your WinRM listener setup before attempting to set up or configure your Ansible control host.

At this stage, Windows should be ready to receive communication from Ansible over WinRM. To complete this process, you will need to also perform some additional configuration on your Ansible control host. First of all, you will need to install the `winrm` Python module, which, depending on your control host's configuration, may or may not have been installed before. The installation method will vary from one operating system to another, but it can generally be installed on most platforms with PIP, as follows:

```
$ python3 -m pip install pywinrm
```

Once this is complete, you will need to define some additional inventory variables for your Windows hosts—don't worry too much about inventories for now as we will cover these later in this book. The following example is just for reference:

```
[windows]
10.0.50.101

[windows:vars]
ansible_user=administrator
```

```
ansible_password=password
ansible_port=5986
ansible_connection=winrm
ansible_winrm_server_cert_validation=ignore
```

Finally, you should be able to run the Ansible `ansible.windows.win_ping` module to perform an end-to-end connectivity test with a command such as the following (adjust for your inventory):

```
$ ansible -i inventory -m ansible.windows.win_ping windows
10.0.50.101 | SUCCESS => {
  "changed": false,
  "ping": "pong"
}
```

This is just the beginning of Windows automation with Ansible—once you decide on your connectivity strategy and way of configuring (whether it be through Group Policy, PowerShell scripts, or otherwise), you will be able to automate your Windows tasks with as much effectiveness as you automate your Linux tasks.

In Ansible 2.8, support was even added for OpenSSH connectivity to Windows hosts, removing the complexity of WinRM configuration and the various authentication mechanisms. While this looks like a great addition to Ansible's Windows automation capabilities, it must be stressed that even now (on release 8.0.0) it is marked as experimental and that the future may bring changes that are not backward compatible with the current code. As such, we will not explore the setup here, but if you are interested in experimenting with this Windows support for yourself, you are encouraged to look at this section of the official Ansible documentation: `https://docs.ansible.com/ansible/latest/os_guide/windows_setup.html#windows-ssh-setup`.

Now that you have learned the fundamental steps to configure Windows hosts for Ansible, let's see how to manage multiple nodes via Ansible in the next section.

Getting to know your Ansible installation

By this stage in this chapter, regardless of your choice of operating system for your Ansible control machine, you should have a working installation of Ansible with which to begin exploring the world of automation. In this section, we will carry out a practical exploration of the fundamentals of Ansible to help you to understand how to work with it. Once you have mastered these basic skills, you will then have the knowledge required to get the most out of the remainder of this book. Let's get started with an overview of how Ansible connects to non-Windows hosts.

Understanding how Ansible connects to hosts

With the exception of Windows hosts (as discussed at the end of the previous section), Ansible uses the SSH protocol to communicate with hosts. The reasons for this choice in the Ansible design are many, not least that just about every Linux/FreeBSD/macOS host has it built in, as do many network devices such as switches and routers. The SSH service is normally integrated with the operating system authentication stack, enabling you to take advantage of host-based identity verification, and a variety of authentication mechanisms, including Kerberos, to improve authentication security. Also, features of OpenSSH such as `ControlPersist` are used to increase the performance of automation tasks and SSH jump hosts/bastions for network isolation and security.

> **Note**
> `ControlPersist` is enabled by default on most modern Linux distributions as part of the OpenSSH server installation. However, on some older operating systems such as RHEL 6 (and CentOS 6), it is not supported, so you will not be able to use it. Ansible automation is still perfectly possible, but longer playbooks might run slower.

Ansible makes use of the same authentication methods that you will already be familiar with, and SSH keys are normally the easiest way to proceed as they remove the need for users to input the authentication password every time a playbook is run. However, this is by no means mandatory, and Ansible supports password authentication through the use of the `--ask-pass` switch. If you are connecting to an unprivileged account on the managed nodes and need to perform the Ansible equivalent of running commands under `sudo` with a password, you can also add `--ask-become-pass` when you run your playbooks to allow this to be specified at runtime as well.

The goal of automation is to be able to run tasks securely but with minimal user intervention. As a result, it is highly recommended that you use SSH keys for authentication, and if you have several keys to manage, then it is advisable to make use of `ssh-agent`.

Every Ansible task, whether it is run individually or as part of a complex playbook, is run against an inventory. An inventory is, quite simply, a list of hosts that you wish to run automation tasks against. Ansible supports a wide range of inventory formats, including the use of dynamic inventories, which can populate themselves automatically from an orchestration provider (for example, you can generate an Ansible inventory dynamically from your Amazon **Elastic Compute Cloud** (**EC2**) instances, meaning you don't have to keep up with all of the changes in your cloud infrastructure).

Dynamic inventory plugins have been written for most major cloud providers (for example, Amazon EC2, **Google Cloud Platform** (**GCP**), and Microsoft Azure), as well as on-premises systems such as OpenShift and OpenStack. There are even plugins for Docker. The beauty of OSS is that for most of the major use cases you can dream of, someone has already contributed the code, so you don't need to figure it out or write it for yourself.

> **Tip**
>
> Ansible's agentless architecture and the fact that it doesn't rely on SSL means that you don't need to worry about DNS not being set up or even time skew problems as a result of the **Network Time Protocol (NTP)** not working—these can, in fact, be tasks performed by an Ansible playbook! Ansible really was designed to get your infrastructure running from a virtually bare operating system image.

For now, let's focus on the INI-formatted inventory. An example is shown here with four servers, each split into two groups. Ansible commands and playbooks can be run against an entire inventory (that is, all four servers), one or more groups (for example, `webservers`), or even a single server:

```
[webservers]
web01.example.org
web02.example.org

[apservers]
app01.example.org
app02.example.org
```

Let's use this inventory file along with the Ansible `ping` module, which is used to test whether Ansible can successfully perform automation tasks on the inventory host in question. The following example assumes you have installed the inventory in the default location, which is normally `/etc/ansible/hosts`. When you run the following `ansible` command against this inventory with the `ping` module, you should see output similar to this:

```
$ ansible webservers -m anisble.builtin.ping
web01.example.org | SUCCESS => {
    "ansible_facts": {
        "discovered_interpreter_python": "/usr/bin/python3"
    },
    "changed": false,
    "ping": "pong"
}
web02.example.org | SUCCESS => {
    "ansible_facts": {
        "discovered_interpreter_python": "/usr/bin/python3"
    },
    "changed": false,
    "ping": "pong"
}
```

Notice that the `ansible.builtin.ping` module was only run on the two hosts in the `webservers` group and not the entire inventory—this was by virtue of us specifying this group name in the command-line parameters.

The `ansible.builtin.ping` module is one of many thousands of modules for Ansible, all of which perform a given set of tasks (from copying files between hosts to text substitution to complex network device configuration). Again, as Ansible is OSS, there is a veritable army of coders out there who are writing and contributing modules, which means if you can dream of a task, there's probably already an Ansible module for it. Even in the instance that no module exists, Ansible supports sending raw shell commands (or PowerShell commands for Windows hosts), and so even in this eventuality, you can complete your desired tasks without having to move away from Ansible.

As long as the Ansible control node can communicate with the managed nodes in your inventory, you can automate your tasks. However, it is worth giving some consideration to where you place your control node. For example, if you are working exclusively with a set of Amazon EC2 machines, it arguably would make more sense for your Ansible control machine to be an EC2 instance—in this way, you are not sending all of your automation commands over the internet. It also means that you don't need to expose the SSH port of your EC2 hosts to the internet, hence keeping them more secure.

We have so far covered a brief explanation of how Ansible communicates with its target hosts, including what inventories are and the importance of SSH communication to all except Windows hosts. In the next section, we will build on this by looking in greater detail at how to verify your Ansible installation.

Verifying the Ansible installation

In this section, you will learn how you can verify your Ansible installation with simple ad hoc commands.

As discussed previously, Ansible can authenticate with your managed nodes in several ways. In this section, we will assume you want to make use of SSH keys and that you have already generated your public and private key pair and applied your public key to all of the managed nodes that you will be automating tasks on.

> **Tip**
> The `ssh-copy-id` utility is incredibly useful for distributing your public SSH key to your target hosts before you proceed any further. An example command might be `ssh-copy-id -i ~/.ssh/id_rsa ansibleuser@web1.example.com`.

To ensure Ansible can authenticate with your private key, you could make use of `ssh-agent`—the following commands show a simple example of how to start `ssh-agent` and add your private key to it. Naturally, you should replace the path with that to your own private key:

```
$ eval $(ssh-agent)
Agent pid 3064
```

```
$ ssh-add ~/.ssh/id_rsa
Identity added: /home/james/.ssh/id_rsa (james@controlnode)
```

As we discussed in the previous section, we must also define an inventory for Ansible to run against. Another simple example is shown here:

```
[webservers]
web01.example.org
web02.example.org
```

The `ansible` command that we used in the previous section has two important switches that you will almost always use: `-m <MODULE_NAME>` to run a module on the managed nodes from your inventory that you specify and, optionally, the module arguments passed using the `-a OPT_ARGS` switch. Commands run using the `ansible` binary are known as ad hoc commands.

The following are three simple examples that demonstrate ad hoc commands—they are also valuable for verifying both the installation of Ansible on your control machine and the configuration of your target hosts, and they will return an error if there is an issue with any part of the configuration. Here, we are introducing the `-i` switch, which is used to tell Ansible that we are specifying a different inventory file from the default— we'll be using this frequently throughout the book from here on:

- **Ping hosts**: You can perform an Ansible `ping` on your inventory hosts using the following command:

  ```
  $ ansible webservers -i /etc/ansible/hosts -m ansible.builtin.
  ping
  ```

- **Display gathered facts**: You can display gathered facts about your inventory hosts using the following command:

  ```
  $ ansible webservers -i /etc/ansible/hosts -m ansible.builtin.
  setup | less
  ```

- **Filter gathered facts**: You can filter gathered facts using the following command:

  ```
  $ ansible webservers -i /etc/ansible/hosts -m ansible.builtin.
  setup -a "filter=ansible_distribution*"
  ```

For every ad hoc command you run, you will get a response in JSON format—the following example output results from running the `ansible.builtin.ping` module successfully:

```
$ ansible webservers -m ansible.builtin.ping
web02.example.org | SUCCESS => {
    "ansible_facts": {
        "discovered_interpreter_python": "/usr/bin/python3"
    },
    "changed": false,
```

```
    "ping": "pong"
}
web01.example.org | SUCCESS => {
    "ansible_facts": {
        "discovered_interpreter_python": "/usr/bin/python3"
    },
    "changed": false,
    "ping": "pong"
}
```

Ansible can also gather and return facts about your target hosts—facts are all manner of useful information about your hosts, from CPU and memory configuration, to network parameters, to disk geometry. These facts are intended to enable you to write intelligent playbooks that perform conditional actions—for example, you might only want to install a given software package on hosts with more than 4 GB of RAM or perhaps perform a specific configuration only on macOS hosts. The following is an example of the filtered facts from a macOS-based host—note the special syntax of the -i inventory parameter; by placing a comma after the hostname, we are telling the ansible command to read the inventory from the command line, rather than a file (a handy shortcut when you're testing and developing):

```
$ ansible -i machost.example.org, -m ansible.builtin.setup -a
"filter=ansible_distribution*" all
machost.example.org | SUCCESS => {
    "ansible_facts": {
        "ansible_distribution": "MacOSX",
        "ansible_distribution_major_version": "13",
        "ansible_distribution_release": "22.4.0",
        "ansible_distribution_version": "13.3.1",
        "discovered_interpreter_python": "/opt/homebrew/bin/
python3.11"
    },
    "changed": false
}
```

Ad hoc commands are incredibly powerful, both for verifying your Ansible installation and for learning Ansible and how to work with modules, as you don't need to write a whole playbook—you can just run a module with an ad hoc command and learn how it responds. Here are some more ad hoc examples for you to consider:

- Copy a file from the Ansible control node to all managed nodes in the webservers group with the following command:

```
$ ansible webservers -m ansible.builtin.copy -a "src=/etc/
hostname dest=/tmp/hostname"
```

- Create a new directory on all hosts in the webservers inventory group, and create it with specific ownership and permissions, as follows:

```
$ ansible webservers -m ansible.builtin.file -a "dest=/tmp/
newpath mode=777 owner=james group=james state=directory"
```

- Delete a specific directory from all hosts in the webservers group with the following command:

```
$ ansible webservers -m ansible.builtin.file -a "dest=/tmp/
newpath state=absent"
```

- Install the apache2 package with apt if it is not already present—if it is present, do not update it. Again, this applies to all hosts in the webservers inventory group. Note the presence of the --become switch—as we're installing packages, we must *become* the root user using sudo. This command assumes that the user account on the managed node can perform passwordless sudo commands:

```
$ ansible webservers -m ansible.builtin.apt -a "name=apache2
state=present" --become
```

- The following command is similar to the previous one, except that changing state=present to state=latest causes Ansible to install the (latest version of the) package if it is not present, and update it to the latest version if it is present:

```
$ ansible webservers -m ansible.builtin.apt -a "name=apache2
state=latest" --become
```

- Display all facts about all the hosts in your inventory (warning—this will produce a lot of JSON!):

```
$ ansible all -m ansible.builtin.setup
```

Now that you have learned more about verifying your Ansible installation and about how to run ad hoc commands, let's proceed to look in a bit more detail at the requirements of nodes that are to be managed by Ansible.

Managed node requirements

So far, we have focused almost exclusively on the requirements for the Ansible control host and have assumed that (except for the distribution of the SSH keys) the target hosts will just work. This, of course, is not always the case, and for example, while a modern installation of Linux installed from an ISO will often just work, cloud operating system images are often stripped down to keep them small, and so might lack important packages such as Python, without which Ansible cannot operate.

If your target hosts are lacking Python, it is usually easy to install it through your operating system's package management system. Ansible requires you to install either Python version 2.7 or 3.5 (and above) on the Ansible-managed nodes but has more stringent requirements for the control node. At the time of writing, ansible-core 2.15 (which accompanies Ansible 8.0.0) requires a version of Python between 3.9 and 3.11 to be installed on the control node. This is likely to change with new releases, so you are advised to always consult the official documentation to check the latest requirements: https://docs.ansible.com/ansible/latest/installation_guide/ intro_installation.html#managed-node-requirements.

> **Tip**
> Again, the exception here is Windows, which relies on PowerShell instead of Python.

If you are working with operating system images on managed nodes that lack Python, the following commands provide a quick guide to getting Python installed:

- To install Python using yum (on older releases of Fedora and CentOS/RHEL 7 and below), use the following command:

    ```
    $ sudo yum -y install python
    ```

- On RHEL and CentOS version 8 and newer versions of Fedora, you would use the dnf package manager instead. Here's the command you'd execute:

    ```
    $ sudo dnf install python
    ```

    You might also elect to install a specific version to suit your needs, as in this example:

    ```
    $ sudo dnf install python39
    ```

- On Debian and Ubuntu systems, you would use the apt package manager to install Python, again specifying a version if required (the example given here is to install Python 3.10 and would work on Ubuntu 22.04):

    ```
    $ sudo apt update
    $ sudo apt install python3.10
    ```

The ansible.builtin.ping module we discussed earlier in this chapter for Ansible not only checks connectivity and authentication with your managed hosts but also uses the managed hosts' Python environment to perform some basic host checks. As a result, it is a fantastic end-to-end test to give you confidence that your managed nodes are configured correctly, with the connectivity and authentication set up perfectly, and to be safe in the knowledge that if Python is missing, the test would return a failed result.

Of course, a perfect question at this stage would be: How can Ansible help if you roll out 100 cloud servers using a stripped-down base image without Python? Does that mean you have to manually go through all 100 nodes and install Python by hand before you can start automating?

Thankfully, Ansible has you covered even in this case, thanks to the ansible.builtin.raw module. This module is used to send raw shell commands to the managed nodes—and it works both with SSH-managed hosts and Windows PowerShell-managed hosts. As a result, you can use Ansible to install Python on a whole set of systems from which it is missing, or even run an entire shell script to bootstrap a managed node. Most importantly, the `ansible.builtin.raw` module is one of very few that does not require Python to be installed on the managed node, so it is perfect for our use case where we must roll out Python to enable further automation.

The following are some examples of tasks in an Ansible playbook that you might use to bootstrap a managed node and prepare it for Ansible management:

```
- name: Bootstrap a host without python3 installed
  ansible.builtin.raw: dnf install -y python3 python3-dnf libselinux-
python3

- name: Run a command that uses non-posix shell-isms (in this example
/bin/sh doesn't handle redirection and wildcards together but bash
does)
  ansible.builtin.raw: cat < /tmp/*txt
  args:
    executable: /bin/bash

- name: safely use templated variables. Always use quote filter to
avoid injection issues.
  ansible.builtin.raw: "{{package_mgr|quote}} {{pkg_flags|quote}}
install {{python|quote}}"
```

We have now covered the basics of setting up Ansible both on the control host and the managed nodes, and we gave you a brief primer on configuring your first connections. It is hoped that you've found this chapter helpful and that it forms the foundation for the rest of your journey through this book.

Summary

Ansible is a powerful and versatile yet simple automation tool, of which the key benefits are its agentless architecture and its simple installation process. Ansible was designed to get you from zero to automation rapidly and with minimal effort, and we have demonstrated the simplicity with which you can get up and running with Ansible in this chapter.

In this chapter, you learned the basics of setting up Ansible—how to install it to control other hosts, and the requirements for nodes being managed by Ansible. You learned about the fundamentals required to set up SSH and WinRM for Ansible automation, as well as how to bootstrap managed nodes to ensure they are suitable for Ansible automation. You also learned about ad hoc commands and their benefits. Finally, you learned how to run the latest version of the code directly from GitHub, which both enables you to contribute directly to the development of Ansible and gives you access to the very latest features should you wish to make use of them on your infrastructure.

In the next chapter, we will learn Ansible language fundamentals to enable you to write your first playbooks and to help you to create templated configurations and start to build up complex automation workflows.

Questions

1. On which operating systems can you set up an Ansible control node? (There are multiple correct answers.)

    A. Ubuntu 22.04

    B. Fedora 35

    C. Windows Server 2022

    D. HP-UX

    E. Mainframe

2. Which protocol does Ansible use to connect to non-Windows managed nodes for running tasks?

    A. HTTP

    B. HTTPS

    C. SSH

    D. TCP

    E. UDP

3. To execute a specific module in the Ansible ad hoc command line, you need to use the -m option.

    A. True

    B. False

Further reading

- For any questions about installation via Ansible's mailing list on Google Groups, refer to the following URL:

  `https://groups.google.com/forum/#!forum/ansible-project`

- Information on how to install the latest version of `pip` can be found here:

  `https://pip.pypa.io/en/stable/installation/`

- Details of specific Windows modules using PowerShell can be found here:

  ```
  https://docs.ansible.com/ansible/latest/collections/ansible/
  windows/index.html
  ```

- If you have a GitHub account and want to follow the GitHub project, you can keep tracking issues, bugs, and ideas for Ansible at the following URL:

  ```
  https://github.com/ansible/ansible
  ```

2
Understanding the Fundamentals of Ansible

At its heart, Ansible is a simple framework that pushes a small program called an **Ansible module** to target nodes. Modules are at the heart of Ansible and are responsible for performing all of the automation's hard work. The Ansible framework goes beyond this, however, and also includes plugins and dynamic inventory management, as well as tying all of this together with playbooks to automate infrastructure provisioning, configuration management, application deployment, network automation, and much more, as shown:

Figure 2.1 – The typical flow and usage of Ansible's automation engine

Even with the addition of Ansible collections since the previous release of this book, this architecture remains unchanged – now, the modules, plugins, and dynamic inventory scripts are simply distributed through collections whereas before everything was distributed as part of the Ansible release itself.

Ansible only needs to be installed on the management node. From there, it distributes the required modules over the network's transport layer (usually SSH or WinRM) to perform tasks and deletes them once the tasks are complete. In this way, Ansible retains its agentless architecture and does not clutter up your target nodes with code that might be required for a one-off automation task.

In this chapter, you will learn more about the composition of the Ansible framework and its various components, as well as how to use them together in playbooks written in YAML syntax. You will learn how to create automation code for your IT operation tasks and learn how to apply this using both ad hoc tasks and more complex playbooks. Finally, you will learn how Jinja2 templating allows you to repeatably build dynamic configuration files using variables and dynamic expressions.

In this chapter, we will cover the following topics:

- Getting familiar with the Ansible framework
- Exploring the configuration file
- Command-line arguments
- Defining variables
- Understanding Jinja2 filters

Technical requirements

This chapter assumes that you have successfully installed the latest version of Ansible (8.0 with `ansible-core` 2.15, at the time of writing) on a Linux node, as discussed in *Chapter 1*, *Getting Started with Ansible*. It also assumes that you have at least one other Linux host to test the automation code on. The more hosts you have available, the more you will be able to develop the examples in this chapter and learn about Ansible. SSH communication between the Linux hosts is assumed, as is a working knowledge of them.

The code bundle for this chapter is available at `https://github.com/PacktPublishing/Practical-Ansible-Second-Edition/tree/main/Chapter%202`.

Getting familiar with the Ansible framework

In this section, you will learn how the Ansible framework fits into IT operations. We will explain how to run Ansible for the first time. Once you understand this framework, you will be ready to start learning about more advanced concepts, such as creating and running playbooks with your own inventory.

In order to run Ansible's ad hoc commands via an SSH connection from your Ansible control machine to multiple remote hosts, you need to ensure you have the latest Ansible version installed on the control host. Use the following command to confirm the latest Ansible version:

```
$ ansible --version
ansible [core 2.15.0] (2.15 82b47c8d5c) last updated 2023/05/19
15:21:43 (GMT +000)
```

```
config file = None
configured module search path = ['/home/james/.ansible/plugins/
modules', '/usr/share/ansible/plugins/modules']
ansible python module location = /home/james/ansible-2.15/ansible/
lib/ansible
ansible collection location = /home/james/.ansible/collections:/usr/
share/ansible/collections
executable location = /home/james/ansible-2.15/ansible/bin/ansible
python version = 3.10.6 (main, Mar 10 2023, 10:55:28) [GCC 11.3.0]
(/usr/bin/python)
jinja version = 3.0.3
libyaml = True
```

You also need to ensure SSH connectivity with each remote host that you will define in the inventory. You can use a simple, manual SSH connection on each of your remote hosts to test the connectivity, as Ansible will make use of SSH during all remote Linux-based automation tasks:

```
$ ssh <username>@web01.example.org
The authenticity of host 'web01.example.org (10.0.50.30)' can't be
established.
ED25519 key fingerprint is SHA256:hU+saFERGFDERW453tasdFPAkpVws.
Are you sure you want to continue connecting (yes/no)? yes
password:<Input_Your_Password>
```

In this section, we will walk you through how Ansible works, starting with some simple connectivity testing. You can learn how the Ansible framework accesses multiple host machines to execute your tasks by following this simple procedure:

1. Create or edit your default inventory file, /etc/ansible/hosts (you can also specify the path with your own inventory file by passing options such as --inventory=/path/ inventory_file). Add some example hosts to your inventory—these must be the IP addresses or hostnames of real machines for Ansible to test against. The following are examples from my network, but you need to substitute these for your own devices. Add one hostname (or IP address) per line:

   ```
   web01.example.org
   web02.example.org
   app01.example.org
   app02.example.org
   ```

All hosts should be specified with a resolvable address—that is, a **Fully Qualified Domain Name** (**FQDN**)—if your hosts have DNS entries (or are in /etc/hosts on your Ansible control node). Alternatively, this can be IP addresses if you do not have DNS or host entries set up. Whatever format you choose for your inventory addresses, you should be able to successfully connect to each host. Unless you have set up stringent firewall rules, a simple ping to each host will suffice as a test. See the following output as an example:

```
$ ping web01.example.org
PING web01.example.org (10.0.50.30) 56(84) bytes of data.
64 bytes from web01.example.org (10.0.50.30): icmp_seq=1 ttl=64
time=1.02 ms
64 bytes from web01.example.org (10.0.50.30): icmp_seq=2 ttl=64
time=1.01 ms
64 bytes from web01.example.org (10.0.50.30): icmp_seq=3 ttl=64
time=0.957 ms
64 bytes from web01.example.org (10.0.50.30): icmp_seq=4 ttl=64
time=1.16 ms
```

2. To make the automation process seamless, we'll generate an SSH authentication key pair so that we don't have to type in a password every time we want to run a playbook. If you do not already have an SSH key pair, you can generate one using the following command:

    ```
    $ ssh-keygen
    ```

    When you run the ssh-keygen tool, you will see an output similar to the following. Note that you should leave the passphrase variable blank when prompted; otherwise, you will need to enter a passphrase every time you want to run an Ansible task, which removes the convenience of authenticating with SSH keys (though it does make them more secure if they ever get into the wrong hands, so please take this into consideration when working with SSH key pairs):

    ```
    $ ssh-keygen
    Generating public/private rsa key pair.
    Enter file in which to save the key (/home/james/.ssh/id_rsa):
    <Enter>
    Enter passphrase (empty for no passphrase): <Press Enter>
    Enter same passphrase again: <Press Enter>
    Your identification has been saved in /home/james/.ssh/id_rsa.
    Your public key has been saved in /home/james/.ssh/id_rsa.pub.
    The key fingerprint is:
    SHA256:1IF0KMMTVAMEQF62kTwcG59okGZLiMmi4Ae/BGBT+24 james@
    controlnode.example.org
    The key's randomart image is:
    +---[RSA 2048]----+
    |=*=*BB==+oo |
    |B=*+*B=.o+ . |
    |=+=o=.o+. . |
    |...=. . |
    ```

```
| o .. S |
| .. |
| E |
| . |
| |
+----[SHA256]-----+
```

3. Although there are conditions under which your SSH keys will be automatically picked up, it is recommended that you make use of `ssh-agent` as this allows you to load multiple keys to authenticate against a variety of targets, without worrying about whether your keys have the right name and path to be picked up. This will be very useful to you in the future, even if it isn't right now. Start `ssh-agent` as follows, and then add your new authentication key (note that you will need to do this for every shell that you open):

    ```
    $ eval $(ssh-agent)
    $ ssh-add ~/.ssh/id_rsa
    ```

4. Before you can perform key-based authentication with your target hosts, you need to apply the public key from the key pair you just generated to each host. You can copy the key to each host, in turn, using the following command:

    ```
    $ ssh-copy-id -i ~/.ssh/id_rsa.pub web01.example.org
    /usr/bin/ssh-copy-id: INFO: Source of key(s) to be installed:
    "~/.ssh/id_rsa.pub"
    /usr/bin/ssh-copy-id: INFO: attempting to log in with the new
    key(s), to filter out any that are already installed
    /usr/bin/ssh-copy-id: INFO: 1 key(s) remain to be installed --
    if you are prompted now it is to install the new keys
    james@web01.example.org's password:

    Number of key(s) added: 1

    Now try logging into the machine, with: "ssh 'web01.example.
    org'"
    and check to make sure that only the key(s) you wanted were
    added.
    ```

5. With this complete, you should now be able to perform an Ansible `ansible.builtin.ping` command on the hosts you put in your inventory file. You will find that you are not prompted for a password at any point as the SSH connections to all the hosts in your inventory are authenticated with your SSH key pair. So, you should see an output similar to the following:

    ```
    $ ansible -i hosts -m ansible.builtin.ping all
    web01.example.org | SUCCESS => {
        "ansible_facts": {
            "discovered_interpreter_python": "/usr/bin/python3"
    ```

```
    },
    "changed": false,
    "ping": "pong"
}
app02.example.org | SUCCESS => {
    "ansible_facts": {
        "discovered_interpreter_python": "/usr/bin/python3"
    },
    "changed": false,
    "ping": "pong"
}
web02.example.org | SUCCESS => {
    "ansible_facts": {
        "discovered_interpreter_python": "/usr/bin/python3"
    },
    "changed": false,
    "ping": "pong"
}
app01.example.org | SUCCESS => {
    "ansible_facts": {
        "discovered_interpreter_python": "/usr/bin/python3"
    },
    "changed": false,
    "ping": "pong"
}
```

This example output is generated with Ansible's default level of verbosity. If you run into problems during this process, you can increase Ansible's level of verbosity by passing one or more -v switches to the `ansible` command when you run it. For most issues, it is recommended that you use -vvvv, which gives you ample debugging information, including the raw SSH commands and the output from them. For example, assume that a certain host (such as web02.example.org) can't be connected to and you receive an error similar to the following:

```
web02.example.org | UNREACHABLE! => {
    "changed": false,
    "msg": "Failed to connect to the host via ssh: ssh: connect
to host web02.example.org port 22: Connection refused",
    "unreachable": true
}
```

The -vvvv flag could potentially produce pages of output and so, to save space, we won't include an example here—experimenting with the verbosity levels is left as an exercise for you. When you generate output with this highest level of verbosity, you will see that it includes many useful details, such as the raw SSH command that was used to generate the connection to the target host in the inventory, along with any error messages that may have resulted from that call. This can be incredibly useful when debugging connectivity or code issues, although the output might be a little overwhelming at first. However, with some practice, you will quickly learn how to interpret it.

By now, you should have a good idea of how Ansible communicates with its clients over SSH. Let's proceed to the next section, where we will look in more detail at the various components that make up Ansible, as this will help us understand how to work with it better.

Breaking down the Ansible components

Ansible allows you to define policies, configurations, task sequences, and orchestration steps in playbooks—the limit is really only your imagination. A playbook can be executed to manage your tasks either synchronously or asynchronously on a remote machine, although you will find that just about all examples are synchronous. In this section, you will learn about the main components of Ansible and understand how Ansible employs those components to communicate with remote hosts.

In order to understand the various components, we first need an inventory to work from. Let's create an example one, ideally with multiple hosts in it—here we will reuse the one we created earlier in this chapter. However, you are free to create your own, and while I have set up name resolution for this example, to give machines more friendly names, remember that you can get started with IP addresses if you don't want to add name resolution just yet.

To really understand how Ansible—as well as its various components—works, we first need to create an Ansible playbook. While the ad hoc commands that we have experimented with so far are useful in their own right, they are just single **tasks**, whereas playbooks are organized groups of tasks that are (usually) run in sequence. Conditional logic can be applied and in any other programming language, playbooks would be considered as your code. At the head of the playbook, you should specify the name of your **play**—although this is not mandatory, it is good practice to name all your plays and tasks as, without this, it would be quite hard for someone else to interpret what the playbook does, or even for you to do so if you come back to it after some time.

Let's get started with building our first example playbook:

1. Specify the play name and inventory hosts to run your tasks against at the very top of your playbook. Also, note the use of - - -, which denotes the beginning of a YAML file (all Ansible playbooks that are written in YAML):

    ```
    ---
    - name: My first Ansible playbook
      hosts: all
    ```

2. After this, we will tell Ansible that we want to perform all the tasks in this playbook as a superuser (usually `root`). We do this with the following statement (to aid your memory, think of `become` as shorthand for `become superuser`):

    ```
    become: yes
    ```

3. After this header, we will specify a task block that will contain one or more tasks to be run in sequence. For now, we will simply create one task to update the version of Apache using the `ansible.builtin.apt` module (because of this, this playbook is only suitable for running against Debian- or Ubuntu-derived hosts). We will also specify a special element of the play called a **handler**. Handlers will be covered in greater detail in *Chapter 4, Playbooks and Roles*, so don't worry too much about them for now. Simply put, a handler is a special type of task that is called only if something changes. So, in this example, the handler code restarts the web server, but only if it is installed or updated, preventing unnecessary restarts if the playbook is run several times and there are no updates for Apache. The following code performs these functions exactly and should form the basis of your first playbook:

    ```
    tasks:
    - name: Install/Update to the latest of Apache Web Server
      ansible.builtin.apt:
        name: apache2
        state: latest
      notify:
        - Restart the Apache Web Server

    handlers:
    - name: Restart the Apache Web Server
      ansible.builtin.service:
        name: apache2
        state: restarted
    ```

Congratulations, you now have your very first Ansible playbook! If you run this now, you should see it iterate through all the web hosts in your inventory, where it will install or update in the `apache2` package as required, and then only restart the service where the package was installed/updated.

In the following command to run the playbook, we have introduced a new switch, `--limit`, which is used when you want to run a playbook on only part of an inventory. In our example, I have four hosts in my inventory, but I only want to install `apache2` on the ones named `web*`, which I specify using the `--limit web*` option. These, of course, are based on the hostnames I have used in my demo environment for this book, and you should change your limit pattern to match your environment:

```
$ ansible-playbook -i hosts --limit web* playbook.yml
PLAY [My first Ansible playbook] ****************************************
*********************
```

```
TASK [Gathering Facts] **********************************************
*****
ok: [web02.example.org]
ok: [web01.example.org]

TASK [Install/Update to the latest of Apache Web Server] *************
********************************************
changed: [web01.example.org]
changed: [web02.example.org]

RUNNING HANDLER [Restart the Apache Web Server] *********************
************************************
changed: [web02.example.org]
changed: [web01.example.org]

PLAY RECAP **********************************************************
web01.example.org          :
ok=3      changed=2      unreachable=0      failed=0      skipped=0
rescued=0      ignored=0
web02.example.org          :
ok=3      changed=2      unreachable=0      failed=0      skipped=0
rescued=0      ignored=0
```

If you examine the output from the playbook, you can see the value in naming not only the play but also each task that is executed, as it makes interpreting the output of the run a very simple task. You will also see that there are multiple possible results from running a task; in the preceding example, we can see two of these results—ok and changed. Most of these results are fairly self-explanatory, with ok meaning the task ran successfully and that nothing changed as a result of the task completing. An example of this in the preceding playbook is the Gathering Facts stage, which is a read-only task that gathers information about the target hosts. As a result, it can only ever return ok or a failed status, such as unreachable, if the host is down. It should never return changed.

However, you can see in the preceding output that both hosts needed to install/upgrade their apache2 package and, as a result of this, the results from the Install/Update to the latest of Apache Web Server task are changed for all the hosts. This changed result means the task ran successfully (as for ok) but that a change was made to the managed node. It also means that our handler instance is notified and so the web server service is restarted.

If we run the playbook a second time straight away, we know that it is hugely unlikely that the apache2 package will need upgrading again. Notice how the playbook output differs this time:

```
PLAY [My first Ansible playbook] *************************************
********************
TASK [Gathering Facts] **********************************************
*************
```

```
ok: [web02.example.org]
ok: [web01.example.org]

TASK [Install/Update to the latest of Apache Web Server] *************
*************************************************
ok: [web01.example.org]
ok: [web02.example.org]

PLAY RECAP ***********************************************************
web01.example.org           :
ok=2      changed=0     unreachable=0      failed=0
skipped=0     rescued=0     ignored=0
web02.example.org           :
ok=2      changed=0     unreachable=0      failed=0
skipped=0     rescued=0     ignored=0
```

You can see that this time, the output from the `Install/Update to the latest of Apache Web Server` task is `ok` for both hosts, meaning no changes were applied (the package was not updated). As a result of this, our handler is not notified and does not run—you can see that it does not even feature in the preceding playbook output. This distinction is important—the goal of an Ansible playbook (and the modules that underpin Ansible) should be to only make changes when they need to be made. If everything is all up to date, then the target host should not be altered. Unnecessary restarts to services should be avoided, as should unnecessary alterations to files. In short, Ansible playbooks are (and should be) designed to be efficient and to achieve a target machine state.

This has very much been a crash course on writing your first playbook, but hopefully, it has given you a taste of what Ansible can do when you move from single ad hoc commands through to more complex playbooks. Before we explore the Ansible language and components any further, let's take a more in-depth look at the YAML language that playbooks are written in.

Learning the YAML syntax

In this section, you will learn how to write a YAML file with the correct syntax, and the various constructs you will see time and again on your Ansible automation journey. Ansible uses YAML because it is easier for humans to read and write than other common data formats, such as XML or JSON. There are no commas, curly braces, or tags to worry about, and the enforced indentation in the code ensures that it is tidy and easy on the eye. In addition, there are libraries available in most programming languages for working with YAML.

This reflects one of the core goals of Ansible—to produce easy-to-read (and write) code that describes the target state of a given host. Ansible playbooks are (ideally) supposed to be self-documenting, as documentation is often an afterthought in busy technology environments—so, what better way to document than through the automation system responsible for deploying code?

Before we dive into the YAML structure, a word on the files themselves. Files written in YAML can optionally begin with - - - (as seen in the example playbook in the previous section) and end with . . . . This applies to all files in YAML, regardless of whether they are consumed by Ansible or another system, and indicates that the file is in the YAML language. You will find that most examples of Ansible playbooks (as well as roles and other associated YAML files) start with - - - but do not end with . . . —the header is sufficient to clearly denote that the file uses the YAML format.

Let's explore the YAML language through the example playbook we created in the preceding section:

1. Lists are an important construct in the YAML language—in fact, although it might not be obvious, the `tasks:` block of the playbook is actually a YAML list. A list in YAML contains all of its items at the same indentation level, with each item in the list preceded by a `-`. For example, we updated the `apache2` package from the preceding playbook using the following code:

    ```
    - name: Install/Update to the latest of Apache Web Server
      ansible.builtin.apt:
        name: apache2
        state: latest
    ```

    However, we could have specified a list of packages to be upgraded as follows:

    ```
    - name: Install/Update to the latest of Apache Web Server
      ansible.builtin.apt:
        name:
          - apache2
          - apache2-utils
        state: latest
    ```

    Now, rather than passing a single value to the `name:` key as a string, we pass a YAML-formatted list containing the names of two packages to be installed/updated. Only certain modules support this so do refer to the documentation to establish which ones you can pass lists to.

2. Dictionaries are another important concept in YAML—they are represented by a `key: value` format, as we have already extensively seen, but all of the items in the dictionary are indented by one more level. This is easiest explained by an example, so consider the following code from our example playbook:

    ```
    ansible.builtin.service:
      name: apache2
      state: restarted
    ```

    In this example (from `handler`), the `ansible.builtin.service` definition is actually a dictionary and both the `name` and `state` keys are indented with two more spaces than the `ansible.builtin.service` key. This higher level of indentation means that the `name` and `state` keys are associated with the `ansible.builtin.service` key, therefore, in this case, telling the `ansible.builtin.service` module which service to operate on (`apache2`) and what to do with it (restart it).

Using these examples, we can see that you can produce quite complicated data structures by mixing lists and dictionaries.

3. As you become more proficient at playbook design (as you progress through the book, you will certainly become more proficient), you may very well start to produce quite complicated variable structures that you will put into their own separate files to keep your playbook code readable. The following is an example of a `variables` file that provides the details of two employees of a company:

```
---
employees:
  - name: daniel
    fullname: Daniel Oh
    role: DevOps Evangelist
    level: Expert
    skills:
      - Kubernetes
      - Microservices
      - Ansible
      - Linux Container
  - name: michael
    fullname: Michael Smith
    role: Enterprise Architect
    level: Advanced
    skills:
      - Cloud
      - Middleware
      - Windows
      - Storage
```

In this example, you can see that we have a dictionary containing the details of each employee. The employees themselves are list items (you can spot this because the lines start with -) and, equally, the employee skills are denoted as list items. You will notice the `fullname`, `role`, `level`, and `skills` keys are at the same indentation level as `name` but do not feature - before them. This tells you that they are in the dictionary with the list item itself, and so they represent the details of the employee.

4. YAML is very literal when it comes to parsing the language and a new line always represents a new line of code. What if you actually need to add a block of text (for example, to a variable)? In this case, you can use a literal block scalar, |, to write multiple lines and YAML will faithfully preserve the new lines, carriage returns, and all the whitespace that follows each line (note, however, that the indentation at the beginning of each line is part of the YAML syntax):

```
Specialty: |
  Agile methodology
```

```
  Cloud-native app development practices
  Advanced enterprise DevOps practices
```

So, if we were to get Ansible to print the preceding content to the screen, it would display as follows (note that the preceding two spaces have gone—they were interpreted correctly as part of the YAML language and not printed):

```
Agile methodology
Cloud-native app development practices
Advanced enterprise DevOps practices
```

Similar to the preceding is the folded block scalar, >, which does the same as the literal block scalar but does not preserve line endings. This is useful for very long strings that you want to print on a single line, but also want to wrap across multiple lines in your code for the purpose of readability. Take the following variation of our example:

```
  Specialty: >
    Agile methodology
    Cloud-native app development practices
    Advanced enterprise DevOps practices
```

Now, if we were to print this, we would see the following:

Agile methodologyCloud-native app development practicesAdvanced enterprise DevOps practices

We could add trailing spaces to the preceding example to stop the words from running into each other, but I have not done this here as I wanted to provide you with an easy-to-interpret example.

As you review playbooks, variable files, and so on, you will see these structures used over and over again. Although simple in definition, they are very important—a missed level of indentation or a missing - instance at the start of a list item can cause your entire playbook to fail to run. As we discovered, you can put all of these various constructs together. One additional example is provided in the following code block of a variables file for you to consider, which shows the various examples we have covered all in one place:

```
---
servers:
  - frontend
  - backend
  - database
  - cache
employees:
  - name: daniel
    fullname: Daniel Oh
    role: DevOps Evangelist
    level: Expert
    skills:
```

```
            - Kubernetes
            - Microservices
            - Ansible
            - Linux Container
     - name: michael
       fullname: Michael Smiths
       role: Enterprise Architect
       level: Advanced
       skills:
            - Cloud
            - Middleware
            - Windows
            - Storage
       Speciality: |
         Agile methodology
         Cloud-native app development practices
         Advanced enterprise DevOps practices
```

You can also express both dictionaries and lists in an abbreviated form, known as **flow collections**. The following example shows exactly the same data structure as our original employees variable file:

```
---
employees: [{"fullname": "Daniel Oh","level": "Expert","name":
"daniel","role": "DevOps Evangelist","skills":
["Kubernetes","Microservices","Ansible","Linux
Container"]},{"fullname": "Michael Smiths","level":
"Advanced","name": "michael","role": "Enterprise
Architect","skills":["Cloud","Middleware","Windows","Storage"]}]
```

Although this displays exactly the same data structure, you can see how difficult it is to read with the naked eye. Flow collections are not used extensively in YAML and I would not recommend you make use of them yourself, but it is important to understand them in case you come across them. You will also notice that although we've started talking about variables in YAML, we haven't expressed any variable types. YAML tries to make assumptions about variable types based on the data they contain, so if you want to assign 1.0 to a variable, YAML will assume it is a floating-point number. If you need to express it as a string (perhaps because it is a version number), you need to put quotation marks around it, which causes the YAML parser to interpret it as a string instead, such as in the following example:

```
version: "2.0"
```

This completes our look at the YAML language syntax. Now that's complete, in the next section, let's take a look at ways that you can organize your automation code to keep it manageable and tidy.

Organizing your automation code

As you can imagine, if you were to write all of your required Ansible tasks in one massive playbook, it would quickly become unmanageable—that is to say, it would be difficult to read, difficult for someone else to pick up and understand, and—most of all—difficult to debug when things go wrong. Ansible provides a number of ways for you to divide your code into manageable chunks; perhaps the most important of these is the use of **roles**. Roles (for the sake of a simple analogy) behave like a library in a conventional high-level programming language. We will go into more detail about roles in *Chapter 4, Playbooks and Roles*.

There are, however, other ways that Ansible supports splitting your code into manageable chunks, which we will explore briefly in this section as a precursor to the more in-depth exploration of roles later in this book.

Let's build up a practical example. To start, we know that we need to create an inventory for Ansible to run against. In this instance, we'll create four notional groups of servers, with each group containing two servers. Our hypothetical example will contain a frontend server and application servers for a fictional application, located in two different geographic locations. Our inventory file will be called `production-inventory` and the example contents are as follows:

```
[frontends_na_zone]
frontend1-na.example.com
frontend2-na.example.com

[frontends_emea_zone]
frontend1-emea.example.com
frontend2-emea.example.com

[appservers_na_zone]
appserver1-na.example.com
appserver2-na.example.com

[appservers_emea_zone]
appserver1-emea.example.com
appserver2-emea.example.com
```

Now, obviously, we could just write one massive playbook to address the required tasks on these different hosts, but as we have already discussed, this would be cumbersome and inefficient.

Let's instead break the task of automating these different hosts down into smaller playbooks:

1. Create a playbook to run a connection test on a specific host group, such as `frontends_na_zone`. Put the following contents into the playbook:

    ```
    ---

    - hosts: frontends_na_zone
      remote_user: james
      gather_facts: no

      tasks:
        - name: simple connection test
          ansible.builtin.ping:
    ```

2. Now, try running this playbook against the hosts. (Note that we have configured it to connect to a remote user on the inventory system, called `james`. If you wish to attempt this example yourself, you will need to set up your own user account and change the `remote_user` line of your playbook accordingly. Also remember to set up SSH keys and authentication as we demonstrated earlier in this chapter.) When you run the playbook after setting up the authentication, you should see output like the following:

    ```
    $ ansible-playbook -i production-inventory frontends-na.yml


    PLAY [frontends_na_
    zone]   ************************************************

    TASK [simple connection test] **********************************
    ******************
    ok: [frontend2-na.example.com]
    ok: [frontend1-na.example.com]


    PLAY RECAP *****************************************
    frontend1-na.example.com   :
    ok=1     changed=0     unreachable=0     failed=0
        skipped=0     rescued=0     ignored=0
    frontend2-na.example.com   :
    ok=1     changed=0     unreachable=0     failed=0
        skipped=0     rescued=0     ignored=0
    ```

3. Now, let's extend our simple example by creating a playbook that will only run on the application servers. Again, we will use the Ansible `ansible.builtin.ping` module to perform a connection test, but in a real-world situation, you would perform more complex tasks, such as installing packages or modifying files. Specify that this playbook is run against this host group from the `appservers_emea_zone` inventory. Add the following contents to the playbook:

    ```
    ---

    - hosts: appservers_emea_zone
      remote_user: james
    ```

```
gather_facts: no

tasks:
  - name: simple connection test
    ansible.builtin.ping:
```

As before, you need to ensure you can access these servers, so either create the `james` user and set up authentication to that account or change the `remote_user` line in the example playbook. Once you have done this, you should be able to run the playbook and you will see output similar to this:

```
$ ansible-playbook -i production-inventory appservers-emea.yml

PLAY [appservers_emea_zone] **************************************
******************

TASK [simple connection test] ***********************************
***************************
ok: [appserver1-emea.example.com]
ok: [appserver2-emea.example.com]

PLAY RECAP ******************************************************
appserver1-emea.example.com : ok=1      changed=0    unreachable=0
failed=0     skipped=0     rescued=0    ignored=0
appserver2-emea.example.com : ok=1      changed=0    unreachable=0
failed=0     skipped=0     rescued=0    ignored=0
```

4. So far, so good. However, we now have two playbooks that we need to run manually, which only address two of our inventory host groups. If we want to address all four groups, we need to create a total of four playbooks, all of which need to be run manually. This is hardly reflective of best automation practices. What if there was a way to take these individual playbooks and run them together from one top-level playbook? This would enable us to divide our code to keep it manageable but also prevent a lot of manual effort when it comes to running the playbooks. Fortunately, we can do exactly that by taking advantage of the `ansible.builtin.` `import_playbook` directive in a top-level playbook that we will call `site.yml`:

```
---

- ansible.builtin.import_playbook: frontends-na.yml
- ansible.builtin.import_playbook: appservers-emea.yml
```

Now, when you run this single playbook using the (by now, familiar) `ansible-playbook` command, you will see that the effect is the same as if we had actually run both playbooks back to back. In this way, even before we explore the concept of roles, you can see that Ansible supports splitting up your code into manageable chunks without needing to run each chunk manually:

```
$ ansible-playbook -i production-inventory site.yml
```

```
PLAY [frontends_na_zone] ********************************************
**************

TASK [simple connection test] **************************************
*******************
ok: [frontend2-na.example.com]
ok: [frontend1-na.example.com]


PLAY [appservers_emea_zone] *****************************************
****************

TASK [simple connection test] **************************************
*********************
ok: [appserver2-emea.example.com]
ok: [appserver1-emea.example.com]


PLAY RECAP *********************************************************
appserver1-emea.example.com :
ok=1      changed=0     unreachable=0      failed=0      skipped=0
rescued=0     ignored=0
appserver2-emea.example.com :
ok=1      changed=0     unreachable=0      failed=0      skipped=0
rescued=0     ignored=0
frontend1-na.example.com    :
ok=1      changed=0     unreachable=0      failed=0      skipped=0
rescued=0     ignored=0
frontend2-na.example.com    :
ok=1      changed=0     unreachable=0      failed=0      skipped=0
rescued=0     ignored=0
```

There's much more that you can do with geographically diverse environments, such as our simple example here, as we have not even touched on things such as placing variables in your inventory (which, for example, associates different parameters with different environments). We will explore this in more detail in *Chapter 3, Defining Your Inventory*.

However, hopefully, this has armed you with enough knowledge that you can start making informed choices about how to organize the code for your playbooks. As you complete further chapters of this book, you will be able to establish whether you wish to make use of roles or the `ansible.builtin.import_playbook` directive (or perhaps even both) as part of your playbook organization.

Let's carry on with our practical introduction to Ansible in the next section, with a look at the configuration file and some of the key directives that you might find valuable.

Exploring the configuration file

Ansible's behavior is, in part, defined by its configuration file. The central configuration file (which impacts the behavior of Ansible for all users on the system) can be found at /etc/ansible/ansible.cfg. However, this is not the only place Ansible will look for its configuration; in fact, it will look in the following locations, from the top to the bottom.

The first instance of the file is the configuration it will use; all of the others are ignored, even if they are present:

- ANSIBLE_CONFIG: The file location specified by the value of this environment variable, if set
- ansible.cfg: In the current working directory
- ~/.ansible.cfg: In the home directory of the user
- /etc/ansible/ansible.cfg: The central configuration that we previously mentioned

If you installed Ansible through a package manager, such as dnf, yum, or apt, you will almost always find a default configuration file called ansible.cfg in /etc/ansible. However, if you built Ansible from the source or installed it via pip, the central configuration file will not exist, and you will need to create it yourself. A good starting point used to be to reference the example Ansible configuration file that was included with the source code. However, since the release of ansible-core 2.12, you can now generate an example configuration file with all the available options present (but commented out) using this command:

```
$ ansible-config init --disabled > ansible.cfg
```

As you will almost certainly be working with a version of ansible-core newer than this, we'll assume this for the remainder of this section. Specifically, we will detail how to locate Ansible's running configuration and how to manipulate it. Most people who install Ansible find that they can get a long way with Ansible before they have to modify the default configuration, as it has been carefully designed to work in a great many scenarios. Indeed, all the example code run so far in this book has been performed on a copy of Ansible installed via PIP, with no configuration changes made.

Nonetheless, it is important to know a little about configuring Ansible in case you come across an issue in your environment that can only be changed by modifying the configuration.

Let's get started by exploring the default configuration that is provided with Ansible:

1. The command in the following code block lists the current configuration parameters supported by Ansible. It is incredibly useful because it tells you both the environment variable that can be used to change the setting (see the `env` field) as well as the configuration file parameter and section that can be used (see the `ini` field). Other valuable information, including the default configuration values and a description of the configuration, is given (see the `default` and `description` fields, respectively). Run the following command to explore the output:

    ```
    $ ansible-config list
    ```

    The following is an example of the kind of output you will see. There are, of course, many pages to it, but a snippet is shown here as an example:

    ```
    $ ansible-config list
    ACTION_WARNINGS:
      default: true
      description:
      - By default Ansible will issue a warning when received from a
    task action (module
          or action plugin)
      - These warnings can be silenced by adjusting this setting to
    False.
      env:
      - name: ANSIBLE_ACTION_WARNINGS
      ini:
      - key: action_warnings
        section: defaults
      name: Toggle action warnings
      type: boolean
      version_added: '2.5'
    AGNOSTIC_BECOME_PROMPT:
      default: true
      description: Display an agnostic become prompt instead of
    displaying a prompt containing
          the command line supplied become method
      env:
      - name: ANSIBLE_AGNOSTIC_BECOME_PROMPT
      ini:
      - key: agnostic_become_prompt
        section: privilege_escalation
      name: Display an agnostic become prompt
      type: boolean
      version_added: '2.5'
      yaml:
        key: privilege_escalation.agnostic_become_prompt
    ```

2. If you want to see a straightforward display of all the possible configuration parameters, along with
    their current values (regardless of whether they are configured from environment variables or a
    configuration file in one of the previously listed locations), you can run the following command:

    ```
    $ ansible-config dump
    ```

    The output shows all the configuration parameters (in an environment variable format), along
    with the current settings. If the parameter is configured with its default value, you are told so
    (see the (default) element after each parameter name). The output is also color-coded by
    default, with parameters at their default displayed in green, while those that have been changed
    are yellow (just like the color coding from an Ansible playbook run):

    ```
    $ ansible-config dump
    ACTION_WARNINGS(default) = True
    AGNOSTIC_BECOME_PROMPT(default) = True
    ANSIBLE_CONNECTION_PATH(default) = None
    ANSIBLE_COW_ACCEPTLIST(default) = ['bud-frogs', 'bunny',
    'cheese', 'daemon', 'default', 'dragon', 'elephant-in-snake',
    'elephant', 'eyes', 'hellok>
    ANSIBLE_COW_PATH(default) = None
    ANSIBLE_COW_SELECTION(default) = default
    ANSIBLE_FORCE_COLOR(default) = False
    ANSIBLE_HOME(default) = /home/james/.ansible
    ...
    CONFIG_FILE() = None
    ...
    ```

3. Let's see the effect on this output by editing one of the configuration parameters. Let's do this
    by setting an environment variable, as follows (this command has been tested in the bash
    shell, but may differ for other shells):

    ```
    $ export ANSIBLE_FORCE_COLOR=True
    ```

    Now, let's rerun the ansible-config command, but this time get it to tell us only the
    parameters that have been changed from their default values:

    ```
    $ ansible-config dump --only-change
    ANSIBLE_FORCE_COLOR(env: ANSIBLE_FORCE_COLOR) = True
    CONFIG_FILE() = None
    ```

    Here, you can see that ansible-config tells us that we have only changed ANSIBLE_
    FORCE_COLOR from the default value, which it is set to True, and that we set it through an
    env variable. Note that CONFIG_FILE has also been changed but no source for the change
    is found – this is because I installed Ansible via PIP, and so /etc/ansible/ansible.
    cfg (and other valid configuration files) do not exist – thus, this is expected behavior. This is
    an incredibly valuable tool, especially if you have to debug configuration issues.

When working with the Ansible configuration file itself, you will note that it is in INI format, meaning it has sections such as `[defaults]`, parameters in the format `key = value`, and comments beginning with either # or ;. You only need to place the parameters you wish to change from their defaults in your configuration file, so if you wanted to create a simple configuration to change the location of your default inventory file, it might look as follows:

```
# Set my configuration variables
[defaults]
inventory = /home/james/ansible-hosts ; Here is the path of the
inventory file
```

As discussed earlier, one of the possible valid locations for the `ansible.cfg` configuration file is in your current working directory. It is likely that this is within your home directory, so on a multi-user system, we strongly recommend you restrict access to the Ansible configuration file to your user account alone. You should take all the usual precautions when it comes to securing important configuration files on a multi-user system, especially as Ansible is normally used to configure multiple remote systems, and so, a lot of damage could be done if a configuration file was inadvertently compromised!

It is also important to note that the behavior of environment variables and configuration files is additive—thus with the configuration file I just mentioned in place, running the dump of the changed configuration again will yield the following:

```
$ ansible-config dump --only-change
ANSIBLE_FORCE_COLOR(env: ANSIBLE_FORCE_COLOR) = True
CONFIG_FILE() = /home/james/code/chapter02/ansible.cfg
DEFAULT_HOST_LIST(/home/james/code/chapter02/ansible.cfg) = ['/home/
james/ansible-hosts']
```

Of course, Ansible's behavior is not just controlled by the configuration files and switches—the command-line arguments that you pass to the various Ansible executables are also of vital importance. In fact, we have already worked with several already. We have shown you how to change where Ansible looks for its inventory file using the `inventory` parameter in `ansible.cfg`. However, in many of the examples that we previously covered in this book, we overrode this with the `-i` switch when running Ansible. So, let's proceed to the next section to look at the use of command-line arguments when running Ansible.

Command-line arguments

In this section, you will learn about the use of command-line arguments for playbook execution and how to employ some of the more commonly used ones to your advantage. We are already very familiar with one of these arguments, the `--version` switch, which we use to confirm that Ansible is installed (and which version is installed).

Just as we were able to learn about the various configuration parameters directly through Ansible, we can also learn about the command-line arguments. Almost all of the Ansible executables have a --help option that you can run to display the valid command-line parameters. Let's try this out now:

1. You can view all the options and arguments when you execute the `ansible` command line. Use the following command:

    $ ansible --help

    You will see a great deal of helpful output when you run the preceding command; a snippet of this is shown in the following code block (you might want to pipe this into a pager, such as `less`, so that you can read it all easily):

```
$ ansible --help
usage: ansible [-h] [--version] [-v] [-b]
                [--become-method BECOME_METHOD]
                [--become-user BECOME_USER]
                [-K | --become-password-file BECOME_PASSWOR
D_FILE]
                [-i INVENTORY] [--list-hosts] [-l SUBSET]
                [-P POLL_INTERVAL] [-B SECONDS] [-o]
                [-t TREE]
                [--private-key PRIVATE_KEY_FILE]
                [-u REMOTE_USER] [-c CONNECTION]
                [-T TIMEOUT]
                [--ssh-common-args SSH_COMMON_ARGS]
                [--sftp-extra-args SFTP_EXTRA_ARGS]
                [--scp-extra-args SCP_EXTRA_ARGS]
                [--ssh-extra-args SSH_EXTRA_ARGS]
                [-k | --connection-password-file CONNECTION
_PASSWORD_FILE]
                [-C] [-D] [-e EXTRA_VARS]
                [--vault-id VAULT_IDS]
```

Figure 2.2 – An example of the output of Ansible's built-in help

2. We could take one example from the preceding code to build on our previous use of the `ansible` command; so far, we have almost exclusively used it to run ad hoc tasks with the -m and -a parameters. However, `ansible` can also perform useful tasks such as telling us about the hosts in a group within our inventory. We could explore this using the `production-inventory` file we used earlier in this chapter:

    **$ ansible -i production-inventory --list-host appservers_emea_
    zone**

When you run this, you should see the members of the `appservers_emea_zone` inventory group listed. Although perhaps a little contrived, this example is incredibly valuable when you start working with dynamic inventory files and you can no longer just `cat` your inventory file to the terminal to view the contents:

```
$ ansible -i production-inventory --list-host appservers_emea_
zone
  hosts (2):
    appserver1-emea.example.com
    appserver2-emea.example.com
```

The same is true for the `ansible-playbook` executable file, too. We have already seen a few of these in the previous examples of this book and there's more that we can do. For example, earlier, we discussed the use of `ssh-agent` to manage multiple SSH authentication keys. While this makes running playbooks simple (as you don't have to pass any authentication parameters to Ansible), it is not the only way of doing this. You can use one of the command-line arguments for `ansible-playbook` to specify the private SSH key file, instead, as follows:

```
$ ansible-playbook -i production-inventory site.yml --private-key ~/
keys/id_rsa
```

Similarly, in the preceding section, we specified the `remote_user` variable for Ansible to connect with in the playbook. However, command-line arguments can also set this parameter for the playbook; so, rather than editing the `remote_user` line in the playbook, we could remove it altogether and instead run it using the following command-line string:

```
$ ansible-playbook -i production-inventory site.yml --user james
```

The ultimate aim of Ansible is to make your life simpler and to complete mundane day-to-day tasks for you. As a result, there is no right or wrong way to do this—you can specify your private SSH key using a command-line argument or make it available using `ssh-agent`. Similarly, you can put the `remote_user` line in your playbook or use the `--user` parameter on the command line. Ultimately, the choice is yours, but it is important to consider that if you are distributing a playbook to multiple users and they all have to remember to specify the remote user on the command line, will they actually remember to do it? What will the consequences be if they don't? If the `remote_user` line is present in the playbook, will that make their lives easier and be less prone to error because the user account has been set in the playbook itself?

As with the configuration of Ansible, you will use a small handful of the command-line arguments frequently and there will be many that you may never touch. The important thing is that you know they are there and how to find out about them, and you can make informed decisions about when to use them. Let's proceed to the next section, where we will look in more detail at ad hoc commands with Ansible.

Understanding ad hoc commands

We have already seen a handful of ad hoc commands so far in this book, but to recap, they are single tasks you can run with Ansible, making use of Ansible modules without the need to create or save playbooks. They are very useful for performing quick, one-off tasks on a number of remote machines or for testing and understanding the behavior of the Ansible modules that you intend to use in your playbooks. They are both a great learning tool and a quick and dirty (because you never document your work with a playbook) automation solution.

As with every Ansible example, we need an inventory to run against. Let's reuse our `production-inventory` file from before:

```
[frontends_na_zone]
frontend1-na.example.com
frontend2-na.example.com

[frontends_emea_zone]
frontend1-emea.example.com
frontend2-emea.example.com

[appservers_na_zone]
appserver1-na.example.com
appserver2-na.example.com

[appservers_emea_zone]
appserver1-emea.example.com
appserver2-emea.example.com
```

Now, let's start with perhaps the quickest and dirtiest of ad hoc commands—running a raw shell command on a group of remote machines. Suppose that you want to check that the date and time of all the frontend servers in EMEA are in sync—you could do this by using a monitoring tool or by manually logging in to each server in turn and checking the date and time. However, you can also use an Ansible ad hoc command:

1. Run the following ad hoc command to retrieve the current date and time from all of the `frontends_emea_zone` servers:

    ```
    $ ansible -i production-inventory frontends_emea_zone -a /usr/
    bin/date
    ```

    You will see that Ansible faithfully logs in to each machine in turn and runs the `date` command, returning the current date and time. Your output will look something like the following:

    ```
    $ ansible -i production-inventory frontends_emea_zone -a /usr/
    bin/date
    ```

```
frontend2-emea.example.com | CHANGED | rc=0 >>
Tue Apr 25 14:26:30 UTC 2023
frontend1-emea.example.com | CHANGED | rc=0 >>
Tue Apr 25 14:26:30 UTC 2023
```

2. This command is run with the user account you are logged in to when the command is run. You can use a command-line argument (discussed in the previous section) to run it as a different user:

```
$ ansible -i production-inventory frontends_emea_zone -a /usr/
sbin/pvs -u james

frontend2-emea.example.com | FAILED | rc=5 >>
  WARNING: Running as a non-root user. Functionality may be
unavailable.
  /run/lock/lvm/P_global:aux: open failed: Permission deniednon-
zero return code
frontend1-emea.example.com | FAILED | rc=5 >>
  WARNING: Running as a non-root user. Functionality may be
unavailable.
  /run/lock/lvm/P_global:aux: open failed: Permission deniednon-
zero return code
```

3. Here, we can see that the james user account does not have the privileges required to successfully run the pvs command. However, we can fix this by adding the --become command-line argument, which tells Ansible to become root on the remote systems:

```
$ ansible -i production-inventory frontends_emea_zone -a /usr/
sbin/pvs -u james --become

frontend2-emea.example.com | FAILED | rc=-1 >>
Missing sudo password
frontend1-emea.example.com | FAILED | rc=-1 >>
Missing sudo password
```

4. We can see that the command still fails because although james is in /etc/sudoers, it is not allowed to run commands as root without entering a sudo password. Luckily, there's a switch to get Ansible to prompt us for this at runtime, meaning we don't need to edit our /etc/sudoers file:

```
$ ansible -i production-inventory frontends_emea_zone -a /usr/
sbin/pvs -u james --become --ask-become-pass
BECOME password:

frontend2-emea.example.com | CHANGED | rc=0 >>
  PV          VG       Fmt  Attr PSize  PFree
  /dev/vdb1  vg_data lvm2 a--  <8.00g <8.00g
frontend1-emea.example.com | CHANGED | rc=0 >>
```

```
PV          VG       Fmt  Attr PSize  PFree
/dev/vdb1   vg_data  lvm2 a--  <8.00g <8.00g
```

5. By default, if you don't specify a module using the -m command-line argument, Ansible assumes you want to use the ansible.builtin.command module (see https://docs.ansible.com/ansible/latest/modules/command_module.html). If you wish to use a specific module, you can add the -m switch to the command-line arguments and then specify the module arguments under the -a switch, as in the following example:

```
$ ansible -i production-inventory frontends_emea_zone -m
ansible.builtin.copy -a "src=/etc/hosts dest=/tmp/hosts"
frontend2-emea.example.com | CHANGED => {
    "ansible_facts": {
        "discovered_interpreter_python": "/usr/bin/python3"
    },
    "changed": true,
    "checksum": "02b369653b5171fe264d0ac91c331531d04f375d",
    "dest": "/tmp/hosts",
    "gid": 1001,
    "group": "james",
    "md5sum": "cd9654dbef8a534df2557531038e03a7",
    "mode": "0664",
    "owner": "james",
    "size": 427,
    "src": "/home/james/.ansible/tmp/ansible-
tmp-1682433595.1356337-8575-192421314639198/source",
    "state": "file",
    "uid": 1001
}
frontend1-emea.example.com | CHANGED => {
    "ansible_facts": {
        "discovered_interpreter_python": "/usr/bin/python3"
    },
    "changed": true,
    "checksum": "02b369653b5171fe264d0ac91c331531d04f375d",
    "dest": "/tmp/hosts",
    "gid": 1001,
    "group": "james",
    "md5sum": "cd9654dbef8a534df2557531038e03a7",
    "mode": "0664",
    "owner": "james",
    "size": 427,
    "src": "/home/james/.ansible/tmp/ansible-
tmp-1682433595.1226285-8574-79002739194384/source",
    "state": "file",
```

```
    "uid": 1001
}
```

The preceding output not only shows that the copy was performed successfully to both hosts but also all the output values from the `ansible.builtin.copy` module. This, again, can be very helpful later when you are developing playbooks as it enables you to understand exactly how the module works and what output it produces in cases where you need to perform further work with that output. As we progress through this book, this will make more sense, so don't worry right now if it doesn't make sense.

You will also note that all arguments passed to the module must be enclosed in quotation marks (`"`). All arguments are specified as `key=value` pairs and no spaces should be added between `key` and `value` (for example, `key = value` is not acceptable). If you need to place quotation marks around one of your argument values, you can escape them using the backslash character (for example, `-a "src=/etc/yum.conf dest=\"/tmp/yum file.conf\""`).

All examples we have performed so far are very quick to execute and run, but this is not always the case with computing tasks. When you have to run an operation for a long time—say, more than two hours—you should consider running it as a background process. In this instance, you can run the command asynchronously and confirm the result of that execution later.

For example, to execute `sleep 2h` asynchronously in the background with a timeout of 7,200 seconds (`-B`) and without polling (`-P`), use this command:

```
$ ansible -i production-inventory frontends_emea_zone -B 7200 -P 0 -a
"sleep 2h"
frontend1-emea.example.com | CHANGED => {
    "ansible_facts": {
        "discovered_interpreter_python": "/usr/bin/python3"
    },
    "ansible_job_id": "809218129417.1291",
    "changed": true,
    "finished": 0,
    "results_file": "/home/james/.ansible_async/809218129417.1291",
    "started": 1
}
frontend2-emea.example.com | CHANGED => {
    "ansible_facts": {
        "discovered_interpreter_python": "/usr/bin/python3"
    },
    "ansible_job_id": "772164843356.1273",
    "changed": true,
    "finished": 0,
    "results_file": "/home/james/.ansible_async/772164843356.1273",
```

```
    "started": 1
}
```

Note that the output from this command gives a unique job ID for each task on each host. Let's now say that we want to see how this task proceeds on the second frontend server. Simply issue the following command from your Ansible control machine:

```
$ ansible -i production-inventory frontend2-emea.example.com -m
ansible.builtin.async_status -a "jid=772164843356.1273"
frontend2-emea.example.com | SUCCESS => {
    "ansible_facts": {
        "discovered_interpreter_python": "/usr/bin/python3"
    },
    "ansible_job_id": "772164843356.1273",
    "changed": false,
    "finished": 0,
    "results_file": "/home/james/.ansible_async/772164843356.1273",
    "started": 1,
    "stderr": "",
    "stderr_lines": [],
    "stdout": "",
    "stdout_lines": []
}
```

Here, we can see that the job has started but not finished. If we now kill the `sleep` command that we issued and check on the status again, we can see the following:

```
$ ansible -i production-inventory frontend2-emea.example.com -a "pkill
sleep"
frontend2-emea.example.com | CHANGED | rc=0 >>

james@controlnode:~/code/chapter02$ ansible -i production-inventory
frontend2-emea.example.com -m ansible.builtin.async_status -a
"jid=772164843356.1273"
frontend2-emea.example.com | FAILED! => {
    "ansible_facts": {
        "discovered_interpreter_python": "/usr/bin/python3"
    },
    "ansible_job_id": "772164843356.1273",
    "changed": true,
    "cmd": [
        "sleep",
        "2h"
    ],
```

```
        "delta": "0:02:06.526826",
        "end": "2023-04-25 14:45:13.024199",
        "finished": 1,
        "msg": "non-zero return code",
        "rc": -15,
        "results_file": "/home/james/.ansible_async/772164843356.1273",
        "start": "2023-04-25 14:43:06.497373",
        "started": 1,
        "stderr": "",
        "stderr_lines": [],
        "stdout": "",
        "stdout_lines": []
    }
```

Here, we see a FAILED status result because the sleep command was killed; it did not exit cleanly and returned a -15 code (see the rc parameter). When it was killed, no output was sent to either stdout or stderr, but if it had been, Ansible would have captured it and displayed it in the preceding code, which would aid you in debugging the failure. Lots of other useful information is included, including how long the task actually ran for, the end time, and so on. Similarly, useful output is also returned when the task exits cleanly.

That concludes our look at ad hoc commands in Ansible. By now, you should have a fairly solid grasp of the fundamentals of Ansible, but there's one important thing we haven't looked at yet, even though we briefly touched on it—variables and how to define them. We'll proceed to look at this in the next section.

Defining variables

In this section, we will explore the topic of variables and how they can be defined in Ansible. You will learn how variables should be defined step by step and understand how to work with them in Ansible.

Although automation removes much of the repetition from previously manual tasks, not every single system is identical. If two systems differ in some minor way, you could write two unique playbooks—one for each system. However, this would be inefficient and wasteful, as well as difficult to manage as time goes on (for example, if the code in one playbook is changed, how can you ensure that it is updated in the second variant?).

Equally, you might need to use a value from one system in another—perhaps you need to obtain the hostname of a database server and make it available to another. All of these issues can be addressed with variables as they allow the same automation code to run with parameter variations, as well as values to pass from one system to another (although this must be handled with some care).

Let's get started with a practical look at defining variables in Ansible.

Variables in Ansible should have well-formatted names that adhere to the following rules:

- The name of the variable must only include letters, underscores, and numbers. Spaces are not allowed.

- The name of the variable can only begin with a letter—it can contain numbers but cannot start with one.

For example, the following are good variable names:

- `external_svc_port`
- `internal_hostname_ap1`

The following examples are all invalid, however, and cannot be used (if you are familiar with Python, you will know that these restrictions also apply to Python code, which Ansible, being written in Python, inherits this from):

- `appserver-zone-na`
- `cache server ip`
- `dbms.server.port`
- `01appserver`

As discussed in the *Learning the YAML syntax* section, variables can be defined in a dictionary structure, such as the following. All values are declared in key-value pairs:

```
region:
  east: app
  west: frontend
  central: cache
```

In order to retrieve a specific field from the preceding dictionary structure, you can use either one of the following notations:

```
# bracket notation
region['east']

# dot notation
region.east
```

There are some exceptions to this; for example, you should use bracket notation if the variable name starts and ends with two underscores (for example, `__variable__`) or contains known public attributes (or even variables that are generated during the playbook run), such as the following:

- `as_integer_ratio`
- `symmetric_difference`

You can find more information on this at `https://docs.ansible.com/ansible/latest/user_guide/playbooks_variables.html#creating-valid-variable-names`.

This dictionary structure is valuable when defining host variables. Although earlier in this chapter we worked with a fictional set of employee records defined as an Ansible `variables` file, you could use this to specify something, such as some `redis` server parameters:

```
---
redis:
- server: cacheserver01.example.com
  port: 6379
  slaveof: cacheserver02.example.com
```

These could then be applied through your playbook and one common playbook could be used for all `redis` servers, regardless of their configuration, as changeable parameters such as the `port` and `master` servers are all contained in the variables.

You can also pass set variables directly in a playbook, and even pass them to roles that you call. For example, the following playbook code calls four hypothetical roles and each assigns a different value to the `username` variable for each one. These roles could be used to set up various administration roles on a server (or multiple servers), with each passing a changing list of usernames as people come and go from the company:

```
roles:
- role: dbms_admin
  vars:
    username: James
- role: system_admin
  vars:
    username: John
- role: security_amdin
  vars:
    username: Rock
- role: app_admin
  vars:
    username: Daniel
```

To access variables from within a playbook, you simply place the variable name inside quoted pairs of curly braces. Consider the following example playbook (based loosely on our previous `redis` example):

```
---
- name: Display redis variables
  hosts: all

  vars:
```

```
  redis:
    server: cacheserver01.example.com
    port: 6379
    slaveof: cacheserver02.example.com

  tasks:
   - name: Display the redis port
     ansible.builtin.debug:
       msg: "The redis port for {{ redis.server }} is {{ redis.port
}}"
```

Here, we define a variable in the playbook itself called `redis`. This variable is a dictionary, containing a number of parameters that might be important for our server. To access the contents of these variables, we use pairs of curly braces around them (as described previously) and the entire string is encased in quotation marks, which means we don't have to individually quote the variables. If you run the playbook on a local machine, you should see an output that looks as follows:

```
$ ansible-playbook -i localhost, -c local redis-playbook.yml

PLAY [Display redis variables] ******************************************
******************

TASK [Gathering Facts] *************************************************
***********
ok: [localhost]

TASK [Display the redis port] ******************************************
*****************
ok: [localhost] => {
    "msg": "The redis port for cacheserver01.example.com is 6379"
}

PLAY RECAP ************************************************************
localhost                  : ok=2    changed=0    unreachable=0
failed=0     skipped=0    rescued=0    ignored=0
```

Although we are accessing these variables here to print them in a debug message, you could use the same curly brace notation to assign them to module parameters, or for any other purpose that your playbook requires them for.

Also note the special inventory format we used here:

- `-i localhost,` – This tells `ansible-playbook` to read a list of literal hostnames from the command line, removing the need to define an inventory file.

- `-c local` – This replaces the need to set up SSH authentication with the local host, by simply using the `local` connection mechanism. This is incredibly useful when running commands on the local machine itself.

Ansible, just like many languages, has specially reserved variables that take on particular meanings in playbooks. In Ansible, these are known as magic variables and you can find a full list of them at `https://docs.ansible.com/ansible/latest/reference_appendices/special_variables.html`. Needless to say, you should not attempt to use any magic variable names for your own variables. Some common magic variables you might come across are as follows:

- `inventory_hostname`: The hostname for the current host that is iterated over in the play
- `groups`: A dictionary of the host groups in the inventory, along with the host membership of each group
- `group_names`: A list of the groups the current host (specified by `inventory_hostname`) is a part of
- `hostvars`: A dictionary of all the hosts in the inventory and the variables assigned to each of them

For example, the host variables for all the hosts can be accessed at any point in the playbook using `hostvars`, even if you are only operating on one particular host. Magic variables are surprisingly useful in playbooks and you will rapidly start to find yourself using them, so it is important to be aware of their existence.

You should also note that you can specify Ansible variables in multiple locations. Ansible has a strict order of variable precedence and you can take advantage of this by setting default values for variables in a place that has low precedence and then overriding them later in the play. This is useful for a variety of reasons, especially where an undefined variable could cause havoc when a playbook is run (or even when the playbook would fail as a result of this). We have not yet discussed all of the places that variables can be stored, so the full list of variable precedence order is not given here.

In addition, it can change between Ansible releases, so it is important that you refer to the documentation when working with and understanding variable precedence—go to `https://docs.ansible.com/ansible/latest/user_guide/playbooks_variables.html#variable-precedence-where-should-i-put-a-variable` for more information.

That concludes our brief overview of variables in Ansible, although we will see them used again in later examples in this book. Let's now round off this chapter with a look at Jinja2 filters, which add a whole world of power to your variable definitions.

Understanding Jinja2 filters

As Ansible is written in Python, it inherits an incredibly useful and powerful templating engine called Jinja2. We will look at the concept of templating later in this book, so for now, we will focus on one particular aspect of Jinja2 known as filtering. Jinja2 filters provide an incredibly powerful framework that you can use to manipulate and transform your data. Perhaps you have a string that you need to convert into lowercase, for example—you could apply a Jinja2 filter to achieve this. You can also use it to perform pattern matching, search and replace operations, and much more. There are many hundreds of filters for you to work with, and in this section, we hope to empower you with a basic understanding of Jinja2 filters and some practical knowledge about how to apply them, as well as showing you where to get more information about them if you wish to explore the subject further.

It is worth noting that Jinja2 operations are performed on the Ansible control node and only the results of the filter operation are sent to the remote hosts. This is done by design, both for consistency and to reduce the workload on the individual nodes as much as possible.

Let's explore this through a practical example. Suppose we have a YAML file containing some data that we want to parse. We can quite easily read a file from the machine filesystem and capture the result using the `register` keyword (`register` captures the result of the task and stores it in a variable—in the case of running the `ansible.builtin.shell` module, it captures all the output from the command that was run).

Our YAML data file might look as follows:

```
tags:
  - key: job
    value: developer
  - key: language
    value: java
```

Now, we could create a playbook to read this file and register the result, but how can we actually turn it into a variable structure that Ansible can understand and work with? Let's consider the following playbook:

```
---
- name: Jinja2 filtering demo 1
  hosts: localhost

  tasks:
    - name: Copy sample data to /tmp
      ansible.builtin.copy:
        src: multiple-document-strings.yaml
        dest: /tmp/multiple-document-strings.yaml
    - name: Read sample data to a variable
      ansible.builtin.shell: cat /tmp/multiple-document-strings.yaml
      register: result
    - name: Print the filtered output in a debug message
      ansible.builtin.debug:
```

```
      msg: '{{ item }}'
    loop: '{{ result.stdout | from_yaml_all | list }}'
```

The `ansible.builtin.shell` module does not necessarily run from the directory that the playbook is stored in, so we cannot guarantee that it will find our `multiple-document-strings.yaml` file even when it is in the same directory as the playbook. The `ansible.builtin.copy` module does, however, source files from the current (playbook) directory, so it is useful to use it to copy it to a known location (such as `/tmp`) for the `ansible.builtin.shell` module to read the file from. The `ansible.builtin.debug` module is then run in a `loop`. The `loop` is used to iterate over all of the lines of `stdout` from the `ansible.builtin.shell` command, applying two Jinja2 filters—`from_yaml_all` and `list` to the output line by line.

The `from_yaml_all` filter parses the source document lines as YAML and then the `list` filter converts the parsed data into a valid Ansible list. If we run the playbook, we should see Ansible's representation of the data structure from within our original file:

```
PLAY [Jinja2 filtering demo 1] ****************************************
*********************

TASK [Gathering Facts] ***********************************************
**************
ok: [localhost]

TASK [Copy sample data to /tmp] **************************************
*********************
changed: [localhost]

TASK [Read sample data to a variable] ********************************
***************************
changed: [localhost]

TASK [Print the filtered output in a debug message] ******************
*******************************************
ok: [localhost] => (item={'tags': [{'key': 'job', 'value':
'developer'}, {'key': 'language', 'value': 'java'}]}) => {
    "msg": {
        "tags": [
            {
                "key": "job",
                "value": "developer"
            },
            {
                "key": "language",
                "value": "java"
            }
```

```
        ]
      }
  }

PLAY RECAP ************************************************
localhost                    :
ok=4    changed=2    unreachable=0    failed=0    skipped=0
rescued=0    ignored=0
```

As you can see, we have generated a list of dictionaries that in themselves contain the key-value pairs.

If this data structure was already stored in our playbook, we could take this one step further and use the `items2dict` filter to turn the list into true `key: value` pairs, removing the `key` and `value` items from the data structure. For example, consider this second playbook:

```
---
- name: Jinja2 filtering demo 2
  hosts: localhost
  vars:
    tags:
      - key: job
        value: developer
      - key: language
        value: java

  tasks:
    - name: Filter the tags variable through items2dict
      ansible.builtin.debug:
        msg: '{{ tags | items2dict }}'
```

Now, if we run this, we can see that our data is converted into a nice, neat set of `key: value` pairs:

```
$ ansible-playbook -i localhost, -c local jinja-filtering2.yml
[WARNING]: Found variable using reserved name: tags

PLAY [Jinja2 filtering demo 2] ****************************************
********************

TASK [Gathering Facts] **********************************************
*****
ok: [localhost]

TASK [Filter the tags variable through items2dict] ******************
***************************************
ok: [localhost] => {
    "msg": {
```

```
            "job": "developer",
            "language": "java"
        }
    }


    PLAY RECAP ***************************************************
    localhost                 :
    ok=2      changed=0    unreachable=0    failed=0    skipped=0
    rescued=0    ignored=0
```

Observe the warning at the top of the playbook. Ansible displays a warning if you attempt to use a reserved name for a variable, as we did here. Normally, you should not create a variable with a reserved name, but the example here demonstrates both how the filter works and how Ansible will attempt to warn you if you do something that might cause problems.

Earlier in this section, we used the `ansible.builtin.shell` module to read a file and used `register` to store the result in a variable. This is perfectly fine, if a little inelegant. Jinja2 contains a series of `lookup` filters that, among other things, can read the contents of a given file. Let's examine the behavior of the following playbook:

```
---
- name: Jinja2 filtering demo 3
  hosts: localhost

  vars:
    ping_value: "{{ lookup('file', '/etc/hosts') }}"

  tasks:
    - name: Display the values obtained from the file lookup
      ansible.builtin.debug:
        msg: "ping value is {{ ping_value }}"
```

When we run this, we can see that Ansible has captured the contents of the `/etc/hosts` file for us, without us needing to resort to the `ansible.builtin.copy` and `ansible.builtin.shell` modules as we did earlier:

```
$ ansible-playbook -i localhost, -c local jinja-filtering3.yml


PLAY [Jinja2 filtering demo 3] *****************************************
********************

TASK [Gathering Facts] ************************************************
*****
ok: [localhost]
```

```
TASK [Display the values obtained from the file lookup] **************
***********************************************
ok: [localhost] => {
    "msg": "ping value is 127.0.0.1 localhost\n\n# The following lines
are desirable for IPv6 capable hosts\n::1 ip6-localhost ip6-loopback\
nfe00::0 ip6-localnet\nff00::0 ip6-mcastprefix\nff02::1 ip6-allnodes\
nff02::2 ip6-allrouters\nff02::3 ip6-allhosts\n\n10.0.50.30
frontend1-na.example.com frontend1-emea.example.com\n10.0.50.31
frontend2-na.example.com frontend2-emea.example.com\n\n10.0.50.40
appserver1-emea.example.com\n10.0.50.41 appserver2-emea.example.com"
}

PLAY RECAP ***********************************************************
localhost                  :
ok=2      changed=0     unreachable=0     failed=0     skipped=0
rescued=0     ignored=0
```

There are many other filters that you might be interested in exploring and a full list can be found in the official Jinja2 documentation (https://jinja.palletsprojects.com/en/3.1.x/). The following are a handful of other examples that will give you an idea of the kinds of things that Jinja2 filters can achieve for you, from quoting strings to concatenating lists, to obtaining useful path information for a file:

```
# Add some quotation in the shell
- shell: echo {{ string_value | quote }}

# Concatenate a list into a specific string
{{ list | join("$") }}

# Obtain the file name of a specific file path
{{ path | basename }}

# Retrieve the directory from a full path
{{ path | dirname }}

# Get the directory from a specific windows path
{{ path | win_dirname }}
```

That concludes our look at Jinja2 filtering. It is a massive topic that deserves a book all to itself, but, as ever, I hope that this practical guide has given you some pointers on how to get started and where to find information.

Summary

Ansible is a very powerful and versatile automation engine that can be used for a wide variety of tasks. Understanding the basics of how to work with it is of paramount importance, before addressing the more complex challenges of playbook creation and large-scale automation. Ansible relies on a language called YAML, a simple-to-read (and write) syntax that supports the rapid development of easy-to-read and easy-to-maintain code and inherits a number of valuable features from the Python language that it is written in, including Jinja2 filtering.

In this chapter, you learned the fundamentals of working with various Ansible programs. You then learned about the YAML syntax and the ways that you can break down your code into manageable chunks to make it easier to read and maintain. We explored the use of ad hoc commands in Ansible, variable definition and structure, and how to make use of Jinja2 filters to manipulate the data in your playbooks.

In the next chapter, we will take a more in-depth look at Ansible inventories and explore some of the more advanced concepts of working with them that you may find useful.

Questions

1. Which component of Ansible allows you to define a block to execute task groups as a play?

   A. `handler`

   B. `service`

   C. `hosts`

   D. `tasks`

   E. `name`

2. Which basic syntax from the YAML format do you use to start a file?

   A. `###`

   B. `---`

   C. `%%%`

   D. `===`

   E. `***`

3. True or false – in order to interpret and transform output data in Ansible, you need to use Jinja2 templates.

   A. True

   B. False

Further reading

To find out about more configuration variables, go to `https://docs.ansible.com/ansible/latest/reference_appendices/config.html#ansible-configuration-settings`.

3

Defining Your Inventory

As we discussed in the preceding two chapters, Ansible cannot do anything until you tell it which hosts it is responsible for. This is, of course, logical—you wouldn't want any automation tool, regardless of how easy it is to use and set up, to simply go out and take control of every single device on your network. Hence, at the bare minimum, you must tell Ansible what hosts it is going to automate tasks on, and this, in the most fundamental terms, is what an inventory is.

However, there is so much more to inventories than just a list of automation targets. Ansible inventories can be provided in several formats; they can be either static or dynamic, and they can contain important variables that define how Ansible interacts with each host (or groups of hosts). Hence, they deserve a chapter to themselves, and in this chapter, we shall perform a practical exploration of inventories and how to use them to your best advantage as you automate your infrastructure with Ansible.

In this chapter, we will cover the following topics:

- Creating an inventory file and adding hosts
- Generating a dynamic inventory file
- Special host management using patterns

Technical requirements

This chapter assumes that you have set up your control host with Ansible, as detailed in *Chapter 1, Getting Started with Ansible*, and you are using the most recent version available—the examples in this chapter were tested with Ansible 8.0 and `ansible-core` 2.15.0. This chapter also assumes that you have at least one additional host to test against, and this should be Linux-based. Although we will give specific examples of hostnames in this chapter, you are free to substitute them with your own hostnames and/or IP addresses, and details of how to do this will be provided in the appropriate places.

The code bundle for this chapter is available here: `https://github.com/PacktPublishing/Practical-Ansible-Second-Edition/tree/main/Chapter%203`.

Creating an inventory file and adding hosts

Whenever you see a reference to "*creating an inventory*" in Ansible, you are normally quite safe to assume that it is a static inventory. Ansible supports two types of inventory—static and dynamic—and we will cover the latter of these two later in this chapter. Static inventories are by their very nature static; they are unchanging unless a human manually edits them. This is great when you are starting out and testing Ansible, as it provides you with a very quick and easy way to get up and running quickly. Even in small, closed environments, static inventories are a great way to manage your environment, especially when changes to the infrastructure are infrequent.

Most Ansible installations will look for a default inventory file in `/etc/ansible/hosts` (though this path is configurable in the Ansible configuration file, as discussed in *Chapter 2, Understanding the Fundamentals of Ansible*). You are welcome to populate this file or to provide your own inventory for each playbook run, and it is commonplace to see inventories provided alongside playbooks—after all, when you start to build them out with variables and groupings, they become a code asset just as your playbooks and roles do, so it makes sense to commit them to source control alongside your other automation code. As you will have seen in the earlier chapters of this book, Ansible commands use the `-i` flag to specify the location of the inventory file if not using the default. We've already seen examples of this in this book, but as a refresher, this might look like the following example:

```
$ ansible -i /home/cloud-user/inventory all -m ansible.builtin.ping
```

Most static inventory files you will come across are created in INI format, though it is important to note that other formats are supported. The most common format you will find after INI-formatted files are YAML ones—more details of the types of inventory files you can work with may be found here: `https://docs.ansible.com/ansible/latest/user_guide/intro_inventory.html`.

In this chapter, we will provide some examples of both INI and YAML formatted inventory files for you to consider, as you must have an awareness of both. Personally, I have worked with Ansible for many years and only worked with either INI-formatted files or dynamic inventories, but they say knowledge is power and so it will do no harm to learn a little about both formats.

Let's start by creating a static inventory file. This inventory file will be separate from the default inventory.

Create an inventory file in `/etc/ansible/my_inventory` using the following INI-formatted code:

```
target1.example.org ansible_host=192.168.81.142 ansible_port=3333

target2.example.org ansible_port=3333 ansible_user=james

target3.example.org ansible_host=192.168.81.143 ansible_port=5555
```

The blank lines between inventory hosts are not required—they have been inserted simply to make the inventory more readable in this book. This inventory file is very simple and does not include any grouping; however, when referencing the inventory, you can still refer to all the hosts together using the special `all` group, which is implicitly defined regardless of how you format and divide your inventory file.

Each line in the preceding file contains one inventory host. The first column contains the inventory hostname that Ansible will use (which can be accessed through the `inventory_hostname` magic variable we discussed in *Chapter 2, Understanding the Fundamentals of Ansible*). All the parameters on the same line after that are variables that are assigned to the host. These can be user-defined variables or special Ansible variables, as we have set here.

There are many such variables, but the preceding examples specifically include the following:

- `ansible_host`: If the inventory hostname cannot be accessed directly—perhaps because it is not in DNS, for example—this variable contains the hostname or IP address that Ansible will connect to instead

- `ansible_port`: By default, Ansible attempts all communication over port 22 for SSH—if you have an SSH daemon running on another port, you can tell Ansible about it using this variable

- `ansible_user`: By default, Ansible will attempt to connect to the remote host using the current user account you are running the Ansible command from—you can override this in several ways, of which this is one

Hence, the preceding three hosts can be summarized as follows:

- The `target1.example.org` host should be connected to using the `192.168.81.142` IP address, on port `3333`

- The `target2.example.org` host should be connected to on port `3333` also, but this time, using the `james` user rather than the account running the Ansible command

- The `target3.example.org` host should be connected to using the `192.168.81.143` IP address, on port `5555`

In this way, even with no further constructs, you can begin to see the power of static INI-formatted inventories.

Now, if you wanted to create exactly the same inventory as the preceding, but this time, format it as YAML, you would specify it as follows (we'll call this file `my_inventory.yaml`):

```
---
ungrouped:
  hosts:
    target1.example.org:
      ansible_host: 192.168.81.142
      ansible_port: 3333
    target2.example.org:
```

```
        ansible_port: 3333
        ansible_user: james
    target3.example.org:
        ansible_host: 192.168.81.143
        ansible_port: 5555
```

You may come across inventory file examples containing parameters such as `ansible_ssh_port`, `ansible_ssh_host`, and `ansible_ssh_user`—these variable names (and others like them) were used in Ansible versions before 2.0. Backward compatibility has been maintained for many of these, but you should update them where possible as this compatibility may be removed at some point in the future.

Now, if you were to run the preceding inventory within Ansible using a simple `ansible.builtin.shell` command, the result would appear as follows:

```
$ ansible -i /etc/ansible/my_inventory.yaml all -m ansible.builtin.
shell -a 'echo hello-yaml' -f 5
target1.example.org | CHANGED | rc=0 >>
hello-yaml
target2.example.org | CHANGED | rc=0 >>
hello-yaml
target3.example.org | CHANGED | rc=0 >>
hello-yaml
```

That covers the basics of creating a simple static inventory file. Let's now expand upon this by adding host groups to the inventory in the next part of this chapter.

Using host groups

There is rarely one playbook that will suit an entire infrastructure, and although it is easy to tell Ansible to use an alternate inventory for a different playbook, this could get very messy, very quickly, with potentially hundreds of small inventory files dotted around your network. You can imagine how quickly this would get unmanageable, and Ansible is supposed to make things more manageable, not the opposite. One possible simple solution to this is to start adding groups to your inventories.

Let's assume you have a simple three-tier web architecture, with multiple hosts in each tier for high availability and/or load balancing. The three tiers in this architecture might be the following:

- Frontend servers
- Application servers
- Database servers

With this architecture set out, let's set about creating an inventory for it, again mixing up the YAML and INI formats to give you experience in both. To keep the examples clear and concise, we'll assume that you can access all servers using their **Fully Qualified Domain Names** (**FQDNs**), and hence won't add any host variables in these inventory files. There is nothing to stop you from doing this, of course, and every example is different.

First of all, let's create the inventory for the three-tier frontend using the INI format. We will call this file `hostsgroups-ini`, and the contents of this file should look something like this:

```
loadbalancer.example.org

[frontends]
web01.example.org
web02.example.org

[apps]
app01.example.org
app02.example.org

[databases]
db01.example.org
db02.example.org
```

In the preceding inventory, we have created three groups, called `frontends`, `apps`, and `databases`. Note that, in INI-formatted inventories, group names go inside square braces. Under each group name goes the server names that belong to each group, so the preceding example shows two servers in each group. Notice the outlier at the top, `loadbalancer.example.org`—this host isn't in any group. All ungrouped hosts must go at the very top of an INI-formatted file.

Before we proceed any further, it's worth noting that inventories can also contain groups of groups, which is incredibly useful for processing certain tasks by a different division. The preceding inventory stands in its own right, but what if our frontend servers are built on Ubuntu, and the app and database servers are built on Fedora? There will be some fundamental differences in the ways we handle these hosts—for example, we might use the `ansible.builtin.apt` module to manage packages on Ubuntu and the `ansible.builtin.dnf` module on Fedora.

We could, of course, handle this case using facts gathered from each host as these will contain the operating system details. We could also create a new version of the inventory, as follows:

```
loadbalancer.example.org

[frontends]
web01.example.org
web02.example.org

[apps]
app01.example.org
```

```
app02.example.org

[databases]
db01.example.org
db02.example.org

[fedora:children]
apps
databases

[ubuntu:children]
frontends
```

With the use of the `children` keyword in the group definition (inside the square braces), we can create groups of groups; hence, we can perform clever groupings to help our playbook design without having to specify each host more than once.

This structure in INI format is quite readable but takes some getting used to when it is converted into YAML format. The code listed next shows the YAML version of the preceding inventory—the two are identical as far as Ansible is concerned, but it is left to you to decide which format you prefer working with:

```
all:
  hosts:
    loadbalancer.example.org:
  children:
    fedora:
      children:
        apps:
          hosts:
            app01.example.org:
            app02.example.org:
        databases:
          hosts:
            db01.example.org:
            db02.example.org:
    ubuntu:
      children:
        frontends:
          hosts:
            web01.example.org:
            web02.example.org:
```

You can see that the `children` keyword is still used in the YAML-formatted inventory, but now the structure is more hierarchical than it was in the INI format. The indentation might be easier for you to follow, but note how the hosts are ultimately defined at quite a high level of indentation—this format could be more difficult to extend, depending on your desired approach.

When you want to work with any of the groups from the preceding inventory, you would simply reference it either in your playbook or on the command line. Extending our previous example, we can run the following:

```
$ ansible -i hostgroups-yaml all -m ansible.builtin.shell -a 'echo
hello-yaml' -f 5
```

Note the `all` keyword in the middle of that line. That is the special `all` group that is implicit in all inventories and is explicitly mentioned in your previous YAML example. If we wanted to run the same command, but this time on just the `fedora` group hosts from the previous YAML inventory, we would run this variation of the command:

```
$ ansible -i hostgroups-yaml fedora -m ansible.builtin.shell -a 'echo
hello-yaml' -f 5
app01.example.org | CHANGED | rc=0 >>
hello-yaml
app02.example.org | CHANGED | rc=0 >>
hello-yaml
db01.example.org | CHANGED | rc=0 >>
hello-yaml
db02.example.org | CHANGED | rc=0 >>
hello-yaml
```

As you can see, this is a powerful way of managing your inventory and making it easy to run commands on just the hosts you want. The possibility of creating multiple groups makes life simple, especially when you want to run different tasks on different groups of servers.

As an aside to developing your inventories, it is worth noting that there is a quick shorthand notation that you can use to create multiple hosts. Let's assume you have 100 app servers, all named sequentially, as follows:

```
[apps]
app01.example.org
app02.example.org
...
app99.example.org
app100.example.org
```

This is entirely possible, but would be tedious and error-prone to create by hand and would produce some very hard to read and interpret inventories. Luckily, Ansible provides a quick shorthand notation to achieve this, and the following inventory snippet actually produces an inventory with the same 100 app servers that we could create manually:

```
[apps]
app[01:100].example.org
```

It is also possible to use alphabetic ranges as well as numeric ones—extending our example to add some cache servers, you might have the following:

```
[cache]
cache-[a:e].example.org
```

This is the same as manually creating the following:

```
[cache]
cache-a.example.org
cache-b.example.org
cache-c.example.org
cache-d.example.org
cache-e.example.org
```

Now that we've completed our exploration of the various static inventory formats and how to create groups (and indeed, child groups), in the next section, let's expand on our previously brief look at host variables.

Adding host and group variables to your inventory

We have already touched upon host variables—we saw them earlier in this chapter when we used them to override connection details such as the user account to connect with, the address to connect to, and the port to use. However, there is so much more you can do with Ansible and inventory variables, and it is important to note that they can be defined not only at the host level but also at the group level, which again provides you with some incredibly powerful ways in which you can efficiently manage your infrastructure from one central inventory.

Let's build on our previous three-tier example and suppose that we need to set two variables for each of our two frontend servers. These are not special Ansible variables but instead are variables entirely of our own choosing, which we will use later on in the playbooks that run against this server. Suppose that these variables are as follows:

- `https_port`, which defines the port that the frontend proxy should listen on
- `lb_vip`, which defines the FQDN of the load balancer in front of the frontend servers

Let's see how this is done:

1. We could simply add these to each of the hosts in the `frontends` part of our inventory file, just as we did before with the Ansible connection variables. In this case, a portion of our INI-formatted inventory might look like this:

   ```
   [frontends]
   web01.example.org https_port=8443 lb_vip=lb.example.org
   web02.example.org https_port=8443 lb_vip=lb.example.org
   ```

   If we run an ad hoc command against this inventory, we can see the contents of both of these variables:

   ```
   $ ansible -i hostvars1-hostgroups-ini frontends -m ansible.
   builtin.debug -a "msg=\"Connecting to {{ lb_vip }}, listening on
   {{ https_port }}\""
   web01.example.org | SUCCESS => {
       "msg": "Connecting to lb.example.org, listening on 8443"
   }
   web02.example.org | SUCCESS => {
       "msg": "Connecting to lb.example.org, listening on 8443"
   }
   ```

   This has worked just as we desired, but the approach is inefficient as you have to add the same variables to every single host.

2. Luckily, you can assign variables to a host group as well as to hosts individually. If we edited the preceding inventory to achieve this, the `frontends` section would now look like this:

   ```
   [frontends]
   web01.example.org
   web02.example.org

   [frontends:vars]
   https_port=8443
   lb_vip=lb.example.org
   ```

   Notice how much more readable that is? Yet, if we run the same command as before against our newly organized inventory, we see that the result is the same:

   ```
   $ ansible -i groupvars1-hostgroups-ini frontends -m ansible.
   builtin.debug -a "msg=\"Connecting to {{ lb_vip }}, listening on
   {{ https_port }}\""
   web01.example.org | SUCCESS => {
       "msg": "Connecting to lb.example.org, listening on 8443"
   }
   web02.example.org | SUCCESS => {
   ```

```
        "msg": "Connecting to lb.example.org, listening on 8443"
    }
```

3. There will be times when you want to work with host variables for individual hosts, and times when group variables are more relevant. It is up to you to determine which is better for your scenario; however, remember that host variables can be used in combination. It is also worth noting that host variables override group variables, so if we need to change the connection port to 8444 on the web01.example.org one, we could do this as follows:

```
[frontends]
web01.example.org https_port=8444
web02.example.org

[frontends:vars]
https_port=8443
lb_vip=lb.example.org
```

    Now, if we run our ad hoc command again with the new inventory, we can see that we have overridden the variable on one host:

```
$ ansible -i groupvars2-hostgroups-ini frontends -m ansible.
builtin.debug -a "msg=\"Connecting to {{ lb_vip }}, listening on
{{ https_port }}\""
web01.example.org | SUCCESS => {
    "msg": "Connecting to lb.example.org, listening on 8444"
}
web02.example.org | SUCCESS => {
    "msg": "Connecting to lb.example.org, listening on 8443"
}
```

    Of course, doing this for one host alone when there are only two might seem a little pointless, but when you have an inventory with hundreds of hosts in it, this method of overriding one host will suddenly become very valuable.

4. Just for completeness, if we were to add the host variables we defined previously to our YAML version of the inventory, the frontends section would appear as follows (the rest of the inventory has been removed to save space):

```
frontends:
  hosts:
    web01.example.org:
      https_port: 8444
    web02.example.org:
  vars:
    https_port: 8443
    lb_vip: lb.example.org
```

Running the same ad hoc command as before, you can see that the result is the same as for our INI-formatted inventory:

```
$ ansible -i groupvars2-hostgroups-yaml frontends -m ansible.
builtin.debug -a "msg=\"Connecting to {{ lb_vip }}, listening on
{{ https_port }}\""
web01.example.org | SUCCESS => {
    "msg": "Connecting to lb.example.org, listening on 8444"
}
web02.example.org | SUCCESS => {
    "msg": "Connecting to lb.example.org, listening on 8443"
}
```

So far, we have covered several ways of providing host variables and group variables to your inventory; however, there is another way that deserves special mention and will become valuable to you as your inventory becomes larger and more complex.

Right now, our examples are small and compact and only contain a handful of groups and variables; however, when you scale this up to a full infrastructure of servers, using a single flat inventory file could, once again, become unmanageable. Luckily, Ansible also provides a solution to this. Two specially named directories, `host_vars` and `group_vars`, are automatically searched for appropriate variable content if they exist within the playbook directory. We can test this out by recreating the preceding frontend variables example using this special directory structure, rather than putting the variables into the inventory file:

1. Let's start by creating a new directory structure for this purpose:

```
$ mkdir vartree
$ cd vartree
```

2. Now, under this directory, we'll create two more directories for the variables:

```
$ mkdir host_vars group_vars
```

3. Now, under the `host_vars` directory, we'll create a file with the name of our host that needs the proxy setting, with `.yml` appended to it (that is, `web01.example.org.yml`). This file should contain the following:

```
---
https_port: 8444
```

4. Similarly, under the `group_vars` directory, create a YAML file named after the group to which we want to assign variables (that is, `frontends.yml`) with the following contents:

```
---
https_port: 8443
lb_vip: lb.example.org
```

5. Finally, we will create our inventory file as before, except that it contains no variables:

```
loadbalancer.example.org

[frontends]
web01.example.org
web02.example.org

[apps]
app01.example.org
app02.example.org

[databases]
db01.example.org
db02.example.org
```

Just for clarity, your final directory structure should look like this:

```
$ tree
.
├── group_vars
│   └── frontends.yml
├── host_vars
│   └── web01.example.org.yml
└── inventory

2 directories, 3 files
```

6. Now, let's try running our familiar ad hoc command and see what happens:

```
$ ansible -i inventory frontends -m ansible.builtin.debug -a
"msg=\"Connecting to {{ lb_vip }}, listening on {{ https_port
}}\""
web01.example.org | SUCCESS => {
    "msg": "Connecting to lb.example.org, listening on 8444"
}
web02.example.org | SUCCESS => {
    "msg": "Connecting to lb.example.org, listening on 8443"
}
```

As you can see, this works exactly as before, and without further instruction, Ansible has traversed the directory structure and ingested all the variable files.

7. If you have many hundreds of variables (or need an even finer-grained approach), you can replace the YAML files with directories named after the hosts and groups. Let's recreate the directory structure, but now with directories instead:

```
$ tree
.
├── group_vars
│   └── frontends
│       ├── https_port.yml
│       └── lb_vip.yml
├── host_vars
│   └── web01.example.org
│       └── main.yml
└── inventory


4 directories, 4 files
```

Notice how we now have directories named after the `frontends` group and the `web01.example.org` host? Inside the `frontends` directory, we have split the variables into two files, and this can be incredibly useful for logically organizing variables in groups, especially as your playbooks get bigger and more complex. Although we have named the variables files by the name of the variable they contain, this has been done purely to help us understand the code structure here. Each variables file may contain any number of variables, and they need not hold any relation to the filename.

The files themselves are simply an adaptation of our previous ones:

```
$ cat host_vars/web01.example.org/main.yml
---
https_port: 8444

$ cat group_vars/frontends/https_port.yml
---
https_port: 8443

$ cat group_vars/frontends/lb_vip.yml
---
lb_vip: lb.example.org
```

Even with this more finely divided directory structure, the result of running the ad hoc command is still the same:

```
$ ansible -i inventory frontends -m ansible.builtin.debug -a
"msg=\"Connecting to {{ lb_vip }}, listening on {{ https_port
}}\""
web01.example.org | SUCCESS => {
```

```
        "msg": "Connecting to lb.example.org, listening on 8444"
    }
web02.example.org | SUCCESS => {
        "msg": "Connecting to lb.example.org, listening on 8443"
    }
```

8. One final thing of note before we conclude this section is, if you define the same variable at both a group level and a child group level, the variable at the child group level takes precedence. This is not as obvious to figure out as it first sounds. Consider our earlier inventory where we used child groups to differentiate between Fedora and Ubuntu hosts—if we add a variable with the same name to both the ubuntu child group and the frontends group (which is a **child** of the ubuntu group) as follows, what will the outcome be? The inventory would look like this:

    ```
    loadbalancer.example.org

    [frontends]
    web01.example.org
    web02.example.org

    [frontends:vars]
    testvar=childgroup

    [apps]
    app01.example.org
    app02.example.org

    [databases]
    db01.example.org
    db02.example.org

    [fedora:children]
    apps
    databases

    [ubuntu:children]
    frontends

    [ubuntu:vars]
    testvar=group
    ```

    Now, let's run an ad hoc command to see what value of testvar is actually set:

    ```
    $ ansible -i hostgroups-children-vars-ini ubuntu -m ansible.
    builtin.debug -a "var=testvar"
    web01.example.org | SUCCESS => {
    ```

```
        "testvar": "childgroup"
    }
    web02.example.org | SUCCESS => {
        "testvar": "childgroup"
    }
```

It's important to note that the `frontends` group is a child of the `ubuntu` group in this inventory (hence, the group is listed under `[ubuntu:children]`), and so the variable value we set at the `frontends` group level wins as this is the child group in this scenario.

By now, you should have a pretty good idea of how to work with static inventory files. However, no look at Ansible's inventory capabilities is complete without a look at dynamic inventories, and we shall do exactly this in the next section.

Generating a dynamic inventory file

In these days of cloud computing and infrastructure-as-code, the hosts you may wish to automate could change on a daily, if not hourly, basis! Keeping a static Ansible inventory up to date could become a full-time job, and hence, in many large-scale scenarios, it becomes unrealistic to attempt to use a static inventory on an ongoing basis.

This is where Ansible's dynamic inventory support comes in. In short, Ansible can gather its inventory data from just about any executable file (though you will find that most dynamic inventories are written in Python)—the only requirement is that the executable returns the inventory data in a specified JSON format. You are free to create your own inventory scripts if you wish, but thankfully, many have been created already for you to use that cover a multitude of potential inventory sources including Amazon EC2, Microsoft Azure, Red Hat Satellite, **Lightweight Directory Access Protocol (LDAP)** directories, and many more systems.

When writing a book, it is difficult to know for certain which dynamic inventory script to use as an example, as it is not a given that everyone will have an Amazon EC2 account they can freely use to test against. As a result, we will use the Cobbler provisioning system by way of example, as this is freely available and easy to roll out on a Fedora system. For those interested, Cobbler is a system for dynamically provisioning and building Linux systems, and it can handle all aspects of this, including DNS, DHCP, PXE booting, and so on. Hence, if you were to use this to provision virtual or physical machines in your infrastructure, it would make sense to also use this as your inventory source, as Cobbler was responsible for building the systems in the first place and so knows all the system names.

This example will demonstrate to you the fundamentals of working with a dynamic inventory, which you can then take forward to use the dynamic inventory scripts for other systems. Let's get started with this process by first installing Cobbler—the process outlined here was tested on Fedora:

1. Your first task is to install the relevant Cobbler packages using `dnf`. Note that, at the time of writing, the SELinux policy provided with Fedora 38 does not support Cobbler's functionality

and blocks some aspects from working. Although this is not something you should do in a production environment, your simplest path to getting this demo up and running is to simply disable SELinux:

```
$ sudo dnf install -y cobbler
$ sudo setenforce 0
```

2. Next, ensure that the `cobblerd` service is configured to listen on the loopback address by checking the settings in `/etc/cobbler/settings`—the relevant snippet of the file is shown here and should appear as follows:

```
# default, localhost
server: 127.0.0.1
```

> **Note**
>
> This is not a public listening address, so please *do not use* 0.0.0.0. You can also set it to the IP address of the Cobbler server.

3. With this step complete, you can start the `cobblerd` service using `systemctl`:

```
$ sudo systemctl enable --now cobblerd.service
$ sudo systemctl status cobblerd.service
```

4. With the Cobbler service up and running, we'll now step through the process of adding a distribution to Cobbler to create some hosts from. This process is fairly simple, but you do need to add a kernel file and an initial RAM disk file. The easiest source to obtain these from is your `/boot` directory, assuming you have installed Cobbler on Fedora 38. On the test system used for this demo, the following commands were used; however, you must replace the version number in the `vmlinuz` and `initramfs` filenames with the appropriate version numbers from your system's `/boot` directory:

```
$ sudo cobbler distro add --name=Fedora38 --kernel=/
boot/vmlinuz-6.2.9-300.fc38.x86_64 --initrd=/boot/
initramfs-6.2.9-300.fc38.x86_64.img

$ sudo cobbler profile add --name=webservers --distro=Fedora38
```

This definition is quite rudimentary and would not necessarily be able to produce working server images; however, it will suffice for our simple demo as we can add some systems based on this notional Fedora 38-based image. Note that the profile name we are creating, `webservers`, will later become our inventory group name in our dynamic inventory.

5. Let's now add those systems to Cobbler. The following two commands will add two hosts called `frontend01` and `frontend02` to our Cobbler system, using the `webservers` profile we created previously:

```
$ sudo cobbler system add --name=frontend01 --profile=webservers
--dns-name=frontend01.example.org --interface=eth0

$ sudo cobbler system add --name=frontend02 --profile=webservers
--dns-name=frontend02.example.org --interface=eth0
```

Note that, for Ansible to work, it must be able to reach the FQDNs specified in the `--dns-name` parameter. To achieve this, I am also adding entries to `/etc/hosts` on the Ansible control node for these two machines to ensure we can reach them later. These entries can point to any two systems of your choosing, as this is just a test.

At this point, you have successfully installed Cobbler, created a profile, and added two hypothetical systems to this profile. The next stage in our process is to download and configure the Ansible dynamic inventory scripts to work with these entries. To achieve this, let's get started on the process given here:

1. Since Ansible 3.0, most dynamic inventory scripts have been moved into Collections as this is the easiest way to distribute and update them while decoupling them from the `ansible-core` distribution. The Cobbler dynamic inventory script is included as part of the `community.general` collection, which you should find was installed as part of the Ansible 8.0 package you installed previously. You can verify this with the following command:

```
$ ansible-galaxy collection list | grep community.general
community.general        6.5.0
```

Here, we can see that the `community.general` collection is installed and is at version 6.5.0 (collection versioning is independent of Ansible versioning).

If you have worked with dynamic inventory scripts in versions of Ansible before 2.9 (before Collections became mainstream), you would almost certainly have located the dynamic inventory script and made it executable, even executing it directly. This is no longer necessary in the new Collections- and Plugins-based architecture, which makes your life much easier, as you shall see shortly.

2. Referring to the documentation for the Cobbler dynamic inventory plugin (`https://docs.ansible.com/ansible/latest/collections/community/general/cobbler_inventory.html`), you will see that, to use the plugin, we must create a configuration file as an inventory source. The filename must end in `.cobbler.yml` or `.cobbler.yaml`, and contain a line referencing the plugin. There are also a whole host of configuration options available (which, in our simple demo setup, aren't necessary), but if you were working with a cloud service provider, you would certainly have to specify your region and credentials in the configuration file. In some cases, you will also have to install additional libraries or software for the inventory plugin to work, and again, the documentation page for

the plugin will tell you whether this is a requirement. In my demo environment, the Cobbler server I built is accessible at the address `cobbler.example.org`, so I shall add this to the configuration file, resulting in the following:

```
$ cat my.cobbler.yml
plugin: community.general.cobbler
url: http://cobbler.example.org/cobbler_api
```

3. This is all that is required! Now, we can run Ansible ad hoc commands just as before, only this time, we will reference the configuration file rather than an inventory file itself. Before we do this, however, let's introduce the `ansible-inventory` command, which you can use to validate the operation of the dynamic inventory:

```
$ ansible-inventory -i my.cobbler.yml --graph
@all:
  |--@ungrouped:
  |--@cobbler:
  |    |--frontend01.example.org
  |    |--frontend02.example.org
  |--@cobbler_webservers:
  |    |--frontend01.example.org
  |    |--frontend02.example.org
  |--@cobbler_:
  |    |--frontend01.example.org
  |    |--frontend02.example.org
```

This is an incredibly powerful and rapid way to query the dynamic inventory operation and what it is returning. Notice also that all group names have had `cobbler_` placed in front of them by the plugin, so we will need to make use of this when we reference the group names.

4. You can now run an Ansible ad hoc command in the manner you are used to—the only difference this time is that you will specify the filename of the dynamic inventory plugin configuration file rather than the name of the static inventory file. Assuming you have set up hosts at the two addresses we entered into Cobbler earlier, your output should look something like that shown here:

```
$ ansible -i my.cobbler.yml cobbler_webservers -m ansible.
builtin.ping
frontend01.example.org | SUCCESS => {
    "ansible_facts": {
        "discovered_interpreter_python": "/usr/bin/python3"
    },
    "changed": false,
    "ping": "pong"
}
```

```
frontend02.example.org | SUCCESS => {
    "ansible_facts": {
        "discovered_interpreter_python": "/usr/bin/python3"
    },
    "changed": false,
    "ping": "pong"
}
```

That's it! You have just implemented your first dynamic inventory in Ansible. Of course, we know that many of you won't be using Cobbler, and some of the other dynamic inventory plugins are a little more complex to get going. For example, the Amazon EC2 dynamic inventory script requires your authentication details for Amazon Web Services (or a suitable IAM account) and the installation of the Python boto and boto3 libraries. How would you know to do all of this? Luckily, it is all documented in the plugin documentation, which you can access via the official Ansible documentation website, or on the command line using a command such as the following:

```
$ ansible-doc -t inventory community.general.cobbler
```

An example of the documentation you will see is shown in the following figure:

```
> COMMUNITY.GENERAL.COBBLER        (/opt/homebrew/Cellar/ansible/8.1.0/li>

        Get inventory hosts from the cobbler service. Uses a
        configuration file as an inventory source, it must end in
        `.cobbler.yml' or `.cobbler.yaml' and have a `plugin: cobbler'
        entry. Adds the primary IP addresses to `cobbler_ipv4_address'
        and `cobbler_ipv6_address' host variables if defined in
        Cobbler. The primary IP address is defined as the management
        interface if defined, or the interface who's DNS name matches
        the hostname of the system, or else the first interface found.

ADDED IN: version 1.0.0 of community.general

OPTIONS (= is mandatory):

- cache
        Toggle to enable/disable the caching of the inventory's source
:
```

Figure 3.1 – The Ansible CLI documentation for the community.general.cobbler plugin

The most fundamental piece of advice I can give is this: whenever you install a new collection containing a dynamic inventory plugin, be sure to check out the documentation, as the requirements will have been documented for you.

Before we end this section, let's have a look at a few other handy hints for working with inventories, starting with the use of multiple inventory sources in the next section.

Using multiple inventory sources in the inventory directories

So far in this book, we have been specifying our inventory file (either static or dynamic) using the -i switch in our Ansible commands. What might not be apparent is that you can specify the -i switch more than once and so use multiple inventories at the same time. This enables you to perform tasks such as running a playbook (or ad hoc command) across hosts from both static and dynamic inventories at the same time. Ansible will work out what needs to be done—static inventories should not be marked as executable and so will not be processed as such, whereas dynamic inventories will be. This small but clever trick enables you to combine multiple inventory sources with ease. Let's move on, in the next section, to looking at the use of static inventory groups in combination with dynamic ones, an extension of this multiple-inventory functionality.

Using static groups with dynamic groups

Of course, the possibility of mixing inventories brings with it an interesting question—what happens to the groups from a dynamic inventory and a static inventory if you define both? The answer is that Ansible combines both, and this leads to an interesting possibility. As you will have observed, our Cobbler inventory script produced an Ansible group called cobbler_webservers from a Cobbler profile that we called webservers. This is common for most dynamic inventory providers; most inventory sources (for example, Cobbler and Amazon EC2) are not Ansible-aware and so do not offer groups that Ansible can directly use—they may also automatically add prefixes or separators to metadata (which may or may not be configurable). As a result, most dynamic inventory scripts will use some facet of information from the inventory source to produce groupings—the Cobbler machine profile being one such example.

Let's extend our Cobbler example from the preceding section by mixing a static inventory. Suppose that we want to make our cobbler_webservers machines a child group of a group called fedora so that we can, in the future, group all Fedora machines together. We know that we only have a Cobbler profile called webservers, and ideally, we don't want to start messing with the Cobbler setup to do something solely Ansible-related.

The answer to this is to create a static inventory file with two group definitions. The first must be the same name as the group you are expecting from the dynamic inventory, except that you should leave it blank. When Ansible combines the static and dynamic inventory contents, it will overlap the two groups and so add the hosts from Cobbler to these groups.

The second group definition should state that cobbler_webservers is a child group of the fedora group. The resulting file should look something like this:

```
[cobbler_webservers]

[fedora:children]
cobbler_webservers
```

Now let's run a simple ad hoc `ansible.builtin.ping` command in Ansible to see how it evaluates the two inventories together. Notice how we will specify the `fedora` group to run `ansible.builtin.ping` against, instead of the `cobbler_webservers` group. We know that Cobbler has no `fedora` group because we never created one, and we know that any hosts in this group must come via the `cobbler_webservers` group when you combine the two inventories, as our static inventory has no hosts in it. The results will look something like this:

```
$ ansible -i my.cobbler.yml -i static-groups-mix-ini fedora -m
ansible.builtin.ping
frontend01.example.org | SUCCESS => {
    "ansible_facts": {
        "discovered_interpreter_python": "/usr/bin/python3"
    },
    "changed": false,
    "ping": "pong"
}
frontend02.example.org | SUCCESS => {
    "ansible_facts": {
        "discovered_interpreter_python": "/usr/bin/python3"
    },
    "changed": false,
    "ping": "pong"
}
```

As you can see from the preceding output, we have referenced two different inventories, one static and the other dynamic. We have combined groups, taking hosts that only exist in one inventory source, and combining them with a group that only exists in another. As you can see, this is an incredibly simple example, and it would be easy to extend this to combine lists of static and dynamic hosts or to add a custom variable to a host that comes from a dynamic inventory.

This is a trick of Ansible that is little known but can be very powerful as your inventories expand and grow. As we have worked through this chapter, you will have observed that we have been very precise about specifying our inventory hosts either individually or by group; for example, we explicitly told the `ansible` command to run the ad hoc command against all hosts in the `cobbler_webservers` group. In the next section, we will build on this to look at how Ansible can manage a set of hosts specified using patterns.

Special host management using patterns

We have already established that you will often want to run either an ad hoc command or a playbook against only a subsection of your inventory. So far, we have been quite precise in doing that, but let's now expand upon this by looking at how Ansible can work with patterns to figure out which hosts a command (or playbook) should be run against.

As a starting point, let's again consider an inventory that we defined earlier in this chapter for the purposes of exploring host groups and child groups. For your convenience, the inventory contents are provided again here:

```
loadbalancer.example.org

[frontends]
web01.example.org
web02.example.org

[apps]
app01.example.org
app02.example.org

[databases]
db01.example.org
db02.example.org

[fedora:children]
apps
databases

[ubuntu:children]
frontends
```

To demonstrate host/group selection by pattern, we shall use the `--list-hosts` switch with the `ansible` command to see which hosts Ansible would operate on. You are welcome to expand the example to use the `ansible.builtin.ping` module, but we'll use `--list-hosts` here in the interests of space and keeping the output concise and readable:

1. We have already mentioned the special `all` group to specify all hosts in the inventory:

```
$ ansible -i hostgroups-ini all --list-hosts
  hosts (7):
    loadbalancer.example.org
    app01.example.org
    app02.example.org
    db01.example.org
    db02.example.org
    web01.example.org
    web02.example.org
```

The asterisk character has the same effect as `all`, but needs to be quoted in single quotes for the shell to interpret the command properly:

```
$ ansible -i hostgroups-ini '*' --list-hosts
  hosts (7):
    loadbalancer.example.org
    app01.example.org
    app02.example.org
    db01.example.org
    db02.example.org
    web01.example.org
    web02.example.org
```

2. Use `:` to specify a logical OR, meaning *"apply to hosts either in this group or that group,"* as in this example:

```
$ ansible -i hostgroups-ini frontends:apps --list-hosts
  hosts (4):
    web01.example.org
    web02.example.org
    app01.example.org
    app02.example.org
```

3. Use `!` to exclude a specific group—you can combine this with other characters such as `:` to show (for example) all hosts except those in the `apps` group. Again, `!` is a special character in the shell and so you must quote your pattern string in single quotes for it to work, as in this example:

```
$ ansible -i hostgroups-ini 'all:!apps' --list-hosts
  hosts (5):
    loadbalancer.example.org
    db01.example.org
    db02.example.org
    web01.example.org
    web02.example.org
```

4. Use `:&` to specify a logical AND between two groups, for example, if we want all hosts that are in the `fedora` group and the `apps` group (again, you must use single quotes in the shell):

```
$ ansible -i hostgroups-ini 'fedora:&apps' --list-hosts
  hosts (2):
    app01.example.org
    app02.example.org
```

5. Use * wildcards in a similar manner to what you would use in the shell, as in this example:

```
$ ansible -i hostgroups-ini 'db*.example.org' --list-hosts
  hosts (2):
    db01.example.org
    db02.example.org
```

Another way you can limit which hosts a command is run on is to use the --limit switch with Ansible. This uses exactly the same syntax and pattern notation as in the preceding but has the advantage that you can use it with the ansible-playbook command, where specifying a host pattern on the command line is only supported for the ansible command itself. Hence, for example, you could run the following:

```
$ ansible-playbook -i hostgroups-ini site.yml --limit frontends:apps

PLAY [A simple playbook for demonstrating inventory patterns] *******
********************************************************************
********

TASK [Ping each host] **********************************************
********************************************************************
********
ok: [web02.example.org]
ok: [web01.example.org]
ok: [app02.example.org]
ok: [app01.example.org]


PLAY RECAP *********************************************************
********************************************************************
********
app01.example.org          :
ok=1    changed=0    unreachable=0    failed=0    skipped=0
rescued=0    ignored=0
app02.example.org          :
ok=1    changed=0    unreachable=0    failed=0    skipped=0
rescued=0    ignored=0
web01.example.org          :
ok=1    changed=0    unreachable=0    failed=0    skipped=0
rescued=0    ignored=0
web02.example.org          :
ok=1    changed=0    unreachable=0    failed=0    skipped=0
rescued=0    ignored=0
```

Patterns are a very useful and important part of working with inventories, and something you will no doubt find invaluable going forward. That concludes our chapter on Ansible inventories; however, it is hoped that this has given you everything you need to work confidently with Ansible inventories.

Summary

Creating and managing Ansible inventories is a crucial part of your work with Ansible, and hence we have covered this fundamental concept early in this book. They are vital as, without them, Ansible would have no knowledge of what hosts it is to run automation tasks against, yet they provide so much more than this. They provide an integration point with configuration management systems, they provide a sensible source for host-specific (or group-specific) variables to be stored, and they provide you with a flexible way of running this playbook.

In this chapter, you learned about creating simple static inventory files and adding hosts to them. We then extended this by learning how to add host groups and assign variables to hosts. We also looked at how to organize your inventories and variables when a single flat inventory file becomes too much to handle. We then learned how to make use of dynamic inventory files, before concluding with a look at useful tips and tricks such as combining inventory sources and using patterns to specify hosts, all of which will make how you work with inventories easier and yet simultaneously more powerful.

In the next chapter, we will learn how to develop playbooks and roles to configure, deploy, and manage remote machines using Ansible.

Questions

1. How do you add the `frontends` group variables to your inventory?

    A. `[frontends::]`

    B. `[frontends::values]`

    C. `[frontends:host:vars]`

    D. `[frontends::variables]`

    E. `[frontends:vars]`

2. What enables you to automate Linux tasks such as provisioning DNS, managing DHCP, updating packages, and configuration management?

    A. Playbook

    B. Yum

    C. Cobbler

    D. Bash

    E. Role

3. Ansible allows you to specify an inventory file location by using the `-i` option on the command line:

    A. True

    B. False

Further reading

Details on using Ansible inventory plugins are available here: `https://docs.ansible.com/ansible/latest/plugins/inventory.html#using-inventory-plugins`

4

Playbooks and Roles

So far in this book, we have worked mostly with ad hoc Ansible commands for simplicity and to help you to understand the fundamentals. However, the lifeblood of Ansible is most certainly the playbook, which is a logical organization of tasks (think ad hoc commands) in a structure that creates a useful outcome. This might be to deploy a web server on a newly built virtual machine, or it might be to apply a security policy. It might even involve handling the whole build process for a virtual machine! The possibilities are endless. Ansible playbooks, as we have already covered, are designed to be simple to write and easy to read – they are intended to be self-documenting and, as such, will form a valuable part of your IT processes.

In this chapter, we will explore playbooks in greater depth, from the basics of their creation to more advanced concepts such as running tasks in loops and blocks, performing conditional logic, and – perhaps one of the most important concepts for playbook organization and code reuse – Ansible roles. We will cover roles in more detail later, but just know that this is something you will want to use as much as possible when creating manageable playbook code.

Specifically, in this chapter, we will cover the following topics:

- Understanding the playbook framework
- Understanding roles – the playbook organizer
- Using conditions in your code
- Repeating tasks with loops
- Grouping tasks using blocks
- Configuring play execution via strategies
- Using `ansible-pull`

Technical requirements

This chapter assumes that you have set up your control host with Ansible, as detailed in *Chapter 1*, *Getting Started with Ansible*, and are using the most recent version available – the examples in this chapter were tested with Ansible 8.0 and `ansible-core` 2.15. This chapter also assumes that you have at least one additional host to test against, and this should be Linux-based. Although we will give specific examples of hostnames in this chapter, you are free to substitute them with your own hostnames and/or IP addresses, and details of how to do this will be provided in the appropriate places.

The code bundle for this chapter is available here: `https://github.com/PacktPublishing/Practical-Ansible-Second-Edition/tree/main/Chapter%204`.

Understanding the playbook framework

A playbook allows you to manage multiple configurations and complex deployments on many machines simply and easily. This is one of the key benefits of using Ansible for the delivery of complex applications. With playbooks, you can organize your tasks in a logical structure, as tasks are (generally) executed in the order they are written, allowing you to have a good deal of control over your automation processes. With that said, it is possible to perform tasks asynchronously, so where tasks are not executed in sequence, we will highlight this. Our goal is that once you complete this chapter, you will understand the best practices to write your own Ansible playbooks.

Although YAML format is easy to read and write, it is very pedantic when it comes to spacing. For example, you cannot use tabs to set indentation even though on the screen a tab and four spaces might look identical – in YAML, they are not. We recommend that you adopt an editor with YAML support to aid you in writing your playbooks if you are doing this for the first time – perhaps Vim, Visual Studio Code, or Eclipse – as these will help you to ensure that your indentation is correct. To test the playbooks we develop in this chapter, we will create a variant of the inventory created in *Chapter 3*, *Defining Your Inventory* (unless stated otherwise):

```
[frontends]
web01.example.org https_port=8443
web02.example.org http_proxy=proxy.example.org

[frontends:vars]
ntp_server=ntp.web.example.org
proxy=proxy.web.example.org

[apps]
app01.example.org
app02.example.org

[webapp:children]
```

```
frontends
apps

[webapp:vars]
proxy_server=proxy.webapp.example.org
health_check_retry=3
health_check_interval=60
```

Let's dive right in and get started writing a playbook. In *Chapter 2, Understanding the Fundamentals of Ansible*, we covered some of the basic aspects of the YAML syntax and structure required to create a playbook, so we won't repeat these in detail here. Rather, we will build on them to show you what playbook development is all about:

1. Create a simple playbook (called myplaybook.yml) to run on the hosts in the frontends host group defined in our inventory file. We can set the user that will access the hosts using the remote_user directive in the playbook, as demonstrated in the following (you can also use the --user switch on the command line, but as this chapter is about playbook development, we'll ignore that for now):

    ```
    ---
    - hosts: frontends
      remote_user: james

      tasks:
      - name: simple connection test
        ansible.builtin.ping:
        remote_user: james
    ```

2. Add another task below the first, which will run the ansible.builtin.shell module (that will, in turn, run the ls command on the remote hosts). We'll also add the ignore_errors directive to this task to ensure that our playbook doesn't fail if the ls command fails (for example, if the directory we're trying to list doesn't exist). Be careful with the indentation and ensure that it matches that of the first part of the file:

    ```
    - name: run a simple command
      ansible.builtin.shell: /bin/ls -al /nonexistent
      ignore_errors: True
    ```

3. Let's see how our newly created playbook behaves when we run it with the following command:

    ```
    $ ansible-playbook -i hosts myplaybook.yml
    ```

The output from this playbook run should look something like the following screenshot:

```
james@controlnode:~/Practical-Ansible-Second-Edition/Chapter 4$ ansible-playbook
 -i hosts myplaybook.yaml

PLAY [frontends] ********************************************************

TASK [Gathering Facts] *************************************************
ok: [web01.example.org]
ok: [web02.example.org]

TASK [simple connection test] *****************************************
ok: [web02.example.org]
ok: [web01.example.org]

TASK [run a simple command] *******************************************
fatal: [web01.example.org]: FAILED! => {"changed": true, "cmd": "/bin/ls -al /no
nexistent", "delta": "0:00:00.007672", "end": "2023-06-21 15:49:51.037501", "msg
": "non-zero return code", "rc": 2, "start": "2023-06-21 15:49:51.029829", "stde
rr": "/bin/ls: cannot access '/nonexistent': No such file or directory", "stderr
_lines": ["/bin/ls: cannot access '/nonexistent': No such file or directory"], "
stdout": "", "stdout_lines": []}
...ignoring
fatal: [web02.example.org]: FAILED! => {"changed": true, "cmd": "/bin/ls -al /no
nexistent", "delta": "0:00:00.008396", "end": "2023-06-21 15:49:51.035995", "msg
": "non-zero return code", "rc": 2, "start": "2023-06-21 15:49:51.027599", "stde
rr": "/bin/ls: cannot access '/nonexistent': No such file or directory", "stderr
_lines": ["/bin/ls: cannot access '/nonexistent': No such file or directory"], "
stdout": "", "stdout_lines": []}
...ignoring

PLAY RECAP ************************************************************
web01.example.org          : ok=3    changed=1    unreachable=0    failed=0    s
kipped=0    rescued=0    ignored=1
web02.example.org          : ok=3    changed=1    unreachable=0    failed=0    s
kipped=0    rescued=0    ignored=1
```

Figure 4.1 – Demonstrating the execution of a playbook where errors are willfully ignored

From the output of the playbook run, you can see that our two tasks were executed in the order in which they were specified. We can see that the `ls` command failed because we tried to list a directory that did not exist, but the playbook did not register any `failed` tasks because we set `ignore_errors` to `true` for this task (and only this task).

Most Ansible modules (with the exception of those that run user-defined commands such as `ansible. builtin.shell`, `ansible.builtin.command`, and `ansible.builtin.raw`) are coded to be idempotent – that is to say, if you run the same task twice, the results will be the same, and the task will not make the same change twice; if it detects that the action it is being requested to perform has been completed, then it does not perform it a second time. This, of course, is not possible for the aforementioned modules, as they could be used to perform just about any conceivable task – hence, how could the module know it was being performed twice?

Every module returns a set of results, and among these results is the task status. You can see these summarized at the bottom of the preceding playbook run output, and their meaning is as follows:

- ok: The task ran successfully and no changes were made

- changed: The task ran successfully and changes were made

- failed: The task failed to run (but the host was reachable)

- unreachable: The host was unreachable to run the task on

- skipped: This task was skipped

- ignored: This task was ignored (for example, in the case of ignore_errors)

- rescued: We will see an example of this later when we look at blocks and rescue tasks

These statuses can be very useful – for example, if we have a task to deploy a new Apache configuration file from a template, we know we must restart the Apache service for the changes to be picked up. However, we only want to do this if the file was actually changed – if no changes were made, we don't want to needlessly restart Apache, as it would interrupt people who might be using the service. Hence, we can use the notify action, which tells Ansible to call a handler when (and only when) the result from a task is changed. In brief, a handler is a special type of task that is run as a result of a notify. However, unlike Ansible playbook tasks, which are performed in sequence, handlers are all grouped together and run at the very end of the play. Also, they can be notified more than once but will only be run once regardless, again preventing needless service restarts. Consider the following playbook:

```
---
- name: Handler demo 1
  hosts: web01.example.org
  gather_facts: no
  become: yes

  tasks:
    - name: Update Apache configuration
      ansible.builtin.template:
        src: template.j2
        dest: /etc/apache2/apache2.conf
      notify: Restart Apache

  handlers:
    - name: Restart Apache
      ansible.builtin.service:
        name: apache2
        state: restarted
```

To keep the output concise, I've turned off fact-gathering for this playbook (we won't use facts in any of the tasks). I'm also running this on just one host again for conciseness, but you are welcome to expand the demo code as you wish. If we run this task for the first time, we will see the following results:

```
$ ansible-playbook -i hosts handlers1.yml


PLAY [Handler demo 1] *********************************************
**********


TASK [Update Apache configuration] *******************************
**********
changed: [web01.example.org]


RUNNING HANDLER [Restart Apache] *********************************
**********
changed: [web01.example.org]


PLAY RECAP *******************************************************
**********
web01.example.org              :
ok=2      changed=2    unreachable=0    failed=0    skipped=0
    rescued=0    ignored=0
```

Note how the handler was run at the end, as the configuration file was updated. However, if we run this playbook a second time without making any changes to the template or configuration file, we will see something like this:

```
$ ansible-playbook -i hosts handlers1.yml


PLAY [Handler demo 1] *********************************************
**********


TASK [Update Apache configuration] *******************************
**********
ok: [web01.example.org]


PLAY RECAP *******************************************************
**********
web01.example.org              :
ok=1      changed=0    unreachable=0    failed=0    skipped=0
rescued=0    ignored=0
```

This time, the handler was not called, as the result from the configuration task was ok. All handlers should have a globally unique name so that the notify action can call the correct handler. You can also call multiple handlers by setting a common name to use the listen directive – this way, you can call either the handler name or the listen string, as demonstrated in the following example:

```
---
- name: Handler demo 1
  hosts: web01.example.org
  gather_facts: no
  become: yes

  handlers:
    - name: restart timesyncd
      ansible.builtin.service:
        name: systemd-timesyncd.service
        state: restarted
      listen: "restart all services"

    - name: restart apache
      ansible.builtin.service:
        name: apache2.service
        state: restarted
      listen: "restart all services"

  tasks:
    - name: restart all services
      ansible.builtin.command: echo "this task will restart all
services"
      notify: "restart all services"
```

We only have one task in the playbook, but when we run it, both handlers are called. Also, remember that we said earlier that ansible.builtin.command was among a set of modules that were a special case because they can't detect whether a change has occurred – as a result, they always return the changed value, and so, in this demo playbook, the handlers will always be notified, even when we run it a second time:

```
$ ansible-playbook -i hosts handlers2.yml


PLAY [Handler demo 1] ***********************************************
***********

TASK [restart all services] ****************************************
***********
```

```
changed: [web01.example.org]


RUNNING HANDLER [restart timesyncd] ********************************
***********
changed: [web01.example.org]


RUNNING HANDLER [restart apache] **********************************
***********
changed: [web01.example.org]


PLAY RECAP ********************************************************
***********
web01.example.org          : ok=3    changed=3    unreachable=0
failed=0     skipped=0    rescued=0    ignored=0
```

These are some of the fundamentals that you need to know to start writing your own playbooks. With these under your belt, let's run through a comparison of ad hoc commands and playbooks in the next section.

Comparing playbooks and ad hoc tasks

Ad hoc commands allow you to quickly create and execute one-off commands, without keeping any record of what was done (other than perhaps your shell history). These serve an important purpose and can be very valuable in getting small changes made quickly and for learning Ansible and its modules.

Playbooks, by contrast, are logically organized sets of tasks (each could conceivably be an ad hoc command), put together in a sequence that performs one bigger action. The addition of conditional logic, error handling, and so on means that, very often, the benefits of playbooks outweigh the usefulness of ad hoc commands. In addition, provided you keep them organized, you will have copies of all previous playbooks that you run, so you will be able to refer back (if you ever need to) to see what you ran and when.

Let's develop a practical example – suppose you want to install Apache 2.4 on Ubuntu Server. There are a number of steps involved even if the default configuration is sufficient (which is unlikely, but for now, we'll keep the example simple). If you were to perform the basic installation by hand, you would need to install the package, open up the firewall, and ensure the service is running (and runs at boot time).

To perform these commands in the shell, you might do the following:

```
$ sudo apt -y install apache2
$ sudo ufw allow http
$ sudo ufw allow https
$ sudo systemctl enable apache2.service
$ sudo systemctl restart apache2.service
```

Now, for each of these commands, there is an equivalent ad hoc Ansible command that you can run. We won't go through all of them here in the interests of space; however, let's say you want to restart the Apache service – if so, you could run an ad hoc command similar to the following (again, we will perform it only on one host for conciseness):

```
$ ansible -i hosts web01* -m ansible.builtin.service -a "name=apache2
state=restarted" --become
```

When run successfully, you will see pages of shell output containing all of the variable data returned from running the `ansible.builtin.service` module. A snippet of the output from running this ad hoc command is shown here for you to check yours against – the key thing being that the command resulted in the `changed` status, meaning that it ran successfully and that the service was indeed restarted:

```
web01.example.org | CHANGED => {
    "ansible_facts": {
        "discovered_interpreter_python": "/usr/bin/python3"
    },
    "changed": true,
    "name": "apache2",
    "state": "started",
```

You, of course, could create and execute a series of ad hoc commands to replicate the multiple shell commands given previously and run them all individually. With a bit of cleverness, you should reduce this from four commands (for example, the Ansible `ansible.builtin.service` module can both enable a service at boot time and restart it in one ad hoc command). However, you would still ultimately end up with at least two or three ad hoc commands, and if you want to run these again later on another server, you will need to refer to your notes to figure out how you did it.

A playbook is, hence, a far more valuable way to approach this – not only will it perform all of the steps in one go but it will also give you a record of how it was done for you to refer to later on. There are multiple ways to do this, but consider the following as an example:

```
---

- name: Install Apache
  hosts: web01.example.org
  gather_facts: no
  become: yes

  tasks:
    - name: Install Apache package
      ansible.builtin.apt:
        name: apache2
        state: latest
```

```
  - name: Open firewall for Apache
    community.general.ufw:
      rule: allow
      port: "{{ item }}"
      proto: tcp
    loop:
      - "http"
      - "https"

  - name: Restart and enable the service
    ansible.builtin.service:
      name: apache2
      state: restarted
      enabled: yes
```

Now, when you run this, you should see that all of our installation requirements have been completed by one fairly simple and easy-to-read playbook. There is a new concept here, loops, which we haven't covered yet, but don't worry – we will cover this later in the chapter:

```
$ ansible-playbook -i hosts installapache.yml

PLAY [Install Apache] ************************************************
**********

TASK [Install Apache package] **************************************
**********
changed: [web01.example.org]

TASK [Open firewall for Apache] ************************************
**********
changed: [web01.example.org] => (item=http)
changed: [web01.example.org] => (item=https)

TASK [Restart and enable the service] ******************************
**********
changed: [web01.example.org]

PLAY RECAP *********************************************************
**********
web01.example.org          :
ok=3     changed=3    unreachable=0    failed=0     skipped=0
rescued=0    ignored=0
```

As you can see, this is far better to capture what was actually done and document it in a format that someone else can easily pick up. Even though we will cover loops later on in the book, it's fairly easy to see from the preceding example how they might work. With this established, let's proceed to the next section to look in more detail at a couple of terms we have used several times to ensure you are clear on their meanings – **plays** and **tasks**.

Defining plays and tasks

So far, when we have worked with playbooks, we have created one single play per playbook (which logically is the minimum you can do). However, you can have more than one play in a playbook, and a "*play*" in Ansible terms is simply a set of tasks (and roles, handlers, and other Ansible facets) associated with a host (or group of hosts). A task is the smallest possible element of a play, and it is responsible for running a single module with a set of arguments to achieve a specific goal. Of course, in theory, this sounds quite complex, but when backed up by a practical example, it becomes quite simple to understand.

If we refer to our example inventory, this describes a simple two-tier architecture (we've left out the database tier for now). Now, suppose we want to write a single playbook to configure both the frontend servers and the application servers. We could use two separate playbooks to configure the frontend and application servers, but this risks fragmenting your code and making it difficult to organize. However, frontend servers and application servers are going to be (by their very nature) fundamentally different and so are unlikely to be configured with the same set of tasks.

The solution to this problem is to create a single playbook with two plays in it. The start of each play can be identified by the line at the lowest indentation (that is, zero spaces in front of it).

Let's get started with building up our playbook:

1. Add the first play to the playbook and define some simple tasks to set up the Apache server on the frontend, as shown here:

    ```
    ---
    - name: Play 1 - configure the frontend servers
      hosts: frontends
      become: yes

      tasks:
      - name: Install the Apache package
        ansible.builtin.apt:
          name: apache2
          state: latest
      - name: Start the Apache server
        ansible.builtin.service:
          name: apache2
          state: started
    ```

2. Immediately below this, in the same file, add the second play to configure the application
    tier servers:

    ```
    - name: Play 2 - configure the application servers
      hosts: apps
      become: true

      tasks:
      - name: Install Tomcat
        ansible.builtin.apt:
          name: tomcat9
          state: latest
      - name: Start the Tomcat server
        ansible.builtin.service:
          name: tomcat9
          state: started
    ```

Now, you have two plays – one to install web servers in the frontends group and one to install
application servers in the apps group, all combined into one simple playbook.

When we run this playbook, we'll see the two plays performed sequentially, in the order they appear
in the playbook. Note the presence of the PLAY keyword, which denotes the start of each play. Use
the following command to run the playbook:

```
$ ansible-playbook -i hosts playandtask.yml
```

The output from your playbook run should look something like the following screenshot:

```
james@controlnode:~/Practical-Ansible-Second-Edition/Chapter 4$ ansible-playbook
 -i hosts playandtask.yml

PLAY [Play 1 - configure the frontend servers] ********************************

TASK [Gathering Facts] ********************************************************
ok: [web02.example.org]
ok: [web01.example.org]

TASK [Install the Apache package] *********************************************
changed: [web02.example.org]
changed: [web01.example.org]

TASK [Start the Apache server] ************************************************
ok: [web02.example.org]
ok: [web01.example.org]

PLAY [Play 2 - configure the application servers] *****************************

TASK [Gathering Facts] ********************************************************
ok: [app01.example.org]
ok: [app02.example.org]

TASK [Install Tomcat] *********************************************************
changed: [app01.example.org]
changed: [app02.example.org]

TASK [Start the Tomcat server] ************************************************
ok: [app01.example.org]
ok: [app02.example.org]

PLAY RECAP ********************************************************************
app01.example.org          : ok=3    changed=1    unreachable=0    failed=0    s
kipped=0    rescued=0    ignored=0
app02.example.org          : ok=3    changed=1    unreachable=0    failed=0    s
kipped=0    rescued=0    ignored=0
web01.example.org          : ok=3    changed=1    unreachable=0    failed=0    s
kipped=0    rescued=0    ignored=0
web02.example.org          : ok=3    changed=1    unreachable=0    failed=0    s
kipped=0    rescued=0    ignored=0
```

Figure 4.2 – Demonstrating the execution of a playbook containing two plays

There we have it – one playbook, yet two distinct plays operating on different sets of hosts from the provided inventory. This is very powerful, especially when combined with roles (which will be covered later in this book). Of course, you can have just one play in your playbook – you don't have to have multiple ones, but it is important to be able to develop multi-play playbooks, as you will almost certainly find them useful as your environment gets more complex.

Playbooks are the lifeblood of Ansible automation – they extend it beyond single tasks/commands (which in themselves are incredibly powerful) to a whole series of tasks organized logically. As you extend your library of playbooks, however, how do you keep your work organized? How do you efficiently reuse the same blocks of code? In the preceding example, we installed Apache, and this might be a requirement on a number of your servers. However, should you attempt to manage them all from one playbook? Or should you perhaps keep copying and pasting the same block of code over and over again? There is a better way, and in Ansible terms, we need to start looking at roles, which we shall do in the very next section.

Understanding roles – the playbook organizer

Roles are designed to enable you to efficiently and effectively reuse Ansible code. They always follow a known structure and often will include sensible default values for variables, error handling, handlers, and so on. Taking our Apache installation example from the previous chapter, we know that this is something that we might want to do over and over again, perhaps with a different configuration file each time, and perhaps with a few other tweaks on a per-server (or per-inventory group) basis. In Ansible, the most efficient way to support the reuse of this code in this way would be to create it as a role.

The process of creating roles is in fact very simple – Ansible will (by default) look within the same directory that you are running your playbook from for a `roles/` directory, and in here, you will create one subdirectory for each role. The role name is derived from the subdirectory name. There is no need to create complex metadata or anything else – it really is that simple. Within each subdirectory goes a fixed directory structure that tells Ansible what the tasks, default variables, handlers, and so on are for each role.

> **Note**
>
> The `roles/` directory is not the only place Ansible will look for roles – this is the first directory it will look in, but it will then look in `/etc/ansible/roles` for any additional roles. This can be further customized through the Ansible configuration file, as discussed in *Chapter 2, Understanding the Fundamentals of Ansible.*

Let's explore this in a little more detail. Consider the following directory structure:

```
site.yml
frontends.yml
dbservers.yml
roles/
    installapache/
      tasks/
      handlers/
      templates/
      vars/
      defaults/
    installtomcat/
      tasks/
      meta/
```

The preceding directory structure shows two roles defined in our hypothetical playbook directory, called installapache and installtomcat. Within each of these directories, you will see a series of subdirectories. These subdirectories do not need to exist (there'll be more on what they mean in a minute, but, for example, if your role has no handlers, then handlers/ does not need to be created). However, where you do require such a directory, you should populate it with a YAML file named main.yml. Each of these main.yml files will be expected to have certain contents, depending on the directory that contained them.

The subdirectories that can exist inside of a role are as follows:

- tasks: This is the most common directory to find in a role, and it contains all of the Ansible tasks that the role should perform.

- handlers: All handlers used in the role should go into this directory.

- defaults: All default variables for the role go in here.

- vars: These are other role variables – these override those declared in the defaults/ directory, as they are higher up the precedence order.

- files: Files needed by the role should go in here – for example, any configuration files that need to be deployed to the target hosts.

- templates: Distinct from the files/ directory, this directory should contain all templates used by the role.

- meta: Any metadata needed for the role goes in here. For example, roles are normally executed in the order they are called from the parent playbook; however, sometimes, a role will have dependency roles that need to be run first, and if this is the case, they can be declared within this directory.

For the examples we will develop in this part of this chapter, we will need an inventory, so let's reuse the inventory we used in the previous section (included here for convenience):

```
[frontends]
web01.example.org https_port=8443
web02.example.org http_proxy=proxy.example.org

[frontends:vars]
ntp_server=ntp.web.example.org
proxy=proxy.web.example.org

[apps]
app01.example.org
app02.example.org

[webapp:children]
```

```
frontends
apps

[webapp:vars]
proxy_server=proxy.webapp.example.org
health_check_retry=3
health_check_interval=60
```

Let's get started with some practical exercises to help you to learn how to create and work with roles. We'll start by creating a role called installapache, which will handle the Apache installation process we looked at in the previous section. However, here, we will expand it to cover the installation of Apache on both Fedora and Ubuntu. This is a good practice, especially if you are looking to submit your roles back to the community, as the more general-purpose they are (and the wider the range of systems they will work on), the more useful they will be to people.

Step through the following process to create your first role:

1. Create the directory structure for the installapache role from within your chosen playbook directory – this is as simple as this:

   ```
   $ mkdir -p roles/installapache/tasks
   ```

2. Now, let's create the mandatory main.yml inside the tasks directory we just created. This won't actually perform the Apache installation – rather, it will call one of two external tasks files, depending on the operating system detected on the target host during the fact-gathering stage. We can use a fact called ansible_distribution, in a when clause, to determine which of the task files to import:

   ```
   ---
   - name: import a tasks based on OS platform
     import_tasks: fedora.yml
     when: ansible_distribution == 'Fedora'
   - import_tasks: ubuntu.yml
     when: ansible_distribution == 'Ubuntu'
   ```

3. Create fedora.yml in roles/installapache/tasks to install the latest version of the Apache web server via the dnf package manager. This should contain the following content:

   ```
   ---
   - name: Install Apache using dnf
     ansible.builtin.dnf:
       name: httpd
       state: latest
   - name: Start the Apache server
     ansible.builtin.service:
   ```

```
        name: httpd
        state: started
```

4. Create a file called `ubuntu.yml` in `roles/installapache/tasks` to install the latest version of the Apache web server via the `apt` package manager on Ubuntu. Note how the content differs between Fedora and Ubuntu hosts:

```
---

- name: Install Apache using apt
  ansible.builtin.apt:
    name: apache2
    state: latest
- name: Start the Apache server
  ansible.builtin.service:
    name: apache2
    state: started
```

For now, we're keeping our code for a role really simple – however, you can see that the preceding tasks' files are just like an Ansible playbook, except that they lack the play definition. As they do not come under a play, they are also at a lower indentation level than in a playbook, but apart from this difference, the code should look very familiar to you. In fact, this is part of the beauty of roles – as long as you pay attention to getting the indentation level right, you can more or less use the same code in a playbook or a role.

Now, roles can't be run directly – we have to create a playbook to call them, so let's write a simple playbook to call our newly created role. This has a play definition just like we saw before, but rather than having a `tasks:` section within the play, we have a `roles:` section where the roles are declared instead. Convention dictates that this file is called `site.yml`, but you are free to call it whatever you like:

```
---

- name: Install Apache using a role
  hosts: frontends
  become: true

  roles:
    - installapache
```

For clarity, your final directory structure should look like this:

```
.
├── hosts
├── roles
│   └── installapache
│       └── tasks
│           ├── fedora.yml
```

```
|                   ├── main.yml
|                   └── ubuntu.yml
└── site.yml
```

With this completed, you can now run your `site.yml` playbook using `ansible-playbook` in
the normal way – you should see output similar to this:

```
$ ansible-playbook -i hosts site.yml

PLAY [Install Apache using a role] *********************************
***********

TASK [Gathering Facts] ********************************************
***********
ok: [web02.example.org]
ok: [web01.example.org]

TASK [installapache : Install Apache using yum] ********************
***********
skipping: [web01.example.org]
skipping: [web02.example.org]

TASK [installapache : Start the Apache server] ********************
***********
skipping: [web01.example.org]
skipping: [web02.example.org]

TASK [installapache : Install Apache using apt] *******************
***********
changed: [web02.example.org]
changed: [web01.example.org]

TASK [installapache : Start the Apache server] *******************
***********
changed: [web02.example.org]
changed: [web01.example.org]

PLAY RECAP *******************************************************
***********
web01.example.org          :
ok=3     changed=2    unreachable=0    failed=0    skipped=2    r
escued=0     ignored=0
web02.example.org          :
ok=3     changed=2    unreachable=0    failed=0    skipped=2
rescued=0     ignored=0
```

That's it – you have created, at the simplest possible level, your first role. Of course (as we discussed earlier), there is much more to a role than just the simple tasks that we have added here, and we will see expanded examples as we work through this chapter. However, the preceding example is intended to show you how quick and easy it is to get started with roles.

Before we look at some of the other aspects relating to roles, let's take a look at some other ways to call your role. Ansible allows you to statically import or dynamically include roles when you write a playbook. The syntax between importing or including a role is subtly different, and notably, both go in the `tasks` section of your playbook rather than in the `roles` section. The following is a hypothetical example that shows both options in a really simple playbook. The `roles/` directory structure, including both the `common` and `approle` roles, is created in a similar manner to the preceding example:

```
---
- hosts: frontends

  tasks:
  - ansible.builtin.import_role:
      name: common
  - ansible.builtin.include_role:
      name: approle
```

These features were not available in versions of Ansible earlier than 2.3, and their usage changed slightly in version 2.4 for consistency with the way that some other Ansible features work. We will not worry about the details of this here, as the core is now on release 2.15, so unless you absolutely have to run a much earlier version of Ansible, it is sufficient to assume that these two statements work, as we shall outline in the following.

Fundamentally, the `ansible.builtin.import_role` statement performs a static import of the role you specify at the time when all playbook code is parsed. Hence, roles brought into your playbook using the `ansible.builtin.import_role` statement are treated just like any other code in a play or role when Ansible begins parsing. Using `ansible.builtin.import_role` is basically the same as declaring your roles after the `roles:` statement in `site.yml`, just as we did in the preceding example.

`ansible.builtin.include_role` is subtly but fundamentally different in that the role you specify is not evaluated when the playbook is parsed initially – rather, it is processed dynamically during the playbook run, at the point at which `ansible.builtin.include_role` is encountered.

Probably the most fundamental reason to choose between the `include` or `import` statements given in the preceding is looping – if you need to run a role within a loop, you cannot do so with `import_role`, so you must use `include_role`. There are, however, both benefits and limitations to both, and you will need to choose the most appropriate one for your scenario – the official Ansible documentation (`https://docs.ansible.com/ansible/latest/user_guide/playbooks_reuse.html#dynamic-vs-static`) will help you to make the right decision.

As we have seen in this section, roles are incredibly simple to get started with and yet offer an incredibly powerful way in which to organize and reuse your Ansible code. In the next section, we will expand upon our simple task-based example by looking at adding role-specific variables and dependencies to your code.

Setting up role-based variables and dependencies

Variables are at the heart of making Ansible playbooks and roles reusable, as they allow the same code to be repurposed with slightly different values or configuration data. The Ansible role directory structure allows for role-specific variables to be declared in two locations. Although, at first, the difference between these two locations may not seem obvious, it is of fundamental importance.

Role-based variables can go in one of two locations:

- `defaults/main.yml`
- `vars/main.yml`

The difference between these two locations is their position in Ansible's variable order of precedence (`https://docs.ansible.com/ansible/latest/user_guide/playbooks_variables.html#variable-precedence-where-should-i-put-a-variable`). Variables that go in the `defaults/` directory are one of the lowest in terms of precedence so are easily overridden. This location is where you would put variables that you want to override easily, but where you don't want to leave a variable undefined. For example, if you install Apache Tomcat, you might build a role to install a specific version. However, you don't want the role to exit with an error if someone forgets to set the version – rather, you would prefer to set a sensible default, such as `9.0`, that can then be overridden with inventory variables or on the command line (using the `-e` or `--extra-vars` switches). In this way, you know the role will work even without someone explicitly setting this variable, but it can easily be changed to a newer Tomcat version if desired.

Variables that go in the `vars/` directory, however, come much higher up on Ansible's variable precedence ordering. These will not be overridden by inventory variables, and so it should be used for variable data that it is more important to keep static. Of course, this is not to say they can't be overridden – the `-e` or `--extra-vars` switches are the highest order of precedence in Ansible so will override anything else that you define.

Most of the time, you will probably make use of the `defaults/` based variables alone, but there will doubtless be times when having the option of variables higher up the precedence ordering becomes valuable to your automation, and so it is vital to know that this option is available to you.

In addition to the role-based variables described previously, there is also the option to add metadata to a role using the `meta/` directory. As before, to make use of this, simply add a file called `main.yml` into this directory. To explain how you might make use of the meta/ directory, let's build and run a practical example that will show how it can be used. Before we get started though, it is important to note that, by default, the Ansible parser will only allow you to run a role once.

This is somewhat similar to the way in which we discussed handlers earlier, which can be called multiple times but ultimately are only run once at the end of the play. Roles are the same in that they can be referred to multiple times but will only actually get run once. There are two exceptions to this – the first is if the role is called more than once but with different variables or parameters, and the other is if the role being called has allow_duplicates set to true in its meta/ directory. We shall see examples of both as we build our example:

1. At the top level of our practical example, we will have a copy of the same inventory we have used throughout this chapter. We will also create a simple playbook called site.yml, which contains the following code:

    ```
    ---
    - name: Role variables and meta playbook
      hosts: web01.example.org

      roles:
        - platform
    ```

    Note that we are simply calling one role called platform from this playbook – nothing else is called from the playbook itself.

2. Let's go ahead and create the platform role – unlike our previous role, this will not contain any tasks or even any variable data; instead, it will just contain a meta directory:

    ```
    $ mkdir -p roles/platform/meta
    ```

    Inside this directory, create a file called main.yml with the following contents:

    ```
    ---
    dependencies:
    - role: linuxtype
      type: "fedora"
    - role: linuxtype
      type: "ubuntu"
    ```

    This code will tell Ansible that the platform role is dependent on the linuxtype role. Note that we specify the dependency twice, but each time we specify it, we pass it a variable called type with a different value – in this way, the Ansible parser allows us to call the role twice because a different variable value has been passed to it each time it is referred to as a dependency.

3. Let's now go ahead and create the linuxtype role – again, this will contain no tasks but more dependency declarations:

    ```
    $ mkdir -p roles/linuxtype/meta/
    ```

Again, create a `main.yml` file in the `meta` directory but this time containing the following:

```
---
dependencies:
- role: version
- role: network
```

Once again, we create more dependencies – this time, when the `linuxtype` role is called, it, in turn, declares dependencies on roles called `version` and `network`.

4. Let's create the `version` role first – this will have both `meta` and `tasks` directories in it:

```
$ mkdir -p roles/version/meta
$ mkdir -p roles/version/tasks
```

In the `meta` directory, we'll create a `main.yml` file with the following contents:

```
---
allow_duplicates: true
```

This declaration is important in this example – as discussed earlier, normally, Ansible will only allow a role to be executed once, even if it is called multiple times. Setting `allow_duplicates` to `true` tells Ansible to allow the execution of the role more than once. This is required because, in the `platform` role, we call (via a dependency) the `linuxtype` role twice, which means, in turn, we will call the `version` role twice.

We'll also create a simple `main.yml` file in the `tasks/` directory, which prints the value of the `type` variable that gets passed to the role:

```
---
- name: Print type variable
  ansible.builtin.debug:
    var: type
```

5. We will now repeat the process with the `network` role – to keep our example code simple, we'll define it with the same contents as the `version` role:

```
$ mkdir -p roles/network/meta
$ mkdir -p roles/network/tasks
```

In the `meta` directory, we'll again create a `main.yml` file with the following contents:

```
---
allow_duplicates: true
```

Again, we'll create a simple `main.yml` file in the `tasks` directory, which prints the value of the `type` variable that gets passed to the role:

```
---
- name: Print type variable
```

```
ansible.builtin.debug:
    var: type
```

At the end of this process, your directory structure should look like this:

```
.
├── hosts
├── roles
│   ├── linuxtype
│   │   └── meta
│   │       └── main.yml
│   ├── network
│   │   ├── meta
│   │   │   └── main.yml
│   │   └── tasks
│   │       └── main.yml
│   ├── platform
│   │   └── meta
│   │       └── main.yml
│   └── version
│       ├── meta
│       │   └── main.yml
│       └── tasks
│           └── main.yml
└── site.yml

11 directories, 8 files
```

Let's see what happens when we run this playbook. The flow should be as follows – our initial playbook statically imports the platform role. The platform role then states that it depends upon the linuxtype role, and the dependency is declared twice with a different value in a variable called type each time. The linuxtype role then states that it depends upon both the network and version roles, which are allowed to run more than once and print the value of type. Hence, we see the network and version roles called twice, printing fedora on the first call and ubuntu the second time (as this is how we originally specified the dependencies in the platform role). You can execute the playbook using the following command:

```
$ ansible-playbook -i hosts site.yml
```

The output should look something like this from this playbook execution:

```
james@controlnode:~/Practical-Ansible-Second-Edition/Chapter 4/role-example2$ an
sible-playbook -i hosts site.yml

PLAY [Role variables and meta playbook] *****************************************

TASK [Gathering Facts] *********************************************************
ok: [web01.example.org]

TASK [version : Print type variable] ********************************************
ok: [web01.example.org] => {
    "type": "fedora"
}

TASK [network : Print type variable] ********************************************
ok: [web01.example.org] => {
    "type": "fedora"
}

TASK [version : Print type variable] ********************************************
ok: [web01.example.org] => {
    "type": "ubuntu"
}

TASK [network : Print type variable] ********************************************
ok: [web01.example.org] => {
    "type": "ubuntu"
}

PLAY RECAP *********************************************************************
web01.example.org          : ok=5    changed=0    unreachable=0    failed=0    s
kipped=0    rescued=0    ignored=0
```

Figure 4.3 – An example of running a playbook using roles with dependencies

This is distinctly different from earlier versions of Ansible (for example, Ansible 2.7), where if you had run the same code, you would have seen only the type printed on the screen as ubuntu. This demonstrates an important point about looking at the code porting guidelines between releases of Ansible/ansible-core and understanding how the behavior may have changed. While, in most cases (excepting the fundamental change around collections), your automation code will work without changes from one version of Ansible to the next, this is not guaranteed, and a subtle change such as this could have catastrophic consequences in a production environment. Ansible code should be treated just as code, including testing new releases of Ansible when they are deployed.

This is quite an advanced example of Ansible role dependencies, but it has been provided to you to demonstrate the importance of knowing a little about variable precedence (that is, where the variable is scoped) and how the parser works. If you write simple, sequentially parsed tasks, then you may never need to know this, but I recommend that you make extensive use of the debug statement and test your playbook design to make sure that you don't fall foul of this during your playbook development.

Now that we have looked in great detail at a number of role aspects, let's take a look in the following section at a centralized store for publicly available Ansible roles – **Ansible Galaxy**.

Ansible Galaxy

No section on Ansible roles would be complete without a mention of Ansible Galaxy. Ansible Galaxy is a community-driven collection of Ansible roles and collections, hosted by Red Hat at `https://galaxy.ansible.com/`. It contains a great many community-contributed Ansible roles and collections, and if you can conceive of an automation task, there is a good chance someone has already written code to do exactly what you want. It is well worth exploring and can get your automation project off the ground quickly, as you can start to work with a set of ready-made roles.

In addition to the website, the `ansible-galaxy` client is included in Ansible, and this provides a quick and convenient way for you to download and deploy roles into your playbook structure. Let's say that you want to update the **message of the day** (**MOTD**) on your target hosts – this is surely something that somebody has already figured out. A quick search on the Ansible Galaxy website returns (at the time of writing) 168 roles to set the MOTD. If we want to use one of these (and I've picked one called `arillso.motd`), we can download it into our roles directory using the following command:

```
$ ansible-galaxy role install -p roles/ arillso.motd
```

That's all you need to do – once the download is complete, you can import or include the role in your playbook, just as you would for the manually created roles we have discussed in this chapter. Note that if you don't specify `-p roles/`, `ansible-galaxy` will install the roles into `~/.ansible/roles`, the central roles directory for your user account. This might be what you want, of course, but if you want the role downloaded directly into your playbook directory structure, you would add this parameter.

Another neat trick is to use `ansible-galaxy` to create an empty role directory structure for you to create your own roles in – this saves all of the manual directory and file creation we undertook in this chapter, as shown in this example:

```
$ ansible-galaxy role init --init-path roles/ testrole
- Role testrole was created successfully
$ tree roles/testrole/
roles/testrole/
├── README.md
├── defaults
│   └── main.yml
├── files
├── handlers
│   └── main.yml
├── meta
│   └── main.yml
```

```
├── tasks
│   └── main.yml
├── templates
├── tests
│   ├── inventory
│   └── test.yml
└── vars
    └── main.yml

8 directories, 8 files
```

That should give you enough information to get started on your journey into Ansible roles. I cannot stress highly enough how important it is to develop your code as roles – it might not seem important initially, but as your automation use cases expand, and your requirement to reuse code grows, you will be glad that you did. In the next section, let's expand our look at Ansible playbooks with a discussion of the ways in which conditional logic can be used in your Ansible code.

Using conditions in your code

In most of our examples so far, we have created simple sets of tasks that always run. However, as you generate tasks (whether in roles or playbooks) that you want to apply to a wider array of hosts, sooner or later, you will want to perform some kind of conditional action. This might be to only perform a task in response to the results of a previous task, or it might be to only perform a task in response to a specific fact gathered from a managed node. In this section, we will provide some practical examples of conditional logic to apply to your Ansible tasks to demonstrate how to use this feature.

As ever, we'll need an inventory to get started, and we'll reuse the inventory we have used throughout this chapter:

```
[frontends]
web01.example.org https_port=8443
web02.example.org http_proxy=proxy.example.org

[frontends:vars]
ntp_server=ntp.web.example.org
proxy=proxy.web.example.org

[apps]
app01.example.org
app02.example.org

[webapp:children]
frontends
```

```
apps

[webapp:vars]
proxy_server=proxy.webapp.example.org
health_check_retry=3
health_check_interval=60
```

Suppose that you want to perform an Ansible task only on certain operating systems. We have already discussed Ansible facts, and these provide the perfect platform to start exploring conditional logic in your playbooks. Consider this – an urgent patch has been released for all of your Fedora systems, and you want to apply it immediately. You could, of course, go through and create a special inventory (or host group) for Fedora hosts, but this is additional work that you don't necessarily need to do.

Instead, let's define the task that will perform our update, adding a when clause containing a Jinja2 expression to it, so that the update is only performed on Fedora-based hosts:

```
---
- name: Play to patch only Fedora systems
  hosts: all
  become: true

  tasks:
  - name: Patch Fedora systems
    ansible.builtin.dnf:
      name: httpd
      state: latest
    when: ansible_facts['distribution'] == "Fedora"
```

Now, when we run this task, if your test system(s) are Fedora-based (and one of mine is), you should see output similar to the following:

```
$ ansible-playbook -i hosts condition.yml


PLAY [Play to patch only Fedora systems] ****************************
***********


TASK [Gathering Facts] *********************************************
***********
ok: [web01.example.org]
ok: [app01.example.org]
ok: [web02.example.org]
ok: [app02.example.org]


TASK [Patch Fedora systems] *****************************************
***********
```

```
skipping: [web02.example.org]
skipping: [app01.example.org]
skipping: [app02.example.org]
ok: [web01.example.org]


PLAY RECAP **************************************************************
***********
app01.example.org          :
ok=1     changed=0    unreachable=0     failed=0     skipped=1
rescued=0     ignored=0
app02.example.org          :
ok=1     changed=0    unreachable=0     failed=0     skipped=1
rescued=0     ignored=0
web01.example.org          :
ok=2     changed=0    unreachable=0     failed=0     skipped=0
rescued=0     ignored=0
web02.example.org          :
ok=1     changed=0    unreachable=0     failed=0     skipped=1
rescued=0     ignored=0
```

The preceding output shows that only one of our systems was Fedora-based, and it returned an ok status, meaning the patch had already been applied. Now, we can make our logic more precise – perhaps it is only our legacy systems that run on Fedora 35 that need the patch applied. In this case, we can expand the logic in our playbook to check both the distribution and major versions, as follows:

```
---
- name: Play to patch only Fedora systems
  hosts: all
  become: true

  tasks:
  - name: Patch Fedora systems
    yum:
      name: httpd
      state: latest
    when: (ansible_facts['distribution'] == "Fedora" and ansible_
facts['distribution_major_version'] == "35")
```

Now, if we run our modified playbook, depending on the systems you have in your inventory, you might see output similar to the following. In this case, all systems were skipped because they did not match my logical expression (and, hence, I am safe in the knowledge that I have no legacy systems in this inventory to worry about):

```
$ ansible-playbook -i hosts condition2.yml


PLAY [Play to patch only Fedora systems] *****************************
***********
```

```
TASK [Gathering Facts] *******************************************
**********
ok: [app01.example.org]
ok: [web01.example.org]
ok: [app02.example.org]
ok: [web02.example.org]


TASK [Patch Fedora systems] ****************************************
**********
skipping: [web01.example.org]
skipping: [web02.example.org]
skipping: [app01.example.org]
skipping: [app02.example.org]


PLAY RECAP ********************************************************
**********
app01.example.org            :
ok=1     changed=0     unreachable=0     failed=0     skipped=1
rescued=0     ignored=0
app02.example.org            :
ok=1     changed=0     unreachable=0     failed=0     skipped=1
rescued=0     ignored=0
web01.example.org            :
ok=1     changed=0     unreachable=0     failed=0     skipped=1
rescued=0     ignored=0
web02.example.org            :
ok=1     changed=0     unreachable=0     failed=0     skipped=1
rescued=0     ignored=0
```

Of course, this conditional logic is not limited to Ansible facts and can be incredibly valuable when using the `ansible.builtin.shell` or `ansible.builtin.command` modules. When you run *any* Ansible module, the module returns data detailing the results of its run. You can capture this in an Ansible variable using the `register` keyword and then process it further later on in the playbook.

Consider the following playbook code. It contains two tasks, the first of which is to obtain the listing of the current directory and capture the output of the `ansible.builtin.shell` module in a variable called `shellresult`. We then print a simple `ansible.builtin.debug` message, but only on the condition that the `hosts` string is in the output of the `ansible.builtin.shell` module run:

```
---
- name: Play to test for hosts file in directory output
  hosts: localhost

  tasks:
```

```
- name: Gather directory listing from local system
  ansible.builtin.shell: "ls -l"
  register: shellresult

- name: Alert if we find a hosts file
  ansible.builtin.debug:
    msg: "Found hosts file!"
  when: '"hosts" in shellresult.stdout'
```

Now, when we run this in the current directory, which if you work from the GitHub repository that accompanies this book will contain a file named `hosts`, then you should see output similar to the following:

```
$ ansible-playbook condition3.yml


PLAY [Play to test for hosts file in directory output]
*************************

TASK [Gathering Facts] *********************************************
***********
ok: [localhost]


TASK [Gather directory listing from local system]
*****************************
changed: [localhost]


TASK [Alert if we find a hosts file] *******************************
***********
ok: [localhost] => {
    "msg": "Found hosts file!"
}


PLAY RECAP ********************************************************
***********
localhost                  :
ok=3     changed=1    unreachable=0     failed=0     skipped=0
rescued=0     ignored=0
```

Yet, if the file doesn't exist, you'll see that the `ansible.builtin.debug` message gets skipped:

```
$ ansible-playbook condition3.yml


PLAY [Play to test for hosts file in directory output]
*************************
```

```
TASK [Gathering Facts] ***********************************************
***********
ok: [localhost]

TASK [Gather directory listing from local system]
******************************
changed: [localhost]

TASK [Alert if we find a hosts file] ********************************
***********
skipping: [localhost]

PLAY RECAP **********************************************************
***********
localhost                   :
ok=2      changed=1     unreachable=0     failed=0      skipped=1
rescued=0     ignored=0
```

You can also create complex conditions for IT operational tasks in production; however, remember that in Ansible, variables are not cast to any particular type by default, so even though the contents of a variable (or fact) might look like a number, Ansible will treat it as a string by default. If you need to perform an integer comparison instead, you must first cast the variable to an integer type. For example, here is a fragment of a playbook that will run a task only on Fedora 35 and newer:

```
tasks:
  - name: Only perform this task on Fedora 35 and later
    ansible.builtin.shell: echo "only on Fedora 35 and later"
    when: ansible_facts['distribution'] == "Fedora" and ansible_
facts['distribution_major_version']|int >= 35
```

There are many different types of conditionals you can apply to your Ansible tasks, and this section just scratches the surface; however, it should give you a sound basis on which to expand your knowledge of applying conditions to your tasks in Ansible. Not only can you apply conditional logic to Ansible tasks but you can also run them in loops over a set of data, which we shall explore in the following section.

Repeating tasks with loops

Oftentimes, we will want to perform a single task but use it to iterate over a set of data. Perhaps you are creating new 15 new user groups on a server for various teams to utilize. It would be incredibly inefficient to have to write 15 individual tasks within an Ansible play to achieve this – and Ansible is all about efficiency and saving the user time. To enable this level of efficiency, Ansible supports looping over datasets to ensure that you can perform large-scale operations using tightly defined code. In this section, we will explore how to make practical use of loops in your Ansible playbooks.

As ever, we must start with an inventory to work against, and we will use our by-now familiar inventory, which we have consistently used throughout this chapter:

```
[frontends]
web01.example.org https_port=8443
web02.example.org http_proxy=proxy.example.org

[frontends:vars]
ntp_server=ntp.web.example.org
proxy=proxy.web.example.org

[apps]
app01.example.org
app02.example.org

[webapp:children]
frontends
apps

[webapp:vars]
proxy_server=proxy.webapp.example.org
health_check_retry=3
health_check_interval=60
```

Let's start with a really simple playbook to show you how to loop over a set of data in a single task. Although this is quite a contrived example, it is intended to be simple to show you the fundamentals of how loops work in Ansible. We will define a single task that runs the ansible.builtin.command module on a single host from the inventory and uses the ansible.builtin.command module to echo the numbers 1 through 6 in turn on the remote system (with some imagination, this could easily be extended to adding user accounts or creating a sequence of files).

Consider the following code:

```
---
- name: Simple loop demo play
  hosts: web01.example.org

  tasks:
    - name: Echo a value from the loop
      ansible.builtin.command: echo "{{ item }}"
      loop:
        - 1
        - 2
        - 3
```

```
    - 4
    - 5
    - 6
```

The `loop:` statement defines the start of the loop, and the items in the loop are defined as a YAML list. Also, note the higher indentation level, which tells the parser they are part of the loop. When working with the loop data, we use a special variable called `item`, which contains the current value from the loop iteration to be echoed. When we run this playbook, we should see output similar to the following:

```
$ ansible-playbook -i hosts loop1.yml

PLAY [Simple loop demo play] ****************************************
***********

TASK [Gathering Facts] *********************************************
***********
ok: [web01.example.org]

TASK [Echo a value from the loop] **********************************
***********
changed: [web01.example.org] => (item=1)
changed: [web01.example.org] => (item=2)
changed: [web01.example.org] => (item=3)
changed: [web01.example.org] => (item=4)
changed: [web01.example.org] => (item=5)
changed: [web01.example.org] => (item=6)

PLAY RECAP *********************************************************
***********
web01.example.org          :
ok=2     changed=1     unreachable=0     failed=0     skipped=0
rescued=0     ignored=0
```

You can combine the conditional logic we discussed in the preceding section with loops, to make the loop operate on just a subset of its data. For example, consider the following iteration of the playbook:

```
---
- name: Simple loop demo play
  hosts: web01.example.org

  tasks:
    - name: Echo a value from the loop
      ansible.builtin.command: echo "{{ item }}"
      loop:
        - 1
```

```
        - 2
        - 3
        - 4
        - 5
        - 6
  when: item|int > 3
```

Now, when we run this, we can see that the task is skipped until we reach the integer value of 4 and higher in the loop contents:

```
$ ansible-playbook -i hosts loop2.yml


PLAY [Simple loop demo play] ****************************************
***********


TASK [Gathering Facts] *********************************************
***********
ok: [web01.example.org]


TASK [Echo a value from the loop] **********************************
***********
skipping: [web01.example.org] => (item=1)
skipping: [web01.example.org] => (item=2)
skipping: [web01.example.org] => (item=3)
changed: [web01.example.org] => (item=4)
changed: [web01.example.org] => (item=5)
changed: [web01.example.org] => (item=6)


PLAY RECAP *********************************************************
***********
web01.example.org          :
ok=2      changed=1    unreachable=0     failed=0     skipped=0
    rescued=0     ignored=0
```

You can, of course, combine this with the conditional logic based on Ansible facts and other variables in the manner we discussed previously. Just as we captured the results of a module's execution using the register keyword before, we can do so with loops. The only difference is that the results will now be stored in a dictionary, with one dictionary entry for each iteration of the loop rather than just one set of results.

Hence, let's see what happens if we further enhance the playbook, as follows:

```
---

- name: Simple loop demo play
  hosts: web01.example.org
```

```
tasks:
  - name: Echo a value from the loop
    ansible.builtin.command: echo "{{ item }}"
    loop:
      - 1
      - 2
      - 3
      - 4
      - 5
      - 6
    when: item|int > 3
    register: loopresult

  - name: Print the results from the loop
    ansible.builtin.debug:
      var: loopresult
```

Now, when we run the playbook, you will see pages of output containing the dictionary with the contents of loopresult. The following output is truncated in the interests of space but demonstrates the kind of results you should expect from running this playbook:

```
$ ansible-playbook -i hosts loop3.yml

PLAY [Simple loop demo play] ****************************************
***********

TASK [Gathering Facts] *********************************************
***********
ok: [web01.example.org]

TASK [Echo a value from the loop] **********************************
***********
skipping: [web01.example.org] => (item=1)
skipping: [web01.example.org] => (item=2)
skipping: [web01.example.org] => (item=3)
changed: [web01.example.org] => (item=4)
changed: [web01.example.org] => (item=5)
changed: [web01.example.org] => (item=6)

TASK [Print the results from the loop] *****************************
***********
ok: [web01.example.org] => {
    "loopresult": {
        "changed": true,
        "msg": "All items completed",
```

```json
    "results": [
        {
            "ansible_loop_var": "item",
            "changed": false,
            "item": 1,
            "skip_reason": "Conditional result was False",
            "skipped": true
        },
        {

            "ansible_loop_var": "item",
            "changed": false,
            "item": 2,
            "skip_reason": "Conditional result was False",
            "skipped": true
        },
```

As you can see, the `results` section of the output is a dictionary, and we can clearly see that the first two items in the list were `skipped` because the result of our when clause (conditional) was `false`.

Hence, we can see so far that loops are easy to define and work with – but you may be asking, *can you create nested loops?* The answer to that question is *yes*, but there is a catch – the special variable named `item` would clash, as both the inner and outer loops would use the same variable name. This would mean the results from your nested loop run would be, at best, unexpected.

Fortunately, there is a `loop` parameter called `loop_control`, which allows you to change the name of the special variable containing the data from the current `loop` iteration from `item` to something of your choosing. Let's create a nested loop to see how this works.

First of all, we'll create a playbook in the usual manner, with a single task to run in a loop. To generate our nested loop, we'll use the `include_tasks` directive to dynamically include a single task from another YAML file, which will also contain a loop. As we intend to use this playbook in a nested loop, we'll use the `loop_var` directive to change the name of the special loop contents variable from `item` to `second_item`:

```yaml
---
- name: Play to demonstrate nested loops
  hosts: localhost

  tasks:
    - name: Outer loop
      ansible.builtin.include_tasks: loopsubtask.yml
      loop:
```

```
      - a
      - b
      - c
  loop_control:
    loop_var: second_item
```

Then, we'll create a second file called `loopsubtask.yml`, which contains the inner loop and is included in the preceding playbook. As we already changed the loop item variable name in the outer loop, we don't need to change it again here. Note that the structure of this file is very much like a tasks file in a role – it is not a complete playbook but, rather, simply a list of tasks:

```
---
- name: Inner loop
  ansible.builtin.debug:
    msg: "second item={{ second_item }} first item={{ item }}"
  loop:
    - 100
    - 200
    - 300
```

Now you should be able to run the playbook, and you will see Ansible iterate over the outer loop first and then process the inner loop over the data defined by the outer loop. Test this playbook by running the following command:

```
$ ansible-playbook loopmain.yml
```

As the loop variable names do not clash, everything works exactly as we would expect:

```
james@controlnode:~/Practical-Ansible-Second-Edition/Chapter 4$ ansible-playbook
 loopmain.yml

PLAY [Play to demonstrate nested loops] *************************************

TASK [Gathering Facts] ******************************************************
ok: [localhost]

TASK [Outer loop] ***********************************************************
included: /home/james/Practical-Ansible-Second-Edition/Chapter 4/loopsubtask.yml
 for localhost => (item=a)
included: /home/james/Practical-Ansible-Second-Edition/Chapter 4/loopsubtask.yml
 for localhost => (item=b)
included: /home/james/Practical-Ansible-Second-Edition/Chapter 4/loopsubtask.yml
 for localhost => (item=c)

TASK [Inner loop] ***********************************************************
ok: [localhost] => (item=100) => {
    "msg": "second item=a first item=100"
}
ok: [localhost] => (item=200) => {
    "msg": "second item=a first item=200"
}
ok: [localhost] => (item=300) => {
    "msg": "second item=a first item=300"
}

TASK [Inner loop] ***********************************************************
ok: [localhost] => (item=100) => {
    "msg": "second item=b first item=100"
}
ok: [localhost] => (item=200) => {
    "msg": "second item=b first item=200"
}
ok: [localhost] => (item=300) => {
    "msg": "second item=b first item=300"
}

TASK [Inner loop] ***********************************************************
ok: [localhost] => (item=100) => {
    "msg": "second item=c first item=100"
}
ok: [localhost] => (item=200) => {
    "msg": "second item=c first item=200"
}
ok: [localhost] => (item=300) => {
    "msg": "second item=c first item=300"
}

PLAY RECAP ******************************************************************
localhost                  : ok=7    changed=0    unreachable=0    failed=0    s
kipped=0    rescued=0    ignored=0

james@controlnode:~/Practical-Ansible-Second-Edition/Chapter 4$
```

Figure 4.4 – Demonstrating nested loops in an Ansible playbook

Loops are simple to work with and yet very powerful, as they allow you to easily use one task to iterate over a large dataset. In the next section, we'll look at another construct of the Ansible language to control playbook flow – blocks.

Grouping tasks using blocks

Blocks in Ansible allow you to logically group a set of tasks together, primarily for one of two purposes. One might be to apply conditional logic to an entire set of tasks; in this example, you could apply an identical when clause to each of the tasks, but this is cumbersome and inefficient – it's far better to place all of the tasks in a block and apply the conditional logic to the block itself. In this way, the logic only needs to be declared once. Blocks are also valuable when it comes to error handling and especially when it comes to recovering from an error condition. We shall explore both of these through simple practical examples in this chapter to get you up to speed with blocks in Ansible.

As ever, let's ensure we have an inventory to work from:

```
[frontends]
web01.example.org https_port=8443
web02.example.org http_proxy=proxy.example.org

[frontends:vars]
ntp_server=ntp.web.example.org
proxy=proxy.web.example.org

[apps]
app01.example.org
app02.example.org

[webapp:children]
frontends
apps

[webapp:vars]
proxy_server=proxy.webapp.example.org
health_check_retry=3
health_check_interval=60
```

Now, let's dive straight in and look at an example of how you would use blocks to apply conditional logic to a set of tasks. At a high level, suppose we want to perform the following actions on all of our Fedora Linux hosts:

- Install the package for the Apache web server
- Install a templated configuration
- Start the appropriate service

We could achieve this with three individual tasks, all with a when clause associated with them, but blocks provide us with a better way. The following example playbook shows the three tasks discussed contained in a block (note the additional level of indentation required to denote their inclusion in the block):

```
---
- name: Conditional block play
  hosts: all
  become: true

  tasks:
  - name: Install and configure Apache
    block:
      - name: Install the Apache package
        ansible.builtin.dnf:
          name: httpd
          state: installed
      - name: Install the templated configuration to a dummy location
        ansible.builtin.template:
          src: templates/src.j2
          dest: /tmp/my.conf
      - name: Start the httpd service
        ansible.builtin.service:
          name: httpd
          state: started
          enabled: True
    when: ansible_facts['distribution'] == 'Fedora'
```

Run your playbook with the following command:

```
$ ansible-playbook -i hosts blocks.yml
```

You should find that the Apache-related tasks are only run on any Fedora hosts you might have in your inventory; you should see that either all three tasks are run or are skipped – depending on the makeup and contents of your inventory, it might look something like this:

```
james@controlnode:~/Practical-Ansible-Second-Edition/Chapter 4$ ansible-playbook
 -i hosts blocks.yml

PLAY [Conditional block play] ************************************************

TASK [Gathering Facts] ******************************************************
ok: [app02.example.org]
ok: [app01.example.org]
ok: [web01.example.org]
ok: [web02.example.org]

TASK [Install the Apache package] *******************************************
skipping: [web01.example.org]
skipping: [web02.example.org]
skipping: [app01.example.org]
skipping: [app02.example.org]

TASK [Install the templated configuration to a dummy location] **************
skipping: [web01.example.org]
skipping: [web02.example.org]
skipping: [app01.example.org]
skipping: [app02.example.org]

TASK [Start the httpd service] **********************************************
skipping: [web01.example.org]
skipping: [web02.example.org]
skipping: [app01.example.org]
skipping: [app02.example.org]

PLAY RECAP ******************************************************************
app01.example.org          : ok=1    changed=0    unreachable=0    failed=0    s
kipped=3    rescued=0    ignored=0
app02.example.org          : ok=1    changed=0    unreachable=0    failed=0    s
kipped=3    rescued=0    ignored=0
web01.example.org          : ok=1    changed=0    unreachable=0    failed=0    s
kipped=3    rescued=0    ignored=0
web02.example.org          : ok=1    changed=0    unreachable=0    failed=0    s
kipped=3    rescued=0    ignored=0
```

Figure 4.5 – A playbook demonstrating the use of blocks in conditional task execution

This is very simple-to-construct but very powerful in terms of the effect it has on your ability to control the flow over large sets of tasks.

This time, let's build a different example to demonstrate how blocks can help Ansible to handle error conditions gracefully. So far, you should have seen that if your playbooks encounter any errors, they are likely to stop executing at the point of failure. This is, in some situations, far from ideal, and you might want to perform some kind of recovery action in this event rather than simply halting the playbook.

Let's create a new playbook, this time with the following contents:

```
---
- name: Play to demonstrate block error handling
  hosts: frontends

  tasks:
```

```
- name: block to handle errors
  block:
    - name: Perform a successful task
      ansible.builtin.debug:
        msg: 'Normally executing....'
    - name: Deliberately create an error
      ansible.builtin.command: /bin/whatever
    - name: This task should not run if the previous one results
in an error
      ansible.builtin.debug:
        msg: 'Never print this message if the above command
fails!!!!'
  rescue:
    - name: Catch the error (and perform recovery actions)
      ansible.builtin.debug:
        msg: 'Caught the error'
    - name: Deliberately create another error
      ansible.builtin.command: /bin/whatever
    - name: This task should not run if the previous one results
in an error
      ansible.builtin.debug:
        msg: 'Do not print this message if the above command
fails!!!!'
  always:
    - name: This task always runs!
      ansible.builtin.debug:
        msg: "Tasks in this part of the play will be ALWAYS
executed!!!!"
```

Note that in the preceding play, we now have additional sections to block – as well as the tasks in block itself, we have two new parts labeled rescue and always. The flow of execution is as follows:

1. All tasks in the block section are executed normally, in the sequence in which they are listed.

2. If a task in the block results in an error, no further tasks in the block are run:

    • Tasks in the rescue section start to run in the order they are listed

    • Tasks in the rescue section do not run if no errors result from the block tasks

3. If an error results from a task being run in the rescue section, no further rescue tasks are executed, and execution moves on to the always section.

4. Tasks in the always section are always run, regardless of any errors in either the block or rescue sections. They even run when no errors are encountered.

Test your playbook code by running the following command:

```
$ ansible-playbook -i hosts blocks-error.yml
```

With this flow of execution in mind, you should see output similar to the following when you execute this playbook, noting that we have deliberately created two error conditions to demonstrate the flow:

```
james@controlnode:~/Practical-Ansible-Second-Edition/Chapter 4$ ansible-playbook
 -i hosts blocks-error.yml

PLAY [Play to demonstrate block error handling] ********************************

TASK [Gathering Facts] ********************************************************
ok: [web01.example.org]
ok: [web02.example.org]

TASK [Perform a successful task] **********************************************
ok: [web01.example.org] => {
    "msg": "Normally executing...."
}
ok: [web02.example.org] => {
    "msg": "Normally executing...."
}

TASK [Deliberately create an error] *******************************************
fatal: [web01.example.org]: FAILED! => {"changed": false, "cmd": "/bin/whatever"
, "msg": "[Errno 2] No such file or directory: b'/bin/whatever'", "rc": 2, "stde
rr": "", "stderr_lines": [], "stdout": "", "stdout_lines": []}
fatal: [web02.example.org]: FAILED! => {"changed": false, "cmd": "/bin/whatever"
, "msg": "[Errno 2] No such file or directory: b'/bin/whatever'", "rc": 2, "stde
rr": "", "stderr_lines": [], "stdout": "", "stdout_lines": []}

TASK [Catch the error (and perform recovery actions)] *************************
ok: [web01.example.org] => {
    "msg": "Caught the error"
}
ok: [web02.example.org] => {
    "msg": "Caught the error"
}

TASK [Deliberately create another error] **************************************
fatal: [web01.example.org]: FAILED! => {"changed": false, "cmd": "/bin/whatever"
, "msg": "[Errno 2] No such file or directory: b'/bin/whatever'", "rc": 2, "stde
rr": "", "stderr_lines": [], "stdout": "", "stdout_lines": []}
fatal: [web02.example.org]: FAILED! => {"changed": false, "cmd": "/bin/whatever"
, "msg": "[Errno 2] No such file or directory: b'/bin/whatever'", "rc": 2, "stde
rr": "", "stderr_lines": [], "stdout": "", "stdout_lines": []}

TASK [This task always runs!] *************************************************
ok: [web01.example.org] => {
    "msg": "Tasks in this part of the play will be ALWAYS executed!!!!"
}
ok: [web02.example.org] => {
    "msg": "Tasks in this part of the play will be ALWAYS executed!!!!"
}

PLAY RECAP ********************************************************************
web01.example.org          : ok=4    changed=0    unreachable=0    failed=1    s
kipped=0    rescued=1    ignored=0
web02.example.org          : ok=4    changed=0    unreachable=0    failed=1    s
kipped=0    rescued=1    ignored=0
```

Figure 4.6 – Demonstrating the use of blocks in error handling in playbooks

Ansible has two special variables, which contain information you might find useful in the `rescue` block to perform your recovery actions:

- `ansible_failed_task`: This is a dictionary containing details of the task from `block` that failed, causing us to enter the `rescue` section. You can explore this by displaying its contents using `ansible.builtin.debug`, so, for example, the name of the failing task can be obtained from `ansible_failed_task.name`.

- `ansible_failed_result`: This is the result of the failed task and behaves the same as if you had added the `register` keyword to the failing task. This saves you from having to add `register` to every single task in the block if it fails.

As your playbooks get more complex and error handling gets more and more important (or, indeed, conditional logic becomes more vital), blocks will become an important part of your arsenal to write robust playbooks. Let's proceed in the next section to explore execution strategies to gain further control of your playbook runs.

Configuring play execution via strategies

As your playbooks become increasingly complex, it becomes more and more important that you have robust ways to debug any issues that might arise. For example, is there a way you can check the contents of a given variable (or variables) during execution without the need to insert `ansible.builtin.debug` statements throughout your playbook? Similarly, we have so far seen that Ansible will ensure that a particular task runs to completion on all inventory hosts that it applies to before moving on to the next task – is there a way to vary this?

When you get started with Ansible, the execution strategy that you see by default (and we have seen this so far in every playbook we have executed, even though we have not mentioned it by name) is known as `linear`. This does exactly what it describes – each task is executed in turn on all applicable hosts before the next task is started. However, there is another less commonly used strategy called `free`, which allows all tasks to be completed as fast as they can on each host, without waiting for other hosts.

The most useful strategy when you start to work with Ansible, however, is going to be the `debug` strategy, and this enables Ansible to drop you straight into its integrated debug environment if an error should occur in the playbook. Let's demonstrate this by creating a playbook that has a deliberate error in it. Note the `strategy: debug` and `debugger: on_failed` statements in the play definition:

```
---
- name: Play to demonstrate the debug strategy
  hosts: web01.example.org
  strategy: debug
  debugger: on_failed
  gather_facts: no
  vars:
```

```
    name: james

tasks:
  - name: Generate an error by referencing an undefined variable
    ansible.builtin.ping: data={{ mobile }}
```

Now, if you execute this playbook, you should see that it starts to run, but then it drops you into the integrated debugger when it encounters the deliberate error it contains. The start of the output should be similar to the following:

```
$ ansible-playbook -i hosts debug.yml
[WARNING]: Found variable using reserved name: name

PLAY [Play to demonstrate the debug strategy] ***********************
***********

TASK [Generate an error by referencing an undefined variable]
*******************
fatal: [web01.example.org]: FAILED! => {"msg": "The task includes
an option with an undefined variable. The error was: 'mobile' is
undefined. 'mobile' is undefined\n\nThe error appears to be in '/
home/james/Practical-Ansible-Second-Edition/Chapter 4/debug.yml':
line 11, column 7, but may\nbe elsewhere in the file depending
on the exact syntax problem.\n\nThe offending line appears to
be:\n\n  tasks:\n    - name: Generate an error by referencing an
undefined variable\n        ^ here\n"}
[web01.example.org] TASK: Generate an error by referencing an
undefined variable (debug)> p
***SyntaxError:SyntaxError('invalid syntax', ('<string>', 0, 0, '', 0,
0))
[web01.example.org] TASK: Generate an error by referencing an
undefined variable (debug)> p task_vars
{'ansible_check_mode': False,
 'ansible_config_file': None,
 'ansible_current_hosts': ['web01.example.org'],
 'ansible_dependent_role_names': [],
 'ansible_diff_mode': False,
 'ansible_facts': {},
 'ansible_failed_hosts': [],
 'ansible_forks': 5,
...

[web01.example.org] TASK: Generate an error by referencing an
undefined variable (debug)> quit
User interrupted execution
$
```

Note that the playbook starts executing but fails on the first task with an error, as the variable is undefined. However, rather than exiting back to the shell, it enters an interactive debugger. We've given a simple example of using the debugger in the preceding output, and if you'd like to learn how to use it more comprehensively, the Ansible documentation has full details of the available commands and how to use them: `https://docs.ansible.com/ansible/latest/user_guide/playbooks_debugger.html`.

To take you through a very simple, practical debugging example, enter the `p task` command at the prompt – this will cause the Ansible debugger to print the name of the failing task, which is very useful if you are in the midst of a large playbook:

```
[web01.example.org] TASK: Generate an error by referencing an
undefined variable (debug)> p task
TASK: Generate an error by referencing an undefined variable
[web01.example.org] TASK: Generate an error by referencing an
undefined variable
```

Now, we know where the play failed, so let's dig a little deeper by issuing the `p task.args` command, which will show us the arguments that were passed to the module in the task:

```
(debug)> p task.args
{'data': '{{ mobile }}'}
[web01.example.org] TASK: Generate an error by referencing an
undefined variable
```

So, we can see that our module was passed the argument called `data`, with the argument value being a variable (denoted by the pairs of curly braces) called `mobile`. Hence, it might be logical to have a look at the variables available to the task to see whether this variable exists and, if so, whether the value is sensible (use the `p task_vars` command to do this):

```
(debug)> p task_vars
{'ansible_check_mode': False,
 'ansible_config_file': None,
 'ansible_current_hosts': ['web01.example.org'],
 'ansible_dependent_role_names': [],
 'ansible_diff_mode': False,
 'ansible_facts': {},
 'ansible_failed_hosts': [],
 'ansible_forks': 5,
```

The preceding output is truncated, and you will find a great many variables associated with the task – this is because any gathered facts, and internal Ansible variables, are all available to the task. However, if you scroll through the list, you will be able to confirm that there is no variable called `mobile`.

Hence, this should be enough information to fix your playbook. Enter q to quit the debugger:

```
[web01.example.org] TASK: Generate an error by referencing an
undefined variable (debug)> q
User interrupted execution
$
```

The Ansible debugger is an incredibly powerful tool, and you should learn to make effective use of it, especially as your playbook complexity grows. This concludes our practical look at the various aspects of playbook design – in the next section, we'll take a look at the ways in which you can integrate Git source code management into your playbooks.

Using ansible-pull

Of course, the ideal way to work with Ansible code is to store it in a version control repository. This is a valuable step that ensures all changes are tracked, and that everyone responsible for automation is working from the same code. However, it also presents an inefficiency – end users must remember to check out (or pull) the latest version of the code and then execute it, and while this isn't difficult, manual tasks are both the enemy of efficiency and make it easy for errors to occur. Luckily, once again, Ansible supports us by providing tooling to ensure the most efficient approach can be achieved, and a special command called `ansible-pull` can be used to both retrieve the latest code from a Git repository and execute it, all using one command. This supports not only greater efficiency for end users (and reduces the chance of human error) but also enables automation jobs to be run unattended (for example, using a scheduler such as `cron`).

An important thing to note, however, is that, while the `ansible` and `ansible-playbook` commands can both operate over an entire inventory and run the playbooks against one or more remote hosts, the `ansible-pull` command is only intended to run the playbooks it obtains from your source control system on `localhost`. Hence, if you want to use `ansible-pull` throughout your infrastructure, you must install it onto every host that needs it.

Nonetheless, let's see how this might work. We'll simply run the command by hand to explore its application, but in reality, you would almost certainly install it in your `crontab` so that it runs on a regular basis, picking up any changes you make to your playbook in the version control system.

As stated, `ansible-pull` is only intended to run the playbook on the local system, so an inventory file is somewhat redundant – instead, we'll use a little-used inventory specification whereby you can simply specify the inventory hosts directory as a comma-separated list on the command line. If you only have one host, you simply specify its name followed by a comma.

Let's use a simple playbook from GitHub that sets the message of the day based on variable content. To do this, we will run the following command (which we'll break down in a minute):

```
$ ansible-pull -d /tmp/ansible-set-motd -i ${HOSTNAME}, -U https://
github.com/jamesfreeman959/ansible-set-motd.git site.yml -e "ag_motd_
content='MOTD generated by ansible-pull'" >> /tmp/ansible-pull.log
2>&1
```

This command breaks down as follows:

- `-d /tmp/ansible-set-motd`: This sets the working directory that will contain the checkout of the code from GitHub. Ensure this is writeable by the user account running the `ansible-pull` command.
- `-i ${HOSTNAME},`: This runs only on the current host, specified by its hostname from the appropriate shell variable.
- `-U https://github.com/jamesfreeman959/ansible-set-motd.git`: We use this URL to obtain the playbooks.
- `site.yml`: This is the name of the playbook to run from the Git repository specified earlier.
- `-e "ag_motd_content='MOTD generated by ansible-pull'"`: This sets the appropriate Ansible variable to generate the MOTD content.
- `>> /tmp/ansible-pull.log 2>&1`: This redirects the output of the command to a log file if we need to analyze it later – this is especially useful if running the command in a cron job where the output would never be printed to the user's terminal.

You can test this with the following command:

```
$ ansible-pull -d /tmp/ansible-set-motd -i ${HOSTNAME}, -U https://
github.com/jamesfreeman959/ansible-set-motd.git site.yml -e "ag_motd_
content='MOTD generated by ansible-pull'"
```

You should see some output similar to the following (note that log redirection has been removed to make it easier to see the output):

```
james@controlnode:~/Practical-Ansible-Second-Edition/Chapter 4$ ansible-pull -d
/tmp/ansible-set-motd -i ${HOSTNAME}, -U https://github.com/jamesfreeman959/ansi
ble-set-motd.git site.yml -e "ag_motd_content='MOTD generated by ansible-pull'"
Starting Ansible Pull at 2023-06-21 16:26:12
/home/james/.local/bin/ansible-pull -d /tmp/ansible-set-motd -i controlnode.exam
ple.org, -U https://github.com/jamesfreeman959/ansible-set-motd.git site.yml -e
ag_motd_content='MOTD generated by ansible-pull'
[WARNING]: Could not match supplied host pattern, ignoring: controlnode
controlnode.example.org | CHANGED => {
    "after": "7d3a191ecb2debe7f84f4fa5817b0f1b49c4cd54",
    "ansible_facts": {
        "discovered_interpreter_python": "/usr/bin/python3"
    },
    "before": null,
    "changed": true
}
[WARNING]: Could not match supplied host pattern, ignoring: controlnode

PLAY [Update the MOTD on hosts] ***********************************************

TASK [Gathering Facts] ********************************************************
ok: [controlnode.example.org]

TASK [ansible.motd : Add 99-footer file] **************************************
skipping: [controlnode.example.org]

TASK [ansible.motd : Delete 99-footer file] **********************************
ok: [controlnode.example.org]

TASK [ansible.motd : Delete /etc/motd file] **********************************
skipping: [controlnode.example.org]

TASK [ansible.motd : Check motd tail supported] ******************************
fatal: [controlnode.example.org]: FAILED! => {"changed": true, "cmd": "test -f /
etc/update-motd.d/99-footer", "delta": "0:00:00.004588", "end": "2023-06-21 16:2
6:20.773218", "msg": "non-zero return code", "rc": 1, "start": "2023-06-21 16:26
:20.768630", "stderr": "", "stderr_lines": [], "stdout": "", "stdout_lines": []}
...ignoring

TASK [ansible.motd : Add motd tail] ******************************************
skipping: [controlnode.example.org]

TASK [ansible.motd : Add motd] ***********************************************
ok: [controlnode.example.org]

PLAY RECAP *******************************************************************
controlnode.example.org    : ok=4    changed=1    unreachable=0    failed=0    s
kipped=3    rescued=0    ignored=1
```

Figure 4.7 – Demonstrating the use of ansible-pull

This command can be a very powerful part of your overall Ansible solution, especially as it means you don't have to worry too much about running all of your playbooks centrally, or ensuring that they are all up to date every time you run them. The ability to schedule this in cron is especially powerful in a large infrastructure where, ideally, automation means things should take care of themselves.

This concludes our practical look at playbooks and how to author your own code – with a little research into Ansible modules, you should now have enough to write your own robust playbooks with ease.

Summary

Playbooks are the lifeblood of Ansible automation, providing a robust framework within which to define logical collections of tasks and handle error conditions cleanly and robustly. The addition of roles into this mix is valuable in terms of not only organizing your code but also in terms of supporting code reuse as your automation requirements grow. Ansible playbooks provide a truly complete automation solution for your technology needs.

In this chapter, you learned about the playbook framework and how to start building your own playbooks. You then learned how to organize your code into roles and design your code to effectively and efficiently support reuse. We then explored some of the more advanced playbook writing topics, such as working with conditional logic, blocks, and loops. Finally, we looked at playbook execution strategies, especially with a view to being able to debug our playbooks effectively, and we wrapped up with a look at how we can run Ansible playbooks on a local machine directly from GitHub.

In the next chapter, we will learn how to consume and create our very own modules, providing you with the skills you need to expand the capabilities of Ansible to suit your own bespoke environments and contribute to the community.

Questions

1. How do you restart the Apache web server in the frontends host group via an ad hoc command?

   A. `ansible frontends -i hosts -a "name=httpd state=restarted"`

   B. `ansible frontends -i hosts -b ansible.builtin.service -a "name=httpd state=restarted"`

   C. `ansible frontends -i hosts -b -m ansible.builtin.service -a "name=httpd state=restarted"`

   D. `ansible frontends -i hosts -b -m ansible.builtin.server -a "name=httpd state=restarted"`

   E. `ansible frontends -i hosts -m restart -a "name=httpd"`

2. Blocks allow you to logically make a group of tasks or perform error handling:

   A. True

   B. False

3. Default strategies are implemented via the relevant modules in the playbook:

    A. True

    B. False

Further reading

`ansible-galaxy` and its documentation can be found here: `https://galaxy.ansible.com/docs/`.

Part 2: Expanding the Capabilities of Ansible

In this section, we will cover the important concepts of Ansible plugins and modules. We will cover both their effective use and how to expand Ansible's capabilities by writing your own plugins, modules, and collections. We'll even look at the requirements for submitting your modules and plugins back to the official Ansible project. We'll also look at coding best practices, as well as some advanced Ansible techniques that allow you to safely automate your infrastructure even when you are working with a clustered environment.

This section contains the following chapters:

- *Chapter 5, Creating and Consuming Modules*
- *Chapter 6, Creating and Consuming Collections*
- *Chapter 7, Creating and Consuming Plugins*
- *Chapter 8, Coding Best Practices*
- *Chapter 9, Advanced Ansible Topics*

5

Creating and Consuming Modules

Throughout this book, we have almost constantly referred to and made use of Ansible modules. We have treated these as *black boxes* – that is to say, we have just accepted that they exist and that they will work in a certain documented manner. However, one of the many great things about Ansible is that it is an open source project, and as such, not only can you view and modify its source code, but you can also develop your own additions. At the time of writing, there are 3,300+ modules available for Ansible, handling everything from simple commands such as copying files and installing packages to configuring highly complex and bespoke networking equipment. This large array of modules has grown out of a genuine need to solve problems with Ansible, and the number included with each release of Ansible increases every time.

Sooner or later, you will come across a specific piece of functionality that doesn't exist in any of the current Ansible modules. Of course, you could attempt to fill this gap functionally, either by writing your own module or by contributing enhancements to one of the existing modules back to the Ansible project for everyone else to benefit from. In this chapter, you will learn the basics of creating modules, as well as how to contribute your code back to the upstream Ansible project if you wish.

Specifically, in this chapter, you will cover the following topics:

- Executing multiple modules using the command line
- Reviewing the module index
- Accessing module documentation from the command line
- Module return values
- Developing custom modules

Let's get started!

Technical requirements

This chapter assumes that you have set up your control host with Ansible, as detailed in *Chapter 1, Getting Started with Ansible*, and are using the most recent version available – the examples in this chapter were tested with `ansible-core` version 2.15. This chapter also assumes that you have at least one additional host to test against. Ideally, this should be Linux-based. Although we will give specific examples of hostnames in this chapter, you are free to substitute them with your own hostname and/or IP address. Details of how to do this will be provided in the appropriate places.

The module development work that will be covered in this chapter assumes the presence of a Python 3 development environment on your computer and that you are running either Linux, FreeBSD, or macOS. Where additional Python modules are needed, their installation is documented. The task of building module documentation has some very specific requirements around Python 3.10 or later, so you will need to install a suitable Python environment if you wish to attempt this.

The code bundle for this chapter is available here: `https://github.com/PacktPublishing/Practical-Ansible-Second-Edition/tree/main/Chapter%205`.

Executing multiple modules using the command line

As this chapter is all about modules and how to create them, let's recap how to use modules. We've done this throughout this book, but we have not drawn attention to some of the specifics related to how they work. One of the key things we have not discussed is how the Ansible engine talks to its modules and vice versa, so let's explore this now.

As ever, when working with Ansible commands, we need an inventory to run our commands against. For this chapter, as our focus is on the modules themselves, we will use a very simple and small inventory, as shown here:

```
[frontends]
frt01.example.com

[appservers]
app01.example.com
```

Now, for the first part of our recap, you can run a module very easily via an ad hoc command and use the `-m` switch to tell Ansible which module you want to run. Hence, one of the simplest commands you can run is the Ansible `ping` command, as shown here:

```
$ ansible -i hosts appservers -m ping
```

Now, let's examine the output of the preceding command:

```
$ ansible -i hosts appservers -m ping
app01.example.com | SUCCESS => {
    "ansible_facts": {
        "discovered_interpreter_python": "/usr/bin/python3"
    },
    "changed": false,
    "ping": "pong"
}
```

Did you notice the structure of the output – the curly braces, colons, and commas? Yes, Ansible uses JSON-formatted data to talk to its modules, and the modules report their data back to Ansible in JSON as well. The preceding output is a subset of the JSON-formatted data returned to the Ansible engine by the `ping` module.

Of course, we never have to worry about this as we work with the modules using either `key=value` pairs on the command line or YAML in playbooks and roles. Hence, the JSON is shielded from us, but this is an important fact to bear in mind as we head into the world of module development later in this chapter.

Ansible modules are just like functions in a high-level programming language, in that they take a well-defined list of arguments as input, perform their function, and then provide a set of output data, which is also well defined and documented. We'll look at this in more detail later in this chapter. Of course, the preceding command didn't include any arguments, so this was the simplest possible invocation of a module via Ansible.

Now, let's run another command that takes an argument and passes that data to the module:

```
$ ansible -i hosts appservers -m command -a "/bin/echo 'hello
modules'"
```

In this case, we provided a single string as an argument to the command module, which Ansible, in turn, converts into JSON and passes down to the command module when it's invoked. When you run this ad hoc command, you will see an output similar to the following:

```
$ ansible -i hosts appservers -m command -a "/bin/echo 'hello
modules'"
app01.example.com | CHANGED | rc=0 >>
hello modules
```

In this instance, the output data does not appear to be JSON formatted; however, what Ansible prints to the Terminal when you run a module is only a subset of the data that each module returns – for example, both the CHANGED status and rc=0 exit code from our command were passed back to Ansible in a JSON-formatted data structure – this was just hidden from us.

This point doesn't need to be labored too much, but it is important to set the context. It is this context that we shall build upon throughout this chapter, so simply remember these key points:

- Communication between Ansible and its modules is done through JSON-formatted data structures
- Modules take input data that controls how they function (arguments)
- Modules always return data – at the very least, the status of the module's execution (for example, `changed`, `ok`, or `failed`)

Of course, before you start coding modules, it makes sense to check whether a module that can perform all (or some) of the functionality you need already exists. We will explore this in the next section.

Reviewing the module index

As discussed in the preceding section, Ansible provides thousands of modules to make it fast and easy to develop playbooks and run them across multiple host machines. How do you go about finding the right module to begin with, though, when there are so many? Fortunately, the Ansible documentation features a well-organized, indexed list of modules that you can consult to find your desired module – this is available here: `https://docs.ansible.com/ansible/latest/collections/index_module.html`.

Let's suppose you want to see whether there is a native Ansible module that can help you configure and manage your Amazon Web Services S3 buckets. That's a fairly precise, well-defined need, so let's approach this logically:

1. Begin by opening the index of all modules in your web browser, as discussed previously: `https://docs.ansible.com/ansible/latest/collections/index_module.html`.

2. Now, we know that `amazon.aws` modules are certainly indexed at the very beginning of this page.

3. There are still thousands of modules listed on this page! So, let's use the find function (*Ctrl + F*) in the browser to see whether the `amazon.aws.s3` keyword appears anywhere:

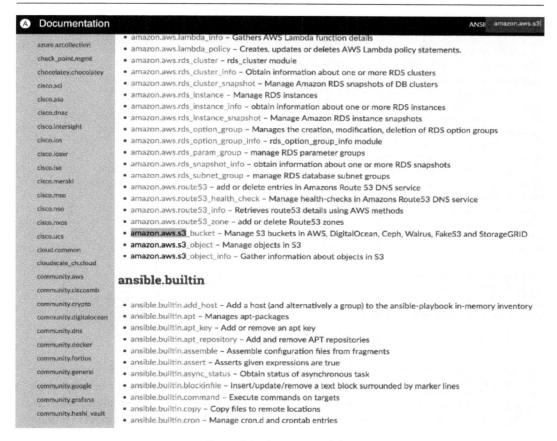

Figure 5.1 – Amazon modules

We now have a shortlist of modules to work with – granted, there are several, so we still need to work out which one (or ones) we will need for our playbook. As shown from the preceding short descriptions, this will depend on what your intended task is.

4. The short descriptions should be enough to give you some clues about whether the module will suit your needs or not. Once you have an idea, you can click on the appropriate document links to view more details about the module and how to work with it:

amazon.aws.s3_object module – Manage objects in S3

> **ⓘ Note**
>
> This module is part of the amazon.aws collection (version 5.4.0).
>
> You might already have this collection installed if you are using the `ansible` package. It is not included in `ansible-core`. To check whether it is installed, run `ansible-galaxy collection list`.
>
> To install it, use: `ansible-galaxy collection install amazon.aws`. You need further requirements to be able to use this module, see Requirements for details.
>
> To use it in a playbook, specify: `amazon.aws.s3_object`.

New in amazon.aws 1.0.0

- Synopsis
- Requirements
- Parameters
- Notes
- Examples
- Return Values

Synopsis

- This module allows the user to manage the objects and directories within S3 buckets. Includes support for creating and deleting objects and directories, retrieving objects as files or strings, generating download links and copying objects that are already stored in Amazon S3.
- Support for creating or deleting S3 buckets with this module has been deprecated and will be removed in release 6.0.0.
- S3 buckets can be created or deleted using the amazon.aws.s3_bucket module.
- Compatible with AWS, DigitalOcean, Ceph, Walrus, FakeS3 and StorageGRID.
- When using non-AWS services, *endpoint_url* should be specified.

Figure 5.2 – Amazon S3 module details

5. As you can see, the documentation page for each module provides a great deal of information, including a longer description. If you scroll down the page, you will see a list of the possible arguments that you can provide the module with, some practical examples of how to use them, and some details about the outputs from the module. Also, note the **Requirements** section – some modules, especially cloud-related ones, require additional Python modules before they will work, and if you attempt to run the `aws_s3` module from a playbook without installing the `boto3` and `botocore` modules on Python 3.6 or later, you will simply receive an error.

All modules must have documentation like this created before they will be accepted as part of the Ansible project, so you must keep this in mind if you intend to submit your own modules. This is also one of the reasons for Ansible's popularity – with easy-to-maintain and well-documented standards, it is the perfect community platform for automation. The official Ansible website isn't the only place you can obtain documentation, however, as it is even available on the command line. We shall look at how to retrieve documentation via this route in the next section.

Accessing module documentation from the command line

As discussed in the preceding section, the Ansible project prides itself on its documentation, and making this documentation readily accessible is an important part of the project itself. Now, suppose you are working on an Ansible task (in a playbook, role, or even an ad hoc command) and you are in a data center environment where you only have access to the shell of the machine you are working on. How would you get access to the Ansible documentation?

Fortunately, part of the Ansible installation that we have not discussed yet is the `ansible-doc` tool, which is installed as standard along with the familiar `ansible` and `ansible-playbook` executables. The `ansible-doc` command includes a complete (text-based) library of documentation for all the modules that ship with the version of Ansible you have installed. This means that the very information you need to work with modules is at your fingertips, even if you are in the middle of a data center and without a working internet connection!

The following are some examples to show you how to interact with the `ansible-doc` tool:

- You can list all of the modules that there's documentation for on your Ansible control machine by simply issuing the following command:

  ```
  $ ansible-doc -l
  ```

  You should see an output similar to the following:

  ```
  amazon.aws.autoscaling_group Create or delete AWS AutoScaling..
  amazon.aws.autoscaling_group_info Gather information about...
  amazon.aws.aws_az_info Gather information about availability...
  amazon.aws.aws_caller_info Get information about the user...
  ```

  There are many pages of output, which shows you just how many modules there are! You can even count them:

  ```
  $ ansible-doc -l | wc -l
  7484
  ```

  That's right – 7,484 modules ship with Ansible 2.15!

- As before, you can search for specific modules using your favorite shell tools to process the index; for example, you could `grep` for `s3` to find all of the S3-related modules, as we did interactively in the web browser in the previous section:

  ```
  $ ansible-doc -l | grep s3

  amazon.aws.s3_bucket Manage S3 buckets in AWS...
  amazon.aws.s3_object_info Gather informatio...
  community.aws.s3_bucket_info Li...
  community.aws.s3_cors Manage CORS ...
  ```

- Now, we can easily look up the specific documentation for the module that interests us. Say we want to learn more about the `aws_s3` module – just as we did on the website, simply run the following:

  ```
  $ ansible-doc aws_s3
  ```

This should produce an output similar to the following:

```
$ ansible-doc aws_s3
> AMAZON.AWS.S3_OBJECT    (/Users/danieloh/Library/Python/3.11/
lib/python/site-packages/ansible_collections/amazon/aws/plugins/
modules/s3_object.py)
        This module allows the user to manage the objects and
directories within S3 buckets. Includes support for creating and
deleting objects and directories, retrieving
        objects as files or strings, generating download links
and copying objects that are already stored in Amazon S3.
Support for creating or deleting S3 buckets with
...
ADDED IN: version 1.0.0 of amazon.aws
  * note: This module has a corresponding action plugin.
OPTIONS (= is mandatory):
- access_key
        AWS access key ID.
        See the AWS documentation for more information about
access tokens https://docs.aws.amazon.com/general/latest/gr/
aws-sec-cred-types.html#access-keys-and-secret-
....
```

Although the formatting is somewhat different, ansible-doc tells us about the module, provides a list of all of the arguments (OPTIONS) that we can pass it, and as we scroll down, even gives some working examples and possible return values. We shall explore the topic of return values in the next section as they are important to understand, especially as we approach the topic of developing modules.

Module return values

As we discussed earlier in this chapter, Ansible modules return their results as structured data, formatted behind the scenes in JSON. You came across this return data in the previous example, both in the form of an exit code and where we used the register keyword to capture the results of a task in an Ansible variable. In this section, we shall explore how to discover the return values for an Ansible module so that we can work with them later on in a playbook, for example, with conditional processing (see *Chapter 4*, *Playbooks and Roles*).

Due to conserving space, we shall choose what is perhaps one of the simplest Ansible modules to work with when it comes to return values – the ping module.

Without further ado, let's use the ansible-doc tool that we learned about in the previous section and see what this says about the return values for this module:

```
$ ansible-doc ping
```

If you scroll to the bottom of the output from the preceding command, you should see something like this:

```
$ ansible-doc ping
> ANSIBLE.BUILTIN.PING      (/home/james/.local/lib/python3.10/site-
packages/ansible/modules/ping.py)
...

RETURN VALUES:

ping:
  description: value provided with the data parameter
  returned: success
sample: pong
  type: str
```

Hence, we can see that the ping module will only return one value, and that is called ping. description tells us what we should expect this particular return value to contain, while the returned field tells us that it will only be returned on success (if it were to be returned on other conditions, these would be listed here). The type return value is a string (denoted by str), and although you can change the value with an argument provided to the ping module, the default return value (and hence sample) is pong.

Now, let's see what this looks like in practice. For example, there's nothing contained in those return values that would tell us whether the module ran successfully and whether anything was changed; however, we know that these are fundamental pieces of information about every module run.

Let's put a very simple playbook together. We're going to run the ping module with no arguments, capture the return values using the register keyword, and then use the debug module to dump the return values onto the Terminal:

```
---
- name: Simple play to demonstrate a return value
hosts: localhost

tasks:
- name: Perform a simple module based task
  ansible.builtin.ping:
  register: pingresult

- name: Display the result
  ansible.builtin.debug:
    var: pingresult
```

Now, let's see what happens when we run this playbook:

```
$ ansible-playbook retval.yml
[WARNING]: provided hosts list is empty, only localhost is available.
Note that
the implicit localhost does not match 'all'


PLAY [Simple play to demonstrate a return value]
*******************************

TASK [Gathering Facts] *********************************
***********
ok: [localhost]


TASK [Perform a simple module based task] ************************
***********
ok: [localhost]


TASK [Display the result] *********************************
***********
ok: [localhost] => {
  "pingresult": {
  "changed": false,
  "failed": false,
  "ping": "pong"
  }
}


PLAY RECAP *************************************************
***********
localhost : ok=3 changed=0 unreachable=0 failed=0 skipped=0 rescued=0
ignored=0
```

Notice that the ping module does indeed return a value called ping, which contains the pong string (as the ping was successful). However, you can see that there are, in fact, two additional return values that were not listed in the Ansible documentation. These accompany every single task run, and are hence implicit – that is to say, you can assume they will be among the data that's returned from every module. The changed return value will be set to true if the module run resulted in a change on the target host, while the failed return value will be set to true if the module run failed for some reason.

Using the debug module to print the output from a module run is an incredibly useful trick if you want to gather more information about a module, how it works, and what sort of data is returned. At this point, we've covered just about all of the fundamentals of working with modules, so in the next section, we'll make a start on developing our very own (simple) module.

Developing custom modules

Now that we're familiar with modules, how to call them, how to interpret their results, and how to find documentation on them, we can make a start on writing a simple module. Although this will not include the deep and intricate functionality of many of the modules that ship with Ansible, it is hoped that this will give you enough information to proceed with confidence when you build out your own, more complex, ones.

One important point to note is that Ansible is written in Python 3, and as such, so are its modules. As a result, you will need to write your module in Python 3; to get started with developing your own module, you will need to make sure you have Python 3 and a few essential tools installed. If you are already running Ansible on your development machine, you probably have the required packages installed, but if you are starting from scratch, you will need to install Python 3, the Python 3 package manager (`pip3`), and perhaps some other development packages. The exact process will vary widely between operating systems, but here are some examples to get you started:

- On Fedora, you would run the following command to install the required packages:

    ```
    $ sudo dnf install python python-devel
    ```

- Similarly, on CentOS, you would run the following command to install the required packages:

    ```
    $ sudo yum install python3 python3-devel
    ```

- On Ubuntu, you would run the following commands to install the packages you need:

    ```
    $ sudo apt-get update
    $ sudo apt-get install python3-pip python3-dev build-essential
    ```

- If you are working on macOS and are using the Homebrew packaging system, the following command will install the packages you need:

    ```
    $ brew install python
    ```

Once you have the required packages installed, you will need to clone the Ansible Git repository to your local machine as there are some valuable scripts in there that we will need later on in the module development process. Use the following command to clone the Ansible repository to your current directory on your development machine:

```
$ git clone https://github.com/ansible/ansible.git
```

Finally (although optionally), it is good practice to develop your Ansible modules in a **virtual environment** (**venv**) as this means any Python packages you need to install go in here, rather than in with your global system Python modules. Installing modules for the entire system in an uncontrolled manner can, at times, cause compatibility issues or even break local tools, so although this is not a required step, it is highly recommended.

The exact command to create a virtual environment for your Python module development work will depend on both the operating system you are running and the version of Python you are using. You should refer to the documentation for your Linux distribution for more information; however, the following commands were tested on CentOS 8 with the default Python 3.11 and higher to create a virtual environment called `moduledev` inside the Ansible source code directory you just cloned from GitHub:

```
$ cd ansible
$ python -m virtualenv moduledev
New python executable in /home/james/ansible/moduledev/bin/python
Installing setuptools, pip, wheel...done.
```

With our development environment set up, let's start writing our first module. This module will be very simple as it's beyond the scope of this book to provide an in-depth discussion about how to write large amounts of Python code. However, we will code something that can use a function from a Python library to copy a file locally on the target machine.

This overlaps heavily with existing module functionality, but it will serve as a nice concise example of how to write a simple Python program in a manner that allows Ansible to make use of it as a module. Now, let's start coding our first module:

1. In your preferred editor, create a new file called (for example) `remote_filecopy.py`:

    ```
    $ vi remote_filecopy.py
    ```

2. Start with a shebang to indicate that this module should be executed with Python:

    ```
    #!/usr/bin/env python
    ```

3. Although not mandatory, it is good practice to add copyright information, as well as your details, in the headers of your new module. By doing this, anyone using it will understand the terms under which they can use, modify, or redistribute it. The text given here is merely an example; you should investigate the various appropriate licenses for yourself and determine which is the best for your module:

    ```
    # Copyright: (c) 2018, Jesse Keating <jesse.keating@example.org>
    # GNU General Public License v3.0+ (see COPYING or https://www.
    gnu.org/licenses/gpl-3.0.txt)
    ```

4. It is also good practice to add an Ansible metadata section that includes `metadata_version`, `status`, and `supported_by` information immediately after the copyright section. Note that the `metadata_version` field represents the Ansible metadata version (which, at the time of writing, should be `1.1`) and is not related to the version of your module or the Ansible version you are using. The values suggested in the following code will be fine for just getting started, but if your module gets accepted into the official Ansible source code, they are likely to change:

```
ANSIBLE_METADATA = {'metadata_version': '1.1',
                    'status': ['preview'],
                    'supported_by': 'community'}
```

5. Remember `ansible-doc` and that excellent documentation that is available on the Ansible documentation website? That all gets automatically generated from special sections you add to this file. Let's get started by adding the following code to our module:

```
DOCUMENTATION = '''
---
module: remote_filecopy
version_added: "2.15"
short_description: Copy a file on the remote host
description:
- The remote_copy module copies a file on the remote host from a
given source to a provided destination.
options:
source:
description:
- Path to a file on the source file on the remote host
required: True
dest:
description:
- Path to the destination on the remote host for the copy
required: True
author:
- Jesse Keating (@omgjlk)
'''
```

Pay particular attention to the `author` dictionary – to pass the syntax checks for inclusion in the official Ansible code base, the author's name should be appended with their GitHub ID in brackets. If you don't do this, your module will still work, but it won't pass the test we'll perform later.

> Notice how the documentation is in YAML format, enclosed between triple single quotes?
>
> The fields listed should be common to just about all modules, but naturally, if your module takes different options, you would specify these so that they match your module.

6. The examples that you will find in the documentation are also generated from this file – they have a special documentation section immediately after DOCUMENTATION and should provide practical examples of how you might create a task using your module, as shown in the following example:

```
EXAMPLES = '''
# Example from Ansible Playbooks
- name: backup a config file
  remote_copy:
    source: /etc/herp/derp.conf
    dest: /root/herp-derp.conf.bak
'''
```

7. The data that's returned by your module to Ansible should also be documented in its own section. Our example module will return the following values:

```
RETURN = '''
source:
  description: source file used for the copy
  returned: success
  type: str
  sample: "/path/to/file.name"
dest:
  description: destination of the copy
  returned: success
  type: str
  sample: "/path/to/destination.file"
gid:
  description: group ID of destination target
  returned: success
  type: int
  sample: 502
group:
  description: group name of destination target
  returned: success
  type: str
  sample: "users"
uid:
  description: owner ID of destination target
```

```
    returned: success
    type: int
    sample: 502
owner:
    description: owner name of destination target
    returned: success
    type: str
    sample: "fred"
mode:
    description: permissions of the destination target
    returned: success
    type: int
    sample: 0644
size:
    description: size of destination target
    returned: success
    type: int
    sample: 20
state:
    description: state of destination target
    returned: success
    type: str
    sample: "file"
'''
```

8. Immediately after we have finished our documentation section, we should import any Python modules we're going to use. Here, we will include the `shutil` module, which will be used to perform our file copy:

```
import shutil
```

9. Now that we've built up the module headers and documentation, we can start working on the code. Now, you can see just how much effort goes into the documentation of every single Ansible module! Our module should start by defining a `main` function, in which we will create an object of the `AnsibleModule` type and use an `argument_spec` dictionary to obtain the options that the module was called with:

```
def main():
    module = AnsibleModule(
        argument_spec = dict(
            source=dict(required=True, type='str'),
            dest=dict(required=True, type='str')
        ),
    )
```

10. At this stage, we have everything we need to write our module's functional code – even the options that it was called with. Hence, we can use the Python `shutil` module to perform the local file copy, based on the arguments provided:

```
shutil.copy(module.params['source'],
            module.params['dest'])
```

11. At this point, we've executed the task our module was designed to complete. However, it is fair to say that we're not done yet – we need to exit the module cleanly and provide our return values to Ansible. Normally, at this point, you would write some conditional logic to detect whether the module was successful and whether it performed a change on the target host or not. However, for simplicity, we'll simply exit with the `changed` status every time – expanding this logic and making the return status more meaningful is left as an exercise for you:

```
module.exit_json(changed=True)
```

The `module.exit_json` method comes from `AnsibleModule`, which we created earlier – remember, we said it was important to know that data was passed back and forth using JSON!

12. As we approach the end of our module code, we must now tell Python where it can import the `AnsibleModule` object from. This can be done with the following line of code:

```
from ansible.module_utils.basic import *
```

13. Now, let's look at the final two lines of code for the module – this is where we tell the module that it should be running the `main` function when it starts:

```
if __name__ == '__main__':
    main()
```

That's it – with a series of well-documented steps, you can write your own Ansible modules in Python. The next step is, of course, to test it (and you will need to write formal tests to merge it with Ansible's GitHub repository). Before we test it in Ansible, let's see whether we can run it manually in the shell. Of course, to make the module think it is being run within Ansible, we must generate some arguments in – you guessed it – JSON format. Create a file with the following contents to provide the arguments:

```
{
    "ANSIBLE_MODULE_ARGS": {
        "source": "/tmp/foo",
        "dest": "/tmp/bar"
    }
}
```

Armed with this little snippet of JSON, you can execute your module directly with Python. If you haven't already done so, you'll need to set up your Ansible development environment as follows. Note that we also manually create the source file, /tmp/foo, so that our module can perform the file copy:

```
$ touch /tmp/foo
$ . moduledev/bin/activate
(moduledev) $ . hacking/env-setup
running egg_info
creating lib/ansible_base.egg-info
writing requirements to lib/ansible_base.egg-info/requires.txt
writing lib/ansible_base.egg-info/PKG-INFO
writing top-level names to lib/ansible_base.egg-info/top_level.txt
writing dependency_links to lib/ansible_base.egg-info/dependency_
links.txt
writing manifest file 'lib/ansible_base.egg-info/SOURCES.txt'
reading manifest file 'lib/ansible_base.egg-info/SOURCES.txt'
reading manifest template 'MANIFEST.in'
warning: no files found matching 'SYMLINK_CACHE.json'
warning: no previously-included files found matching 'docs/docsite/
rst_warnings'
warning: no previously-included files matching '*' found under
directory 'docs/docsite/_build'
warning: no previously-included files matching '*.pyc' found under
directory 'docs/docsite/_extensions'
warning: no previously-included files matching '*.pyo' found under
directory 'docs/docsite/_extensions'
warning: no files found matching '*.ps1' under directory 'lib/ansible/
modules/windows'
warning: no files found matching '*.psm1' under directory 'test/
support'
writing manifest file 'lib/ansible_base.egg-info/SOURCES.txt'

Setting up Ansible to run out of checkout...

PATH=/home/james/ansible/bin:/home/james/ansible/moduledev/bin:/usr/
local/sbin:/usr/local/bin:/usr/sbin:/usr/bin:/home/james/bin
PYTHONPATH=/home/james/ansible/lib
MANPATH=/home/james/ansible/docs/man:/usr/local/share/man:/usr/share/
man

Remember, you may wish to specify your host file with -i

Done!
```

Now, you're finally ready to run your module for the first time. You can do this as follows:

```
(moduledev) $ python remote_filecopy.py args.json
{"invocation": {"module_args": {"dest": "/tmp/bar", "source": "/tmp/
foo"}}, "changed": true}

(moduledev) $ ls -l /tmp/bar
-rw-r--r-- 1 root root 0 Apr 26 12:35 /tmp/bar
```

Success! Your module works – and it both ingests and produces JSON data, as we discussed earlier in this chapter. Of course, there's much more to add to your module – we've not addressed `failed` or `ok` returns from the module, nor does it support check mode. However, we're off to a flying start. If you want to learn more about Ansible modules and fleshing out your functionality, you can find more details here: `https://docs.ansible.com/ansible/latest/dev_guide/developing_modules_general.html`.

Note that when it comes to testing your module, creating arguments in a JSON file is hardly intuitive, although, as we have seen, it does work well. Luckily for us, it is easy to run our Ansible module in a playbook! By default, Ansible will check the playbook directory for a subdirectory called `library/` and will run referenced modules from here. Hence, we might create the following:

```
$ cd ~
$ mkdir testplaybook
$ cd testplaybook
$ mkdir library
$ cp ~/ansible/moduledev/remote_filecopy.py library/
```

Now, create a simple inventory file in this playbook directory, just as we did previously, and add a playbook with the following contents:

```
---
- name: Playbook to test custom module
  hosts: all

tasks:
- name: Test the custom module
  remote_filecopy:
    source: /tmp/foo
    dest: /tmp/bar
  register: testresult

- name: Print the test result data
```

```
ansible.builtin.debug:
  var: testresult
```

For clarity, your final directory structure should look like this:

```
testplaybook
├── hosts
├── library
|  └── remote_filecopy.py
└── testplaybook.yml
```

Now, try running the playbook in the usual manner and see what happens:

```
$ ansible-playbook -i hosts testplaybook.yml

PLAY [Playbook to test custom module] ****************************
***********

TASK [Gathering Facts] ******************************************
***********
ok: [frt01.example.com]
ok: [app01.example.com]

TASK [Test the custom module] ***********************************
***********
changed: [app01.example.com]
changed: [frt01.example.com]

TASK [Print the test result data] *******************************
***********
ok: [app01.example.com] => {
 "testresult": {
 "changed": true,
 "failed": false
 }
}
ok: [frt01.example.com] => {
 "testresult": {
 "changed": true,
 "failed": false
 }
}
```

```
PLAY RECAP ****************************************************************
***********
app01.example.com : ok=3 changed=1 unreachable=0 failed=0 skipped=0
rescued=0 ignored=0
frt01.example.com : ok=3 changed=1 unreachable=0 failed=0 skipped=0
rescued=0 ignored=0
```

Success! Not only have you tested your Python code locally, but you have also successfully run it on two remote servers in an Ansible playbook. That was really easy, which proves just how straightforward it is to get started expanding your Ansible modules so that they meet your own bespoke needs.

Despite the success of running this piece of code, we've not checked the documentation yet, nor tested its operation from Ansible. Before we address these issues in more detail, in the next section, we'll take a look at some of the common pitfalls of module development and how to avoid them.

Avoiding common pitfalls

Your modules must be well thought out and handle error conditions gracefully – people are going to rely on your module someday to automate a task on perhaps thousands of servers, so the last thing they want is to spend significant amounts of time debugging errors, especially trivial ones that could have been trapped or handled gracefully. In this section, we'll look specifically at error handling and ways to do this so that playbooks will still run and exit gracefully.

One piece of overall guidance before we get started is that just like documentation receives a high degree of attention in Ansible, so should your error messages. They should be meaningful and easy to interpret, and you should steer clear of meaningless strings such as Error!.

So, right now, if we remove the source file that we're attempting to copy and then rerun our module with the same arguments, I think you'll agree that the output is neither pretty nor meaningful unless you happen to be a hardened Python developer:

```
(moduledev) $ rm -f /tmp/foo
(moduledev) $ python3 remote_filecopy.py args.json


Traceback (most recent call last):
  File "remote_filecopy.py", line 101, in <module>
    main()
    ^^^^^^
  File "remote_filecopy.py", line 94, in main
    shutil.copy(module.params['source'],
    ^^^^^^^^^^^^^^^^^^^^^^^^^^^^^^^^^^^^^^
```

```
    File "/opt/homebrew/Cellar/python@3.11/3.11.4/Frameworks/Python.
framework/Versions/3.11/lib/python3.11/shutil.py", line 419, in copy
        copyfile(src, dst, follow_symlinks=follow_symlinks)
    File "/opt/homebrew/Cellar/python@3.11/3.11.4/Frameworks/Python.
framework/Versions/3.11/lib/python3.11/shutil.py", line 256, in
copyfile
        with open(src, 'rb') as fsrc:
             ^^^^^^^^^^^^^^^^

FileNotFoundError: [Errno 2] No such file or directory: '/tmp/foo'
```

We can, without a doubt, do better. Let's make a copy of our module and add a little code to it. First of all, replace the shutil.copy lines of code with the following:

```
try:
    shutil.copy(module.params['source'], module.params['dest'])
except:
    module.fail_json(msg="Failed to copy file")
```

This is some incredibly basic exception handling in Python, but what it does is allow the code to try the shutil.copy task. However, if this fails and an exception is raised, rather than exiting with a traceback, we exit cleanly using the module.fail_json call. This will tell Ansible that the module failed and cleanly send a JSON-formatted error message back. Naturally, we could do a lot to improve the error message; for example, we could obtain the exact error message from the shutil module and pass it back to Ansible, but again, this is left as an exercise for you to complete.

Now, when we try and run the module with a non-existent source file, we will see the following cleanly formatted JSON output:

```
(moduledev) $ rm -f /tmp/foo
(moduledev) $ python3 better_remote_filecopy.py args.json

{"msg": "Failed to copy file", "failed": true, "invocation": {"module_
args": {"dest": "/tmp/bar", "source": "/tmp/foo"}}}
```

However, the module still works in the same manner as before if the copy succeeds:

```
(moduledev) $ touch /tmp/foo
(moduledev) $ python3 better_remote_filecopy.py args.json

{"invocation": {"module_args": {"dest": "/tmp/bar", "source": "/tmp/
foo"}}, "changed": true}
```

With this simple change to our code, we can now cleanly and gracefully handle the failure of the file copy operation and report something more meaningful back to the user rather than using a traceback. Some additional pointers for exception handling and processing in your modules are as follows:

- Fail quickly – don't attempt to keep processing after an error

- Return the most meaningful possible error messages using the various module JSON return functions

- Never return a traceback if there's any way you can avoid it

- Try making errors meaningful in the context of the module and what it does (for example, for our module, `File copy error` is more meaningful than `File error` – and I think you'll easily come up with even better error messages)

- Don't bombard the user with errors; instead, try to focus on reporting the most meaningful ones, especially when your module code is complex

That completes our brief yet practical look at error handling in Ansible modules. In the next section, we shall return to the documentation we included in our module, including how to build it into HTML documentation so that it can go on the Ansible website (and indeed, if your module gets accepted into the Ansible source code, this is exactly how the web documentation will be generated).

Testing and documenting your module

We have already put a great deal of work into documenting our module, as we discussed earlier in this chapter. However, how can we see it, and how can we check that it compiles correctly into the HTML that would go on the Ansible website if it were accepted as part of the Ansible source code?

Before we get into actually viewing our documentation, we should make use of a tool called `ansible-test`, which was newly added in the 2.15 release. This tool can perform a sanity check on our module code to ensure that our documentation meets all the standards required by the Ansible project team and that the code is structured correctly (for example, the Python `import` statements should always come after the documentation blocks). Let's get started:

1. To run the sanity tests, assuming you have cloned the official repository, change into this directory and set up your environment. Note that if your standard Python binary isn't Python 3, the `ansible-test` tool will not run, so you should ensure Python 3 is installed and, if necessary, set up a virtual environment to ensure you are using Python 3. This can be done as follows:

    ```
    $ cd ansible$ python 3 -m venv venv
    $ . venv/bin/activate
    (venv) $ source hacking/env-setup
    running egg_info
    creating lib/ansible.egg-info
    ```

```
writing lib/ansible.egg-info/PKG-INFO
writing dependency_links to lib/ansible.egg-info/dependency_
links.txt
writing requirements to lib/ansible.egg-info/requires.txt
writing top-level names to lib/ansible.egg-info/top_level.txt
writing manifest file 'lib/ansible.egg-info/SOURCES.txt'
reading manifest file 'lib/ansible.egg-info/SOURCES.txt'
reading manifest template 'MANIFEST.in'
warning: no files found matching 'SYMLINK_CACHE.json'
writing manifest file 'lib/ansible.egg-info/SOURCES.txt'

Setting up Ansible to run out of checkout...

PATH=/home/james/ansible/bin:/home/james/ansible/venv/bin:/usr/
local/sbin:/usr/local/bin:/usr/sbin:/usr/bin:/home/james/bin
PYTHONPATH=/home/james/ansible/lib
MANPATH=/home/james/ansible/docs/man:/usr/local/share/man:/usr/
share/man

Remember, you may wish to specify your host file with -i

Done!
```

2. Next, use `pip` to install the Python requirements so that you can run the `ansible-test` tool:

    ```
    (venv) $ pip install -r test/runner/requirements/sanity.txt
    ```

3. Now, provided you have copied your module code into the appropriate location in the source tree (an example copy command is shown here), you can run the sanity tests as follows:

    ```
    (venv) $ cp ~/moduledev/remote_filecopy.py ./lib/ansible/
    modules/files/
    (venv) $ ansible-test sanity --test validate-modules remote_
    filecopy
    Sanity check using validate-modules
    WARNING: Cannot perform module comparison against the base
    branch. Base branch not detected when running locally.
    WARNING: Reviewing previous 1 warning(s):
    WARNING: Cannot perform module comparison against the base
    branch. Base branch not detected when running locally.
    ```

From the preceding output, you can see that apart from one warning related to us not having a base branch to compare against, the module code that we developed earlier in this chapter has passed all the tests. If you had an issue with the documentation (for example, the author's name format was incorrect), this would be given as an error.

Now that we have passed the sanity checks with `ansible-test`, let's see whether the documentation looks right by using the `ansible-doc` command. This is very easy to do. First of all, exit your virtual environment, if you are still in it, and change to the Ansible source code directory you cloned from GitHub earlier. Now, you can manually tell `ansible-doc` where to look for modules instead of the default path. This means that you could run the following:

```
$ cd ~/ansible
$ ansible-doc -M moduledev/ remote_filecopy
```

You should be presented with the textual rendering of the documentation we created earlier – an example of the first page is shown here to give you an idea of how it should look:

```
> REMOTE_FILECOPY (/home/james/ansible/moduledev/remote_filecopy.py)

  The remote_copy module copies a file on the remote host from a
  given source to a provided destination.

  * This module is maintained by The Ansible Community
OPTIONS (= is mandatory):

= dest
 Path to the destination on the remote host for the copy


= source
 Path to a file on the source file on the remote host
```

Excellent! So, we can already access our module documentation using `ansible-doc` and indeed confirm that it renders correctly in text mode. However, how do we go about building the HTML version? Fortunately, there is a well-defined process for this, which we shall outline here:

1. Under `lib/ansible/modules/`, you will find a series of categorized directories that modules are placed under – ours fits best under the `files` category, so copy it to this location in preparation for the build process to come:

   ```
   $ cp moduledev/remote_filecopy.py lib/ansible/modules/files/
   ```

2. Change to the `docs/docsite/` directory as the next step in the documentation creation process:

   ```
   $ cd docs/docsite/
   ```

3. Build a documentation-based Python file. Use the following command to do so:

   ```
   $ MODULES=hello_module make webdocs
   ```

Now, in theory, making the Ansible documentation should be this simple to get the `make webdocs` command to run at all.

Even in this environment, on CentOS 7, the `make webdocs` command fails unless you have some very specific Python 3 requirements in place. These are not well documented, but from testing, I can tell you that Sphinx v2.4.4 works. The version that's supplied with CentOS 7 is too old and fails, while the newest version available from the Python module repositories is not compatible with the build process and fails.

Once I'd started working from the Ansible source tree, I had to make sure I had removed any preexisting `sphinx` modules from my Python 3 environment (you need Python 3.11 or above to build the documentation locally – if you don't have this installed on your node, please do this before proceeding) and then ran the following commands:

```
$ pip3 uninstall sphinx
$ pip3 install sphinx==2.4.4
$ pip3 install sphinx-notfound-page
```

With this in place, you will be able to successfully run `make webdocs` to build your documentation. You will see pages of output. A successful run should end with something like the output shown here:

```
generating indices... genindex py-modindexdone
writing additional pages... search/home/james/ansible/docs/docsite/_
themes/sphinx_rtd_theme/search.html:21: RemovedInSphinx30Warning:
To modify script_files in the theme is deprecated. Please insert a
<script> tag directly in your theme instead.
  {% endblock %}
  opensearchdone
copying images... [100%] dev_guide/style_guide/images/thenvsthan.jpg
copying downloadable files... [ 50%] network/getting_started/sample_
files/first_copying downloadable files... [100%] network/getting_
started/sample_files/first_playbook_ext.yml
copying static files... ... done
copying extra files... done
dumping search index in English (code: en)... done
dumping object inventory... done
build succeeded, 35 warnings.

The HTML pages are in _build/html.
make[1]: Leaving directory `/home/james/ansible/docs/docsite'
```

Now, notice how, at the end of this process, the `make` command tells us where to look for the compiled documentation. If you look in here, you will find the following:

```
$ find /home/james/ansible/docs/docsite -name remote_filecopy*
/home/james/ansible/docs/docsite/rst/modules/remote_filecopy_module.
```

```
rst
/home/james/ansible/docs/docsite/_build/html/modules/remote_filecopy_
module.html
/home/james/ansible/docs/docsite/_build/doctrees/modules/remote_
filecopy_module.doctree
```

Try opening the HTML file in your web browser – you should see that the page renders just like one of the documentation pages from the official Ansible project documentation! This enables you to check that your documentation builds correctly and looks and reads well in the context that it will be viewed. It also gives you confidence that, when you submit your code to the Ansible project (if you are doing so), you are submitting something consistent with Ansible's documentation quality standards.

More information on building the documentation locally is provided here: `https://docs.ansible.com/ansible/latest/community/documentation_contributions.html#building-the-documentation-locally`.

The current process of building the documentation is a little fussy around the environments that are supported; however, hopefully, this is something that will be resolved in due course. In the meantime, the process outlined in this section has given you a tested and working process to start from.

The module checklist

In addition to the pointers and good practices that we have covered so far, there are a few more things you should adhere to in your module code to produce something that will be considered of a high standard for potential inclusion with Ansible. The following list is not exhaustive but will give you a good idea of the practices you should adhere to as a module developer:

- Test your modules as much as you can, both in cases that will succeed and in those that cause errors. You can test them using JSON data, as we did in this chapter, or make use of them within a test playbook.

- Try and keep your Python requirements to a minimum. Sometimes, there is no way to avoid the need for additional Python dependencies (such as the `boto` requirements of the AWS-specific modules), but in general, the less you can use, the better.

- Don't cache data for your module – the execution strategies of Ansible across differing hosts mean you are unlikely to get good results from doing this. Expect to gather all of the data you need on each run.

- Modules should be a single Python file – they shouldn't be distributed across multiple files.

- Make sure you investigate and run the Ansible integration tests when you are submitting your module code. More information on these is available here: `https://docs.ansible.com/ansible/latest/dev_guide/testing_integration.html`.

- Make sure you include exception handling at the appropriate points in your module code, as we did in this chapter, to prevent issues.

Armed with the information you've gained from this chapter, you should have everything you need to start creating modules. You may not decide to submit them to the Ansible project, and there is certainly no requirement to do so. However, even if you don't, following the practices outlined in this chapter will ensure that you build a good-quality module, regardless of its intended audience. Finally, on the basis that you do want to submit your source code to the Ansible project, in the next section, we'll look at how to do this through a pull request to the Ansible project.

Contributing upstream – submitting a GitHub pull request

When you've worked hard on your module and thoroughly tested and documented it, you might feel that it is time to submit it to the Ansible project for inclusion. Doing this means creating a pull request on the official Ansible repository. Although the intricacies of working with GitHub are beyond the scope of this book, we will give you a practically focused outline of the basic procedures involved.

> **Note**
>
> Following the process outlined here will generate a real request against the Ansible project on GitHub so that the code you are committing can be merged with their code. *Do not* follow this process unless you genuinely have a new module that is ready for submission to the Ansible code base.

To submit your module as a pull request of the Ansible repository, you need to fork the collection repository.

Now, we will walk through the commands you need to run to add your module code to it. Then, we'll show you how to create the required **pull requests** (also known as **PRs**) so that you can merge your new module with the upstream Ansible project:

1. Fork a collection repository that you want to create a PR for using GitHub (`https://github.com/ansible-collections`). For example, if you need to create a PR in the `community.mysql` collection, you need to select **Fork**:

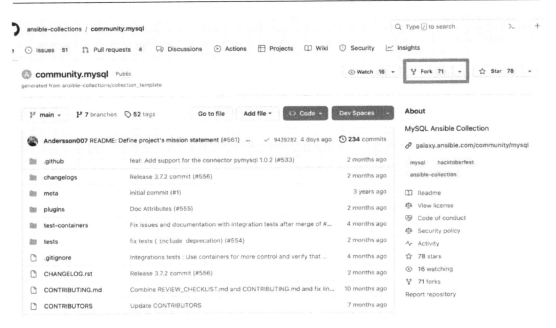

Figure 5.3 – The community.mysql collection

2. Clone the forked repository to your local machine. Use a command similar to the following, but be sure to replace the URL with the one that matches your own GitHub account:

```
$ git clone https://github.com/YOUR_ACCOUNT/COLLECTION_
REPO.git ~/YOUR_WORKING_DIRECTORY
```

3. Add the upstream repository after you go to your cloned repository:

```
$ cd ~/ YOUR_WORKING_DIRECTORY
$ git remote add upstream https://github.com/ansible-
collections/COLLECTION_REPO.git
```

4. Update your local branch:

```
$ git fetch upstream
$ git rebase upstream/YOUR_BRANCH
```

5. Create a branch for the PR:

```
$ git checkout -b name_of_my_branch
```

6. Change your code in the collection.

7. Submit your pull request:

```
$ git add . && git commit -m "Add a new feature or fix a bug..."
&& git push origin YOUR_BRANCH
```

8. Go to the upstream repository (http://github.com/ansible-collections/ COLLECTION_REPO). Then, select the **Pull requests** tab. Fill out the PR template with your changes. Then, select **create a pull request**. Note that if your PR looks good to the community, it will be merged:

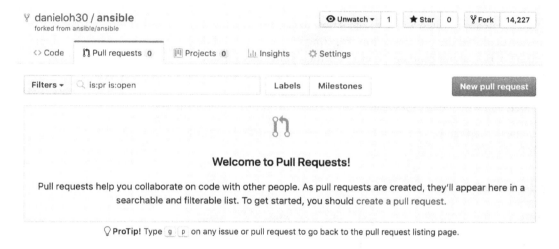

Figure 5.4 – The Pull requests tab

There are many more ways to contribute to the Ansible project other than creating pull requests for custom modules. Here are some examples of other ways you can contribute to the project:

- Review the Ansible documentation and report any bugs you find in it (one was filed in the creation of *Chapter 4, Playbooks and Roles*)

- Create a local Ansible MeetUp to spread your knowledge about Ansible. If you are lucky enough to have one in your area already, consider attending it regularly.

- Spread Ansible knowledge and awareness via social media with the appropriate account references and hashtags; for example, @ansible, #ansible, and so on.

That completes our journey of learning how to create modules, from the very first steps of looking into the theory of module operation, all the way through to contributing your new module code to the official Ansible project on GitHub. We hope you have found this journey informative and valuable and that it enhances your ability to work with Ansible and extend its functionality where required.

Summary

Modules are the very lifeblood of Ansible – without them, Ansible could not perform all of the complex and varied tasks it performs so well across a wide variety of systems. By being an open source project, it is incredibly easy to extend the functionality of Ansible by yourself, and in this chapter, we explored how you can, with a little Python knowledge, write a custom module from scratch. Ansible is, at the time of writing, incredibly feature-rich, but this ease of customization and extension makes Ansible virtually limitless in terms of its potential, especially given the power and popularity of Python as a programming language.

In this chapter, we started with a recap of how to execute multiple modules using the command line. We then explored the process of interrogating the current module index, as well as how to obtain documentation about modules to evaluate their suitability for our needs, regardless of whether we have an active internet connection or not. We then explored module data and its JSON format, before finally going on a journey through which we put together the code for a simple custom module. This provided you with a basis for creating modules in the future if you so desire.

In the next chapter, we will explore the process of using and creating another core Ansible feature, known as plugins.

Questions

Answer the following questions to test your knowledge of this chapter:

1. Which command line can be passed down as a parameter to a module?

    A. `ansible dbservers -m command "/bin/echo 'hello modules'"`

    B. `ansible dbservers -m command -d "/bin/echo 'hello modules'"`

    C. `ansible dbservers -z command -a "/bin/echo 'hello modules'"`

    D. `ansible dbservers -m command -a "/bin/echo 'hello modules'"`

    E. `ansible dbservers -a "/bin/echo 'hello modules'"`

2. Which of the following practices is not recommended when you create a custom module and address exceptions?

    A. Design a custom module simply and never provide a traceback to the user, if you can avoid it.

    B. Fail your module code quickly, and verify that you are providing helpful and understandable exception messages.

    C. Only display error messages for the most relevant exceptions, rather than all possible errors.

    D. Ensure that your module documentation is relevant and easy to understand.

    E. Delete playbooks that result in errors and then recreate them from scratch.

3. True or false: To contribute to the Ansible upstream project, you need to submit your code to the `devel` branch.

   A. True

   B. False

Further reading

To learn more about the topics that were covered in this chapter, take a look at the following resources:

- Documentation regarding the common return values of modules in Ansible can be found here: `https://docs.ansible.com/ansible/latest/reference_appendices/common_return_values.html#common`

- Check out the following documentation for all the existing modules on Windows machines that you can use: `https://docs.ansible.com/ansible/latest/collections/ansible/windows/index.html`

6

Creating and Consuming Collections

If you were familiar with Ansible releases before 2.9, so far, much of this book will have looked very familiar to you. If you're a newcomer to the world of Ansible automation, then, of course, all of this will look new and shiny. Regardless of your experience with Ansible to date, no book on this would be complete without an in-depth look at collections. Collections are the solution to the problems that started to manifest as a result of Ansible's own popularity and success, and they are now at the heart of every modern Ansible installation. Whether you realized it or not, you've been working with them throughout this book so far, and they are here to stay, so it benefits us to take a deep dive into them.

In this chapter, we will explore collections in depth, looking in more detail at the problem that they solve and how they came about, before taking a more technical look at their structure and makeup. We will conclude the chapter with a hands-on example of creating your own collection so that you have a solid understanding of how they are created, built, maintained, and used. As a result, you will be able to work with this powerful new addition to Ansible with ease and take advantage of collections in your own automation solutions.

Specifically, in this chapter, we will cover the following topics:

- An introduction to Ansible collections
- Understanding fully qualified collection names
- Managing collections on your control node
- Updating your Ansible collections and core installation
- Creating your own collections

Technical requirements

This chapter assumes that you have set up your control host with Ansible, as detailed in *Chapter 1*, *Getting Started with Ansible*, and are using the most recent version available – the examples in this chapter were tested with Ansible 8.0 and `ansible-core` 2.15. This chapter also assumes that you have at least one additional host to test against, and this should be Linux-based. Although we will give specific examples of hostnames in this chapter, you are free to substitute them with your own hostnames and/or IP addresses, and details of how to do this will be provided in the appropriate places.

The code bundle for this chapter is available here: `https://github.com/PacktPublishing/Practical-Ansible-Second-Edition/tree/main/Chapter 6`

Introduction to Ansible collections

Although we've mentioned some of this earlier in this book, our goal is for this to be a complete one-stop source of information for collections – thus, if you've skipped directly to this chapter, don't worry – we've got you covered. Let's start with some history as this is important to understand the intention behind collections.

With Ansible releases prior to 2.9, everything was managed in one huge monolithic code base. While the core Ansible team owned this code base, the modules that really form the lifeblood of Ansible (after all, they are what enable it to automate so many disparate systems with ease) were not. Let's say a network device vendor wanted to release a new module. Perhaps they added a new feature or fixed a bug in a prior release. They would have to make these changes, test them, and then submit them as a pull request to the main Ansible repository – not only is this a significant undertaking, depending on the number of **Pull Requests** (**PRs**) and amount of code to be merged, but it can also take a long time, slowing down release cycles.

At this point, the owners of the repository would have to merge the code, test it themselves, and perform a release. This way of working was fine in the early days of Ansible, but as its adoption got greater, it became impossible to scale in this manner. Imagine that a large enterprise user of Ansible has a problem with an Ansible module and they need a fix now, or perhaps the vendor has an exciting new launch coming up and they want Ansible support from day one. Neither of these was possible with this way of working. Coupled with the fact that Ansible 2.8 had thousands of modules, the task of managing Ansible code became an unenviable task.

This assumes, of course, that code was eligible to be integrated into the main code base. If something was confidential in nature, or needed distributing in a hurry to fix a problem, then there was no easy way to integrate it into the Ansible installation (to be clear, there were methods, but they were not as simple and straightforward as collections have made this process).

It was out of these needs that collections were born. In brief, collections empower individual teams and vendors to develop, test, and release contributions to Ansible at their own pace, and independent of the release cycle of the core Ansible code. To be specific, collections provide a mechanism to package and distribute the following:

- Roles
- Plugins
- Modules
- Playbooks
- Documentation

As with all aspects of Ansible, the design of collections is simple and easy to work with. A collection is simply a set of directories containing the files that contain the required functionality. These are then packaged up into a gzipped tarball (a well-known and understood file format) for easy distribution. Collections can be installed and managed locally (as we shall see later, in the *Managing collections on your control node* section) and via Ansible Galaxy (`https://galaxy.ansible.com`).

Anyone familiar with Ansible from its pre-collection days will know that roles were distributed via Ansible Galaxy and were easy to manage using the `ansible-galaxy` command-line utility. Thus, a valid question might be, if you develop your own role, should you distribute it as a role, or a role contained within a collection? After all, both are currently viable solutions, and both can be distributed via Ansible Galaxy. Although both routes are entirely possible at this time, it is the opinion of the author that, in time, roles will be distributed as collections, as these offer much greater scope for expansion – for example, if you need to develop a plugin to extend the capabilities of your role, then you can add this to the collection you have already created. On the other hand, distributing the role as is would necessitate a later migration to a collection, and thus, you future-proof your code by packaging it as a collection in the first place.

It is very easy for developers, vendors, and enterprises to build their Ansible functionality into collections for packaging and distribution. They can then contribute this back to the community if they so desire (and in the spirit of open source software, this is certainly the goal), but if they contain confidential information, they are just as easy to host and maintain in an internal repository.

With this introduction complete, you have gained a good idea of what a collection is and its intended purpose. We will now proceed in the next section of this chapter to begin a look at the practical aspects of creating and consuming collections to further your understanding.

Understanding fully qualified collection names

Before collections existed, every module that was created and contributed to Ansible had to have a unique name. Thus, it was very common to see modules named like this (both were taken from the Ansible 2.8 release):

- `ios_bgp`

- `eos_bgp`

- `fortios_router_bgp`

All three of these modules are to modify the **Border Gateway Protocol** (**BGP**) configuration of network devices, but they all have the device name added in front of `bgp` to do the following:

- Ensure their names are unique

- Ensure Ansible coders can understand what their code does

Collections remove the need for unique module names, so it is now possible for contributors to create modules with names that overlap. This is valuable because it removes the need for such long and verbose module names, but it creates the risk of unexpected code behavior. For example, we often use the `debug` module to understand what our playbook code does and print something out during the execution. It would be entirely possible for us to create our own collection with a module called `debug`, which does something slightly (or entirely) different. Imagine the confusion that would result if your playbook performed differently on different control nodes, or didn't work at all.

It is for this reason that throughout this book, in earlier versions of Ansible code, you would be used to seeing code like this:

```
- name: Print some debug output
  debug:
    msg: "Hello World!"
```

This still works in Ansible today (you are welcome to test this!), and support for short-form module names has been retained for backward compatibility so that any legacy code that you have can be run. While this is valuable in empowering users to upgrade their Ansible code at their own pace without needing multiple versions of Ansible on the control node, the risk of unexpected behavior due to a module name clash is not insignificant, so it is important to start using fully qualified collection names as soon as possible.

For example, in place of the previously provided example code, we would now write the following:

```
- name: Print some debug output
  ansible.builtin.debug:
    msg: "Hello World!"
```

The functionality of this code is identical, but the risk of module name clash is now removed because the fully qualified collection name has been specified.

What is a **Fully Qualified Collection Name (FQCN)** though? The best way to explain this is to break it down into its component parts, which look like this:

```
<namespace>.<collection_name>.<module_name>
```

Let's start with the namespace – this is a unique namespace used to identify the developer of the collections. This might be your name if you are an individual developer, or the name of a company if you are contributing to a vendor. All namespaces must be unique, and this is reasonable as a limitation – when you look on Ansible Galaxy, you want to know that modules with the `cisco` namespace are all managed by Cisco, and thus, you can be certain of who owns and manages the code. Similarly, the `ansible` namespace (from which we make use of `ansible.builtin.debug`) is owned and managed by the Ansible project itself.

Now, it's also safe to assume that each namespace will have one or more collections. It makes sense for collections to be divided up by functionality; otherwise, we head back to the problems of monolithic code base management we discussed earlier in this chapter. For example, within the `cisco` namespace, there is an `ios` collection to manage Cisco IOS devices and a separate `asa` collection to manage their **Adaptive Security Appliance (ASA)** family of devices. These are maintained separately and enable the vendor to make changes to them independently of each other, as new devices and/or firmware for each device family are released. Collection names must be unique with a namespace but do not need to be unique across namespaces. For example, if I wrote my own module to add an automation functionality I needed to a Cisco ASA device, I could call my collection `asa`, but I could not put it in the `cisco` namespace on Ansible Galaxy.

The third and final part of the FQCN is the module name itself. This serves the same function as it always has in Ansible and must be unique within a collection. We have already used modules a number of times in this book, and we will continue to do so; thus, we will assume here that you are happy with the concept of an Ansible module.

Putting this all together, whereas in Ansible 2.8 (or earlier) you would have used the `ios_bgp` module for BGP configuration on a Cisco IOS device, the FQCN for this module is now `cisco.ios.ios_bgp`. A valid question you may be asking about this FQCN is, why, given the unique namespace and collection name within it, is the module still called `ios_bgp` and not simply `bgp`? The answer lies in backward compatibility – Ansible 8.0 still supports playbooks written for 2.8 and earlier and, as such, still supports module names that are not fully qualified. Thus, if Cisco changed the module name to `bgp`, they would break backward compatibility.

Despite this backward compatibility functionality, it is important to start making friends with FQCNs as soon as possible. Module names must be unique within a collection, but that is the only limitation. There is nothing to stop me from creating my own module called `ios_bgp`, in my own `ios` collection, and calling it something like `practicalansible.ios.ios_bgp`. In this instance, you could not guarantee which module you were calling if you only specified the module by the name `ios_bgp` in your playbooks and roles, and as such, it is vital to use FQCNs to make sure you don't come across any unexpected or erroneous behavior.

Although these concepts relating to FQCNs are simple, they are foundational knowledge, and we will rely on this understanding as we proceed through this chapter, so it is important that we get them out of the way early on. Now that we've achieved this, we'll look in the next section at how to manage collections on your control node.

Managing collections on your control node

As we discussed in *Chapter 1*, *Getting Started with Ansible*, when you install Ansible, it actually installs a set of collections, providing equivalent functionality to the latest 2.x release so that backward compatibility is maintained (alongside `ansible-core`, of course). This process is invisible to the user, and this accompanying collection set also gets updated as you update your Ansible installation.

Given this, you could be forgiven for wondering why you need to learn about managing collections at all – after all, Ansible comes with a huge set by default, and the collections get updated as you update your installation. Yet this is the beauty of collections – if they do exactly what you need to do, then you need to take further action. In contrast, if you actually do need to extend the functionality of your Ansible control node, you can do just that – the power lies in the choice and flexibility, just as it always has with Ansible.

To help us understand the management of our collections, let's start by looking at the locations in which they get installed. Like everything in Ansible, the paths in which collections get installed are configurable, and you can install collections wherever you like (provided you've set the correct setting of course).

If we log into our demo node, where I installed Ansible under my local user account using `pip3`, I can query the Ansible collection paths as follows:

```
$ ansible-config dump | grep COLLECTIONS_PATHS
COLLECTIONS_PATHS(default) = ['/home/james/.ansible/collections', '/
usr/share/ansible/collections']
```

What you can see here is that the `COLLECTIONS_PATHS` environment variable is not set (denoted by `(default)` displayed in the output), and thus, it has defaulted to two known locations:

- `~/.ansible/collections`
- `/usr/share/ansible/collections`

The collections paths are searched in the order specified, so the location under my home directory will be searched prior to the path under `/usr/share`. You can set the location for your collections by setting the environment variable we just queried previously, or you can create an entry in your `ansible.cfg` file in the `[default]` section, using the `collections_paths` key. Please refer to this link for more information: `https://docs.ansible.com/ansible/latest/reference_appendices/config.html#collections-paths`.

On my demo node, I have not performed any work on collections so far, and as a result, if I try to list the previous paths, I will find that neither of them exists. Nonetheless, let's try and install the `gns3` collection from user `davidban77` and see what happens (`https://galaxy.ansible.com/davidban77/gns3`):

```
$ ansible-galaxy collection install davidban77.gns3
Starting galaxy collection install process
Process install dependency map
Starting collection install process
Downloading https://galaxy.ansible.com/download/davidban77-gns3-
1.5.0.tar.gz to /home/james/.ansible/tmp/ansible-local-919n6_zrnbj/
tmpgf0fuin6/davidban77-gns3-1.5.0-hlfzoaen
Installing 'davidban77.gns3:1.5.0' to '/home/james/.ansible/
collections/ansible_collections/davidban77/gns3'
davidban77.gns3:1.5.0 was installed successfully
```

Here, we can see that the collection was installed successfully, and the `ansible-galaxy` tool even tells us helpfully where it was installed. However, note that it was installed only for my local user account, so if another user on this box wants to make use of this collection, they must install their own copy. This is fine, but it risks creating issues further down the road if they install a different version (which might happen because they install the same collection but later on, after an update has been made).

However, we can get around this. The first way is to install the collection(s) you need centrally so that all users can access them. We know that, by default, the `COLLECTIONS_PATHS` variable will search `/usr/share/ansible/collections`, and this will be accessible to all users, so any collections that need to be available globally can be installed here. The path won't exist by default, but you can easily create it and install the collection here by running the following commands:

```
$ sudo mkdir -p /usr/share/ansible/collections
$ sudo chmod a+w /usr/share/ansible/collections/
$ ansible-galaxy collection install -p /usr/share/ansible/collections
davidban77.gns3
Starting galaxy collection install process
Process install dependency map
Starting collection install process
Downloading https://galaxy.ansible.com/download/davidban77-gns3-
1.5.0.tar.gz to /home/james/.ansible/tmp/ansible-local-1036ifclq7yb/
tmpi34u42w5/davidban77-gns3-1.5.0-nvsahsw0
Installing 'davidban77.gns3:1.5.0' to '/usr/share/ansible/collections/
ansible_collections/davidban77/gns3'
davidban77.gns3:1.5.0 was installed successfully
```

Note that the `chmod` command used is a blunt-force method to grant all users access to install collections in this shared directory. It is recommended that you set up suitable access controls to this directory as is appropriate for your environment, but as this will differ in every scenario, this is left as an exercise for you to complete.

What you will notice now is that we added the `-p` flag to the command we ran before, telling `ansible-galaxy` to install our collection in a different location than the default (which is the first entry in the `COLLECTIONS_PATHS` variable). As such, we have successfully installed the collection in a central location for all users to work with.

We can validate this using the following command (output truncated for readability):

```
$ ansible-galaxy collection list

# /home/james/.local/lib/python3.10/site-packages/ansible_collections
Collection                      Version
------------------------------- -------
amazon.aws                      5.4.0
ansible.netcommon               4.1.0
...
# /usr/share/ansible/collections/ansible_collections
Collection      Version
--------------- -------
davidban77.gns3 1.5.0

# /home/james/.ansible/collections/ansible_collections
Collection      Version
--------------- -------
davidban77.gns3 1.5.0
```

Note how the output of this command lists the collections in each of its known locations, which includes all paths listed by the `COLLECTIONS_PATHS` variable, and also the install location of Ansible (which is included first and is implicit in the configuration – you do not need to specify this).

There is no uninstall option when it comes to collections, but the beauty of Ansible has always been in its simplicity, and collections, like roles, are simply a set of directories and files in a known structure (there'll be more on this later in the chapter). As a result, if we wanted to uninstall the centrally available `davidban77.gns3` collection, you would simply run the following:

```
$ rm -rf /usr/share/ansible/collections/ansible_collections/
davidban77/gns3/
```

If you rerun the collection listing, you'll see that this collection no longer appears in the output. What happens if you want to install a specific version of a collection though? Well, say you wanted to install the 1.4.0 release of the collection we've been testing with – you would simply run this command to install it:

```
$ ansible-galaxy collection install davidban77.gns3:1.4.0
Starting galaxy collection install process
Process install dependency map
Starting collection install process
Downloading https://galaxy.ansible.com/download/davidban77-gns3-
1.4.0.tar.gz to /home/james/.ansible/tmp/ansible-local-1081bdunqhfz/
tmp41a0hc01/davidban77-gns3-1.4.0-cg29hr0y
Installing 'davidban77.gns3:1.4.0' to '/home/james/.ansible/
collections/ansible_collections/davidban77/gns3'
davidban77.gns3:1.4.0 was installed successfully
```

Here, we have successfully installed version 1.4.0 of this collection, and it has overwritten version 1.5.0, which we installed earlier. Upgrading collections is as simple as either specifying the latest version in place of the earlier one we used previously, or forcing a reinstallation (which, by its very nature, installs the latest version of the collection):

```
$ ansible-galaxy collection install --force davidban77.gns3
Starting galaxy collection install process
Process install dependency map
Starting collection install process
Downloading https://galaxy.ansible.com/download/davidban77-gns3-
1.5.0.tar.gz to /home/james/.ansible/tmp/ansible-local-116881rshtvg/
tmpzaaelkpw/davidban77-gns3-1.5.0-3moa8p5j
Installing 'davidban77.gns3:1.5.0' to '/home/james/.ansible/
collections/ansible_collections/davidban77/gns3'
davidban77.gns3:1.5.0 was installed successfully
```

You can even specify version ranges – if, for example, we've established we need to use a version of this collection newer than the 1.2.0 release, but older than the 1.5.0 release, we can run the following:

```
$ ansible-galaxy collection install 'davidban77.gns3:>1.2.0,<1.5.0'
Starting galaxy collection install process
Process install dependency map
Starting collection install process
Downloading https://galaxy.ansible.com/download/davidban77-gns3-
1.4.0.tar.gz to /home/james/.ansible/tmp/ansible-local-1210j61dbhwq/
tmpznhg7oik/davidban77-gns3-1.4.0-u800o2wa
Installing 'davidban77.gns3:1.4.0' to '/home/james/.ansible/
collections/ansible_collections/davidban77/gns3'
davidban77.gns3:1.4.0 was installed successfully
```

Here, the latest version within the range we specified has been installed – a very useful and powerful feature to maintain dependencies.

This discussion on installing and maintaining collection versions brings us neatly back to our original concern – how to ensure users are all installing the correct version of collections required (or sanctioned) for playbook development. We've established that you can install collections centrally, and this is certainly one viable route. However, this method breaks down as soon as someone starts developing and/or running playbooks on another machine. It is clear then that a different method will be required.

Thankfully, the `ansible-galaxy` command also supports working with requirements files – these are simply a list of the required collections (and versions) that you need to have installed, and as they are simple text files, they can be committed to source control along with all your other automation code. Then, all the people involved in your playbook need to do is run a single command to install the required collection, and they can then proceed with development and/or running the playbooks with the confidence that they have the correct collections installed, and with the correct versions. Let's add one more collection to the previous example and create a file called `requirements.yml` with the following content:

```
---
collections:
- name: davidban77.gns3
  version: '>1.2.0,<1.5.0'
- marmorag.ansodium
```

In this file, we state that we need the `davidban77.gns3` collection with the version constraints we tested earlier, and also the `marmorag.ansodium` collection. You can see that we omitted the `name:` key with the second collection – this is only required if you specify additional parameters such as `version:`; thus, a useful shorthand if you don't need this is to simply create a list of collection names. Once you have this file, you can ensure the collections meet the stated requirements by running the following:

```
$ ansible-galaxy collection install -r requirements.yml
Starting galaxy collection install process
Process install dependency map
Starting collection install process
Downloading https://galaxy.ansible.com/download/marmorag-ansodium-
1.0.2.tar.gz to /home/james/.ansible/tmp/ansible-local-1242d4dc7w5j/
tmp0rltoudk/marmorag-ansodium-1.0.2-q01qc8if
'davidban77.gns3:1.4.0' is already installed, skipping.
Installing 'marmorag.ansodium:1.0.2' to '/home/james/.ansible/
collections/ansible_collections/marmorag/ansodium'
marmorag.ansodium:1.0.2 was installed successfully
```

Here, you can see that the requirements for the `davidban77.gns3` collection were already met, so no further action was taken. However, the `marmorag.ansodium` collection, which we didn't previously install, now gets installed.

As a side note, all the collections we are working from here are publicly available at `https://galaxy.ansible.com` – however, it is important to note that you can also specify your own server or even a local tarball to install collections with, and we shall see examples of the latter in action later in the chapter.

That concludes our look at managing collections on your control node, and armed with this information, you should be able to set up a consistent environment for all your automation needs. In the next section, we will look at a subtle variation on this theme – how to update the collections that were installed at the time you installed the Ansible package.

Updating your Ansible collections and core installation

You may very well be asking what happens to the collections you installed at the time of installing Ansible – how do you maintain or upgrade them? Naturally, one way is to wait for the next release of the `ansible` package, and then upgrade it with `pip` – however, this is a brute-force method and may not provide you with the results you are looking for. Let's take a more fine-grained approach.

Let's say you want to get access to the latest features in the `amazon.aws` collection, which is bundled with the `ansible` package when you install it – you would simply install it (again!) as follows:

```
$ ansible-galaxy collection install amazon.aws
Starting galaxy collection install process
Process install dependency map
Starting collection install process
Downloading https://galaxy.ansible.com/download/amazon-aws-6.1.0.tar.
gz to /home/james/.ansible/tmp/ansible-local-12589si7_qld/tmpytach2d5/
amazon-aws-6.1.0-mihyh1f0
Installing 'amazon.aws:6.1.0' to '/home/james/.ansible/collections/
ansible_collections/amazon/aws'
amazon.aws:6.1.0 was installed successfully
```

Now, if you query the installed collections, you will see the following:

```
$ ansible-galaxy collection list

# /home/james/.local/lib/python3.10/site-packages/ansible_collections
Collection                      Version
------------------------------- -------
amazon.aws                      5.4.0

...
# /home/james/.ansible/collections/ansible_collections
Collection        Version
----------------- -------
amazon.aws        6.1.0
```

Thus, you can see that the original version of the collection has been retained, but the newer version has been installed in our local collections directory (as specified by COLLECTIONS_PATHS). Ansible will use manually installed collections in locations specified by this variable in precedence over the originally installed collections, so this way, it is easy to upgrade collections that are bundled with the Ansible package. If you feel at all nervous about which collection is used, there is a handy lookup plugin that you can use to query the version of a collection being used by Ansible. Consider the following code:

```
---
- name: Play to check collection version
  hosts: localhost
  gather_facts: no

  tasks:
    - name: Get the version of the amazon.aws collection
      ansible.builtin.debug:
        msg: "amazon.aws version {{ lookup('community.general.
collection_version', 'amazon.aws') }}"
```

Most of this code should now be familiar to you. All we do here is use a lookup plugin called community.general.collection_version, passing it the value of the collection name we want to query (in our case, amazon.aws). If we run this, it will kindly reassure us that we're on the version we just installed:

```
$ ansible-playbook check-collection-version.yml

PLAY [Play to check collection version] *****************************
********************************************************************
***********************************

TASK [Get the version of the amazon.aws collection] *****************
********************************************************************
***********************************
ok: [localhost] => {
    "msg": "amazon.aws version 6.1.0"
}

PLAY RECAP *********************************************************
********************************************************************
***********************************
localhost                  :
ok=1    changed=0    unreachable=0    failed=0    skipped=0
       rescued=0    ignored=0
```

If we downgrade the collection to an older version than that installed with the ansible package (an unlikely scenario, but just for example), we can see then that Ansible faithfully adheres to its path search order and does not default to the `amazon.aws` collection that was installed as part of the Ansible installation, even though this version is newer:

```
$ ansible-galaxy collection install amazon.aws:5.0.0
Starting galaxy collection install process
Process install dependency map
Starting collection install process
Downloading https://galaxy.ansible.com/download/amazon-aws-5.0.0.tar.
gz to /home/james/.ansible/tmp/ansible-local-1291avom1yll/tmpn2juwhhj/
amazon-aws-5.0.0-nzac4kq1
Installing 'amazon.aws:5.0.0' to '/home/james/.ansible/collections/
ansible_collections/amazon/aws'
amazon.aws:5.0.0 was installed successfully
james@controlnode:~/Practical-Ansible-Second-Edition/Chapter 6$
ansible-playbook check-collection-version.yml


PLAY [Play to check collection version] *****************************
*******************************************************************
**********************************

TASK [Get the version of the amazon.aws collection] *****************
*******************************************************************
**********************************
ok: [localhost] => {
    "msg": "amazon.aws version 5.0.0"
}


PLAY RECAP *********************************************************
*******************************************************************
**********************************
localhost                  :
ok=1    changed=0    unreachable=0    failed=0    skipped=0
rescued=0    ignored=0
```

Although simple, this management of collections installed at the time of installing Ansible is fundamental to maintaining your control nodes, and as such, it is important that we cover it. Now that you've learned all about collections, what they are, why they are important, and how to administer them, let's create our very own collection to work with in the next section.

Creating your own collections

We have learned a great deal about collections and how to manage and maintain them. Let's now complete your knowledge on this topic by creating your own one from scratch, thus giving you a full overview of how they are put together and how they work.

As with roles (see *Chapter 4*, *Playbooks and Roles*), collections are simply an organized set of files within directories. Although you can look up all these directories and create them by hand, we can also get the `ansible-galaxy` utility to create a blank template for us to work with.

Let's start with the fundamentals. We know that we need both a namespace and a collection name. If we publish on the Ansible Galaxy website, then the namespace will be our GitHub handle, as Ansible Galaxy takes this and uses it as your namespace. In our case, we won't be publishing to Ansible Galaxy, so I'll choose the namespace `practicalansible`, but feel free to substitute this with your GitHub handle in all the following example code and commands if you want to publish your work.

Once we've decided on the namespace, the next step is a collection name. Normally, this would be used to indicate what a collection is for, and here, we will use this to amalgamate examples found elsewhere in this book, so we'll simply call the collection `examples`.

We'll create an empty directory to work in to separate this from the rest of our code, and then we'll create the skeleton directory structure as follows:

```
$ mkdir collection-development
$ cd collection-development/
$ ansible-galaxy collection init practicalansible.examples
- Collection practicalansible.examples was created successfully
If we examine this directory structure, we can see that it looks as
follows:
$ tree
.
└── practicalansible
    └── examples
        ├── README.md
        ├── docs
        ├── galaxy.yml
        ├── meta
        │   └── runtime.yml
        ├── plugins
        │   └── README.md
        └── roles

6 directories, 4 files
```

Here, you can see the following:

- The top-level directory is the namespace we chose.

- The next-level directory is the collection name.

- Under these top-level directories, we have the following:

  - A README.md file (mandatory documentation if you submit to Ansible Galaxy, and advisable in just about every scenario)

- A `galaxy.yml` file that will contain important metadata about the role, such as tags, a license, and a documentation page so that your entry on Ansible Galaxy is populated correctly

- We then have a `docs/` directory – this should be used for all documentation and will be referenced by the `ansible-doc` command, so it should be populated according to best practices.

- There is also a `meta/` directory – this is prepopulated with a `runtime.yml` file that is used for submissions to Ansible Galaxy and contains important information about the minimum version of `ansible-core` required, as well as other artifacts related to deprecation and code upgrade.

- Last but by no means least, we have the `plugins/` and `roles/` directories, and this is where the code that you are going to distribute will be placed.

Not created in the skeleton directory structure are two directories called `playbooks/` and `tests/`. The `playbooks/` directory is used to distribute playbooks with the collection (yes, you can even do this!), which you can run directly from the command line (provided you're using `ansible-core` 2.11 or newer) or via the `import_playbook` statement within a playbook.

The `tests/` directory is used to contain automated tests for your code, to be run by the `ansible-test` tool. We won't focus on these in this book, but if you'd like to learn more about this topic, this is a great place to start: `https://docs.ansible.com/ansible/latest/dev_guide/developing_collections_testing.html`.

As not everyone will be able to (or want to) submit to Ansible Galaxy, our focus in this chapter will be on the use of collections to distribute and use code such as modules and roles. Let's get started on this.

Throughout the book so far, you have already seen many examples of running modules from collections – this is the most common use case for most users, so we will start here.

In *Chapter 5*, *Creating and Consuming*, we created a simple module to test called `remotecopy`. We know that collections are the standard way to distribute these, so let's integrate this into our new collection. We do this by creating a directory called `modules/` under the `plugins/` directory and then copying our code there. The end results should look like this:

```
$ mkdir plugins/modules
$ cp ~/Practical-Ansible-Second-Edition/Chapter\ 5/testplaybook/
library/remote_filecopy.py plugins/modules/
$ tree
.
├── README.md
├── docs
├── galaxy.yml
├── meta
│   └── runtime.yml
```

```
├── plugins
│   ├── README.md
│   └── modules
│       └── remote_filecopy.py
└── roles


5 directories, 5 files
```

Note that we didn't change the code at all in the module from that used in *Chapter 5, Creating and Consuming*. No modifications to your code are necessary to work with collections – it's simply a matter of making sure you put your files in the correct subdirectory. With that done, we can now package up our collection for testing. This is done by changing to the root directory of the collection itself and then issuing the `ansible-galaxy collection build` command:

```
$ cd ~/Practical-Ansible-Second-Edition/Chapter\ 6/collection-
development/practicalansible/examples/
$ ansible-galaxy collection build
Created collection for practicalansible.examples at /home/james/
Practical-Ansible-Second-Edition/Chapter 6/collection-development/
practicalansible/examples/practicalansible-examples-1.0.0.tar.gz
```

Note that Ansible has appended a version number of `1.0.0` to the filename – this was obtained from the `galaxy.yml` file and is the default value. We'll edit this in a future example, but for now, it serves our purpose.

With the collection built, it's time to test it. First of all, we need to create an empty directory to work in. Once we're in there, we can use the `ansible-galaxy` command to install our new collection:

```
$ mkdir ~/Practical-Ansible-Second-Edition/Chapter\ 6/collection-test/
$ cd ~/Practical-Ansible-Second-Edition/Chapter\ 6/collection-test/
$ ansible-galaxy collection install ~/Practical-Ansible-Second-
Edition/Chapter\ 6/collection-development/practicalansible/examples/
practicalansible-examples-1.0.0.tar.gz
Starting galaxy collection install process
Process install dependency map
Starting collection install process
Installing 'practicalansible.examples:1.0.0' to '/home/james/.ansible/
collections/ansible_collections/practicalansible/examples'
practicalansible.examples:1.0.0 was installed successfully
```

Congratulations! You've just created and installed your very first collection! From here, we need to create a playbook to test it out. We will create this in the same way we did before, making sure to use the FQCN of our newly built and installed collection:

```
---
- name: Playbook to test custom module
  hosts: localhost
  gather_facts: no

  tasks:
    - name: Test the custom module
      practicalansible.examples.remote_filecopy:
        source: /tmp/foo
        dest: /tmp/bar
      register: testresult

    - name: Print the test result data
      ansible.builtin.debug:
        var: testresult
```

Now, we will run the playbook in the normal manner – again, no other special commands or configurations are required, even though we've just built and installed our own collection:

```
$ ansible-playbook collection-test1.yml

PLAY [Playbook to test custom module] ******************************
**********

TASK [Test the custom module] *************************************
**********
changed: [localhost]

TASK [Print the test result data] *********************************
**********
ok: [localhost] => {
    "testresult": {
        "changed": true,
        "failed": false
    }
}

PLAY RECAP ********************************************************
**********
```

```
localhost                      :
ok=2      changed=1    unreachable=0    failed=0    skipped=0
    rescued=0    ignored=0
```

We can see that our module works perfectly, and thus, you can feel accomplished that you have just successfully built, installed, and integrated your first collection using code we already provided in the book.

You can also query the documentation that was built into this module in the normal manner:

```
$ ansible-doc practicalansible.examples.remote_filecopy
> PRACTICALANSIBLE.EXAMPLES.REMOTE_FILECOPY     (/home/james/.ansible/
collections/ansible_collections/practicalansible/examples/plugins/
modules/remote_filecopy.py)


        The remote_copy module copies a file on the remote host from a
given source to a provided destination.

ADDED IN: version 2.15 of practicalansible.examples

OPTIONS (= is mandatory):

= dest
        Path to the destination on the remote host for the copy

= source
        Path to a file on the source file on the remote host

...
```

Of course, we've built our first collection but also written a separate playbook as a test harness for it. In many cases, you wouldn't just write a simple test harness as we have here – you would write a playbook to solve an actual use case, or even provide some example code to show how the collection can be used. Let's do this now by adding our playbook to the collection:

```
$ cd ~/Practical-Ansible-Second-Edition/Chapter\ 6/collection-
development/practicalansible/examples/
$ mkdir playbooks/
$ cp ~/Practical-Ansible-Second-Edition/Chapter\ 6/collection-test/
collection-test1.yml playbooks/collection_test1.yml
$ sed -i 's/version: .*$/version: 1.1.0/g' galaxy.yml
$ tree
.
├── README.md
├── docs
├── galaxy.yml
├── meta
```

```
|      └── runtime.yml
├── playbooks
|      └── collection_test1.yml
├── plugins
|      ├── README.md
|      └── modules
|            └── remote_filecopy.py
└── roles


6 directories, 6 files
```

Although we don't modify the playbook code, our playbook has a hardcoded `hosts` line in the play definition set to `localhost` – you'd probably never do this in a real collection, and the Ansible documentation itself recommends using a variable to define the hosts so that users can specify their own pattern here. We're just distributing example code via the collection though, so in our case, we can justify this decision.

While not changing the playbook file contents, we change the filename as part of the `cp` command. This is done because Ansible does not support the use of hyphens (`-`) in filenames when you refer to objects in a collection – an important point that might trip you up later! Also, note here that we've used the `sed` command to change the version number in the `galaxy.yml` file to make it easy to read the code in the book, but you are welcome to edit it with your favorite text editor. With this done, we can repackage the collection in the same manner as we did before:

```
$ ansible-galaxy collection build
Created collection for practicalansible.examples at /home/james/
Practical-Ansible-Second-Edition/Chapter 6/collection-development/
practicalansible/examples/practicalansible-examples-1.1.0.tar.gz
Now that we've built the new tarball, we can install it as follows:
$ ansible-galaxy collection install practicalansible-examples-
1.1.0.tar.gz
Starting galaxy collection install process
Process install dependency map
Starting collection install process
Installing 'practicalansible.examples:1.1.0' to '/home/james/.ansible/
collections/ansible_collections/practicalansible/examples'
practicalansible.examples:1.1.0 was installed successfully
```

You can now run the playbook from the command line by simply providing the fully qualified playbook name:

```
$ ansible-playbook practicalansible.examples.collection_test1
[WARNING]: running playbook inside collection practicalansible.
examples
```

```
PLAY [Playbook to test custom module] ******************************
***********

TASK [Test the custom module] ***************************************
***********
changed: [localhost]

TASK [Print the test result data] **********************************
***********
ok: [localhost] => {
    "testresult": {
        "changed": true,
        "failed": false
    }
}


PLAY RECAP *********************************************************
***********
localhost                  :
ok=2    changed=1    unreachable=0    failed=0    skipped=0
    rescued=0    ignored=0
```

You have now successfully added a playbook to your collection, bumped up the version number, and upgraded your local installation. You've even run the playbook from the collection directly rather than from a local file, as we have throughout all other examples in the book. We hope you feel a sense of accomplishment at this point! Let's now extend our collection with another example – integrating a plugin. Once again, we'll make use of code provided elsewhere in this book – specifically, *Chapter 7, Creating and Consuming Plugins*.

To do this, we need to copy the code we need into our collection. While you would expect plugins to go under the `plugins/` directory, they must actually be placed under a subdirectory within this, named by the plugin type. We will copy over a `lookup` plugin, so we must create a directory called `lookup/` before we can copy the plugin code to it:

```
$ cd ~/Practical-Ansible-Second-Edition/Chapter\ 6/collection-
development/practicalansible/examples/
$ mkdir plugins/lookup
$ cp ~/Practical-Ansible-Second-Edition/Chapter\ 7/lookup_plugins/
firstchar.py plugins/lookup/
$ sed -i 's/version: .*$/version: 1.2.0/g' galaxy.yml
$ tree
.
├── README.md
├── docs
├── galaxy.yml
├── meta
```

```
|       └── runtime.yml
├── playbooks
|   └── collection_test1.yml
├── plugins
|   ├── README.md
|   ├── lookup
|   |       └── firstchar.py
|   └── modules
|       └── remote_filecopy.py
└── roles


7 directories, 7 files
```

Once again, we haven't modified the plugin code at all – we have just placed it into our directory structure. Again, we've bumped up the version number of the collection using `sed` to edit the `galaxy.yml` file in place. With this done, we can build and install the new version of the collection in the normal manner:

```
$ ansible-galaxy collection build
Created collection for practicalansible.examples at /home/james/
Practical-Ansible-Second-Edition/Chapter 6/collection-development/
practicalansible/examples/practicalansible-examples-1.2.0.tar.gz
$ ansible-galaxy collection install practicalansible-examples-
1.2.0.tar.gz
Starting galaxy collection install process
Process install dependency map
Starting collection install process
Installing 'practicalansible.examples:1.2.0' to '/home/james/.ansible/
collections/ansible_collections/practicalansible/examples'
practicalansible.examples:1.2.0 was installed successfully
```

With that completed, it is once again time to test our newly enhanced collection via a playbook. This time, we won't build the playbook into the collection – we'll simply create it and run it from the test directory we created earlier. The playbook code should look like the following – again, you should find it unchanged from *Chapter 7, Creating and Consuming Plugins*, except that we've put the FQCN of the `lookup` plugin into the playbook rather than the short form name you might otherwise use:

```
---
- name: Play to demonstrate our custom lookup plugin
  hosts: localhost
  gather_facts: false

  tasks:
    - name: make a statement
      ansible.builtin.debug:
```

```
        msg: "{{ lookup('practicalansible.examples.firstchar',
'testdoc.txt')}}"
```

Remember to also create a file called `testdoc.txt` in the same directory as the playbook for the `lookup` plugin to reference – our example contains the following:

```
$ cat testdoc.txt
I can Ansible!
```

Finally, run the playbook in the normal manner, and you should find that the plugin works as desired:

```
$ ansible-playbook collection-test2.yml


PLAY [Play to demonstrate our custom lookup plugin]
****************************


TASK [make a statement] ***********************************
***********
ok: [localhost] => {
    "msg": "73"
}


PLAY RECAP ************************************************
***********
localhost                  :
ok=1    changed=0    unreachable=0    failed=0    skipped=0
rescued=0    ignored=0
```

As you can see, our `lookup` plugin works perfectly as part of our newly expanded collection. To round off our look at building our own collection, we will expand it further still by adding a role to it.

To provide a little background, `ansible-galaxy` (both the tool and the Ansible Galaxy website) were originally envisaged to be used to manage, distribute, and install roles. Given that the processes for managing collections, and that their purpose as reusable Ansible code artifacts is very similar to the original roles for which they were designed, it makes perfect sense to use the same tooling for collection management.

At the time of writing, the Galaxy tools and website support both roles and collections and are likely to for the foreseeable future. However, collections provide a number of advantages, including the option to package multiple roles in a single collection, and you also can use them to distribute any plugins (or even modules) that might be needed for the roles.

The process to migrate a role to a collection is incredibly easy, and if you have a simple role that only includes objects such as tasks, files, templates, handlers, and variables, then you can copy the code over as is (to the correct place, naturally) without any modifications. However, special care needs to be taken if you included plugins with your role previously, as these will need to be moved aside from the role and integrated into the collection itself at the top level (in exactly the same way as we integrated our demo `lookup` plugin a little earlier in this section).

To extend our example, we'll take one of the roles that we demonstrated in *Chapter 4, Playbooks and Roles*, to show how it can be integrated and tested. As before, we need to change to our collection directory and copy the role over (retaining its directory structure) into a `roles/` directory within the collection. You can do this as follows:

```
$ cd ~/Practical-Ansible-Second-Edition/Chapter\ 6/collection-
development/practicalansible/examples/
$ cp -r ~/Practical-Ansible-Second-Edition/Chapter\ 4/role-example1/
roles/installapache/ roles/
$ sed -i 's/version: .*$/version: 1.3.0/g' galaxy.yml
$ tree
.
├── README.md
├── docs
├── galaxy.yml
├── meta
│   └── runtime.yml
├── playbooks
│   └── collection_test1.yml
├── plugins
│   ├── README.md
│   ├── lookup
│   │   ├── firstchar.py
│   │   └── firstchar.pyc
│   └── modules
│       └── remote_filecopy.py
└── roles
    └── installapache
        └── tasks
            ├── fedora.yml
            ├── main.yml
            └── ubuntu.yml

9 directories, 11 files
```

As you can see, the role is now copied into place and retains the same structure as before, under the `roles/` subdirectory within the collection. With this complete, we can now build the new collection (we have incremented the version number again) and install it:

```
$ ansible-galaxy collection build
Created collection for practicalansible.examples at /home/james/
Practical-Ansible-Second-Edition/Chapter 6/collection-development/
```

```
practicalansible/examples/practicalansible-examples-1.3.0.tar.gz
$ ansible-galaxy collection install practicalansible-examples-
1.3.0.tar.gz
Starting galaxy collection install process
Process install dependency map
Starting collection install process
Installing 'practicalansible.examples:1.3.0' to '/home/james/.ansible/
collections/ansible_collections/practicalansible/examples'
practicalansible.examples:1.3.0 was installed successfully
```

With the newly updated role in place, all that remains to do is test it. We will borrow the same playbook we used to test it before, with a small modification to call the role from the collection:

```
---
- name: Install Apache using a role
  hosts: frontends
  become: true

  roles:
    - practicalansible.examples.installapache
```

As this is a role to install Apache on external nodes, we will need to copy over the inventory we used before – if you use the GitHub repository that accompanies this book, that has been done for you. All that remains is to run the code, which should return something like this:

```
$ ansible-playbook -i hosts collection-test3.yml

PLAY [Install Apache using a role] **********************************
***********

TASK [Gathering Facts] **********************************************
***********
ok: [web01.example.org]
ok: [web02.example.org]

TASK [practicalansible.examples.installapache : Install Apache using
yum] ******
skipping: [web01.example.org]
skipping: [web02.example.org]

TASK [practicalansible.examples.installapache : Start the Apache
server] *******
skipping: [web01.example.org]
skipping: [web02.example.org]
```

```
TASK [practicalansible.examples.installapache : Install Apache using
apt] ******
ok: [web01.example.org]
ok: [web02.example.org]

TASK [practicalansible.examples.installapache : Start the Apache
server] *******
ok: [web01.example.org]
ok: [web02.example.org]

PLAY RECAP ********************************************************
***********
web01.example.org            :
ok=3     changed=0     unreachable=0     failed=0     skipped=2
rescued=0     ignored=0
web02.example.org            :
ok=3     changed=0     unreachable=0     failed=0     skipped=2
rescued=0     ignored=0
```

No changes will be made if you ran this role previously as part of *Chapter 4, Playbooks and Roles*, but you can clearly see from the preceding that we successfully call the role from the collection and it works perfectly.

With that, we have successfully integrated a plugin, a module, a playbook, and a role into a collection, taking you through the entire process of building and adding to your own collection. That wraps up our look at collections in depth, but I hope that this has given you enough information to proceed with your own testing and development, ultimately building your own collections.

Summary

Collections are now a vitally important part of Ansible's overall architecture, and they provide an easy and effective mechanism for all code to be distributed and managed on control nodes everywhere. Learning about collections is vital to your understanding of the architecture of any modern version of Ansible, and armed with this information, you can manage, build, and maintain collections on your control nodes, even contributing them back to the community if you so desire.

In this chapter, you learned about the history of collections, how they came about, and why they are so important to Ansible. You then learned how to reference objects from within collections using FQCNs, before moving on to learning about the installation and management of collections on your control node. Finally, we looked at the process involved in building, installing, and testing your own collection, such that you can progress to contributing collections to the wider Ansible community if you so desire.

In the next chapter, we will learn how to consume and create our very own plugins, providing you with the skills you need to expand the capabilities of Ansible to suit your own bespoke environments and contribute to the community.

Questions

1. Collections are an optional feature of Ansible versions later than 2.9:

    A. True

    B. False

2. What does the acronym FQCN stand for?

    A. Fully Qualified Collection Namespace

    B. Fully Qualified Control Node

    C. Fully Qualified Collection Name

    D. Fully Qualified Control Name

3. Collections are installed and managed with which command?

    A. `ansible-galaxy`

    B. `ansible-collection`

    C. `ansible`

    D. `collection-manager`

Further reading

`ansible-galaxy` and its documentation can be found here: `https://galaxy.ansible.com/docs/`

7

Creating and Consuming Plugins

Modules have been a very obvious and key part of our journey through Ansible so far. They are used to execute well-defined tasks and can be used either in one-off commands (using ad hoc commands) or as part of a much larger playbook. Plugins are just as important to Ansible, and we have used them in all of our testing so far without even realizing it! While modules are always used to create some kind of task in Ansible, the way that plugins are used depends on their use case. There are many different types of plugins; we will introduce them to you in this chapter and give you an idea of their purpose. But, as a tester, did you realize that when Ansible connects to a remote server using SSH, functionality is provided by a connection plugin? This demonstrates the important role that plugins play.

In this chapter, we will provide you with an in-depth introduction to plugins, as well as show you how to explore the various plugins that come with Ansible. We'll then expand on this by demonstrating how you can create your own plugins and use them in an Ansible project, in very much the same way as we did with our custom module in the previous chapter. This will hopefully help you understand the limitless possibilities that open source software such as Ansible provides.

In this chapter, we will cover the following topics:

- Discovering the plugin types
- Finding the included plugins
- Creating custom plugins

Technical requirements

This chapter assumes that you have set up your control host with Ansible, as detailed in *Chapter 1, Getting Started with Ansible*, and that you are using the most recent version available. The examples in this chapter have been tested with `ansible-core` version 2.15. This chapter also assumes that you have at least one additional host to test against; ideally, this should be Linux-based.

Although we will give specific examples of hostnames in this chapter, you are free to substitute them with your own hostname and/or IP addresses, and details of how to do this are provided at the appropriate places. The plugin development work covered in this chapter assumes the presence of a Python 3 development environment on your computer, and that you are running either Linux, FreeBSD, or macOS. Where additional Python modules are needed, their installation is documented. The task of building module documentation has some very specific requirements in Python 3.10 or later, so it is assumed you can install a suitable Python environment if you wish to attempt this.

The code bundle for this chapter is available at `https://github.com/PacktPublishing/Practical-Ansible-Second-Edition/tree/main/Chapter%207`.

Discovering the plugin types

Ansible's code has always been designed to be modular—indeed, this is one of its core strengths. Whether that is through the use of modules to perform tasks or through plugins (as we will see shortly), Ansible's modular design allows it to be as versatile and powerful as it has demonstrated itself to be so far in this book. As with modules, Ansible plugins are all written in Python and are expected to ingest and return data in a certain well-defined format (more on this later). Ansible's plugins are often invisible in their function in that you rarely call them by name in your commands or playbooks, yet they are responsible for some of the most important features Ansible has to offer, including SSH connectivity, the ability to parse inventory files (in INI format, YAML, or otherwise), and the ability to run `jinja2` filters on your data.

As ever, let's validate the presence of a suitably installed version of Ansible on your test machine before proceeding further:

```
$ ansible-doc --version
ansible-doc [core 2.15.0]
  config file = None
  configured module search path = ['/Users/danieloh/Library/
Python/3.11/bin/plugins/modules', '/usr/share/ansible/plugins/
modules']
  ansible python module location = /Users/danieloh/Library/
Python/3.11/lib/python/site-packages/ansible
  ansible collection location = /Users/danieloh/Library/Python/3.11/
bin/collections:/usr/share/ansible/collections
  executable location = /Users/danieloh/Library/Python/3.11/bin/
ansible-doc
```

```
python version = 3.11.3 (main, Apr  7 2023, 20:13:31) [Clang 14.0.0
(clang-1400.0.29.202)] (/opt/homebrew/opt/python@3.11/bin/python3.11)
jinja version = 3.1.2
libyaml = True
```

As much work goes into documenting the plugins as it does into documenting the modules, so you will be pleased to know that there is a plugin index available at https://docs.ansible.com/ansible/latest/plugins/plugins.html.

You can also use the ansible-doc command as we did before, only you need to add the -t with the module's name, too. Plugins are always placed in an appropriate category as their function is radically different between categories. If you don't specify the -t switch with ansible-doc, you end up specifying the ansible-doc -t module, which returns a list of the available modules.

At the time of writing, the following plugin types can be found in Ansible:

- become: Responsible for enabling Ansible to obtain super-user access (for example, through sudo)
- cache: Responsible for caching facts retrieved from backend systems to improve automation performance
- callback: Allows you to add new behaviors when responding to events – for example, changing the format that data is printed in in the output of an Ansible playbook run
- cliconf: Provides abstractions to the command-line interfaces of various network devices, giving Ansible a standard interface to operate on
- connection: Provides connectivity from Ansible to remote systems (for example, over SSH, WinRM, Docker, and many more)
- httpapi: Tells Ansible how to interact with a remote system's API (for example, for a Fortinet firewall)
- inventory: Provides Ansible with the ability to parse various static and dynamic inventory formats
- lookup: Allows Ansible to look up data from an external source (for example, by reading a flat text file)
- netconf: Provides Ansible with abstractions to enable it to work with NETCONF-enabled networking devices
- shell: Provides Ansible with the ability to work with various shells on different systems (for example, powershell on Windows versus sh on Linux)
- strategy: Provides plugins to Ansible with different execution strategies (for example, the debug strategy we saw in *Chapter 4, Playbooks and Roles*)
- vars: Provides Ansible with the ability to source variables from certain sources, such as the host_vars and group_vars directories we explored in *Chapter 3, Defining Your Inventory*

We will leave exploring the plugin documentation on the Ansible website as an exercise for you to complete. However, if you want to explore the various plugins using the `ansible-doc` tool, you would need to run the following commands:

1. To use the `ansible-doc` command to list all the plugins available in a given category, you can run the following command:

```
$ ansible-doc -t connection -l
```

This will return a textual index of the connection plugins, similar to what we saw when we were looking at the module documentation. The first few lines of the index output are shown here:

```
ansible.builtin.local             execute on controller
ansible.builtin.paramiko_ssh      Run tasks via python ssh (paramiko)
ansible.builtin.psrp              Run tasks over Microsoft PowerShell Remoting Protocol
ansible.builtin.ssh               connect via SSH client binary
ansible.builtin.winrm             Run tasks over Microsoft's WinRM
ansible.netcommon.grpc            Provides a persistent connection using the gRPC protocol
ansible.netcommon.httpapi         Use httpapi to run command on network appliances
ansible.netcommon.libssh          Run tasks using libssh for ssh connection
ansible.netcommon.netconf         Provides a persistent connection using the netconf protocol
ansible.netcommon.network_cli     Use network_cli to run command on network appliances
ansible.netcommon.persistent      Use a persistent unix socket for connection
community.aws.aws_ssm             execute via AWS Systems Manager
community.docker.docker           Run tasks in docker containers
community.docker.docker_api       Run tasks in docker containers
community.docker.nsenter          execute on host running controller container
community.general.chroot          Interact with local chroot
community.general.funcd           Use funcd to connect to target
community.general.iocage          Run tasks in iocage jails
community.general.jail            Run tasks in jails
community.general.lxc             Run tasks in lxc containers via lxc python library
community.general.lxd             Run tasks in lxc containers via lxc CLI
community.general.qubes           Interact with an existing QubesOS AppVM
community.general.saltstack       Allow ansible to piggyback on salt minions
community.general.zone            Run tasks in a zone instance
community.libvirt.libvirt_lxc     Run tasks in lxc containers via libvirt
community.libvirt.libvirt_qemu    Run tasks on libvirt/qemu virtual machines
community.okd.oc                  Execute tasks in pods running on OpenShift
community.vmware.vmware_tools     Execute tasks inside a VM via VMware Tools
containers.podman.buildah         Interact with an existing buildah container
containers.podman.podman          Interact with an existing podman container
kubernetes.core.kubectl          Execute tasks in pods running on Kubernetes
```

Figure 7.1 – Ansible documentation for connection

2. You can then explore the documentation for a given plugin. For example, if we want to learn about the `paramiko_ssh` plugin, we can issue the following command:

```
$ ansible-doc -t connection paramiko_ssh
```

You will find that the plugin documentation takes on a very familiar format, similar to what we saw for the modules in *Chapter 5, Creating and Consuming Modules*:

```
> ANSIBLE.BUILTIN.PARAMIKO    (/Users/danieloh/Library/Python/3.11/lib/python/site-packages/ansible/plugins/connection/paramiko_ssh.py)

        Use the python ssh implementation (Paramiko) to connect to targets The paramiko transport is provided because many distributions, in particular
        EL6 and before do not support ControlPersist in their SSH implementations. This is needed on the Ansible control machine to be reasonably
        efficient with connections. Thus paramiko is faster for most users on these platforms. Users with ControlPersist capability can consider using
        -c ssh or configuring the transport in the configuration file. This plugin also borrows a lot of settings from the ssh plugin as they both cover
        the same protocol.

ADDED IN: version 0.1 of ansible-core

OPTIONS (= is mandatory):

- banner_timeout
        Configures, in seconds, the amount of time to wait for the SSH banner to be presented. This option is supported by paramiko version 1.15.0 or
        newer.
        set_via:
          env:
          - name: ANSIBLE_PARAMIKO_BANNER_TIMEOUT
          ini:
          - key: banner_timeout
            section: paramiko_connection
        default: 30
        type: float
        added in: version 2.14 of ansible-core

- host_key_auto_add
        Automatically add host keys
        set_via:
          env:
          - name: ANSIBLE_PARAMIKO_HOST_KEY_AUTO_ADD
          ini:
          - key: host_key_auto_add
            section: paramiko_connection
        default: null
        type: boolean

- host_key_checking
        Set this to "False" if you want to avoid host key checking by the underlying tools Ansible uses to connect to the host
        set_via:
          env:
          - name: ANSIBLE_HOST_KEY_CHECKING
          - name: ANSIBLE_SSH_HOST_KEY_CHECKING
          - name: ANSIBLE_PARAMIKO_HOST_KEY_CHECKING
          ini:
          - key: host_key_checking
            section: defaults
          - key: host_key_checking
            section: paramiko_connection
          vars:
```

Figure 7.2 – Ansible documentation for the paramiko_ssh connection

Thanks to all the hard work and effort that goes into documenting every area of Ansible, you can easily find out about the plugins that are included with Ansible and how to work with them. So far, we have seen that the documentation for plugins is no less complete than it is for modules. In the next section of this chapter, we'll dive a bit deeper into how to find the plugin code that accompanies your Ansible distribution.

Finding included plugins

As we discussed in the preceding section, plugins are not as apparent in Ansible as their module counterparts are, and yet we have been using them behind the scenes in every single Ansible command we've issued so far! Let's build on our work in the previous section, where we looked at the plugin documentation, by looking at where we can find the source code for the plugins. This, in turn, will serve as a precursor to us building a simple plugin of our own.

If you installed Ansible on a Linux system using a package manager (that is, via an RPM or DEB package), then the location of your plugins will depend on your OS. For example, on my test CentOS 8 system where I installed Ansible from the official RPM package, I can see the plugins installed here:

```
$ ls /usr/lib/python3.11/site-packages/ansible/plugins/
action cliconf httpapi inventory lookup terminal
become connection __init__.py loader.py netconf test
cache doc_fragments __init__.pyc loader.pyc shell vars
callback filter __init__.pyo loader.pyo strategy
```

Notice how the plugins are separated into subdirectories, all named after their categories. If we want to look up the paramiko_ssh plugin, which we reviewed the documentation of in the preceding section, we can look in the connection/ subdirectory:

```
$ ls -l /usr/lib/python3.11/site-packages/ansible/plugins/connection/
paramiko_ssh.py
-rw-r--r--1 root root 23544 Mar 5 05:39 /usr/lib/python3.11/site-
packages/ansible/plugins/connection/paramiko_ssh.py
```

However, in general, I do not recommend that you edit or change the files that are installed from a package as you might all too easily overwrite them when upgrading the package. As one of our goals in this chapter is to write a simple custom plugin, let's look at how to find the plugins in the official Ansible source code:

1. Clone the official Ansible repository from GitHub, as we did previously, and change the directory to the location of your clone:

    ```
    $ git clone https://github.com/ansible/ansible.git
    $ cd ansible
    ```

2. Within the official source code directory structure, you will find that the plugins are all contained (again, in categorized subdirectories) under lib/ansible/plugins/:

    ```
    $ cd lib/ansible/plugins
    ```

3. We can explore the connection-based plugins by looking in the connection directory:

    ```
    $ ls -al connection/
    ```

    The exact contents of this directory will depend on the version of the Ansible source code that you have cloned. At the time of writing, it looks as follows, with one Python file for each plugin (similar to how we saw one Python file for each module in *Chapter 5*, *Creating and Consuming Modules*):

    ```
    $ ls -al connection/
    total 176
    drwxr-xr-x 2 root root 109 May 15 17:24 .
    ```

```
drwxr-xr-x 19 root root 297 May 15 17:24 ..
-rw-r--r-- 1 root root 16411 May 15 17:24 __init__.py
-rw-r--r-- 1 root root 6855 May 15 17:24 local.py
-rw-r--r-- 1 root root 23525 May 15 17:24 paramiko_ssh.py
-rw-r--r-- 1 root root 32839 May 15 17:24 psrp.py
-rw-r--r-- 1 root root 55367 May 15 17:24 ssh.py
-rw-r--r-- 1 root root 31277 May 15 17:24 winrm.py
```

4. You can review the contents of each plugin to learn more about how they work, which is again part of the beauty of open source software:

    ```
    $ less connection/paramiko_ssh.py
    ```

    An example of the beginning of this file is shown in the following code block to give you an idea of the kind of output you should be seeing if this command runs correctly:

    ```
    # (c) 2012, Michael DeHaan <michael.dehaan@gmail.com>
    # (c) 2017 Ansible Project
    # GNU General Public License v3.0+ (see COPYING or https://www.
    gnu.org/licenses/gpl-3.0.txt)
    from __future__ import (absolute_import, division, print_
    function)
    __metaclass__ = type

    DOCUMENTATION = """
        author: Ansible Core Team
        connection: paramiko
        short_description: Run tasks via python ssh (paramiko)
        description:
            - Use the python ssh implementation (Paramiko) to
    connect to targets
            - The paramiko transport is provided because many
    distributions, in particular EL6 and before do not support
    ControlPersist
            in their SSH implementations.
    ....
    ```

Notice the DOCUMENTATION block, which is very similar to what we saw when we were working with the module source code. If you explore the source code of each plugin, you will find that the structure bears some similarity to the module code structure. However, rather than simply taking this statement at face value, in the next section, we'll build our very own custom plugin to learn, through a practical example, how they are put together.

Creating custom plugins

In this section, we will take you through a practical guide to creating a plugin. The example will be, by necessity, simple. However, hopefully, it will serve you well in guiding you in the principles and best practices of plugin development and give you a solid foundation to build more complex plugins. We will even show you how to integrate these with your playbooks and, when you're ready, submit them to the official Ansible project for inclusion.

As we noted when we built a module, Ansible is written in Python, and its plugins are no exception. As a result, you will need to write your plugin in Python; so, to get started on developing a plugin, you will need to make sure you have Python and a few essential tools installed. If you already have Ansible running on your development machine, you probably have the required packages installed.

Let's get started with creating a plugin. Although there are many similarities between coding modules and plugins, there are also fundamental differences. Each of the different types of plugins that Ansible can work with is coded slightly differently and has different recommendations. Sadly, we don't have space to go through each one in this book, but you can find out more about the requirements for each plugin type by reading the official Ansible documentation at `https://docs.ansible.com/ansible/latest/dev_guide/developing_plugins.html`.

For our simple example, we'll create a filter plugin that replaces a given string with another. If you refer to the preceding documentation link, filter plugins are perhaps some of the easiest ones to code because there isn't a stringent requirement on the documentation in the same way that there is for modules. However, if we were to create a `lookup` plugin, we would be expected to create the same DOCUMENTATION, EXAMPLES, and RETURN documentation sections that we created in *Chapter 5, Creating and Consuming Modules*. We would also need to test and build our web documentation in the same way.

We have already covered this, so it doesn't serve to repeat the entirety of this process in this chapter. Instead, we will focus on creating a filter plugin. In contrast with other Ansible plugins and modules, you can have several filters defined in a single Python plugin file. Filters are, by nature, quite compact to code. They are also numerous, so having one file per filter doesn't scale well. However, if you want to code other types of plugins (such as `lookup` plugins), you *will* need to create one Python file per plugin.

Let's start creating our simple filter plugin. As we are only creating one, it will live in its own single Python file. You could propose a modification to one of the Ansible core filter Python files if you want to submit your code back to the Ansible project; but for now, we'll leave that as a project for you to complete yourself. Our filter file will be called `custom_filter.py` and it will live in a directory called `filter_plugins`, which must be created in the same directory as your playbook.

For clarity, your final directory structure should look as follows:

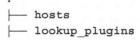
```
.
├── hosts
├── lookup_plugins
```

```
|   └── firstchar.py
├── myplugin2.yml
└── testdoc.txt
```

Perform the following steps to create and test your plugin code:

1. Start your plugin file with a header so that people will know who wrote the plugin and what license it is released under. Naturally, you should update both the copyright and license fields with values appropriate to your plugin, but the following text is given as an example for you to get started with:

    ```
    # (c) 2020, James Freeman <james.freeman@example.com>
    # GNU General Public License v3.0+ (see COPYING or https://www.
    gnu.org/licenses/gpl-3.0.txt)
    ```

2. Next, we'll add a very simple Python function – yours can be as complex as you want it to be, but for ours, we will simply use the Python `.replace` function to replace one string with another inside a `string` variable. The following example looks for instances of `Puppet` and replaces them with `Ansible`:

    ```
    def improve_automation(a):
    return a.replace("Puppet", "Ansible")
    ```

3. Next, we need to create an object of the `FilterModule` class, which is how Ansible will know that this Python file contains a filter. Within this object, we can create a `filters` definition and return the value of our previously defined filter function to Ansible:

    ```
    class FilterModule(object):
    '''improve_automation filters'''
    def filters(self):
    return {'improve_automation': improve_automation}
    ```

4. As you can see, this code is all incredibly simple and we're able to use built-in Python functions, such as `replace`, to manipulate the strings. There isn't a specific test harness for plugins in Ansible, so we will test out our plugin code by writing a simple playbook that will implement it. The following playbook code defines a simple string that includes the word `Puppet` in it and prints this to the console using the `debug` module, applying our newly defined filter to the string:

    ```
    ---
    - name: Play to demonstrate our custom filter
      hosts: frontends
      gather_facts: false
      vars:
        statement: "Puppet is an excellent automation tool!"

      tasks:
    ```

```
- name: make a statement
  debug:
    msg: "{{ statement | improve_automation }}"
```

Now, before we attempt to run this, let's recap what the directory structure should look like. Just as we were able to utilize the custom module that we created in *Chapter 5, Creating and Consuming Modules,* by creating a `library/` subdirectory to house our module, we can also create a `filter_plugins/` subdirectory for our plugin. Your directory tree structure, when you have finished coding the various file details in the preceding code block, should look something like this:

```
.
├── filter_plugins
│   ├── custom_filter.py
├── hosts
├── myplugin.yml
```

Now, let's run our little test playbook and see what output we get. If all goes well, it should look something like the following:

```
$ ansible-playbook -i hosts myplugin.yml

PLAY [Play to demonstrate our custom filter] ************************
**********

TASK [make a statement] ********************************************
**********
ok: [frt01.example.com] => {
    "msg": "Ansible is an excellent automation tool!"
}

PLAY RECAP *********************************************************
**********
frt01.example.com : ok=1 changed=0 unreachable=0 failed=0 skipped=0
rescued=0 ignored=0
```

As you can see, our new filter plugin replaced the `Puppet` string in our variable's contents and replaced it with the `Ansible` string. This, of course, is just a silly test and not one you are likely to contribute back to the Ansible project. However, it shows how, in just six lines of code and with a modicum of Python knowledge, we have created a filter plugin to manipulate a string. You could come up with something far more complex and useful, I'm sure!

Other plugin types require more effort than this; although we won't go through the process of creating a filter plugin here, you'll find coding a filter plugin more akin to coding a module, as you need to do the following:

- Include the DOCUMENTATION, EXAMPLES, and RETURN sections with the appropriate documentation

- Ensure you have incorporated appropriate and sufficient error handling in the plugin
- Test it thoroughly, including both the failure and success cases

As an example of this, we'll repeat the preceding process but create a `lookup` plugin instead. This plugin will be based heavily on a simplified version of the file `lookup` plugin. However, we want to adapt our version so that it only returns the first character of a file. You could adapt this example to perhaps read the header from a file, or you could add arguments to the plugin so that you can extract a substring using character indexes. We will leave this enhancement activity as an exercise for you to carry out yourself.

Let's get started! Our new lookup plugin will be called `firstchar`, and as `lookup` plugins have a one-to-one mapping with their Python files, the plugin file will be called `firstchar.py`. (In fact, Ansible will use this filename as the name of the plugin – you won't find a reference to it in the code anywhere!). If you intend to test this from a playbook, as executed previously, you should create this in a directory called `lookup_plugins/`:

1. Start by adding a header to the plugin file, as before, so that the maintainer and copyright details are clear. We are borrowing a large chunk of the original `lookup` plugin code from `file.py` for our example, so we must include the relevant credit:

```
# (c) 2023, Daniel Oh <daniel.oh@example.com>
# (c) 2020, James Freeman <james.freeman@example.com>
# (c) 2012, Daniel Hokka Zakrisson <daniel@hozac.com>
# (c) 2017 Ansible Project
# GNU General Public License v3.0+ (see COPYING or https://www.
gnu.org/licenses/gpl-3.0.txt)
```

2. Next, add the Python 3 headers – these are an absolute requirement if you intend to submit your plugin via a **Pull Request** (**PR**) to the Ansible project:

```
from __future__ import (absolute_import, division, print_
function)
__metaclass__ = type
```

3. Next, add a DOCUMENTATION block to your plugin so that other users can understand how to interact with it:

```
DOCUMENTATION = """
  lookup: firstchar
  author: James Freeman <james.freeman@example.com>
  version_added: "2.15"
  short_description: read the first character of file contents
  description:
    - This lookup returns the first character of the contents
from a file on the Ansible controller's file system.
  options:
```

```
    _terms:
        description: path(s) of files to read
        required: True
    notes:
        - if read in variable context, the file can be interpreted
as YAML if the content is valid to the parser.
        - this lookup does not understand 'globing', use the
fileglob lookup instead.
    """
```

4. Add the relevant EXAMPLES blocks to show how to use your plugin, just as we did with our modules:

```
EXAMPLES = """
- debug: msg="the first character in foo.txt is
{{lookup('firstchar', '/etc/foo.txt') }}"


"""
```

5. Also, make sure you document the RETURN values from your plugin:

```
RETURN = """
_raw:
description:
- first character of content of file(s)
"""
```

6. With the documentation complete, we can now start working on our Python code. We will start by importing all the Python modules we need to make our module work. We'll also set up the display object, which is used for verbose output and debugging. This should be used in place of the print statements in your plugin code if you need to display the debug output:

```
from ansible.errors import AnsibleError, AnsibleParserError
from ansible.plugins.lookup import LookupBase
from ansible.utils.display import Display

display = Display()
```

7. We will now create an object of the LookupModule class. Define a default function within this called run (this is expected for the Ansible lookup plugin framework) and initialize an empty array for our return data:

```
class LookupModule(LookupBase):

    def run(self, terms, variables=None, **kwargs):

        ret = []
```

8. With this in place, we will start a loop to iterate over each of the terms (which, in our simple plugin, will be the filenames passed to the plugin). Although we will only test this on simple use cases, the way that lookup plugins can be used means that they need to support the lists of terms to operate on. Within this loop, we display valuable debugging information and, most importantly, define an object with the details of each of the files we will open, called lookupfile:

```
for term in terms:
    display.debug("File lookup term: %s" % term)

    lookupfile = self.find_file_in_search_path(variables,
'files', term)

    display.vvvv(u"File lookup using %s as file" % lookupfile)
```

9. Now, we will read in the file contents. This could be as simple as using one line of Python code, but we know from our work on modules in *Chapter 5, Creating and Consuming Modules*, that we should not take it for granted that we will be passed a file we can read. As a result, we will put the statement to read our file contents into a try block and implement exception handling to ensure that the behavior of the plugin is sensible, even in error cases, and that easy-to-understand error messages are passed back to the user, rather than to Python tracebacks:

```
try:
    if lookupfile:
        contents, show_data = self._loader._get_file_
contents(lookupfile)
        ret.append(contents.rstrip()[0])
    else:
        raise AnsibleParserError()
except AnsibleParserError:
    raise AnsibleError("could not locate file in lookup: %s"
% term)
```

Notice that here, we append the first character of the file contents (denoted by the [0] index) to our empty array. We also remove any training spaces using rstrip.

10. Finally, we must return the character we gathered from the file to Ansible with a return statement:

```
return ret
```

11. Once again, we can create a simple test playbook to test out our newly created plugin:

```
---

- name: Play to demonstrate our custom lookup plugin
  hosts: frontends
  gather_facts: false
```

```
tasks:
  - name: make a statement
    debug:
      msg: "{{ lookup('firstchar', 'testdoc.txt')}}"
```

Again, we are using the debug module to print output to the console and referencing our `lookup` plugin to obtain the output.

12. Create the text file referenced in the previous code block, called `testdoc.txt`. This can contain anything you like – mine contains the following simple text:

```
Hello
```

13. Now, when we run our new playbook, we should see an output similar to the following:

```
$ ansible-playbook -i hosts myplugin2.yml

PLAY [Play to demonstrate our custom lookup plugin]
***************************

TASK [make a statement] *****************************************
****************
ok: [frt01.example.com] => {
  "msg": "H"
}

PLAY RECAP ******************************************************
****************
frt01.example.com : ok=1 changed=0 unreachable=0 failed=0
skipped=0 rescued=0 ignored=0
```

If all goes well, your playbook should return the first character of the text file you created. Naturally, there is a lot we could do to enhance this code, but this serves as a nice, simple example to get you started.

With this foundation in place, you should now have a reasonable idea of how to get started with writing your plugins for Ansible. The next logical step for us is to look in greater depth at how we can test our newly written plugins. We will do this in the next section.

Learning to integrate custom plugins with Ansible source code

So far, we have only tested our plugin in a standalone manner. This is all well and good, but what if you wanted to add it either to your own fork of the Ansible source code – or, better yet, submit it back to the Ansible project for inclusion with a PR? Fortunately, this process is very similar to the one we covered in *Chapter 5*, *Creating and Consuming Modules*, only with slightly different folder structures.

Next, you will need to copy your plugin code into one of the appropriate plugin directories:

- For example, our example filter would be copied to the following directory in the source code you just cloned:

```
$ cp ~/custom_filter.py ./lib/ansible/plugins/filter/
```

- Similarly, our custom `lookup` plugin would go into the `lookup` plugin's directory, using a command such as the following:

```
$ cp ~/firstchar.py ./lib/ansible/plugins/lookup/
```

With your code copied into place, you need to test the documentation (that is, whether your plugin includes it) as before. You can build the `webdocs` documentation in the same way as we did in *Chapter 5, Creating and Consuming Modules*, so we will not recap this here. However, as a refresher, we can quickly check whether the documentation renders correctly using the `ansible-doc` command, as follows:

```
$ . hacking/env-setup
running egg_info
creating lib/ansible.egg-info
writing requirements to lib/ansible.egg-info/requires.txt
writing lib/ansible.egg-info/PKG-INFO
writing top-level names to lib/ansible.egg-info/top_level.txt
writing dependency_links to lib/ansible.egg-info/dependency_links.txt
writing manifest file 'lib/ansible.egg-info/SOURCES.txt'
reading manifest file 'lib/ansible.egg-info/SOURCES.txt'
reading manifest template 'MANIFEST.in'
warning: no files found matching 'SYMLINK_CACHE.json'
writing manifest file 'lib/ansible.egg-info/SOURCES.txt'

Setting up Ansible to run out of checkout...

PATH=/home/james/ansible/bin:/usr/local/sbin:/usr/local/bin:/usr/
sbin:/usr/bin:/root/bin
PYTHONPATH=/home/james/ansible/lib
MANPATH=/home/james/ansible/docs/man:/usr/local/share/man:/usr/share/
man

Remember, you may wish to specify your host file with -i

Done!

$ ansible-doc -t lookup firstchar
> FIRSTCHAR (/home/james/ansible/lib/ansible/plugins/lookup/firstchar.
py)
```

```
        This lookup returns the first character of the contents from a
        file on the Ansible controller's file system.

  * This module is maintained by The Ansible Community
 OPTIONS (= is mandatory):

 = _terms
        path(s) of files to read
```

As you have seen so far, there is a great deal of overlap between plugin development and module development in Ansible. It is especially important to pay attention to error handling with exceptions to produce good quality, easy-to-understand error messages and to adhere to and uphold Ansible's high documentation standards. One additional item that we have not covered here is the plugin's output. All plugins must return strings in Unicode; this ensures that they can run through the `jinja2` filters correctly. Further guidance can be found in the official Ansible documentation at `https://docs.ansible.com/ansible/latest/dev_guide/developing_plugins.html`.

Armed with this knowledge, you should now be well placed to begin your plugin development work, and even submit your code back to the community, if you desire. We'll offer a brief recap of this in the next section.

Sharing plugins with the community

You may wish to submit your new plugin to the Ansible project, just as we considered for our custom modules in *Chapter 5, Creating and Consuming Modules*. The process for doing this with plugins is almost identical to what you do for modules, which this section will recap.

> **Note**
> Using the following process will submit a real request to the Ansible project on GitHub to merge the code you submit with their code. Do *not* follow this process unless you genuinely have a new module that is ready to be submitted to the Ansible code base.

To submit your plugin as a PR of the Ansible repository, you need to fork the `devel` branch of the official Ansible repository. To do this, log in to your GitHub account on your web browser (or create an account if you don't already have one), and then navigate to `https://github.com/ansible/ansible.git`. Click on **Fork** at the top-right corner of the page:

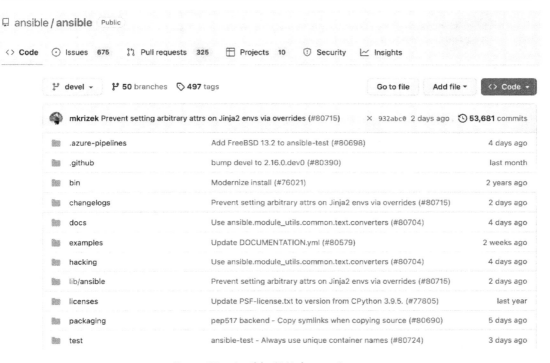

Figure 7.3 – Ansible GitHub repository

Once you have forked the repository to your account, we will walk you through the commands you need to run to add your module code to it and then create the required PRs to merge your new module with the upstream Ansible project:

1. Clone the `devel` branch that you just forked to your local machine. Use a command similar to the following, but be sure to replace the URL with one that matches your own GitHub account:

   ```
   $ git clone https://github.com/<your GitHub account>/ansible.git
   ```

2. Copy your module code into the appropriate `plugins/` directory. The `copy` command used in the following code block is just an example to give you an idea as to what to do – in reality, you should choose the appropriate category subdirectory for your plugin as it won't necessarily fit into the `lookup` category. Once you've added your Python file, perform a `git add` command to make Git aware of the new file, and then commit it with a meaningful `commit` message. Some example commands are shown here:

   ```
   $ cd ansible
   $ cp ~/ansible-development/plugindev/firstchar.py ./lib/ansible/
   plugins/lookup
   $ git add lib/ansible/plugins/lookup/firstchar.py
   ```

```
$ git commit -m 'Added tested version of firstchar.py for pull
request creation'
```

3. Now, be sure to push the code to your forked repository using the following command:

```
$ git push
```

4. Return to GitHub in your web browser and navigate to the **Pull requests** page, as shown in the following screenshot. Click on the **New pull request** button:

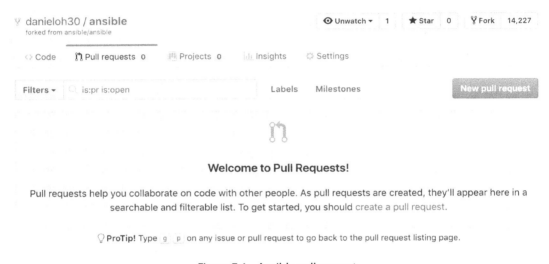

Figure 7.4 – Ansible pull request

Follow the PR creation process, as guided by the GitHub website. Once you have successfully submitted your PR, you should be able to navigate to the list of PRs on the official Ansible source code repository and find yours there. An example of the PR list is shown in the following screenshot for your reference:

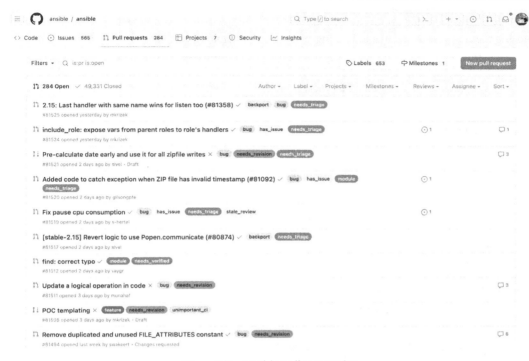

Figure 7.5 – Ansible pull request list

As discussed previously, don't be alarmed if it takes a long time for your PR to be reviewed – this is simply due to how many PRs there are to review and process. You can always use your plugin code locally by adding it to a local `*_plugins/` directory, as we demonstrated earlier, so that the processing speed of your PR doesn't hinder your work with Ansible. Further details of where to place your plugin code when working locally can be found at `https://docs.ansible.com/ansible/latest/dev_guide/developing_locally.html`.

That completes our look at creating plugins, including two working examples. Hopefully, you have found this journey informative and valuable and it has enhanced your ability to work with Ansible and extend its functionality where required.

Summary

Ansible plugins are a core part of Ansible's functionality and as we discovered in this chapter, we have been working with them throughout this book without even realizing it! Ansible's modular design makes it easy to extend and add functionality, regardless of whether you are working with modules or the various types of plugins that are currently supported. Whether it's to add a new filter for string processing or a new way of looking up data (or perhaps even a new connection mechanism to new technology), Ansible plugins provide a complete framework that can extend Ansible far beyond its already extensive capabilities.

In this chapter, we learned about the various types of plugins that are supported by Ansible, before exploring them in greater detail and looking at we you can obtain documentation and information on the existing ones. We then completed two practical examples to create two different types of plugins for Ansible while looking at the best practices for plugin development and how this overlaps with module development. We finished off by recapping how to submit our new plugin code as a PR back to the Ansible project.

In the next chapter, we will explore the best practices that you should adhere to when writing your Ansible playbooks to ensure that you produce manageable, high-quality automation code.

Questions

Answer the following questions to test your knowledge of this chapter:

1. Which of the following `ansible-doc` commands can you use to list the names of all the cache plugins?

    A. `ansible-doc -a cache -l`

    B. `ansible-doc cache -l`

    C. `ansible-doc -a cache`

    D. `ansible-doc -t cache -l`

    E. `ansible-doc cache`

2. Which class do you need to add to your `lookup` plugin's code to include the bulk of the plugin code, including `run()`, the `items` loop, `try`, and `except`?

    A. `LookupModule`

    B. `RunModule`

    C. `StartModule`

    D. `InitModule`

    E. `LoadModule`

3. True or false: To create custom plugins with complex operations rather than printing simple hello world text using Python, you need to install Python with the relevant dependencies on your OS.

    A. True

    B. False

Further reading

You can find all of the plugins on Ansible by accessing the Ansible repository directly at `https://github.com/ansible/ansible/tree/devel/lib/ansible/plugins`.

8

Coding Best Practices

Ansible can help you automate almost all your daily IT tasks, from mundane tasks, such as applying patches or deploying configuration files, to deploying entirely new infrastructure as code. The use of, and engagement with, Ansible has been growing year by year as more and more people realize its power and simplicity. You will find many examples of Ansible playbooks, roles, blog articles, and so on across the internet, and combined with resources such as this book, you will become proficient at writing your own Ansible playbooks.

Yet, how can you tell whether an example you found on the internet is actually a good way of doing things? In this chapter, we will take you through a practical guide of the best practices in Ansible, showing you what is currently considered good practice when it comes to directory structure and playbook layout, how to make effective use of inventories (especially on the cloud), and how best to differentiate your environments. By the end of this chapter, you should be able to proceed with confidence in writing everything from small single-task playbooks to large-scale playbooks for complex environments.

In this chapter, we will cover the following topics:

- The preferred directory layout
- Differentiating between different environment types
- The proper approach to defining group and host variables
- Using top-level playbooks
- Leveraging version control tools
- Setting OS and distribution variances
- Porting between Ansible versions

Technical requirements

This chapter assumes that you have set up your control host with Ansible, as in *Chapter 1*, *Getting Started with Ansible*, and that you are using the most recent version available; the examples in this chapter were tested on Ansible 2.15. This chapter also assumes that you have at least one additional host to test against; ideally, this should be Linux-based. Although we will give specific examples of hostnames in this chapter, you are welcome to substitute them with your own hostname and/or IP addresses, and details of how to do this are provided in the appropriate places.

The code bundle used in this chapter is available at `https://github.com/PacktPublishing/ Practical-Ansible-Second-Edition/tree/main/Chapter%208`.

The preferred directory layout

As we have explored Ansible throughout this book, we have shown many times that the more your playbook grows in size and scale, the more likely you are to want to divide it up into multiple files and directories. A great example of this is roles, which we covered in *Chapter 4*, *Playbooks and Roles*, where we defined roles to not only enable us to reuse common automation code but also to split up what could potentially be a massive, single playbook into smaller, logically organized, manageable chunks. We also looked, in *Chapter 3*, *Defining Your Inventory*, at the process of defining your inventory file and how you can also split this up across multiple files and directories. What we have not looked at, however, is how we can put all of this together. All of this is documented in the official Ansible documentation at `https://docs.ansible.com/ansible/latest/user_guide/ playbooks_best_practices.html#content-organization`.

However, in this chapter, let's get started with a practical example of this to show you a great way of setting up your directory structure for a simple role-based playbook that has two different inventories—one for a development environment and one for a production environment (you would want to keep these separate in any real-world use case; although, ideally, you should be able to execute the same plays on both for consistency and for testing purposes).

Let's get started by building the directory structure:

1. Create a directory tree for your development inventory with the following commands:

    ```
    $ mkdir -p inventories/development/group_vars
    $ mkdir -p inventories/development/host_vars
    ```

2. Next, we'll define an INI-formatted inventory file for our development inventory—in our example, we'll keep this really simple with just two servers. The file to create is `inventories/ development/hosts`:

    ```
    [app]
    app01.dev.example.com
    app02.dev.example.com
    ```

3. To further our example, we'll add a group variable to our app group. As discussed in *Chapter 3, Defining Your Inventory*, create a file called app.yml in the group_vars directory we created in the previous step:

    ```
    ---
    http_port: 8080
    ```

4. Next, create a production directory structure using the same method:

    ```
    $ mkdir -p inventories/production/group_vars
    $ mkdir -p inventories/production/host_vars
    ```

5. Create an inventory file called hosts in the newly created production directory with the following contents:

    ```
    [app]
    app01.prod.example.com
    app02.prod.example.com
    ```

6. Now, we'll define a different value for the http_port group variable for our production inventory. Add the following contents to inventories/production/group_vars/app.yml:

    ```
    ---
    http_port: 80
    ```

That completes our inventory definition. Next, we will add any custom modules or plugins that we might find useful for our playbook. Suppose we want to use the remote_filecopy.py module we created in *Chapter 5, Creating and Consuming Modules*. Just as we discussed in that chapter, we first create the directory for this module:

```
$ mkdir library
```

Then, we add the remote_filecopy.py module to this library. We won't relist the code here to save space, but you can copy it from the section called *Developing custom modules* from *Chapter 5, Creating and Consuming Modules*, or take advantage of the example code that accompanies this book on GitHub.

The same can be done for the plugins; if we also want to use the filter plugin that we created in *Chapter 6, Creating and Consuming Plugins*, we would create an appropriately named directory:

```
$ mkdir filter_plugins
```

Then, copy the filter plugin code into this directory.

Finally, we'll create a role to use in our new playbook structure. Naturally, you will have many roles, but we'll create one as an example and then you can repeat the process for each role. We'll call our role `installapp` and use the `ansible-galaxy` command (covered in *Chapter 4, Playbooks and Roles*) to create the directory structure for us:

```
$ mkdir roles
$ ansible-galaxy role init --init-path roles/ installapp
- Role installapp was created successfully
```

Then, in our `roles/installapp/tasks/main.yml` file, we'll add the following contents:

```
---
- name: Display http_port variable contents
  debug:
    var: http_port

- name: Create /tmp/foo
  file:
    path: /tmp/foo
    state: file

- name: Use custom module to copy /tmp/foo
  remote_filecopy:
    source: /tmp/foo
  dest: /tmp/bar

- name: Define a fact about automation
  set_fact:
    about_automation: "Puppet is an excellent automation tool"

- name: Tell us about automation with a custom filter applied
  debug:
    msg: "{{ about_automation | improve_automation }}"
```

In the preceding code, we've reused a number of examples from earlier chapters of this book. You can also define the handlers, variables, default values, and so on to the role, as discussed previously, but for our example, this will suffice.

The final stage in creating our best practice directory structure is to add a top-level playbook to run. By convention, this will be called `site.yml` and it will have the following simple contents (note that the directory structure we have built takes care of many things, allowing the top-level playbook to be incredibly simple):

```
---
- name: Play using best practice directory structure
  hosts: all
```

```
roles:
  - installapp
```

For the purpose of clarity, your resulting directory structure should look as follows:

```
.
├── filter_plugins
│   ├── custom_filter.py
│   └── custom_filter.pyc
├── inventories
│   ├── development
│   │   ├── group_vars
│   │   │   └── app.yml
│   │   ├── hosts
│   │   └── host_vars
│   └── production
│       ├── group_vars
│       │   └── app.yml
│       ├── hosts
│       └── host_vars
├── library
│   └── remote_filecopy.py
├── roles
│   └── installapp
│       ├── defaults
│       │   └── main.yml
│       ├── files
│       ├── handlers
│       │   └── main.yml
│       ├── meta
│       │   └── main.yml
│       ├── README.md
│       ├── tasks
│       │   └── main.yml
│       ├── templates
│       ├── tests
│       │   ├── inventory
│       │   └── test.yml
│       └── vars
│           └── main.yml
└── site.yml
```

Now, we can simply run our playbook in the normal manner. For example, to run it on the `development` inventory, execute the following:

```
$ ansible-playbook -i inventories/development/hosts site.yml

PLAY [Play using best practice directory structure]
****************************

TASK [Gathering Facts] *********************************************
***********
ok: [app02.dev.example.com]
ok: [app01.dev.example.com]

TASK [installapp : Display http_port variable contents]
************************
ok: [app01.dev.example.com] => {
 "http_port": 8080
}
ok: [app02.dev.example.com] => {
 "http_port": 8080
}

TASK [installapp : Create /tmp/foo] *********************************
***********
changed: [app02.dev.example.com]
changed: [app01.dev.example.com]

TASK [installapp : Use custom module to copy /tmp/foo]
*************************
changed: [app02.dev.example.com]
changed: [app01.dev.example.com]

TASK [installapp : Define a fact about automation]
*****************************
ok: [app01.dev.example.com]
ok: [app02.dev.example.com]

TASK [installapp : Tell us about automation with a custom filter
applied] ******
ok: [app01.dev.example.com] => {
 "msg": "Ansible is an excellent automation tool"
}
ok: [app02.dev.example.com] => {
 "msg": "Ansible is an excellent automation tool"
}
```

```
PLAY RECAP *********************************************************
***********
app01.dev.example.com : ok=6 changed=2 unreachable=0 failed=0
skipped=0 rescued=0 ignored=0
app02.dev.example.com : ok=6 changed=2 unreachable=0 failed=0
skipped=0 rescued=0 ignored=0
```

Similarly, run the following for the production inventory:

```
$ ansible-playbook -i inventories/production/hosts site.yml

PLAY [Play using best practice directory structure]
***************************

TASK [Gathering Facts] *********************************************
***********
ok: [app02.prod.example.com]
ok: [app01.prod.example.com]

TASK [installapp : Display http_port variable contents]
************************
ok: [app01.prod.example.com] => {
  "http_port": 80
}
ok: [app02.prod.example.com] => {
  "http_port": 80
}


TASK [installapp : Create /tmp/foo] ********************************
***********
changed: [app01.prod.example.com]
changed: [app02.prod.example.com]

TASK [installapp : Use custom module to copy /tmp/foo]
**************************
changed: [app02.prod.example.com]
changed: [app01.prod.example.com]

TASK [installapp : Define a fact about automation]
*****************************
ok: [app01.prod.example.com]
ok: [app02.prod.example.com]


TASK [installapp : Tell us about automation with a custom filter
applied] ******
```

```
ok: [app01.prod.example.com] => {
  "msg": "Ansible is an excellent automation tool"
}
ok: [app02.prod.example.com] => {
  "msg": "Ansible is an excellent automation tool"
}


PLAY RECAP ********************************************************
***********
app01.prod.example.com : ok=6 changed=2 unreachable=0 failed=0
skipped=0 rescued=0 ignored=0
app02.prod.example.com : ok=6 changed=2 unreachable=0 failed=0
skipped=0 rescued=0 ignored=0
```

Notice how the appropriate hosts and associated variables are picked up for each inventory and how tidy and well organized our directory structure is. This is the ideal way for you to lay out your playbooks and will ensure that they can be scaled up to whatever size you need them to be, without them becoming unwieldy and difficult to manage or troubleshoot. In the next section, we will explore differentiating between different environment types.

Differentiating between different environment types

In almost every business, you will need to split your technology environment by type. For example, you will almost certainly have a development environment, where all the testing and development work is performed, and a production environment, where all of the stable test code is run. The environments should (in a best-case scenario) make use of the same Ansible playbooks—after all, the logic is that if you can successfully deploy and test an application in your development environment, then you should be able to deploy it in the same way in a production environment and have it work just as well. However, there are always differences between the two environments, not just in the hostnames but also sometimes in the parameters, the load balancer names, the port numbers, and so on—the list can seem endless.

In the *The preferred directory layout* section of this chapter, we covered a way of differentiating between a development and production environment using two separate inventory directory trees. This is how you should proceed when it comes to differentiating these environments; obviously, we won't repeat the examples, but it's important to note that when working with multiple environments, your goals should be as follows:

- Try and reuse the same playbooks for all of your environments that run the same code. For example, if you deploy a web app in your development environment, you should be confident that your playbooks will deploy the same app in the production environment (and your **Quality Assurance (QA)** environment, as well as any others that it might need to be deployed in).

- This means that not only are you testing your application deployments and code but you are also testing your Ansible playbooks and roles as part of your overall testing process.

- Your inventories for each environment should be kept in separate directory trees (as we saw in the *The preferred directory layout* section of this chapter), but all roles, playbooks, plugins, and modules (if used) should be in the same directory structure (this should be the case for both environments).

- It is normal for different environments to require different authentication credentials; you should keep these separate not only for security but also to ensure that playbooks are not accidentally run in the wrong environment.

- Your playbooks should be in your version control system, just as your code is. This enables you to track changes over time and ensure that everyone is working from the same copy of the automation code.

If you pay attention to these simple pointers, you will find that your automation workflow becomes a real asset to your business and ensures reliability and consistency across all of your deployments. Conversely, failure to follow these pointers puts you at risk of experiencing the dreaded, *it worked in development but it doesn't work in production* deployment failures that so often plague the technology industry. Let's now build on this discussion in the next section by looking at best practices when handling host and group variables—something that, as we saw in the *The preferred directory layout* section, you need to apply, especially when working with multiple environments.

The proper approach to defining group and host variables

When working with group and host variables, you can split them up using the directory-based approach we used in the *The preferred directory layout* section. However, there are a few additional pointers to managing this that you should be aware of. First and foremost, you should always pay attention to variable precedence. A detailed list of variable precedence order can be found at `https://docs.ansible.com/ansible/latest/user_guide/playbooks_variables.html#variable-precedence-where-should-i-put-a-variable`. However, the key takeaways for working with multiple environments are as follows:

- Host variables are always of a higher order of precedence than group variables, so you can override any group variable with a host variable. This behavior is useful if you take advantage of it in a controlled manner, but can yield unexpected results if you are not aware of it.

- There is a special group variables definition called `all`, which is applied to all inventory groups. This has a lower order of precedence than specifically defined group variables.

- What happens if you define the same variable twice in two groups? If this happens, both groups have the same order of precedence, so which one wins? To demonstrate this (and our earlier examples), we will create a simple practical example for you to follow.

To get started, let's create a directory structure for our inventories. To keep this example as concise as possible, we will only create a development environment. However, you are free to expand on these concepts by building on the more complete example we covered in the *The preferred directory layout* section of this chapter:

1. Create an inventory directory structure with the following commands:

    ```
    $ mkdir -p inventories/development/group_vars
    $ mkdir -p inventories/development/host_vars
    ```

2. Create a simple inventory file with two hosts in a single group in the `inventories/development/hosts` file; the contents should be as follows:

    ```
    [app]
    app01.dev.example.com
    app02.dev.example.com
    ```

3. Now, let's create a special group variable file for all the groups in the inventory; this file will be called `inventories/development/group_vars/all.yml` and should contain the following content:

    ```
    ---
    http_port: 8080
    ```

4. Finally, let's create a simple playbook called `site.yml` to query and print the value of the variable we just created:

    ```
    ---
    - name: Play using best practice directory structure
      hosts: all

      tasks:
        - name: Display the value of our inventory variable
          debug:
            var: http_port
    ```

5. Now, if we run this playbook, we'll see that the variable (which we only defined in one place) takes the value we would expect:

    ```
    $ ansible-playbook -i inventories/development/hosts site.yml
    ```

```
PLAY [Play using best practice directory structure]
****************************

TASK [Gathering Facts] *****************************************
****************
ok: [app01.dev.example.com]
ok: [app02.dev.example.com]

TASK [Display the value of our inventory variable]
****************************
ok: [app01.dev.example.com] => {
  "http_port": 8080
}
ok: [app02.dev.example.com] => {
  "http_port": 8080
}

PLAY RECAP *********************************************************
****************
app01.dev.example.com : ok=2 changed=0 unreachable=0 failed=0
skipped=0 rescued=0 ignored=0
app02.dev.example.com : ok=2 changed=0 unreachable=0 failed=0
skipped=0 rescued=0 ignored=0
```

6. So far, so good! Now, let's add a new file to our inventory directory structure, with the `all.yml` file remaining unchanged. Let's also create a new file located in `inventories/development/group_vars/app.yml`, which will contain the following content:

   ```
   ---
   http_port: 8081
   ```

7. We have now defined the same variable twice—once in a special group called `all` and once in the `app` group (which both servers in our `development` inventory belong to). So, what happens if we now run our playbook? The output should appear as follows:

   ```
   $ ansible-playbook -i inventories/development/hosts site.yml

   PLAY [Play using best practice directory structure]
   ****************************

   TASK [Gathering Facts] *****************************************
   ****************
   ok: [app02.dev.example.com]
   ok: [app01.dev.example.com]
   ```

```
TASK [Display the value of our inventory variable]
*****************************
ok: [app01.dev.example.com] => {
  "http_port": 8081
}
ok: [app02.dev.example.com] => {
  "http_port": 8081
}


PLAY RECAP *****************************************************
****************
app01.dev.example.com : ok=2 changed=0 unreachable=0 failed=0
skipped=0 rescued=0 ignored=0
app02.dev.example.com : ok=2 changed=0 unreachable=0 failed=0
skipped=0 rescued=0 ignored=0
```

8. As expected, the variable definition in the specific group won, which is in line with the order of precedence documented for Ansible. Now, let's see what happens if we define the same variable twice in two specifically named groups. To complete this example, we'll create a child group, called `centos`, and another group that could notionally contain hosts built to a new build standard, called `newcentos`, of which both application servers will be a member. This means modifying `inventories/development/hosts` so that it now looks as follows:

    ```
    [app]
    app01.dev.example.com
    app02.dev.example.com

    [centos:children]
    app

    [newcentos:children]
    app
    ```

9. Now, let's redefine the `http_port` variable for the `centos` group by creating a file called `inventories/development/group_vars/centos.yml`, which contains the following content:

    ```
    ---
    http_port: 8082
    ```

10. Just to add to the confusion, let's also define this variable for the `newcentos` group in `inventories/development/group_vars/newcentos.yml`, which will contain the following content:

    ```
    ---
    http_port: 8083
    ```

11. We've now defined the same variable four times at the group level! Let's rerun our playbook and see which value comes through:

```
$ ansible-playbook -i inventories/development/hosts site.yml

PLAY [Play using best practice directory structure]
****************************

TASK [Gathering Facts] *****************************************
****************
ok: [app01.dev.example.com]
ok: [app02.dev.example.com]

TASK [Display the value of our inventory variable]
****************************
ok: [app01.dev.example.com] => {
  "http_port": 8083
}
ok: [app02.dev.example.com] => {
  "http_port": 8083
}

PLAY RECAP *****************************************************
****************
app01.dev.example.com : ok=2 changed=0 unreachable=0 failed=0
skipped=0 rescued=0 ignored=0
app02.dev.example.com : ok=2 changed=0 unreachable=0 failed=0
skipped=0 rescued=0 ignored=0
```

12. The value we entered in newcentos.yml won—but why? The Ansible documentation states that where identical variables are defined at the group level in the inventory (the one place you can do this), the one from the last-loaded group wins. Just for completeness, we can override all of this by leaving the group_vars directory untouched, but adding a file called inventories/development/host_vars/app01.dev.example.com.yml, which will contain the following content:

```
---
http_port: 9090
```

13. Now, if we run our playbook one final time, we will see that the value we defined at the host level completely overrides any value that we set at the group level for app01.dev.example.com. app02.dev.example.com is unaffected as we did not define a host variable for it, so the next highest level of precedence—the group variable from the newcentos group—won:

```
$ ansible-playbook -i inventories/development/hosts site.yml
```

```
PLAY [Play using best practice directory structure]
****************************

TASK [Gathering Facts] *****************************************
****************
ok: [app01.dev.example.com]
ok: [app02.dev.example.com]

TASK [Display the value of our inventory variable]
****************************
ok: [app01.dev.example.com] => {
  "http_port": 9090
}
ok: [app02.dev.example.com] => {
  "http_port": 8083
}

PLAY RECAP *****************************************************
****************
app01.dev.example.com : ok=2 changed=0 unreachable=0 failed=0
skipped=0 rescued=0 ignored=0
app02.dev.example.com : ok=2 changed=0 unreachable=0 failed=0
skipped=0 rescued=0 ignored=0
```

With this knowledge, you can now make advanced decisions about how to structure your variables within your inventory to make sure you achieve the desired results at both a host and group level. It's important to know about variable precedence ordering, as these examples have demonstrated, but following the documented order will also allow you to produce powerful, flexible playbook inventories that work well across multiple environments. Now, you may have noticed that, throughout this chapter, we have used a top-level playbook in our directory structure, called site.yml. We will look at this playbook in greater detail in the next section.

Using top-level playbooks

In all of the examples so far, we have built out using the best practice directory structure recommended by Ansible and continually referred to a top-level playbook, typically called site.yml. The idea behind this playbook (and, indeed, its common name across all of our directory structures) is so that it can be used across your entire server estate—that is to say, your **site**.

Of course, this is not to say that you have to use the same set of playbooks across every server in your infrastructure or for every single function; rather, it means only you can make the best decision as to what suits your environment best. However, the whole aim of Ansible automation is that the created solution is simple to run and operate. Imagine handing a playbook directory structure with 100 different playbooks to a new system administrator—how would they know which ones to run and in which circumstances? The task of training someone to use the playbooks would be immense and would simply move complexity from one area to another.

At the other end of the spectrum, you could make use of the when clauses with facts and inventory grouping, such that your playbook knows exactly what to run on each server in every possible circumstance. This, of course, is unlikely to happen, and the truth is that your automation solution will end up somewhere in the middle.

The most important thing is that, on receipt of a new playbook directory structure, a new operator at least knows what the starting point for both running the playbooks and understanding the code is. If the top-level playbook they encounter is always `site.yml`, then at least everyone knows where to start. Through the clever use of roles and the `import_*` and `include_*` statements, you can split your playbook up into logical portions of reusable code, as we previously discussed, all from one playbook file.

Now that you have learned about the importance of top-level playbooks, let's take a look, in the next section, at how to take advantage of version control tools to ensure good practices are adhered to when it comes to centralizing and maintaining your automation code.

Leveraging version control tools

As we discussed earlier in this chapter, it is vital that you version control and test not only your code but also your Ansible automation code. This should include inventories (or dynamic inventory collections), any custom modules, plugins, roles, and playbook code. The reason for this is simple—the ultimate goal of Ansible automation is likely to be to deploy an entire environment using a playbook (or set of playbooks). This might even involve deploying infrastructure as code, especially if you are deploying to a cloud environment.

Any changes to your Ansible code could mean big changes to your environment and possibly even determine whether an important production service works or not. As a result, it is vital that you maintain a version history of your Ansible code and that everyone works from the same version. You are free to choose the version control system that suits you best; most corporate environments will already have some kind of version control system in place. However, if you haven't worked with version control systems before, we recommend that you sign up for a free account somewhere such as GitHub or GitLab, which both offer version control repositories for free, along with more advanced paid-for plans.

A complete discussion of version control with Git is beyond the scope of this book, but there are entire books devoted to the subject. However, we will take you through the simplest possible use case. It is assumed, in the following examples, that you are using a free account on GitHub, but if you are using a different provider, simply change the URLs to match those given to you by your version control repository host.

In addition to this, you will need to install the command-line Git tools on your Linux host.

On CentOS, you would install these as follows:

```
$ sudo yum install git
```

On Ubuntu, the process is similarly straightforward:

```
$ sudo apt-get update
$ sudo apt-get install git
```

On macOS, you can use the `brew` package manager to install Git tools as follows:

```
$ brew install git
```

Once the tools are installed and your account is set up, your next task is to clone a Git repository to your machine. If you want to start working with your own repository, you will need to set this up with your provider—excellent documentation is provided by both GitHub and GitLab and you should follow this to set up your first repository.

Once it is set up and initialized, you can clone a copy to your local machine to make changes to your code. This local copy is called a working copy, and you can work through the process of cloning it and making changes as follows (note that these are purely hypothetical examples to give you an idea of the commands you will need to run; you should adapt them for your own use case):

1. Clone your `git` repository to your local machine to create a working copy using a command such as the following:

   ```
   $ git clone https://github.com/<YOUR_GIT_ACCOUNT>/<GIT_REPO>.git
   Cloning into '<GIT_REPO>'...
   remote: Enumerating objects: 7, done.
   remote: Total 7 (delta 0), reused 0 (delta 0), pack-reused 7
   Unpacking objects: 100% (7/7), done.
   ```

2. Change to the directory of the code you cloned (the working copy) and make any code changes you need to make:

   ```
   $ cd <GIT_REPO>
   $ vim myplaybook.yml
   ```

3. Be sure to test your code and, when you are happy with it, add the changed files that are ready for committing a new version using a command such as the following:

   ```
   $ git add myplaybook.yml
   ```

4. The next step is to commit the changes you have made. A commit is basically a new version of code within the repository, so it should be accompanied by a meaningful commit message (specified in quotes after the -m switch), as follows:

```
$ git commit -m 'Added new spongle-widget deployment to
myplaybook.yml'
[master ed14138] Added new spongle-widget deployment to
myplaybook.yml
Committer: Daniel Oh <doh@danieloh.redhat.com>
Your name and email address were configured automatically based
on your username and hostname. Please check that they are
accurate.
You can suppress this message by setting them explicitly. Run
the
following command and follow the instructions in your editor to
edit
your configuration file:

git config --global --edit

After doing this, you may fix the identity used for this commit
with:

git commit --amend --reset-author

1 file changed, 1 insertion(+), 1 deletion(-)
```

5. Right now, all of these changes live solely in the working copy on your local machine. This is good by itself, but it would be better if the code was available to everyone who needs to view it on the version control system. To push your updated commits back to (for example) GitHub, run the following command:

```
$ git push
Enumerating objects: 5, done.
Counting objects: 100% (5/5), done.
Delta compression using up to 8 threads
Compressing objects: 100% (3/3), done.
Writing objects: 100% (3/3), 297 bytes | 297.00 KiB/s, done.
Total 3 (delta 2), reused 0 (delta 0)
remote: Resolving deltas: 100% (2/2), completed with 2 local
objects.
To https://github.com/<YOUR_GIT_ACCOUNT>/<GIT_REPO>.git
0d00263..ed14138 master -> master
```

That's all there is to it!

6. Now, other collaborators can clone your code just as we did in *Step 1*. Alternatively, if they already have a working copy of your repository, they can update their working copy using the following command (you can also do this if you want to update your working copy to see changes made by someone else):

```
$ git pull
```

There are some incredibly advanced topics and use cases for Git that are beyond the scope of this book. However, you will find that roughly 80% of the time, the preceding commands are all the Git command-line knowledge you need. There are also a number of graphical frontends to Git, as well as code editors and **Integrated Development Environments** (**IDEs**), that integrate with Git repositories and can assist you further in taking advantage of them. With that complete, let's take a look at how to ensure you can use the same playbook (or role) across multiple hosts, even though they might have different OSs and versions.

Setting OS and distribution variances

As stated earlier, our goal is to try to use the same automation code as widely as possible. However, as much as we try to standardize our technology environments, variants always creep in. For example, it is impossible to simultaneously perform a major upgrade on all your servers in one go, so when a major new OS version comes out, such as **Red Hat Enterprise Linux** (**RHEL**) 8 or Ubuntu Server 20.04, it is inevitable that some machines will remain on older versions as others are upgraded. Similarly, an environment might be standardized on Ubuntu, but then an application is introduced that has only been certified to run on CentOS. In short, as important as standardization is, variances will always creep in.

When writing Ansible playbooks, especially roles, your goal should be for them to be as widely applicable as possible throughout your environment. A classic example of this is package management—let's say you are writing a role to install the Apache 2 web server. If you have to support both Ubuntu and CentOS with this role, not only do you have different package managers to deal with (yum and apt) but you also have different package names (httpd and apache2).

In *Chapter 4*, *Playbooks and Roles*, we looked at how to apply conditions to tasks using the when clause, along with facts gathered by Ansible, such as ansible_distribution. However, there is another way of running tasks on specific hosts that we haven't yet looked at. In the same chapter, we also looked at the concept of defining multiple plays in one playbook—there is a special module that can create inventory groups for us based on Ansible facts, and we can leverage this along with multiple plays to create a playbook that runs the appropriate tasks on each host based on its type. This is best explained by a practical example, so let's get started.

Assume that we are using the following simple inventory file for this example, which has two hosts in a single group called app:

```
[app]
app01.dev.example.com
app02.dev.example.com
```

Let's now build a simple playbook that demonstrates how you can group the groups using an Ansible fact so that the OS distribution determines which play in a playbook is run.

Follow these steps to create this playbook and observe its operation:

1. Start by creating a new playbook—we'll call it osvariants.yml—with the following Play definition. It will also contain a single task, as shown:

    ```
    ---
    - name: Play to demonstrate group_by module
      hosts: all

      tasks:
      - name: Create inventory groups based on host facts
        group_by:
          key: os_{{ ansible_facts['distribution'] }}
    ```

    The playbook structure will be, by now, incredibly familiar to you. However, the use of the group_by module is new. It dynamically creates new inventory groups based on the key that we specify—in this example, we are creating groups based on a key comprising the os_ fixed string, followed by the OS distribution fact obtained from the Gathering Facts stage. The original inventory group structure is preserved and unmodified, but all the hosts are also added to the newly created groups according to their facts.

    So, the two servers in our simple inventory remain in the app group, but if they are based on Ubuntu, they will be added to a newly created inventory group called os_Ubuntu. Similarly, if they are based on CentOS, they will be added to a group called os_CentOS.

2. Armed with this information, we can go ahead and create additional plays based on the newly created groups. Let's add the following Play definition to the same playbook file to install Apache on CentOS:

    ```
    - name: Play to install Apache on CentOS
      hosts: os_CentOS
      become: true

      tasks:
      - name: Install Apache on CentOS
        yum:
    ```

```
      name: httpd
      state: present
```

This is a perfectly normal `Play` definition that uses the `yum` module to install the `httpd` package (as required on CentOS). The only thing that differentiates it from our earlier work is the `hosts` definition at the top of the play. This uses the newly created inventory group created by the `group_by` module in the first play.

3. Similarly, we can add a third `Play` definition—this time, for installing the `apache2` package on Ubuntu using the `apt` module:

```
- name: Play to install Apache on Ubuntu
  hosts: os_Ubuntu
  become: true

  tasks:
    - name: Install Apache on Ubuntu
    apt:
      name: apache2
      state: present
```

4. If our environment is based on CentOS servers and we run this playbook, the results are as follows:

```
$ ansible-playbook -i hosts osvariants.yml

PLAY [Play to demonstrate group_by module] ********************
****************

TASK [Gathering Facts] ****************************************
****************
ok: [app02.dev.example.com]
ok: [app01.dev.example.com]

TASK [Create inventory groups based on host facts]
******************************
ok: [app01.dev.example.com]
ok: [app02.dev.example.com]

PLAY [Play to install Apache on CentOS] ***********************
****************

TASK [Gathering Facts] ****************************************
****************
ok: [app01.dev.example.com]
ok: [app02.dev.example.com]
```

```
TASK [Install Apache on CentOS] ********************************
****************
changed: [app02.dev.example.com]
changed: [app01.dev.example.com]
[WARNING]: Could not match supplied host pattern, ignoring: os_
Ubuntu

PLAY [Play to install Apache on Ubuntu] **********************
****************
skipping: no hosts matched

PLAY RECAP ****************************************************
****************
app01.dev.example.com : ok=4 changed=2 unreachable=0 failed=0
skipped=0 rescued=0 ignored=0
app02.dev.example.com : ok=4 changed=2 unreachable=0 failed=0
skipped=0 rescued=0 ignored=0
```

Notice how the task to install Apache on CentOS was run. It was run this way because the group_by module created a group called os_CentOS and our second play only runs on hosts in the group called os_CentOS. As there were no servers running on Ubuntu in the inventory, the os_Ubuntu group was never created and so the third play does not run. We receive a warning about the fact that there is no host pattern that matches os_Ubuntu, but the playbook does not fail—it simply skips this play.

We provided this example to show you another way of managing the inevitable variance in OS types that you will come across in your automation coding. At the end of the day, it is up to you to choose the coding style most appropriate to you. You can make use of the group_by module, as detailed here, or write your tasks in blocks and add a when clause to the blocks so that they only run when a certain fact-based condition is met (for example, the OS distribution is CentOS)—or perhaps even a combination of the two. The choice is ultimately yours, and these different examples are provided to empower you with multiple options that you can choose between to create the best possible solution for your scenario.

Finally, let's round off this chapter with a look at porting your automation code between Ansible versions.

Porting between Ansible versions

Ansible is a fast-moving project, and with releases and new features added, new modules (and module enhancements) are released and the inevitable bugs that come with the software are fixed. There is no doubt that you will end up writing your code against one version of Ansible only to need to run it on a newer version again at some point. By way of example, when we started writing the second edition, the current release of Ansible was 2.15.

Often, you will find that your code from an earlier version *just about works* when you upgrade it, but this isn't always a given. Modules are sometimes deprecated (although usually not without warning) and features do change. You can find more details on the 2.15 release notes here: `https://github.com/ansible/ansible/blob/v2.15.2/changelogs/CHANGELOG-v2.15.rst`.

So, the question remains—how can you ensure that your playbooks, roles, modules, and plugins still work when you update your Ansible installation?

The first part of the answer is to establish which version of Ansible you are starting from. For example, let's say you are preparing for the release of Ansible 2.10. If you query the version of Ansible you already have installed and see something like the following, then you know you are starting from Ansible release 2.15.0:

```
$ ansible [core 2.15.0]
  config file = None
  configured module search path = ['/Users/danieloh/Library/
Python/3.11/bin/plugins/modules', '/usr/share/ansible/plugins/
modules']
  ansible python module location = /Users/danieloh/Library/
Python/3.11/lib/python/site-packages/ansible
  ansible collection location =
/Users/danieloh/Library/Python/3.11/bin/collections:/usr/share/
ansible/collections
  executable location = /Users/danieloh/Library/Python/3.11/bin/
ansible
  python version = 3.11.3 (main, Apr  7 2023, 20:13:31) [Clang 14.0.0
(clang-1400.0.29.202)] (/opt/homebrew/opt/python@3.11/bin/python3.11)
  jinja version = 3.1.2
libyaml = True
```

So, your first port of call should be to review the porting guide for the Ansible release; a porting guide is normally written for every major release (such as 2.10, 8, and so on). Note that Ansible 8 includes Ansible Core 2.15.

The guide for Ansible 8 can be found at `https://docs.ansible.com/ansible/latest/porting_guides/porting_guide_8.html`.

If we review this document, we can see that there are a number of changes coming—whether they are significant to you really depends on the code you are running. For example, if we review the *Added Collections* section of the guide, we can see that the `grafana.grafana` (version `2.0.0`) collection has been added.

As seen in the preceding link, there are several known issues in the eight releases of Ansible. To that end, it is also important to note that the porting guides are written from the perspective of an upgrade from the previous major release. If you query your Ansible version and it returns the following, you are porting from Ansible 2.8:

```
$ ansible --version
ansible 2.8.4
```

```
config file = /etc/ansible/ansible.cfg
configured module search path = [u'/home/james/.ansible/plugins/
modules', u'/usr/share/ansible/plugins/modules']
ansible python module location = /usr/lib/python2.7/site-packages/
ansible
executable location = /usr/bin/ansible
python version = 2.7.5 (default, Aug 7 2019, 00:51:29) [GCC 4.8.5
20150623 (Red Hat 4.8.5-39)]
```

If you move straight to Ansible 8 (Core 2.15), then you need to review the porting guides for both 2.9 (which covers the changes required to your code between releases 2.8 and 2.9) and 2.10 (which covers the changes required to upgrade from 2.9 to 2.10). An index of all the porting guides can be found on the official Ansible website at `https://docs.ansible.com/ansible/devel/porting_guides/porting_guides.html`.

Another great source of information, especially more fine-grained information, on the changes between releases is the changelogs. These are released and updated for every minor release and can currently be found in the official Ansible GitHub repository on the `stable` branch for the release you wish to query. For example, if you wish to review all the changelogs for Ansible 2.15, you would need to go to `https://github.com/ansible/ansible/blob/stable-2.15/changelogs/CHANGELOG-v2.15.rst`.

The trick to porting code between Ansible releases (if, indeed, you can call it a trick) is simply to read the excellent documentation released by the Ansible project team. A lot of effort goes into creating this documentation, so you are advised to make good use of it. That concludes our look at the best practices for working with Ansible. We hope you have found this chapter valuable.

Summary

Ansible automation projects often start out small, but as people come to realize the power and simplicity of Ansible, both the code and the inventories tend to grow at an exponential pace (at least in my experience). It is important that in the push for greater automation, the Ansible automation code and the infrastructure itself don't become another headache. By embedding a few good practices early on and applying them consistently throughout your automation journey with Ansible, you will find that managing your Ansible automation is easy and is a true benefit to your technology infrastructure.

In this chapter, you learned new ways of differentiating environments by OS type, as well as more about variable precedence and how to leverage it when working with host and group variables. You then explored the importance of the top-level playbook, before looking at how to make use of version control tools to manage your automation code. Finally, you explored the new techniques for creating single playbooks that will manage servers of different OS versions and distributions, before finally looking at the important topic of porting your code to new Ansible versions.

In the next chapter, we will look at some of the more advanced ways that you can use Ansible to take care of some special cases that may arise on your automation journey.

Questions

1. What is a safe and easy way to manage (that is, modify, fix, and create) code changes continuously and share them with others?

   A. Playbook revision

   B. Task history

   C. Ad hoc creation

   D. With a Git repository

   E. Log management

2. True or false? Ansible Galaxy supports sharing roles with other users from a central, community-supported repository:

   A. True

   B. False

3. True or false? Ansible modules are guaranteed to be available in all future releases of Ansible:

   A. True

   B. False

Further reading

Manage multiple repositories, versions, or tasks by creating branches and tags to control multiple versions effectively. Refer to the following links for more details:

- How to use Git tagging: `https://git-scm.com/book/en/v2/Git-Basics-Tagging`
- How to use Git branches: `https://git-scm.com/docs/git-branch`

9

Advanced Ansible Topics

Up to this point, we have worked hard to give you a solid foundation in Ansible so that, whatever your desired automation task, you can implement it with ease and confidence. However, when you really start to ramp up your automation, how do you ensure that you can handle any condition that arises in a graceful manner? For example, how can you ensure that when you have to initiate long-running actions, you can run them asynchronously and come back to them to check on the results reliably later? Or, if you are updating a large group of servers, how can you ensure that the play fails early if a handful of servers suffer failures? The last thing you want to do is to roll out a broken update (let's face it, problems do occur with everyone's code from time to time) across 100 servers—far better to detect that a small percentage have failed and abort the entire play on this basis than attempt to continue and break an entire load-balanced cluster.

In this chapter, we will look at how to solve these particular issues, as well as many more, using some of the more advanced features of Ansible to control playbook flow and error handling. We will explore, through practical examples, how to perform rolling updates with Ansible, how to work with proxies and jump hosts (which is vital for secure environments and often for core network configuration), and how to secure sensitive Ansible data at rest using the native Ansible Vault technology. By the end of this chapter, you will have a full picture of how to run Ansible not only in a small environment but also in a large, secure, mission-critical environment.

In this chapter, we will cover the following topics:

- Asynchronous versus synchronous actions
- Controlling play execution for rolling updates
- Configuring the maximum failure percentage
- Setting task execution delegation
- Using the `run_once` option
- Running playbooks locally
- Working with proxies and jump hosts

- Configuring playbook prompts
- Placing tags in the plays and tasks
- Securing data with Ansible Vault

Technical requirements

This chapter assumes that you have set up your control host with Ansible, as detailed in *Chapter 1, Getting Started with Ansible*, and are using the most recent version available. The examples in this chapter are tested with Ansible 2.15. This chapter also assumes that you have at least one additional host to test against and, ideally, this should be Linux-based. Although we will give specific examples of hostnames in this chapter, you are free to substitute them with your own hostname and/or IP addresses; details of how to do this are provided at the appropriate places.

The code bundle for this chapter is available at `https://github.com/PacktPublishing/Practical-Ansible-Second-Edition/tree/main/Chapter%209`.

Asynchronous versus synchronous actions

As we have seen in this book so far, Ansible plays are executed in sequence, with each task running to completion before the next task is started. Although this is often advantageous for flow control and logical sequencing, there are times when you may not want this. In particular, it might be the case that a particular task runs for longer than the configured SSH connection timeout, and as Ansible uses SSH to perform its automation tasks on most platforms, this would be an issue.

Fortunately, Ansible tasks can be run asynchronously—that is to say, tasks can be run in the background on the target host and polled on a regular basis. This is in contrast to synchronous tasks, where the connection to the target host is kept open until the task completes (which runs the risk of a timeout occurring).

As ever, let's explore this through a practical example. Suppose we have two servers in a simple INI-formatted inventory:

```
[frontends]
frt01.example.com
frt02.example.com
```

Now, in order to simulate a long-running task, we'll run the `sleep` command using the `shell` module. However, rather than have it run with the SSH connection blocked for the duration of the `sleep` command, we'll add two special parameters to the task, as shown:

```
---
- name: Play to demonstrate asynchronous tasks
  hosts: frontends
  become: true
```

```
tasks:
  - name: A simulated long running task
    shell: "sleep 20"
    async: 30
    poll: 5
```

The two new parameters are `async` and `poll`. The `async` parameter tells Ansible that this task should be run asynchronously (so that the SSH connection will not be blocked) for a maximum of 30 seconds. If the task runs for longer than this configured time, Ansible considers the task to have failed and the play is failed, accordingly. When `poll` is set to a positive integer, Ansible checks the status of the asynchronous task at the specified interval—in this example, every 5 seconds. If `poll` is set to 0, then the task is run in the background and never checked—it is up to you to write a task to manually check its status later on.

> **Note**
>
> If you don't specify the `poll` value, it will be set to the default value defined by the `DEFAULT_POLL_INTERVAL` configuration parameter of Ansible (which is 10 seconds).

When you run this playbook, you will find that it runs just like any other playbook; from the terminal output, you won't be able to see any difference. But behind the scenes, Ansible checks the task every 5 seconds until it succeeds or reaches the `async` timeout value of 30 seconds:

```
$ ansible-playbook -i hosts async.yml

PLAY [Play to demonstrate asynchronous tasks] ***********************
***********

TASK [Gathering Facts] *********************************************
***********
ok: [frt02.example.com]
ok: [frt01.example.com]

TASK [A simulated long running task] *******************************
***********
changed: [frt02.example.com]
changed: [frt01.example.com]

PLAY RECAP *********************************************************
***********
frt01.example.com : ok=2 changed=1 unreachable=0 failed=0 skipped=0
rescued=0 ignored=0
frt02.example.com : ok=2 changed=1 unreachable=0 failed=0 skipped=0
rescued=0 ignored=0
```

If you want to check on the task later (that is, if `poll` is set to 0), you could add a second task to your playbook so that it looks as follows:

```
---
- name: Play to demonstrate asynchronous tasks
  hosts: frontends
  become: true

tasks:
  - name: A simulated long running task
    shell: "sleep 20"
    async: 30
    poll: 0
    register: long_task

  - name: Check on the asynchronous task
  async_status:
    jid: "{{ long_task.ansible_job_id }}"
  register: async_result
  until: async_result.finished
  retries: 30
```

In this playbook, the initial asynchronous task is defined as before, except we have now set `poll` to 0. We have also chosen to register the result of this task to a variable called `long_task`—this is so that we can query the job ID for the task when we check it later on. The next (new) task in the play uses the `async_status` module to check on the job ID we registered from the first task and loops until the job either finishes or reaches 30 retries—whichever comes first. When using these in a playbook, you almost certainly wouldn't add the two tasks back to back like this—usually, you would perform additional tasks in between them—but to keep this example simple, we will run the two tasks sequentially. Running this playbook should yield an output similar to the following:

```
$ ansible-playbook -i hosts async2.yml

PLAY [Play to demonstrate asynchronous tasks] ***********************
***********

TASK [Gathering Facts] *********************************************
***********
ok: [frt01.example.com]
ok: [frt02.example.com]

TASK [A simulated long running task] *******************************
***********
changed: [frt02.example.com]
changed: [frt01.example.com]
```

```
TASK [Check on the asynchronous task] *****************************
***********
FAILED - RETRYING: Check on the asynchronous task (30 retries left).
FAILED - RETRYING: Check on the asynchronous task (30 retries left).
FAILED - RETRYING: Check on the asynchronous task (29 retries left).
FAILED - RETRYING: Check on the asynchronous task (29 retries left).
FAILED - RETRYING: Check on the asynchronous task (28 retries left).
FAILED - RETRYING: Check on the asynchronous task (28 retries left).
FAILED - RETRYING: Check on the asynchronous task (27 retries left).
FAILED - RETRYING: Check on the asynchronous task (27 retries left).
changed: [frt01.example.com]
changed: [frt02.example.com]


PLAY RECAP ********************************************************
***********
frt01.example.com : ok=3 changed=2 unreachable=0 failed=0 skipped=0
rescued=0 ignored=0
frt02.example.com : ok=3 changed=2 unreachable=0 failed=0 skipped=0
rescued=0 ignored=0
```

In the preceding code block, we can see that the long-running task is left running and the next task polls its status until the conditions we set are met. In this case, we can see that the task finished successfully and the overall play result was successful. Asynchronous actions are especially useful for large downloads, package updates, and other tasks that might take a long time to run. You may find them useful in your playbook development, especially in more complex infrastructures.

With this under our belt, let's take a look at another advanced technique that might be useful in large infrastructures—performing rolling updates with Ansible.

Controlling play execution for rolling updates

By default, Ansible parallelizes tasks on multiple hosts at the same time to speed up automation tasks in large inventories. The setting for this is defined by the `forks` parameter in the Ansible configuration file, which defaults to 5 (so, by default, Ansible attempts to run its automation job on five hosts at the same time).

In a load-balanced environment, this is not ideal, especially if you want to avoid downtime. Suppose we have five frontend servers in an inventory (or perhaps even fewer). If we allow Ansible to update all of these at the same time, the end users may experience a loss of service. So, it is important to consider updating all of the servers at different times. Let's reuse our inventory from the previous section with just two servers in it. Obviously, if these were in a load-balanced environment, it would be vital that we only update one of these at a time; if both were taken out of service simultaneously, then end users would definitely lose access to the service until the Ansible play completes successfully.

The answer to this is to use the `serial` keyword in the play definition to determine how many hosts are operated on at once. Let's demonstrate this through a practical example:

1. Create the following simple playbook to run two commands on the two hosts in our inventory. The content of the command is not important at this stage, but if you run the `date` command using the `command` module, you will be able to see the time that each task is run, as well as if you specify `-v` to increase the verbosity when you run the play:

    ```
    ---
    - name: Simple serial demonstration play
      hosts: frontends
      gather_facts: false

      tasks:
        - name: First task
          command: date
        - name: Second task
          command: date
    ```

2. Now, if you run this play, you will see that it performs all the operations on each host simultaneously, as we have fewer hosts than the default number of forks—5. This behavior is normal for Ansible, but not really what we want as our users will experience a service outage:

    ```
    $ ansible-playbook -i hosts serial.yml

    PLAY [Simple serial demonstration play] ************************
    ****************

    TASK [First task] *********************************************
    ****************
    changed: [frt02.example.com]
    changed: [frt01.example.com]

    TASK [Second task] ********************************************
    ****************
    changed: [frt01.example.com]
    changed: [frt02.example.com]


    PLAY RECAP ****************************************************
    ****************
    frt01.example.com : ok=2 changed=2 unreachable=0 failed=0
    skipped=0 rescued=0 ignored=0
    frt02.example.com : ok=2 changed=2 unreachable=0 failed=0
    skipped=0 rescued=0 ignored=0
    ```

3. Now, modify the play definition, as shown. We will leave the `tasks` sections exactly as they were in *Step 1*:

```
---
- name: Simple serial demonstration play
  hosts: frontends
  serial: 1
  gather_facts: false
```

4. Notice the presence of the `serial: 1` line. This tells Ansible to complete the play on `1` host at a time before moving on to the next. If we run the play again, we can see this in action:

```
$ ansible-playbook -i hosts serial.yml

PLAY [Simple serial demonstration play] ************************
****************

TASK [First task] *********************************************
****************
changed: [frt01.example.com]

TASK [Second task] ********************************************
****************
changed: [frt01.example.com]

PLAY [Simple serial demonstration play] ************************
****************

TASK [First task] *********************************************
****************
changed: [frt02.example.com]

TASK [Second task] ********************************************
****************
changed: [frt02.example.com]

PLAY RECAP ****************************************************
****************
frt01.example.com : ok=2 changed=2 unreachable=0 failed=0
skipped=0 rescued=0 ignored=0
frt02.example.com : ok=2 changed=2 unreachable=0 failed=0
skipped=0 rescued=0 ignored=0
```

Much better! If you imagine that this playbook actually disables these hosts on a load balancer, performs an upgrade, and then re-enables the hosts on the load balancer, this is exactly how you would want the operation to proceed. Doing so without the `serial: 1` directive would result in all the hosts being removed from the load balancer at once, causing a loss of service.

It is useful to note that the `serial` directive can also take a percentage instead of an integer. When you specify a percentage, you are telling Ansible to run the play on that percentage of hosts at one time. So, if you have four hosts in your inventory and specify `serial: 25%`, Ansible will only run the play on one host at a time. If you have eight hosts in your inventory, it will run the play on two hosts at a time. I'm sure you get the idea!

You can even build on this by passing a list to the `serial` directive. Consider the following code:

```
serial:
- 1
- 3
- 5
```

This tells Ansible to run the play on 1 host, initially, then on the next 3, and then on batches of 5 at a time until the inventory is completed for deploying a new change to particular servers. You can also specify a list of percentages in place of the integer numbers of hosts. In doing this, you will build up a robust playbook that can perform rolling updates without causing a loss of service to end users. With this complete, let's further build on this knowledge by looking at controlling the maximum failure percentage that Ansible can tolerate before it aborts a play, which will again be useful in highly available or load-balanced environments such as this.

Configuring the maximum failure percentage

In its default mode of operation, Ansible continues to execute a play on a batch of servers (the batch size is determined by the `serial` directive we discussed in the preceding section) as long as there are hosts in the inventory and a failure isn't recorded. Obviously, in a highly available or load-balanced environment (such as the one we discussed previously), this is not ideal. If there is a bug in your play, or perhaps a problem with the code being rolled out, the last thing that you want is for Ansible to faithfully roll it out to all servers in the cluster, causing a service outage because all the nodes suffered a failed upgrade. It would be far better, in this kind of environment, to fail early on and leave at least some hosts in the cluster untouched until someone can intervene and resolve the issue.

For our practical example, let's consider an expanded inventory with 10 hosts in it. We'll define this as follows:

```
[frontends]
frt[01:10].example.com
```

Now, let's create a simple playbook to run on these hosts. We will set our batch size to 5 and `max_fail_percentage` to `50%` in the play definition:

1. Create the following play definition to demonstrate the use of the `max_fail_percentage` directive:

    ```
    ---
    - name: A simple play to demonstrate use of max_fail_percentage
    ```

```
hosts: frontends
gather_facts: no
serial: 5
max_fail_percentage: 50
```

We have defined 10 hosts in our inventory, so it will process them in batches of 5 (as specified by `serial: 5`). The play will be aborted, and processing will stop if more than 50% of the hosts in one batch fail.

> **Note**
>
> The percentage of failed hosts must exceed the value of `max_fail_percentage`; if it is equal, the play continues.

2. Next, we will define two simple tasks. The first task has a special clause under it that we use to deliberately simulate a failure—this line starts with `failed_when` and we use it to tell the task that if it runs this task on the first three hosts in the batch, then it should deliberately fail this task, regardless of the result; otherwise, it should allow the task to run as normal:

```
tasks:
- name: A task that will sometimes fail
  debug:
    msg: This might fail
  failed_when: inventory_hostname in ansible_play_batch[0:3]
```

3. Finally, we will add a second task that will always succeed. This is run if the play is allowed to continue, but not if it is aborted:

```
- name: A task that will succeed
  debug:
    msg: Success!
```

So, we have deliberately constructed a playbook that will run on a 10-host inventory in batches of 5 hosts at a time, but the play is aborted if more than 50% of the hosts in any given batch experience a failure. We have also deliberately set up a failure condition that causes 3 of the hosts in the first batch of 5 (60%) to fail.

4. Run the playbook and observe what happens:

```
$ ansible-playbook -i morehosts maxfail.yml

PLAY [A simple play to demonstrate use of max_fail_percentage]
*****************

TASK [A task that will sometimes fail] *************************
*****************
fatal: [frt01.example.com]: FAILED! => {
```

```
  "msg": "This might fail"
}
fatal: [frt02.example.com]: FAILED! => {
 "msg": "This might fail"
}
fatal: [frt03.example.com]: FAILED! => {
 "msg": "This might fail"
}
ok: [frt04.example.com] => {
 "msg": "This might fail"
}
ok: [frt05.example.com] => {
 "msg": "This might fail"
}


NO MORE HOSTS LEFT *********************************************
****************

NO MORE HOSTS LEFT *********************************************
****************

PLAY RECAP ****************************************************
****************
frt01.example.com : ok=0 changed=0 unreachable=0 failed=1
skipped=0 rescued=0 ignored=0
frt02.example.com : ok=0 changed=0 unreachable=0 failed=1
skipped=0 rescued=0 ignored=0
frt03.example.com : ok=0 changed=0 unreachable=0 failed=1
skipped=0 rescued=0 ignored=0
frt04.example.com : ok=1 changed=0 unreachable=0 failed=0
skipped=0 rescued=0 ignored=0
frt05.example.com : ok=1 changed=0 unreachable=0 failed=0
skipped=0 rescued=0 ignored=0
```

Notice the results of this playbook. We deliberately failed three of the first batch of five, exceeding the threshold for max_fail_percentage that we set. This immediately causes the play to abort and the second task is not performed on the first batch of five. You will also notice that the second batch of 5, out of the 10 hosts, is never processed, so our play was truly aborted. This is exactly the behavior you would want to see to prevent a failed update from rolling out across a cluster. Through the careful use of batches and max_fail_percentage, you can safely run automated tasks across an entire cluster without the fear of breaking the entire cluster in the event of an issue. In the next section, we will take a look at another feature of Ansible that can be incredibly useful when it comes to working with clusters—task delegation.

Setting task execution delegation

In every play we have run so far, we have assumed that all the tasks are executed on each host in the inventory in turn. However, what if you need to run one or two tasks on a different host? For example, we have talked about the concept of automating upgrades on clusters. Logically, however, we would want to automate the entire process, including the removal of each host in turn from the load balancer and their return after the task is completed.

Although we still want to run our play across our entire inventory, we certainly don't want to run the load balancer commands from those hosts. Let's once again explain this in more detail with a practical example. We'll reuse the two simple host inventories that we used earlier in this chapter:

```
[frontends]
frt01.example.com
frt02.example.com
```

Now, to work on this, let's create two simple shell scripts in the same directory as our playbook. These are only examples, as setting up a load balancer is beyond the scope of this book. However, imagine that you have a shell script (or other executables) that you can call that can add and remove hosts to and from a load balancer:

1. For our example, create a script called `remove_from_loadbalancer.sh`, which will contain the following:

    ```
    #!/bin/sh
    echo Removing $1 from load balancer...
    ```

2. We will also create a script called `add_to_loadbalancer.sh`, which will contain the following:

    ```
    #!/bin/sh
    echo Adding $1 to load balancer...
    ```

    Obviously, in a real-world example, there would be much more code in these scripts!

3. Now, create a playbook that will perform the logic we outlined here. We will first create a quite simple play definition (you are free to experiment with the `serial` and `max_fail_percentage` directives as you wish) and an initial task:

    ```
    ---

    - name: Play to demonstrate task delegation
      hosts: frontends

      tasks:
        - name: Remove host from the load balancer
          command: ./remove_from_loadbalancer.sh {{ inventory_
    hostname }}
    ```

```
    args:
      chdir: "{{ playbook_dir }}"
  delegate_to: localhost
```

Notice the task structure—most of it will be familiar to you. We are using the `command` module to call the script we created earlier, passing the hostname from the inventory being removed from the load balancer to the script. We use the `chdir` argument with the `playbook_dir` magic variable to tell Ansible that the script is to be run from the same directory as the playbook.

The special part of this task is the `delegate_to` directive, which tells Ansible that even though we're iterating through an inventory that does not contain `localhost`, we should run this action on `localhost` (we are not copying the script to our remote hosts, so it will not run if we attempt to run it from there).

4. After this, we add a task where the upgrade work is carried out. This task has no `delegate_to` directive, so it is run on the remote host from the inventory (as desired):

```
- name: Deploy code to host
  debug:
    msg: Deployment code would go here....
```

5. Finally, we add the host back to the load balancer using the second script we created earlier. This task is almost identical to the first:

```
- name: Add host back to the load balancer
  command: ./add_to_loadbalancer.sh {{ inventory_hostname }}
  args:
    chdir: "{{ playbook_dir }}"
  delegate_to: localhost
```

6. See this playbook in action:

```
$ ansible-playbook -i hosts delegate.yml


PLAY [Play to demonstrate task delegation] ********************
****************


TASK [Gathering Facts] ****************************************
****************
ok: [frt01.example.com]
ok: [frt02.example.com]


TASK [Remove host from the load balancer] *********************
****************
changed: [frt02.example.com -> localhost]
changed: [frt01.example.com -> localhost]
```

```
TASK [Deploy code to host] **************************************
****************
ok: [frt01.example.com] => {
  "msg": "Deployment code would go here...."
}
ok: [frt02.example.com] => {
  "msg": "Deployment code would go here...."
}

TASK [Add host back to the load balancer] **********************
****************
changed: [frt01.example.com -> localhost]
changed: [frt02.example.com -> localhost]

PLAY RECAP *****************************************************
****************
frt01.example.com : ok=4 changed=2 unreachable=0 failed=0
skipped=0 rescued=0 ignored=0
frt02.example.com : ok=4 changed=2 unreachable=0 failed=0
skipped=0 rescued=0 ignored=0
```

Notice how even though Ansible is working through the inventory (which doesn't feature localhost), the load balancer-related scripts are actually run from localhost, while the upgrade task is performed directly on the remote host. This, of course, isn't the only thing you can do with task delegation, but it's a common example of a way that it can help you.

In truth, you can delegate any task to localhost, or even another non-inventory host. You could, for example, run an rsync command delegated to localhost to copy files to remote hosts using a similar task definition to the previous one. Also, note that you can choose to use a form of shorthand notation in your playbooks (and roles) for delegate_to, called local_action. This allows you to specify a task on a single line that would ordinarily be run with delegate_to: localhost added below it. Wrapping this all up into a second example, our playbook will look as follows:

```
---
- name: Second task delegation example
  hosts: frontends

  tasks:
  - name: Perform an rsync from localhost to inventory hosts
    local_action: command rsync -a /tmp/ {{ inventory_hostname }}:/
tmp/target/
```

The preceding shorthand notation is equivalent to the following:

```
tasks:
- name: Perform an rsync from localhost to inventory hosts
```

```
command: rsync -a /tmp/ {{ inventory_hostname }}:/tmp/target/
delegate_to: localhost
```

If we run this playbook, we can see that `local_action` simply runs a module on the machine running Ansible (which is often `localhost`, but not necessarily always), enabling us to efficiently copy whole directory trees across to remote servers in the inventory:

```
$ ansible-playbook -i hosts delegate2.yml

PLAY [Second task delegation example] ******************************
***********

TASK [Gathering Facts] *********************************************
***********
ok: [frt02.example.com]
ok: [frt01.example.com]

TASK [Perform a rsync from localhost to inventory hosts]
***********************
changed: [frt02.example.com -> localhost]
changed: [frt01.example.com -> localhost]

PLAY RECAP *********************************************************
***********
frt01.example.com: ok=2 changed=1 unreachable=0 failed=0 skipped=0
rescued=0 ignored=0
frt02.example.com: ok=2 changed=1 unreachable=0 failed=0 skipped=0
rescued=0 ignored=0
```

This concludes our look at task delegation; although, as stated, these are just two common examples. I'm sure you can think up some more advanced use cases for this capability. Let's continue looking at controlling the flow of Ansible code by proceeding, in the next section, to look at the special `run_once` option.

Using the run_once option

When working with clusters, you will sometimes encounter a task that should only be executed once for the entire cluster. For example, you might want to upgrade the schema of a clustered database or issue a command to reconfigure a Pacemaker cluster, which would typically be issued on one node and then automatically propagated to all other nodes by the cluster management software. You could, of course, address this with a special inventory with only one host in it, or even by writing a special play that references one host from the inventory, but this is inefficient and starts to make your code fragmented.

Instead, you can write your code as you normally would but make use of the special `run_once` directive for any tasks you want to run only once on your inventory. For example, let's reuse the 10-host inventory that we defined earlier in this chapter. Now, let's proceed to demonstrate this option, as follows:

1. Create the simple playbook as in the following code block. We are using a `debug` statement to display some output, but in real life, you would insert your script or command that performs your one-off cluster function here (for example, upgrading a database schema):

```
---
- name: Play to demonstrate the run_once directive
  hosts: frontends

  tasks:
    - name: Upgrade database schema
      debug:
        msg: Upgrading database schema...
      run_once: true
```

2. Now, run this playbook and see what happens:

```
$ ansible-playbook -i morehosts runonce.yml

PLAY [Play to demonstrate the run_once directive]
********************************

TASK [Gathering Facts] *****************************************
*****************
ok: [frt02.example.com]
ok: [frt05.example.com]
ok: [frt03.example.com]
ok: [frt01.example.com]
ok: [frt04.example.com]
ok: [frt06.example.com]
ok: [frt08.example.com]
ok: [frt09.example.com]
ok: [frt07.example.com]
ok: [frt10.example.com]

TASK [Upgrade database schema] **********************************
*****************
ok: [frt01.example.com] => {
  "msg": "Upgrading database schema..."
}
---
```

```
PLAY RECAP *****************************************************
****************
frt01.example.com : ok=2 changed=0 unreachable=0 failed=0
skipped=0 rescued=0 ignored=0
frt02.example.com : ok=1 changed=0 unreachable=0 failed=0
skipped=0 rescued=0 ignored=0
frt03.example.com : ok=1 changed=0 unreachable=0 failed=0
skipped=0 rescued=0 ignored=0
frt04.example.com : ok=1 changed=0 unreachable=0 failed=0
skipped=0 rescued=0 ignored=0
frt05.example.com : ok=1 changed=0 unreachable=0 failed=0
skipped=0 rescued=0 ignored=0
frt06.example.com : ok=1 changed=0 unreachable=0 failed=0
skipped=0 rescued=0 ignored=0
frt07.example.com : ok=1 changed=0 unreachable=0 failed=0
skipped=0 rescued=0 ignored=0
frt08.example.com : ok=1 changed=0 unreachable=0 failed=0
skipped=0 rescued=0 ignored=0
frt09.example.com : ok=1 changed=0 unreachable=0 failed=0
skipped=0 rescued=0 ignored=0
frt10.example.com : ok=1 changed=0 unreachable=0 failed=0
skipped=0 rescued=0 ignored=0
```

Notice that, just as desired, although the playbook was run on all 10 hosts (and, indeed, gathered facts from all 10 hosts), Ansible only ran the upgrade task on one host.

3. It is important to note that the run_once option applies per batch of servers, so if we add serial: 5 to our play definition (running our play in 2 batches of 5 on our inventory of 10 servers), the schema upgrade task runs twice! It runs once as requested, but once per batch of servers, not once for the entire inventory. Be careful of this nuance when working with this directive in a clustered environment.

    Add serial: 5 to your play definition and rerun the playbook. The output should appear as follows:

    ```
    $ ansible-playbook -i morehosts runonce.yml


    PLAY [Play to demonstrate the run_once directive]
    *******************************


    TASK [Gathering Facts] *********************************
    ****************
    ok: [frt04.example.com]
    ok: [frt01.example.com]
    ok: [frt02.example.com]
    ok: [frt03.example.com]
    ok: [frt05.example.com]
    ```

```
TASK [Upgrade database schema] ********************************
****************
ok: [frt01.example.com] => {
  "msg": "Upgrading database schema..."
}


PLAY [Play to demonstrate the run_once directive]
******************************

TASK [Gathering Facts] ***********************************
****************
ok: [frt08.example.com]
ok: [frt06.example.com]
ok: [frt07.example.com]
ok: [frt10.example.com]
ok: [frt09.example.com]

TASK [Upgrade database schema] ********************************
****************
ok: [frt06.example.com] => {
  "msg": "Upgrading database schema..."
}


PLAY RECAP ***************************************************
****************
frt01.example.com : ok=2 changed=0 unreachable=0 failed=0
skipped=0 rescued=0 ignored=0
frt02.example.com : ok=1 changed=0 unreachable=0 failed=0
skipped=0 rescued=0 ignored=0
frt03.example.com : ok=1 changed=0 unreachable=0 failed=0
skipped=0 rescued=0 ignored=0
frt04.example.com : ok=1 changed=0 unreachable=0 failed=0
skipped=0 rescued=0 ignored=0
frt05.example.com : ok=1 changed=0 unreachable=0 failed=0
skipped=0 rescued=0 ignored=0
frt06.example.com : ok=2 changed=0 unreachable=0 failed=0
skipped=0 rescued=0 ignored=0
frt07.example.com : ok=1 changed=0 unreachable=0 failed=0
skipped=0 rescued=0 ignored=0
frt08.example.com : ok=1 changed=0 unreachable=0 failed=0
skipped=0 rescued=0 ignored=0
frt09.example.com : ok=1 changed=0 unreachable=0 failed=0
skipped=0 rescued=0 ignored=0
frt10.example.com : ok=1 changed=0 unreachable=0 failed=0
skipped=0 rescued=0 ignored=0
```

This is how the `run_once` option is designed to work—you can observe, in the preceding output, that our schema upgrade ran twice, which is probably not something we wanted! However, with this awareness, you should be able to take advantage of this option to control your playbook flow across clusters and still achieve the results you want. Let's now move away from cluster-related Ansible tasks and look at the subtle but important difference between running playbooks locally and running them on `localhost`.

Running playbooks locally

It is important to note that when we talk about running a playbook locally with Ansible, it is not the same as talking about running it on `localhost`. If we run a playbook on `localhost`, Ansible actually sets up an SSH connection to `localhost` (it doesn't differentiate its behavior or attempt to detect whether a host in the inventory is local or remote—it simply tries faithfully to connect).

Indeed, we can try creating a `local` inventory file with the following contents:

```
[local]
localhost
```

Now, if we attempt to run the `ping` module in an ad hoc command against this inventory, we see the following:

```
$ ansible -i localhosts -m ping all --ask-pass
The authenticity of host 'localhost (::1)' can't be established.
ECDSA key fingerprint is
SHA256:DUwVxH+45432pSr9qsN8Av4l0KJJ+r5jTo123n3XGvZs.
ECDSA key fingerprint is
MD5:78:d1:dc:23:cc:28:51:42:eb:fb:58:49:ab:92:b6:96.
Are you sure you want to continue connecting (yes/no)? yes
SSH password:
localhost | SUCCESS => {
 "ansible_facts": {
 "discovered_interpreter_python": "/usr/bin/python"
 },
 "changed": false,
 "ping": "pong"
}
```

As you can see, Ansible set up an SSH connection that needed the host key to validate, as well as our SSH password. Now, although you could add the host key (as we did in the preceding code block), add key-based SSH authentication to your `localhost`, and so on, there is a more direct way of doing this.

We can now modify our inventory so that it looks as follows:

```
[local]
localhost ansible_connection=local
```

We've added a special variable to our `localhost` entry—the `ansible_connection` variable—which defines which protocol is used to connect to this inventory host. So, we have told it to use a direct local connection instead of SSH-based connectivity (which is the default).

It should be noted that `ansible_connection` specifies the type of communication, such as `local/ssh/etc`. So, if we change our inventory to look as follows, Ansible will not even attempt to connect to the remote host called `frt01.example.com`—it will connect locally to the machine running the playbook (without SSH):

```
[local]
frt01.example.com ansible_connection=local
```

We can demonstrate this very simply. Let's first check for the absence of a test file in our local `/tmp` directory:

```
ls -l /tmp/foo
ls: cannot access /tmp/foo: No such file or directory
```

Now, let's run an ad hoc command to touch this file on all hosts in the new inventory we just defined:

```
$ ansible -i localhosts2 -m file -a "path=/tmp/foo state=touch" all
frt01.example.com | CHANGED => {
 "ansible_facts": {
 "discovered_interpreter_python": "/usr/bin/python"
 },
 "changed": true,
 "dest": "/tmp/foo",
 "gid": 0,
 "group": "root",
 "mode": "0644",
 "owner": "root",
 "size": 0,
 "state": "file",
 "uid": 0
}
```

The command ran successfully, so let's see whether the test file is present on the local machine:

```
$ ls -l /tmp/foo
-rw-r--r-- 1 root root 0 Apr 24 16:28 /tmp/foo
```

It is! So, the ad hoc command did not attempt to connect to `frt01.example.com`, even though this hostname was in the inventory. The presence of `ansible_connection=local` meant that this command was run on the local machine without using SSH.

This ability to run commands locally without the need to set up SSH connectivity, SSH keys, and so on can be incredibly valuable, especially if you need to get things up and running quickly on your local machine. With this complete, let's take a look at how you can work with proxies and jump hosts using Ansible.

Working with proxies and jump hosts

Often, when it comes to configuring core network devices, these are isolated from the main network via a proxy or jump host. Ansible lends itself well to automating network device configuration as most of it is performed over SSH; however, this is only helpful in a scenario where Ansible can either be installed and operated from the jump host or, better yet, can operate via a host such as this.

Fortunately, Ansible can do exactly that. Let's assume that you have two Cumulus Networks switches in your network (these are based on a special distribution of Linux for switching hardware, which is very similar to Debian). These two switches have the `cmls01.example.com` and `cmls02.example.com` hostnames, but both can only be accessed from a host called `bastion.example.com`.

The configuration to support our `bastion` host is performed in the inventory, rather than in the playbook. We begin by defining an inventory group with the switches in, in the normal manner:

```
[switches]
cmls01.example.com
cmls02.example.com
```

However, we can now start to get clever by adding some special SSH arguments into the inventory variables for this group. Add the following code to your inventory file:

```
[switches:vars]
ansible_ssh_common_args='-o ProxyCommand="ssh -W %h:%p -q bastion.
example.com"'
```

This special variable content tells Ansible to add extra options when it sets up an SSH connection, including to proxy via the `bastion.example.com` host. The `-W %h:%p` options tell SSH to proxy the connection and to connect to the host specified by `%h` (this is either `cmls01.example.com` or `cmls02.example.com`) on the port specified by `%p` (usually port 22).

Now, if we attempt to run the Ansible `ping` module against this inventory, we can see whether it works:

```
$ ansible -i switches -m ping all
cmls02.example.com | SUCCESS => {
  "ansible_facts": {
```

```
  "discovered_interpreter_python": "/usr/bin/python"
  },
  "changed": false,



cmls01.example.com | SUCCESS => {
 "ansible_facts": {
 "discovered_interpreter_python": "/usr/bin/python"
 },
 "changed": false,
 "ping": "pong"
}
```

You will notice that we can't actually see any differences in Ansible's behavior from the command-line output. On the surface, Ansible works just as it normally does and connects successfully to the two hosts. However, behind the scenes, it proxies via bastion.example.com.

Note that this simple example assumes that you are connecting to both the bastion host and switches using the same username and SSH credentials (or in this case, keys). There are ways to provide separate credentials for both variables, but this involves more advanced usage of OpenSSH, which is beyond the scope of this book. However, this section intends to give you a starting point and demonstrate the possibility of this, and you are free to explore OpenSSH proxying by yourself.

Let's now change track and explore how it is possible to set up Ansible to prompt you for data during a playbook run.

Configuring playbook prompts

So far, all of our playbooks have had their data specified for them at runtime in variables we defined within the playbook. However, what if you actually want to obtain information from someone during a playbook run? Perhaps you want a user to select a version of a package to install? Or, perhaps you want to obtain a password from a user for an authentication task without storing it anywhere. (Although Ansible Vault can encrypt the data at rest, some companies may forbid the storing of passwords and other such credentials in tools that they have not evaluated.) Fortunately, for these instances (and many more), Ansible can prompt you for user input and store the input in a variable for future processing.

Let's reuse the two host frontend inventories we defined at the beginning of this chapter. Now, let's demonstrate how to capture data from users during a playbook run with a practical example:

1. Create a simple play definition in the usual manner, as follows:

```
   ---
   - name: A simple play to demonstrate prompting in a playbook
     hosts: frontends
```

2. Now, we will add a special section to the play definition. We previously defined a `vars` section, but this time, we will define one called `vars_prompt` (which enables you to do just that—define variables through user prompts). In this section, we will prompt for two variables—one for a user ID and one for a password. One will be echoed to the screen, while the other will not be, by setting `private: yes`:

```
vars_prompt:
  - name: loginid
    prompt: "Enter your username"
    private: no
  - name: password
    prompt: "Enter your password"
    private: yes
```

3. We will now add a single task to our playbook to demonstrate this prompting process of setting the variables:

```
tasks:
- name: Proceed with login
  debug:
    msg: "Logging in as {{ loginid }}..."
```

4. Now, run the playbook and see how it behaves:

```
$ ansible-playbook -i hosts prompt.yml
Enter your username: james
Enter your password:

PLAY [A simple play to demonstrate prompting in a playbook]
********************

TASK [Gathering Facts] *****************************************
****************
ok: [frt01.example.com]
ok: [frt02.example.com]

TASK [Proceed with login] **************************************
****************
ok: [frt01.example.com] => {
  "msg": "Logging in as james..."
}
ok: [frt02.example.com] => {
  "msg": "Logging in as james..."
}


PLAY RECAP *****************************************************
****************
```

```
frt01.example.com : ok=2 changed=0 unreachable=0 failed=0
skipped=0 rescued=0 ignored=0
frt02.example.com : ok=2 changed=0 unreachable=0 failed=0
skipped=0 rescued=0 ignored=0
```

As you can see, we are prompted for both variables, yet the password is not echoed to the terminal, which is important for security reasons. We can then make use of the variables later in the playbook. Here, we just used a simple `debug` command to demonstrate that the variables have been set; however, you would instead implement an actual authentication function in place of this.

With this complete, let's proceed to the next section and look at how you can selectively run your tasks from within your plays with the use of tags.

Placing tags in the plays and tasks

We have discussed, at many points in this book, that as your confidence and experience with Ansible grows, it is likely that your playbooks will grow, both in scale and complexity. While this is undoubtedly a good thing, there may be times when you only want to run a subset of a playbook, rather than running it from beginning to end. We discussed how to conditionally run tasks based on the value of a variable or fact, but is there a way we can run them based on a selection made when the playbook is run?

Tags in Ansible plays are the solution to this, and in this section, we will build a simple playbook with two tasks—each bearing a different tag—to show you how tags work. We will work with the two simple host inventories that we worked with previously:

1. Create the following simple playbook to perform two tasks—one to install the `nginx` package and the other to deploy a configuration file from a template:

```
---
- name: Simple play to demonstrate use of tags
  hosts: frontends

  tasks:
    - name: Install nginx
      yum:
        name: nginx
        state: present
      tags:
        - install

    - name: Install nginx configuration from template
      template:
        src: templates/nginx.conf.j2
        dest: /etc/nginx.conf
      tags:
        - customize
```

2. Now, run the playbook in the usual manner, but with one difference—this time, we will add the `--tags` switch to the command line. This switch tells Ansible to only run the tasks that have tags matching the ones that are specified. So, for example, run the following command:

```
$ ansible-playbook -i hosts tags.yml --tags install

PLAY [Simple play to demonstrate use of tags] *****************
****************

TASK [Gathering Facts] ****************************************
****************
ok: [frt02.example.com]
ok: [frt01.example.com]

TASK [Install nginx] ******************************************
***************
changed: [frt02.example.com]
changed: [frt01.example.com]

PLAY RECAP ****************************************************
****************
frt01.example.com : ok=2 changed=1 unreachable=0 failed=0
skipped=0 rescued=0 ignored=0
frt02.example.com : ok=2 changed=1 unreachable=0 failed=0
skipped=0 rescued=0 ignored=0
```

Notice that the task to deploy the configuration file does not run. This is because it is tagged with customize and we did not specify this tag when running the playbook.

3. There is also a `--skip-tags` switch that does the reverse of the previous switch—it tells Ansible to skip the tags listed. So, if we run the playbook again but skip the customize tag, we should see an output like the following:

```
$ ansible-playbook -i hosts tags.yml --skip-tags customize

PLAY [Simple play to demonstrate use of tags] *****************
****************

TASK [Gathering Facts] ****************************************
****************
ok: [frt02.example.com]
ok: [frt01.example.com]

TASK [Install nginx] ******************************************
***************
ok: [frt02.example.com]
ok: [frt01.example.com]
```

```
PLAY RECAP *****************************************************
****************
frt01.example.com : ok=2 changed=0 unreachable=0 failed=0
skipped=0 rescued=0 ignored=0
frt02.example.com : ok=2 changed=0 unreachable=0 failed=0
skipped=0 rescued=0 ignored=0
```

This play run is identical because, rather than including only the install-tagged tasks, we skipped the tasks tagged with customize.

Note that if you do not specify either --tags or --skip-tags, then all the tasks are run, regardless of their tag.

A few notes about tags. First of all, each task can have more than one tag, so we see them specified in a YAML list format. If you use the --tags switch, a task will run if any of its tags match the tag that was specified on the command line. Secondly, tags can be reused, so we could have five tasks that are all tagged install, and all five tasks would be performed or skipped if you requested them to do so via --tags or --skip-tags, respectively.

You can also specify more than one tag on the command line, running all the tasks that match any of the specified tags. Although the logic behind tags is relatively simple, it can take a little while to get used to it, and the last thing you want to do is run your playbook on real hosts to check whether you understand tagging! A great way to figure this out is to add --list-tasks to your command, which, rather than running the playbook, lists the tasks from the playbook that would perform if you run it. Some examples are provided for you in the following code block, based on the example playbook we just created:

```
$ ansible-playbook -i hosts tags.yml --skip-tags customize --list-
tasks

playbook: tags.yml

  play #1 (frontends): Simple play to demonstrate use of tags TAGS: []
  tasks:
  Install nginx TAGS: [install]

$ ansible-playbook -i hosts tags.yml --tags install,customize --list-
tasks

playbook: tags.yml

  play #1 (frontends): Simple play to demonstrate use of tags TAGS: []
  tasks:
  Install nginx TAGS: [install]
  Install nginx configuration from template TAGS: [customize]
```

```
$ ansible-playbook -i hosts tags.yml --list-tasks

playbook: tags.yml

  play #1 (frontends): Simple play to demonstrate use of tags TAGS: []
  tasks:
  Install nginx TAGS: [install]
  Install nginx configuration from template TAGS: [customize]
```

As you can see, not only does `--list-tasks` show you which tasks would run but it also shows you which tags are associated with them, which helps you further understand how tagging works and ensure that you achieve the playbook flow that you wanted. Tags are an incredibly simple yet powerful way to control which parts of your playbook run and, often, when it comes to creating and maintaining large playbooks, it is better to be able to run only selected parts of the playbook at once. From here, we will move on to the final section of this chapter, where we will look at securing your variable data at rest by encrypting it with Ansible Vault.

Securing data with Ansible Vault

Ansible Vault is a tool included with Ansible that allows you to encrypt your sensitive data at rest, while also using it in a playbook. Often, it is necessary to store login credentials or other sensitive data in a variable to allow a playbook to run unattended. However, this risks exposing your data to people who might use it with malicious intent. Fortunately, Ansible Vault secures your data at rest using AES-256 encryption, meaning your sensitive data is safe from prying eyes.

Let's proceed with a simple example that shows you how you can use Ansible Vault:

1. Start by creating a new vault to store sensitive data in; we will call this file `secret.yml`. You can create this using the following command:

   ```
   $ ansible-vault create secret.yml
   New Vault password:
   Confirm New Vault password:
   ```

   Enter the password you have chosen for the vault when prompted and confirm it by entering it a second time (the vault that accompanies this book on GitHub is encrypted with the `secure` password).

2. When you have entered the password, you will be sent to your normal editor (defined by the `EDITOR` shell variable). On my test system, this is `vi`. Within this editor, you should create a `vars` file, in the normal manner, containing your sensitive data:

   ```
   ---
   secretdata: "Ansible is cool!"
   ```

3. Save and exit the editor (press *Esc*, then `:wq` in `vi`). You will exit the shell. Now, if you look at the contents of your file, you will see that they are encrypted and are safe from anyone who should not be able to read the file:

```
$ cat secret.yml
$ANSIBLE_VAULT;1.1;AES256
63333734623764633865633237333166333634353334373862346334646363130
3163653931306138
6334356465396463643936323163323132373836336461370a34323638626631
3331653964326334
6236373766316533653963332623666363833643436633963356436356234636 2
6336643732613830
6139363035373736370a6466613964643863646539356363663663666326163
3538626230616630
3534646534643063646332383861303738663633333343562656239646337633 3
3532366561323266
3664613662643263383464643734633632383138363663323730
```

4. However, the important thing about Ansible Vault is that you can use this encrypted file in a playbook as if it were a normal `variables` file (although, obviously, you must tell Ansible your vault password). Create a simple playbook as follows:

```
---
- name: A play that makes use of an Ansible Vault
  hosts: frontends

  vars_files:
  - secret.yml

  tasks:
  - name: Tell me a secret
    debug:
      msg: "Your secret data is: {{ secretdata }}"
```

The `vars_files` directive is used in the same way as it would be if you were using an unencrypted `variables` file. Ansible reads the headers of the `variables` files at runtime and determines whether they are encrypted or not.

5. Try running the playbook without telling Ansible what the vault password is—in this instance, you should receive an error such as this:

```
$ ansible-playbook -i hosts vaultplaybook.yml
ERROR! Attempting to decrypt but no vault secrets found
```

6. Ansible correctly understands that we are trying to load a `variables` file that is encrypted with `ansible-vault`, but we must manually tell it about the password for it to proceed. There are several ways of specifying passwords for vaults (more on this in a minute), but for simplicity, try running the following command and enter your vault password when prompted:

```
$ ansible-playbook -i hosts vaultplaybook.yml --ask-vault-pass
Vault password:

PLAY [A play that makes use of an Ansible Vault]
********************************

TASK [Gathering Facts] *******************************
****************
ok: [frt01.example.com]
ok: [frt02.example.com]

TASK [Tell me a secret] *******************************
****************
ok: [frt01.example.com] => {
  "msg": "Your secret data is: Ansible is cool!"
}
ok: [frt02.example.com] => {
  "msg": "Your secret data is: Ansible is cool!"
}

PLAY RECAP ********************************************
****************
frt01.example.com : ok=2 changed=0 unreachable=0 failed=0
skipped=0 rescued=0 ignored=0
frt02.example.com : ok=2 changed=0 unreachable=0 failed=0
skipped=0 rescued=0 ignored=0
```

Success! Ansible decrypted our vault file and loaded the variables into the playbook, which we can see from the `debug` statement we created. This is a very simple example of what you can do with vaults. There are multiple ways that you can specify passwords; you don't have to be prompted for them on the command line—they can be provided either by a plain text file that contains the vault password or via a script that could obtain the password from a secure location at runtime (think of a dynamic inventory script, only for returning a password rather than a hostname). The `ansible-vault` tool itself can also be used to edit, view, and change the passwords in a vault file, or even decrypt it and turn it back into plain text. The user guide for Ansible Vault is a great place to start for more information (`https://docs.ansible.com/ansible/latest/user_guide/vault.html`).

One thing to note is that you don't actually have to have a separate vault file for your sensitive data; you can include it inline in your playbook. For example, let's try re-encrypting our sensitive data for inclusion in an otherwise unencrypted playbook (again, use the `secure` password for the vault if you are testing the examples from the GitHub repository accompanying this book). Run the following command in your shell (it should produce an output similar to what is shown):

```
$ ansible-vault encrypt_string 'Ansible is cool!' --name secretdata
New Vault password:
Confirm New Vault password:
secretdata: !vault |
  $ANSIBLE_VAULT;1.1;AES256
  34393431303339353735656236656130336664666337363732376262343837663738
  393465623930
  33666230613063646439666666565316235313136633264310a623736643362663035
  373861343435
  62346264313638656363323835323833363326463656136633932633235643038373
  4653030306637
  37363365336536230380a316364313831666463643534633530393337346164356634
  613065396434
  33316338336266636666635333346438653638303465666663313037636435643230
  65
Encryption successful
```

You can copy and paste the output of this command into a playbook. So, if we modify our earlier example, it would appear as follows:

```
---
- name: A play that makes use of an Ansible Vault
  hosts: frontends

  vars:
    secretdata: !vault |
        $ANSIBLE_VAULT;1.1;AES256
        343934313033393537356562366561303366646663373637323763262343837
        663738393465623930
        336662306130636464396666666565316235313136633264310a623736643362
        663035373861343435
        62346264313638656363323835323833363326463656136633932633235643430
        383734653030306637
        37363365336536230380a316364313831666463643534633530393337346164
        35663461306539433
        33316338336266636666635333346438653638303465666663313037636435643
        323065

  tasks:
    - name: Tell me a secret
```

```
        debug:
          msg: "Your secret data is: {{ secretdata }}"
```

Now, when you run this playbook in exactly the same manner as we did before (specifying the vault password using a user prompt), you should see that it runs just as when we used an external encrypted `variables` file:

```
$ ansible-playbook -i hosts inlinevaultplaybook.yml --ask-vault-pass
Vault password:

PLAY [A play that makes use of an Ansible Vault]
********************************

TASK [Gathering Facts] *********************************************
***********
ok: [frt02.example.com]
ok: [frt01.example.com]

TASK [Tell me a secret] ********************************************
***********
ok: [frt01.example.com] => {
  "msg": "Your secret data is: Ansible is cool!"
}
ok: [frt02.example.com] => {
  "msg": "Your secret data is: Ansible is cool!"
}

PLAY RECAP ********************************************************
***********
frt01.example.com : ok=2 changed=0 unreachable=0 failed=0 skipped=0
rescued=0 ignored=0
frt02.example.com : ok=2 changed=0 unreachable=0 failed=0 skipped=0
rescued=0 ignored=0
```

Ansible Vault is a powerful and versatile tool for encrypting your sensitive playbook data at rest and should enable you (with a little care) to run most of your playbooks unattended without ever leaving passwords or other sensitive data in the clear. If you add multiple encrypted files in your `group_vars` directory, all files need to contain the same password. That concludes this section and this chapter; I hope that it has been useful to you.

Summary

Ansible has many advanced features that allow you to run your playbooks in a variety of scenarios, whether that is upgrading a cluster of servers in a controlled manner; working with devices on a secure, isolated network; or controlling your playbook flow with prompts and tags. Ansible has been adopted by a large and ever-growing user base and, as such, is designed and evolved around solving real-world problems. Most of the advanced features of Ansible we discussed are centered around exactly this—solving real-world problems.

In this chapter, you learned about running tasks asynchronously in Ansible, before looking at the various features available for running playbooks to upgrade a cluster, such as running tasks on small batches of inventory hosts, failing a play early if a certain percentage of hosts fail, delegating tasks to a specific host, and even running tasks once, regardless of your inventory (or batch) size. You also learned about the difference between running playbooks locally as opposed to on `localhost` and how to use SSH-proxying to automate tasks on an isolated network via a `bastion` host. Finally, you learned about handling sensitive data without storing it unencrypted at rest, either through prompting the user at runtime or through the use of Ansible Vault. You even learned about running a subset of your playbook tasks with tagging.

In the next chapter, we will explore a topic we touched on briefly in this chapter in more detail—automating network device management with Ansible.

Questions

1. Which parameter allows you to configure the maximum number of hosts in a batch that will fail before a play is aborted?

    A. `percentage`

    B. `max_fail`

    C. `max_fail_percentage`

    D. `max_percentage`

    E. `fail_percentage`

2. True or false? You can use the `--ask-vault-pass` parameter to use the vault to keep sensitive data at rest:

    A. True

    B. False

3. True or false? To run a playbook asynchronously, you need to use the `async` keyword:

    A. True

    B. False

Further reading

If you install Passlib, which is a password-hashing library for Python 3, `vars_prompt` is encrypted with any crypt scheme (such as `descrypt`, `md5crypt`, `sha56_crypt`, and more). You can learn more about this here:

`https://passlib.readthedocs.io/en/stable/`

Part 3: Using Ansible in an Enterprise

In this section, we will take a practical look at how to get the most out of Ansible in an enterprise environment. We will start by looking at how to automate your network devices with Ansible, before moving on to the use of Ansible to manage both cloud and container environments. We will then look at some of the more advanced testing and troubleshooting strategies that will assist you in your use of Ansible in an enterprise, before looking at the Ansible Automation Controller/ **Ansible Web eXecutable (AWX)** product, which provides rich **Role-Based Access Control (RBAC)** and auditing capabilities in enterprise settings in a variety of execution environments. Finally, we will deep dive into execution environments.

This section contains the following chapters:

- *Chapter 10, Network Automation with Ansible*
- *Chapter 11, Container and Cloud Management*
- *Chapter 12, Troubleshooting and Testing Strategies*
- *Chapter 13, Getting Started with Ansible Automation Controller*
- *Chapter 14, Execution Environments*

10

Network Automation with Ansible

Years ago, the standard practice was to configure every single network device by hand. This way of managing devices was possible mainly because the routers and switches were routing the traffic of physical servers, so only a little configuration was needed on each networking device, and changes were slow-paced. In addition, humans were the only ones with enough information on machines to set up networking. Everything was very manual in terms of both planning and execution.

Virtualization changed this paradigm, as it has resulted in thousands of machines being connected to the same switch or router, each with potentially different networking requirements. Changes are fast paced and expected frequently, and with virtual infrastructures defined in code, it becomes a full-time job for a human administrator just to keep up with the changes to the infrastructure. Virtualization orchestration platforms have far better knowledge of the machine's location and can even generate an inventory for us, as we saw in earlier chapters. Practically speaking, there is no way a human being can memorize or manage a modern, large-scale, virtualized infrastructure. As a result, it becomes clear that automation is required when configuring the network infrastructure.

We will learn more about this and what we can do to automate our network in this chapter by covering the following topics:

- Why automate network management?
- How Ansible manages networking devices
- How to enable network automation
- The available Ansible networking modules
- Connecting to network devices
- Environment variables for network devices
- Custom conditional statements for networking devices

Let's get started!

Technical requirements

This chapter assumes that you have set up your control host with Ansible, as detailed in *Chapter 1, Getting Started with Ansible*, and are using the most recent version available – the examples in this chapter were tested with Ansible 2.15. This chapter also assumes that you have at least one additional host to test against; ideally, this should be Linux-based. Since this chapter is network device-centric, we understand that not everyone will have access to specific networking equipment to test on (for example, Cisco switches).

Where examples are given, and you have access to such devices, please feel free to explore the examples. However, if you do not have access to any network hardware, we will give an example using the freely available Cumulus VX, which offers a fully-featured demo of Cumulus Networks' switching environment. Although we will give specific examples of hostnames in this chapter, you are free to substitute them with your hostname and/or IP address. Details of how to do this will be provided in the appropriate places.

The code bundle for this chapter is available here: `https://github.com/PacktPublishing/Practical-Ansible-2/tree/master/Chapter%2010`.

Why automate network management?

How we design data centers has radically changed in the last 30 years. In the 90s, a typical data center was full of physical machines, each with a particular purpose. In many companies, the servers were bought from different vendors based on the purpose of the machine. This meant that every time there was a need for new servers, network devices, and storage devices, those devices were bought, provisioned, configured, and delivered.

The big drawback here was the significant lag between identifying the need for the server and its delivery. At the time, this was acceptable since most companies had very few systems, and they tended to change very rarely. Also, this approach was costly as a lot of devices were underutilized.

With the progress of society and companies in the world of technology, it has become necessary for companies to get more efficiency from their infrastructure and cut their infrastructure deployment time and costs. These new requirements paved the way for a new idea: virtualization. By creating a virtualization cluster, you do not need physical hosts of the right size, so you can provision a number of them upfront, add them to a resource pool, and then create the right-sized machines in your virtualization platform. This decoupling means that when a new server is needed, you can create it with a few clicks and it will be ready in seconds.

This shift also allowed enterprises to move from a per-project infrastructure, with each project being deployed with its unique data center requirements, to one large central infrastructure that can have its behavior defined by software and configuration. This new architecture means that a single network infrastructure can support many projects, regardless of their scale. We call this a **virtual data center infrastructure**; in this infrastructure, we use generic design patterns as much as possible. The virtual data center infrastructure allows enterprises to deploy, switch, and serve infrastructure at a large scale to enable a multitude of projects so that they can be successfully implemented by simply subdividing them (for example, by creating virtual servers).

Another significant advantage of virtualization is the decoupling of workloads and physical hosts. Historically, since a workload was tied to a physical host, if the host died, the workload itself died if not correctly replicated on different hardware. Virtualization solved this problem since the workload is now tied to one or more virtual hosts, but those can be moved freely from one physical host to another by the virtualization controller.

This ability to provision servers quickly and the ability to move them from one host to another created an issue with networking configuration management. Before, it was acceptable for a human to tweak the configuration details while installing the new machine, but now, machines move from one host to another (and therefore from one physical switch port to another) without any human intervention. This peculiarity means that the system needs to update network configurations as well.

At the same time, and for similar reasons, VLANs affirmed their presence in networking, which allowed the utilization of network devices to be dramatically improved, and its costs to therefore be optimized.

Today, we work at an even larger scale, where virtual objects (machines, containers, functions, and so on) move in our data centers, fully managed by software systems, and where humans are less and less involved in the process.

In this kind of environment, automating the network configuration is a crucial part of its success.

Today, some companies (the famous *cloud providers*) work at a scale where manual network management is not only impracticable but impossible, even when employing huge teams of network engineers. On the other hand, there are many environments where it would be technically possible to manage network configurations manually, at least partially so, but it's still impractical.

Aside from the time required to configure a network device, the biggest advantage – from my perspective – of network automation is the opportunity to drastically reduce human errors. If a human has to configure a VLAN on 100 devices, chances are they will make a few errors in the process. This is normal but problematic since those configurations must be thoroughly tested and amended. Often, the problem doesn't stop here because when a device breaks and needs to be replaced, a human has to configure the new device in the same way as the old one was configured. Often – over time – the configurations change, and there is very often no clear way to trace this, so while replacing a faulty network device, there might be problems with some rules that were present in the previous device but are not present in the new one.

Now that we have discussed the need to automate network management, let's look at how to manage networking devices with Ansible.

How Ansible manages networking devices

Ansible allows you to manage many different networking devices, including Arista EOS, Cisco ASA, Cisco IOS, Cisco IOS XR, Cisco NX-OS, Dell OS 6, Dell OS 9, Dell OS 10, Extreme EXOS, Extreme IronWare, Extreme NOS, Extreme SLX-OS, Extreme VOSS, F5 BIG-IP, F5 BIG-IQ, Junos OS, Lenovo CNOS, Lenovo ENOS, MikroTik RouterOS, Nokia SR OS, Pluribus Netvisor, and VyOS, as well as all OSs that support NETCONF. As you can imagine, we can make Ansible communicate with them in various ways.

Also, we have to remember that Ansible networking modules run on the controller host (the one where you issued the `ansible` command), while usually, the Ansible modules run on the target host. This difference is crucial because it allows Ansible to use different connection mechanisms based on the target device type. Remember that even when you have a host with SSH management capabilities (that many switches have), Ansible needs Python to be present on the target host to be able to run modules on it. Since most switches (and embedded hardware) do not have Python, Ansible will often use specific connection protocols. The key ones supported by Ansible for network device management are given here.

There are five main connection types that Ansible uses for connecting to those network devices, as follows:

- `ansible.netcommon.network_cli`
- `ansible.netcommon.netconf`
- `ansible.netcommon.httpapi`
- `local`
- `ssh`

When you create a connection with your networking device, you need to choose the connection mechanism based on the ones supported by your devices and your needs:

- `ansible.netcommon.network_cli` is supported by most modules, and it is the most similar to how Ansible usually works with non-networking modules. This mode uses a CLI via SSH. This protocol creates a persistent connection at the beginning of the execution, which is kept alive for the whole execution so that you don't have to provide credentials for every task.

- `ansible.netcommon.netconf` is supported by some modules. This mode uses XML via SSH, so it applies XML-based configurations to the device. This protocol creates a persistent connection at the beginning of the execution, which is kept alive for the whole execution so that you don't have to provide credentials for every task.

- `ansible.netcommon.httpapi` is supported by a few modules. This mode uses the HTTP API that the device publishes. This protocol creates a persistent connection at the beginning of the execution, which is kept alive for the whole execution so that you don't have to provide credentials for every task.

- `local` is supported by most devices, but it is a deprecated connection mode. This connection mode is vendor-dependent and usually requires some vendor-specific packages to be present on Ansible's execution host. This mode does not create a persistent connection, so you must provide the credentials at every task. When possible, avoid this mode.

- `ssh` must not be forgotten as an option. Although a large number of devices depend upon the connection modes listed before, a new breed of network devices is being created that runs Linux natively on **white box** switch hardware. One such example is Cumulus Networks (now part of NVIDIA), and as its software is Linux-based, all configurations can be performed over SSH as if the switch was just another Linux box.

Knowing how Ansible connects to and communicates with your networking hardware is essential, as it gives you the understanding you need to build your Ansible playbooks and debug issues when things go wrong.

In this section, we covered the communication protocols you will come across when working with networking hardware. In the next section, we will build on this by looking at the fundamentals of starting our network automation journey with Ansible.

How to enable network automation

Before using Ansible for network automation, you must ensure you have everything you need. We need different requirements based on the kind of connection method we will use. For our example, we will use a Cisco IOS device with `network_cli` connectivity.

The only requirements for Ansible network automation to work are as follows:

- Ansible 2.5+

- Proper connectivity with the network device

First, we need to check the Ansible version:

1. To ensure that you have a recent Ansible version, you can run the following command:

   ```
   $ ansible --version
   ```

   This command will tell you the version of your Ansible installation.

2. If it's 2.5 or newer, you can issue the following command (with the appropriate options) to check the connectivity of your network device:

   ```
   $ ansible all -i n1.example.org, -c network_cli -u my_user -k -m
   cisco.ios.ios_facts -e ansible_network_os=cisco.ios.ios all
   ```

This command should return your device's facts, proving that we can connect. As for any other target, Ansible can retrieve facts, which is usually the first thing Ansible does when interacting with a target.

In this particular case, we are using the -k parameter to inform Ansible that we want to be prompted for a password to be used for SSH login.

Retrieving facts is a key step since this allows Ansible to know the current state of the device and act appropriately.

By running the `cisco.ios.ios_facts` module on our target device, we are just executing this first standard step (so no changes are performed), but this confirms that Ansible can connect to the device and perform commands on it.

As you might have imagined, you can only run the preceding command and explore its behavior if you have access to a network device running Cisco IOS. We understand that not everyone has the same networking equipment available for testing purposes (or any at all!). Fortunately for us, a new breed of switches is becoming available – white box switches. These switches are created by various manufacturers and are based on standardized hardware where you can install your network operating system. One such operating system is NVIDIA Cumulus Linux, and a freely available test version of this, called NVIDIA Cumulus VX, is available for you to download.

> **Note**
>
> At the time of writing, the download link for NVIDIA Cumulus VX is `https://www.nvidia.com/en-us/networking/ethernet-switching/cumulus-vx/`. You will need to register to download it, but doing so gives you free access to the world of open networking.

Download the image appropriate to your hypervisor (for example, VirtualBox) and then run it just as you would run any other Linux virtual machine. Once you've done this, you can connect to the NVIDIA Cumulus VX switch, just like you would any other SSH device. For example, to run an ad hoc command to gather facts about all the switch port interfaces (that are enumerated as `swp1`, `swp2`, and `swpX` on Cumulus VX), you would run the following command:

```
$ ansible -i vx01.example.org, -u cumulus -m ansible.builtin.setup -a
'filter=ansible_swp*' all --ask-pass
```

If successful, this should result in pages of information about the switch port interface for your Cumulus VX-powered virtual switch. On my test system, the first part of this output looks like this:

```
vx01.example.org | SUCCESS => {
  "ansible_facts": {
    "ansible_swp1": {
      "active": false,
      "device": "swp1",
      "features": {
```

```
    "esp_hw_offload": "off [fixed]",
    "esp_tx_csum_hw_offload": "off [fixed]",
    "fcoe_mtu": "off [fixed]",
    "generic_receive_offload": "on",
    "generic_segmentation_offload": "on",
    "highdma": "off [fixed]",
    ...
```

As you can see, working with white box switches using an operating system such as NVIDIA Cumulus Linux has the advantage that you can connect using the standard SSH protocol and even use the `ansible.builtin.setup` module to gather facts about it. Working with other proprietary hardware is not much more difficult but requires more parameters to be specified, as we showed earlier in this chapter.

Now that you know the fundamentals of enabling network automation, let's learn how to discover the appropriate networking modules for our desired automation task in Ansible.

The available Ansible networking modules

With the advent of Galaxy and collections, we have seen a huge increase in available Ansible content for networking. Currently, there are more than 150 collections and more than 1,000 roles on Galaxy. You can also find the most important collections on the official Ansible documentation. To find the collections, you should take the following steps:

- First of all, check the official documentation. By visiting `https://docs.ansible.com/ansible/latest/network/user_guide/platform_index.html`, you can find the different device families and which connection types they use.

- If the device you would like to manage is not on the list, you can search on Galaxy by going to `https://galaxy.ansible.com` and using the website's search feature.

The list of collections and modules is way too long and family-specific for us to discuss them in depth. Also, those lists are in constant update, and they tend to get continuously longer.

If you are familiar with configuring the device manually, you will quickly find the name of the modules reasonably natural, so it will be easy for you to understand what they do. However, let's go through a handful of examples from the collection of Cisco IOS modules – specifically, with reference to `https://galaxy.ansible.com/cisco/ios`:

- `cisco.ios.ios_banner`: As the name suggests, this module will allow you to tweak and modify the login banner (which in many systems is called *motd*).

- `cisco.ios.ios_bgp`: This module allows you to configure BGP routes.

- cisco.ios.ios_command: This is the IOS equivalent of the ansible.builtin.command module and it allows you to perform many different commands. As for the ansible.builtin.command module, this is a very powerful module, but it's better to use specific modules for the operations we are going to perform if they are available.

- cisco.ios.ios_config: This module allows us to make any changes to the device's configuration file. Similarly to the cisco.ios.ios_command module, this is a very powerful module, but it's better to use specific modules for the operation we are going to perform if they are available. The idempotency for this module is only guaranteed if no abbreviated commands are used.

- cisco.ios.ios_vlan: This module allows the configuration of VLANs.

These are just a few examples, but there are many more modules for Cisco IOS, and if you cannot find a specific module to perform the operation you want, you can always fall back to cisco.ios.ios_command and cisco.ios.ios_config, which, thanks to their flexibility, will allow you to perform any operation you can think of.

In contrast, if you are working with a Cumulus Linux switch, you'll find there are fewer modules since they are more generic.

As always, the Ansible documentation is your friend, and it should be your first port of call when you are learning how to automate commands on a new class of devices. In this section, we have demonstrated a simple process for finding out which Ansible modules are available for your network device, using Cisco as a specific example (though you could apply these principles to any other device). Now, let's look at how Ansible connects to network devices.

Connecting to network devices

As we have seen, there are some peculiarities in Ansible networking, so specific configurations are required.

To manage network devices with Ansible, you need to have at least one to test on. Let's assume we have a Cisco IOS system available to us. It is accepted that not everyone will have such a device to test on, so the following is offered as a hypothetical example only.

Going by the https://docs.ansible.com/ansible/latest/network/user_guide/platform_index.html page, we can see that the correct ansible_network_os for this device is cisco.ios.ios and that we can connect to it using both network_cli and local. Since local is deprecated, we are going to use network_cli. Follow these steps to configure Ansible so that you can manage IOS devices:

1. First, let's create the inventory file with our devices in the routers group:

    ```
    [routers]
    n1.example.org
    ```

```
n2.example.org

[cumulusvx]
vx01.example.org
```

2. To know which connection parameters to use, we will set Ansible's special connection variables so that they define the connection parameters. We'll do this in a group variables subdirectory of our playbook, so we will need to create the `group_vars/routers.yml` file with the following content:

```
---
ansible_connection: network_cli
ansible_network_os: cisco.ios.ios
ansible_become: True
ansible_become_method: enable
```

Thanks to these special variables, Ansible will know how to connect to your devices. We covered some of these examples earlier in this book, but as a recap, Ansible uses the values of those variables to determine their behavior in the following ways:

- `ansible_connection`: This variable is used by Ansible to decide how to connect to the device. By choosing `network_cli`, we are instructing Ansible to connect to the CLI in SSH mode.

- `ansible_network_os`: This variable is used by Ansible to understand the device family of the device we are going to use. By choosing `cisco.ios.ios`, we are instructing Ansible to expect a Cisco IOS device.

- `ansible_become`: This variable is used by Ansible to decide whether to perform privilege escalation on the device or not. By specifying `True`, we are telling Ansible to perform privilege escalation.

- `ansible_become_method`: There are many different ways to perform privilege escalation on the various devices (normally `sudo` on a Linux server – this is the default setting), and for Cisco IOS, we must set this to `enable`.

With that, you have learned the necessary steps to connect to network devices.

To validate that the connection is working as expected (assuming you have access to a router running Cisco IOS), you can run this simple playbook, called `ios_facts.yaml`:

```
---
- name: Play to return facts from a Cisco IOS device
  hosts: routers
  gather_facts: False
  tasks:
```

```
- name: Gather IOS facts
  cisco.ios.ios_facts:
    gather_subset: all
```

You can run this using a command such as the following:

```
$ ansible-playbook -i hosts ios_facts.yml --ask-pass
```

If it returns successfully, this means that your configuration is correct and you've been able to give Ansible the necessary authorization to manage your IOS device.

Similarly, if you wanted to connect to a Cumulus VX device, you could add another group variables file called group_vars/cumulusvx.yml containing the following code:

```
---
ansible_user: cumulus
become: false
```

An analogous playbook that returns all the facts about our Cumulus VX switches could look like this:

```
---
- name: Simply play to gather Cumulus VX switch facts
  hosts: cumulusvx
  gather_facts: no
  tasks:
  - name: Gather facts
    ansible.builtin.setup:
      gather_subset: all
```

You can run this in a normal manner by using a command such as the following:

```
$ ansible-playbook -i hosts cumulusvx_facts.yml --ask-pass
```

If successful, you should see the following output from your playbook run:

```
SSH password:

PLAY [Simply play to gather Cumulus VX switch facts] ***************
*****************************************************************
**********

TASK [Gather facts] **********************************************
**********************************************
ok: [vx01.example.org]
```

```
PLAY RECAP ******************************************************
***************************************
vx01.example.org : ok=1 changed=0 unreachable=0 failed=0 skipped=0
rescued=0 ignored=0
```

This demonstrates the techniques for connecting to two different types of network devices in Ansible, including one you can test by yourself without access to any special hardware.

Now, let's build on this by looking at how to set environment variables for network devices in Ansible.

Environment variables for network devices

Very often, the complexity of networks is high, and the network systems are very varied. For those reasons, Ansible has many variables that can help you tweak it to make Ansible fit your environment.

Let's suppose you have two different networks (one for computing and one for network devices) that can't communicate directly but have to pass through a bastion host to reach one from the other. Since we have Ansible in the computing network, we must jump networks using the bastion host to configure an IOS router in the management network. Also, our target switch needs a proxy set to reach the internet.

To connect to the IOS router in the management network, we will need to create a new group for our network devices, which are on a separate network. For this example, this might be specified as follows:

```
[bastion_routers]
n1.example.org
n2.example.org

[bastion_cumulusvx]
vx01.example.org
```

Following the creation of our updated inventory, we can create a new group variables file, such as `group_vars/bastion_routers.yaml`, with the following content:

```
---
ansible_connection: network_cli
ansible_network_os: cisco.ios.ios
ansible_become: True
ansible_become_method: enable
ansible_ssh_common_args: '-o ProxyCommand="ssh -W %h:%p -q bastion.
example.org"'
proxy_env:
http_proxy: http://proxy.example.org:8080
```

We can also do the same for our Cumulus VX switches if they are behind a bastion server by creating a `group_vars/bastion_cumulusvx.yml` file:

```
---
ansible_user: cumulus
ansible_become: false
ansible_ssh_common_args: '-o ProxyCommand="ssh -W %h:%p -q bastion.
example.org"'
proxy_env:
http_proxy: http://proxy.example.org:8080
```

In addition to the options we discussed in the previous section, we now have two additional options:

- `ansible_ssh_common_args`: This is a very powerful option that allows us to add additional options to the SSH connections to tweak their behavior. These options should be pretty straightforward to identify since you are already using them in your SSH configurations to simply SSH to the target machine. In this specific case, we are adding `ProxyCommand`, which is the SSH directive to perform a jump to a host (usually a bastion host) so that we can enter the target host securely.

- `http_proxy`: This option, which is below the `proxy_env` option, is key in environments where network isolation is strong, and therefore your machines can't interact with the internet unless they use a proxy.

Assuming you have set up passwordless (for example, SSH key-based) access to your bastion host, you should be able to run an ad hoc Ansible `ping` command against your Cumulus VX host, as follows:

```
$ ansible -i hosts -m ping -u cumulus bastion_cumulusvx

vx01.example.org | SUCCESS => {
    "ansible_facts": {
    "discovered_interpreter_python": "/usr/bin/python"
  },
  "changed": false,
  "ping": "pong"
}
```

Note that using the bastion server becomes transparent – you can automate with Ansible as if you were on the same flat network. If you have access to a Cisco IOS-based device, you should be able to run a similar command against the `bastion_routers` group and achieve similarly positive results.

Now that you have learned the necessary steps to set environment variables for network devices and access them with Ansible, even when they are on isolated networks, let's learn how to set conditional statements for networking devices.

Custom conditional statements for networking devices

Although there are no networking-specific Ansible conditionals, conditionals frequently come into play in networking-related Ansible usage.

In networking, it's common to enable and disable ports. To have data be able to pass through the cable, both ports at the ends of the cable should be enabled, resulting in a connected state (some vendors will use different names for this, but the idea is the same).

Let's suppose we have two Arista Networks EOS devices, and we issued the ON status on the ports and need to wait for the connection to be up before proceeding.

To wait for the `Ethernet4` interface to be enabled, we will need to add the following task to our playbook:

```
- name: Wait for interface to be enabled
  arista.eos.eos_command:
    commands:
    - show interface Ethernet4 | json
    wait_for:
    - "result[0].interfaces.Ethernet4.interfaceStatus eq connected"
```

`arista.eos.eos_command` is the module that allows us to issue free-formed commands to an Arista Networks EOS device. The command itself needs to be specified in an array in the `commands` option. With the `wait_for` option, we can specify a condition and Ansible will reiterate on the specified task until the condition is satisfied. Since the command's output is redirected to the `json` utility, the output will be a JSON, so we can traverse its structure using Ansible's ability to manipulate JSON data.

We can achieve similar results on Cumulus VX – for example, we can query the facts gathered from the switch to see whether the `swp2` port is enabled. If it is not, then we will enable it; however, if it is enabled, we will skip the command. We can do this with a simple playbook, as follows:

```
---
- name: Simple play to demonstrate conditional on Cumulus Linux
  hosts: cumulusvx
  tasks:
  - name: Enable swp2 if it is disabled
    community.network.nclu:
      commands:
      - add int swp2
    commit: true
    when: not ansible_swp2.active
```

Notice the use of the when clause in our task, meaning we should only issue the configuration directive if swp2 is not active. If we were to run this playbook for the first time on an unconfigured Cumulus Linux switch, we should see an output similar to the following:

```
PLAY [Simple play to demonstrate conditional on Cumulus Linux] *******
**********************************************************

TASK [Gathering Facts]
**********************************************************************
ok: [vx01.example.org]

TASK [Enable swp2 if it is disabled] ******************************
******************************
changed: [vx01.example.org]

PLAY RECAP
*********************************************************************
vx01.example.org : ok=2 changed=1 unreachable=0 failed=0 skipped=0
rescued=0 ignored=0
```

As we can see, the Enable swp2 task, if it is disabled based on the community.network.nclu module, returned a changed state, which means that it changed the switch configuration. However, if we were to run the playbook a second time, the output should be more like this:

```
PLAY [Simple play to demonstrate conditional on Cumulus Linux] *******
**********************************************************

TASK [Gathering Facts]
**********************************************************************
ok: [vx01.example.org]

TASK [Enable swp2 if it is disabled] ******************************
******************************
skipping: [vx01.example.org]

PLAY RECAP
*********************************************************************
vx01.example.org : ok=1 changed=0 unreachable=0 failed=0 skipped=1
rescued=0 ignored=0
```

This time, the task was skipped as the Ansible facts show that the swp2 port is already enabled. This example is elementary, but it shows how you can work with conditionals on a network device, as you have already seen conditionals being used on Linux servers earlier in this book.

That concludes our brief look at network device automation with Ansible – more in-depth work would require a look at network configurations and necessitate more hardware, which is beyond the scope of this book. However, I hope this information demonstrates that Ansible can be used effectively to automate and configure a wide array of network devices.

Summary

Modern large-scale infrastructures that change rapidly necessitate the automation of network tasks. Fortunately, Ansible supports a wide array of network devices, from proprietary hardware such as Cisco IOS-based devices, to open standards such as white box switches that run operating systems such as Cumulus Linux. Ansible is a powerful and supportive tool to manage your network configuration and allows you to implement changes quickly and safely. You can even replace entire devices in your network and be confident in your ability to put the correct configuration on the new device, thanks to your Ansible playbooks.

In this chapter, you learned about the reasons for automating network management. You then looked at how Ansible manages network devices, how to enable network automation in Ansible, and how to locate the Ansible modules necessary to perform the automation tasks you wish to complete. Then, through practical examples, you learned how to connect to network devices, set environment variables (and connect to isolated networks via bastion hosts), and apply conditional statements to Ansible tasks for network device configuration.

In the next chapter, we will learn how to manage Linux containers and cloud infrastructures using Ansible.

Questions

1. Which of these is NOT one of the four major connection types that Ansible uses for connecting to network devices?

    A. `netconf`

    B. `network_cli`

    C. `local`

    D. `netstat`

    E. `httpapi`

2. True or false: The `ansible_network_os` variable is used by Ansible to understand the device family of the device we are going to use.

    A. True

    B. False

3. True or false: To connect to an IOS router in a separate network, you need to specify the special connection variables for the host, possibly as inventory group variables.

    A. True

    B. False

Further reading

The official documentation about Ansible networking is available here: `https://docs.ansible.com/ansible/latest/network/index.html`.

11

Container and Cloud Management

Ansible is a very flexible automation tool and can be easily used to automate any aspect of your infrastructure. In the last few years, container-based workloads and cloud workloads have become more and more popular, and for this reason, we will look at how you can automate tasks related to those kinds of workloads with Ansible. This chapter will start by designing and building containers with Ansible. We will then look at how to run those containers, and finally, we will look at ways to manage various cloud platforms with Ansible.

Specifically, we will be covering the following topics in this chapter:

- Automating Docker and Podman with Ansible
- Managing Kubernetes with Ansible
- Exploring container-focused modules
- Automating against Amazon Web Services
- Complementing Google Cloud Platform with automation
- Seamless automation integration with Azure
- Expanding your environment with Rackspace Cloud
- Using Ansible to orchestrate OpenStack

Let's get started!

Technical requirements

This chapter assumes that you have set up your control host with Ansible, as detailed in *Chapter 1, Getting Started with Ansible*, and are using the most recent version available – the examples in this chapter were tested with Ansible 2.15. Although we will give specific examples of hostnames in this chapter, you are free to substitute them with your own hostname and/or IP address. Details of how to do this will be provided in the appropriate places. This chapter also assumes you have access to Docker, Podman, Kubernetes, and the different clouds. Since the majority of processes will be very similar across the different clouds, you will be able to gain the majority of the information even if you will read the whole chapter and just test those playbooks on the couple of environments you have access to.

All the examples in this chapter can be found in this book's GitHub repository at `https://github.com/PacktPublishing/Practical-Ansible-Second-Edition/tree/main/Chapter%2011`.

Automating Docker and Podman with Ansible

In today's world, simply being able to run an image is not considered a production-ready setup.

To be able to call a deployment **production-ready**, you need to demonstrate that the service your application delivers will run reasonably, even in the case of a single application crash, as well as hardware failure. Often, you'll have even more reliability constraints from your customer.

Luckily, your software is not the only one that has those requirements, so orchestration solutions have been developed for this purpose.

Today, the most successful one is Kubernetes, due to its various distributions/versions, so we are going to focus on it primarily.

The idea of Kubernetes is that you inform the Kubernetes control plane that you want X number of instances of Y application. Kubernetes will count how many instances of Y application are running on the Kubernetes Nodes to ensure that the number of instances is X. If there are too few instances, Kubernetes will take care of starting more instances. At the same time, if there are too many instances, the exceeding instances will be stopped.

Since Kubernetes constantly checks that the requested amount of instances is running, in the case of an application failure or a node failure, Kubernetes will start new instances to replace the lost instances.

Due to the complexity of installing and managing Kubernetes, multiple companies have started to sell distributions of Kubernetes that simplify their operations and that they are willing to support.

Every Kubernetes node runs an instance of a container engine. For this reason, we will start to see how the two most widely used standalone containers engine can be automated.

Managing Docker

Docker is now a very common, ubiquitous tool for development usage and you can leverage Ansible to easily manage your Docker instance. Since we are going to manage a Docker instance, we need to make sure we have one at hand and that the Docker command on our machine is configured correctly. We need to do this to ensure this is enough to run `docker images` on the terminal. Let's say you get a result similar to the following:

```
REPOSITORY TAG IMAGE ID CREATED SIZE
```

This means that everything is working properly. More lines may be provided as output if you have already-cloned images.

On the other hand, let's say it returns something like this:

```
Cannot connect to the Docker daemon at unix:///var/run/docker.sock. Is
the docker daemon running?
```

This means that we don't have a Docker daemon running or that our Docker console has been configured incorrectly.

Also, it's important to ensure that you have the `docker` Python module installed since Ansible tries to use it to communicate with the Docker daemon. Let's take a look:

1. First of all, we need to create a playbook called `start-docker-container.yaml` that contains the following code:

   ```
   ---
   - hosts: localhost
     tasks:
     - name: Start a container with a command
       community.docker.docker_container:
         name: test-container
         image: alpine
         command:
         - echo
         - "Hello, World!"
   ```

2. Now that we have the Ansible playbook, we just need to execute it:

   ```
   $ ansible-playbook start-docker-container.yaml
   ```

   As you may expect, it will give you an output similar to the following:

   ```
   PLAY [localhost] ************************************************
   *********************
   ```

```
TASK [Gathering Facts] *****************************************
************************
ok: [localhost]

TASK [Start a container with a command] ***********************
************************
changed: [localhost]

PLAY RECAP ****************************************************
************************
localhost : ok=2 changed=1 unreachable=0 failed=0 skipped=0
rescued=0 ignored=0
```

3. We can now check that our command executed properly, as follows:

    ```
    $ docker container list -a
    ```

    This will show the container that was run:

    ```
    CONTAINER ID IMAGE COMMAND CREATED STATUS PORTS NAMES
    c706ec55fc0d alpine "echo Hello, World!" 3 minutes ago Exited
    (0) About a minute ago test-container
    ```

    This proves that a container was executed.

4. To check that the echo command was executed, we can run the following code:

    ```
    $ docker logs test-container
    ```

    This will return the following output:

    ```
    Hello, World!
    ```

In this section, we executed the community.docker.docker_container module. This is not the only module Ansible has to control the Docker daemon, but it is probably one of the most widely used since it's used to control containers running on Docker.

Other modules include the following:

- community.docker.docker_config: Used to change the configurations of the Docker daemon
- community.docker.docker_container_info: Used to gather information from (inspect) a container
- community.docker.docker_network: Used to manage Docker networking configuration

There are also many modules in the `community.docker` collection, but they are actually used to manage Docker Swarm clusters and not Docker instances. Some examples are as follows:

- `community.docker.docker_node`: Used to manage a node in a Docker Swarm cluster
- `community.docker.docker_node_info`: Used to retrieve information about a specific node in a Docker Swarm cluster
- `community.docker.docker_swarm_info`: Used to retrieve information about a Docker Swarm cluster

As we will see in the next section, there are many more modules that can be used to manage containers that are orchestrated in various ways.

Now that you have learned how to automate Docker with Ansible, we will see how to work with Podman, a Docker alternative.

Managing Podman

Podman is a container engine competitor to Docker. The reason why Red Hat started to develop an alternative container engine is due to the design of Docker. Although Docker changed some design decisions over the years, at the time, Docker was running as a daemon that required root access to the machine, and the CLI `docker` command was just a client. The risk with this approach, at least from Red Hat's standpoint, was that a bug in the Docker daemon could have endangered the whole system's security.

Podman, differently from Docker, does not have a daemon running, and all utilities Podman provides are discrete. This approach allows Podman to be much more secure than Docker, allowing containers to be run without any root access.

One of the critical decisions made at the very beginning of Podman development was the CLI and API compatibility between Podman and Docker. This aspect dramatically increases the simplicity of moving from one to the other without much effort.

As you might have imagined, from an Ansible standpoint, it is also going to be very similar.

Due to the simpler design Podman has, to ensure that it is present and usable on your system, it is enough to run the `podman` command. If it returns the following, it means that you do not have it installed:

```
bash: podman: command not found
```

If it returns all the command options, this means that Podman is properly installed on your system.

We can therefore create our first Ansible Playbook to manage Podman, which we will call `start-podman-container.yaml`, with the following content:

```
---
- hosts: localhost
  tasks:
  - name: Start a container with a command
    containers.podman.podman_container:
      name: test-container
      image: alpine
      command:
      - echo
      - "Hello, World!"
```

We can now run the playbook by executing the following:

```
$ ansible-playbook start-podman-container.yaml
```

As you may expect, it will give you an output similar to this:

```
PLAY [localhost] *******************************************
*********
***********************************************************
*********
********************************

TASK [Gathering Facts] *************************************
*********
***********************************************************
*********
********************************
ok: [localhost]

TASK [Start a container with a command] ********************
*********
***********************************************************
*********
********************************
changed: [localhost]

PLAY RECAP *************************************************
*********
***********************************************************
*********
********************************
localhost                  :
ok=2    changed=1    unreachable=0    failed=0
    skipped=0    rescued=0    ignored=0
```

As we did for Docker, we can check that the command executed properly by running the following:

```
$ podman container list -a
```

And this command will return the information of the container that ran:

```
CONTAINER ID  IMAGE
COMMAND            CREATED        STATUS                PORTS
      NAMES96531f2f960e  docker.io/library/alpine:latest
                      echo Hello, World...  2 minutes ago
Exited (0) 2 minutes ago
test-container
```

The fact that it exited with 0 means that it successfully ran, as we were expecting.

Similarly to Docker, there are many other modules usable in the `containers.podman` collection. Differently from Docker, though, there is no such thing as Podman Swarm, and therefore all Docker modules focusing on Swarm will not have a Podman counterpart.

Now that we have explored the two major standalone container engines that you might encounter in development and test environments, we will discuss Kubernetes since it is the most widely used container platform in production environments.

Managing Kubernetes with Ansible

We will assume that you have access to either a Kubernetes or OpenShift cluster for testing. Setting these up is out of the scope of this book, so you might want to look at a distribution such as Minikube or Minishift, both of which are designed to be quick and easy to set up so that you can start learning these technologies rapidly. We also need to have the `kubectl` client or the `oc` client, depending on whether we have deployed Kubernetes or OpenShift, properly configured.

Installing Ansible Kubernetes dependencies

First of all, you need to ensure you are running a fairly updated version of Python 3 (>=3.6) and install the required Python packages (you can install it either via PIP or your OS packaging system):

- Kubernetes >= 12.0.0
- PyYAML >= 3.11
- `jsonpatch`

Since the `kubernetes.core` collection is not generally shipped with Ansible, you'll need to install it by running this:

```
$ ansible-galaxy collection install kubernetes.core
```

We are now ready for our first Kubernetes playbook!

Listing Kubernetes namespaces with Ansible

A Kubernetes cluster has multiple namespaces internally, and you can usually find the ones a cluster has with `kubectl get namespaces`. You can do the same with Ansible by creating a file called `k8s-ns-show.yaml` with the following content:

```
---
- hosts: localhost
  tasks:
  - name: Get information from K8s
    kubernetes.core.k8s_info:
      api_version: v1
      kind: Namespace
      register: ns
  - name: Print info
    ansible.builtin.debug:
      var: ns
```

We can now execute this as follows:

```
$ ansible-playbook k8s-ns-show.yaml
```

You will now see information regarding the namespaces in the output.

Notice that in the seventh line of the code (`kind: Namespace`), we are specifying the type of resources we are interested in. You can specify other Kubernetes object types to see them (for example, you can try this with Deployments, Services, and Pods).

Creating a Kubernetes namespace with Ansible

So far, we have learned how to show existing namespaces, but usually, Ansible is used in a declarative way to achieve a desired state. So, let's create a new playbook called `k8s-ns.yaml` with the following content:

```
---
- hosts: localhost
  tasks:
  - name: Ensure the myns namespace exists
    kubernetes.core.k8s:
      api_version: v1
      kind: Namespace
      name: myns
      state: present
```

Before running it, we can execute `kubectl get ns` so that we can ensure `myns` is not present. In my case, the output is as follows:

```
$ kubectl get ns
NAME STATUS AGE
default Active 69m
kube-node-lease Active 69m
kube-public Active 69m
kube-system Active 69m
```

We can now run the playbook with the following command:

```
$ ansible-playbook k8s-ns.yaml
```

The output should resemble the following one:

```
PLAY [localhost] **************************************************
**************

TASK [Gathering Facts] *******************************************
**************
ok: [localhost]

TASK [Ensure the myns namespace exists] **************************
**************
changed: [localhost]

PLAY RECAP *******************************************************
**************
localhost : ok=2 changed=1 unreachable=0 failed=0 skipped=0 rescued=0
ignored=0
```

As you can see, Ansible reports that it changed the namespace state. If I execute `kubectl get ns` again, it is clear that Ansible created the namespace we were expecting:

```
$ kubectl get ns
NAME STATUS AGE
default Active 74m
kube-node-lease Active 74m
kube-public Active 74m
kube-system Active 74m
myns Active 22s
```

Now, let's create a service.

Creating a Kubernetes service with Ansible

So far, we have seen how to create namespaces from Ansible, so now, let's put a service in the namespace we just created. Let's create a new playbook called `k8s-svc.yaml` with the following content:

```
---
- hosts: localhost
  tasks:
  - name: Ensure the Service mysvc is present
    kubernetes.core.k8s:
      state: present
      definition:
        apiVersion: v1
        kind: Service
        metadata:
          name: mysvc
          namespace: myns
        spec:
          selector:
            app: myapp
            service: mysvc
          ports:
          - protocol: TCP
            targetPort: 800
            name: port-80-tcp
            port: 80
```

Before running it, we can execute `kubectl get svc` to ensure that the namespace has no services. Make sure you're in the right namespace before running it! In my case, the output is as follows:

```
$ kubectl get svc
No resources found in myns namespace.
```

We can now run it with the following command:

```
$ ansible-playbook k8s-svc.yaml
```

The output should resemble the following one:

```
PLAY [localhost] ********************************************************
**************

TASK [Gathering Facts] *************************************************
**************
ok: [localhost]
```

```
TASK [Ensure the myns namespace exists] *****************************
**************
changed: [localhost]


PLAY RECAP **********************************************************
**************
localhost : ok=2 changed=1 unreachable=0 failed=0 skipped=0 rescued=0
ignored=0
```

As you can see, Ansible reports that it changed the service state. If I execute `kubectl get svc` again, it is clear that Ansible created the service we were expecting:

```
$ kubectl get svc
NAME TYPE CLUSTER-IP EXTERNAL-IP PORT(S) AGE
mysvc ClusterIP 10.0.0.84 <none> 80/TCP 10s
```

As you can see, we followed the same procedure that we used in the namespace case, but we specified a different Kubernetes object type and specified the various parameters that are needed for the Service type. You can do the same for all other Kubernetes object types.

Now that you have learned how to deal with Kubernetes clusters, you'll learn how to automate Docker with Ansible.

Exploring container-focused modules

Often, when organizations grow, they start to use multiple technologies in different parts of the organization. Another thing that usually happens is that after a department has found that a vendor worked well for them, they will be more inclined to try new technologies offered by that vendor. A mix of those two factors and time (usually, fewer technology cycles) will end up creating multiple solutions for the same problem within the same organization.

If your organization is in this situation with containers, Ansible can come to the rescue, thanks to its ability to interoperate with the majority of, if not all, container platforms.

Often, the biggest obstacle to doing something with Ansible is finding the name of the modules you need to use to achieve what you want to achieve. In this section, we will try to help in this effort, mainly in terms of the containerization space, but this might help you in the quest to find different kinds of modules.

The starting point for all Ansible module research should be the official Ansible documentation and eventually Ansible Galaxy.

Many Ansible modules relative to container services are in the cloud collections category (ECS, Docker, LXC, or LXD), containers (at the moment only Podman), or in their own one, such as Kubernetes.

To help you further, let's take a look at some of the main container platforms and the main modules Ansible provides.

Amazon Web Services (AWS), back in 2014, launched **Elastic Container Service (ECS)**, which is a way to deploy and orchestrate Docker containers within their infrastructure. In the following year, AWS also launched **Elastic Container Registry (ECR)**, a managed Docker Registry service. The service did not become as ubiquitous as AWS hoped, so in 2018, AWS launched **Elastic Kubernetes Service (EKS)** to allow people that wanted to run Kubernetes on AWS to have a managed service.

If you are using or plan to use EKS, this is just a standard managed Kubernetes cluster, so you can use the Kubernetes-specific modules that we are going to cover shortly. If you decide to use ECS, there are several modules that could help you. The most important ones are `community.aws.ecs_cluster`, which allows you to create or terminate ECS clusters; `community.aws.ecs_ecr`, which allows you to manage ECR; `community.aws.ecs_service`, which allows you to create, terminate, start, or stop a service in ECS; and `community.aws.ecs_task`, which allows you to run, start, or stop a task in ECS. In addition to those, there is `community.aws.ecs_service_info`, which allows Ansible to list or describe services in ECS.

Microsoft Azure, in 2018, announced **Azure Container Service (ACS)** and then announced **Azure Kubernetes Service (AKS)**. These services are managed Kubernetes solutions, so they can both be managed with the Kubernetes modules. In addition to those, Ansible provided two specific modules: the `azure.azcollection.azure_rm_aks` module allows us to create, update, and delete AKS instances.

Google Cloud launched **Google Kubernetes Engine (GKE)** in 2015. GKE is the **Google Cloud Platform (GCP)** version of managed Kubernetes, and is therefore compatible with Ansible Kubernetes modules. In addition to those, there are various GKE-specific modules, some of which are as follows:

- `google.cloud.gcp_container_cluster`: Allows you to create a GCP cluster
- `google.cloud.gcp_container_cluster_info`: Allows you to gather facts for a GCP cluster
- `google.cloud.gcp_container_node_pool`: Allows you to create a GCP node pool
- `google.cloud.gcp_container_node_pool_info`: Allows you to gather facts for a GCP node pool

Red Hat started OpenShift in 2011, and at the time, it was based on its own container runtime. Version 3, which was released in 2015, was completely based on Kubernetes, so all Ansible Kubernetes modules work. In addition to those, there is the `oc` module, which is currently still present but in a deprecated state, giving preference to the Kubernetes modules.

In 2015, Google released Kubernetes and, quickly, a huge community started to build around it. Ansible allows you to manage your Kubernetes clusters with some modules:

- `kubernetes.core.k8s`: Allows you to manage any kind of Kubernetes object

- `kubernetes.core.k8s_auth`: Allows you to authenticate to Kubernetes clusters that require an explicit login step

- `kubernetes.core.k8s_facts`: Allows you to inspect Kubernetes objects

- `kubernetes.core.k8s_scale`: Allows you to set a new size for a Deployment, ReplicaSet, Replication Controller, or Job

- `kubernetes.core.k8s_service`: Allows you to manage Services on Kubernetes

LXC and LXD are also systems that can be used to run containers in Linux. These systems are also supported by Ansible, thanks to the following modules:

- `community.general.lxc_container`: Allows you to manage LXC containers

- `community.general.lxd_container`: Allows you to manage LXD containers

- `community.general.lxd_profile`: Allows you to manage LXD profiles

Now that you have learned how to explore container-focused modules, you'll learn how to automate with AWS.

Automating with Amazon Web Services

In many organizations, cloud providers are used widely, while in others, they are just being introduced. However, in one way or another, you will probably have to deal with a cloud provider while doing your job. AWS is the biggest and oldest, and is perhaps something you will have to work with.

Installation

To be able to use Ansible to automate your AWS estate, you'll need to install the `boto3` library. To do so, run the following command:

```
$ pip install boto3
```

As for collections, at the moment, there are two collections to interact with AWS services: `community.aws` and `amazon.aws`. In many cases, you will need both of them, since many features of the former have not yet been implemented in the latter:

```
$ ansible-galaxy collection install community.aws amazon.aws
```

Now that you have all the necessary software installed, you can set up authentication.

Authentication

The `boto` library looks up the necessary credentials in the `~/.aws/credentials` file. There are two different ways to ensure that the credentials file is configured properly.

It is possible to use the AWS CLI tool. Alternatively, this can be done with a text editor of your choice by creating a file with the following structure:

```
[default]
aws_access_key_id = [YOUR_KEY_HERE]
aws_secret_access_key = [YOUR_SECRET_ACCESS_KEY_HERE]
```

Now that you've created the file with the necessary credentials, `boto` will be able to work against your AWS environment. Since Ansible uses `boto` for every single communication with AWS systems, this means that Ansible will be appropriately configured, even without you having to change any Ansible-specific configuration.

Creating your first machine

Now that Ansible is able to connect to your AWS environment, you can proceed with the actual playbook by following these steps:

1. Create the `aws.yaml` Playbook with the following content, ensuring you use your public key in the `key_material` value in the first task:

    ```
    ---
    - hosts: localhost
      tasks:
      - name: Ensure key pair is present
        amazon.aws.ec2_key:
          name: fale
          key_material: "{{ lookup('file', '~/.ssh/fale.pub') }}"
      - name: Gather information of the EC2 VPC net in eu-west-1
        amazon.aws.ec2_vpc_net_info:
          region: eu-west-1
        register: aws_simple_net
      - name: Gather information of the EC2 VPC subnet in eu-west-1
        amazon.aws.ec2_vpc_subnet_info:
          region: eu-west-1
          filters:
            vpc-id: '{{ aws_simple_net.vpcs.0.id }}'
        register: aws_simple_subnet
      - name: Ensure wssg Security Group is present
        amazon.aws.ec2_security_group:
          name: wssg
    ```

```
        description: Web Security Group
        region: eu-west-1
        vpc_id: '{{ aws_simple_net.vpcs.0.id }}'
        rules:
        - proto: tcp
          from_port: 22
          to_port: 22
          cidr_ip: 0.0.0.0/0
        - proto: tcp
          from_port: 80
          to_port: 80
          cidr_ip: 0.0.0.0/0
        - proto: tcp
          from_port: 443
          to_port: 443
          cidr_ip: 0.0.0.0/0
        rules_egress:
        - proto: all
          cidr_ip: 0.0.0.0/0
        register: aws_simple_wssg
    - name: Setup instance
      amazon.aws.ec2_instance:
        assign_public_ip: true
        image: ami-3548444c
        region: eu-west-1
        exact_count: 1
        key_name: fale
        count_tag:
          Name: ws01.ansible2cookbook.com
        instance_tags:
          Name: ws01.ansible2cookbook.com
        instance_type: t2.micro
        group_id: '{{ aws_simple_wssg.group_id }}'
        vpc_subnet_id: '{{ aws_simple_subnet.subnets.0.id }}'
        volumes:
        - device_name: /dev/sda1
          volume_type: gp2
          volume_size: 10
          delete_on_termination: True
```

2. Run it using the following command:

```
$ ansible-playbook aws.yaml
```

This command will return something like the following:

```
PLAY [localhost] ******************************************
**********************************

TASK [Gathering Facts] ***********************************
**********************************
ok: [localhost]

TASK [Ensure key pair is present] ************************
**********************************
ok: [localhost]

TASK [Gather information of the EC2 VPC net in eu-west-1] ******
**********************************
ok: [localhost]

TASK [Gather information of the EC2 VPC subnet in eu-west-1]
**************************************
ok: [localhost]

TASK [Ensure wssg Security Group is present] ******************
**********************************
ok: [localhost]

TASK [Setup instance] ************************************
**********************************
changed: [localhost]

PLAY RECAP ***********************************************
**********************************
localhost : ok=6 changed=1 unreachable=0 failed=0 skipped=0
rescued=0 ignored=0
```

If you check the AWS console, you will see that you now have one machine up and running!

To launch a virtual machine in AWS, we need a few things to be in place:

- An SSH key pair
- A network
- A subnetwork
- A security group

By default, a network and a subnetwork are already available in your account, but you need to retrieve their IDs.

That's why we started by uploading the public part of an SSH key pair to AWS, queried for information about the network and the subnetwork, then ensured that the security group we wanted to use was present, and lastly triggered the machine build.

Now you have learned how to automate against AWS, you'll learn how to complement GCP with automation.

Complementing Google Cloud Platform with automation

Another global cloud provider is Google, with its GCP. Google's approach to the cloud is different from other providers' since Google does not try to simulate the data center in a virtual environment. This is because Google wants to rethink the concept of cloud provision in order to simplify it.

Installation

You need to ensure that you have the proper components installed before you can start using GCP with Ansible. More specifically, you will require the Python `requests` and `google-auth` modules. To install these modules, run the following command:

```
$ pip install requests google-auth
```

We can now proceed to install the Google Cloud collection:

```
$ ansible-galaxy collection install google.cloud
```

Now that you have all the dependencies present, you can start the authentication process.

Authentication

There are three different approaches to obtaining a working set of credentials in GCP:

- The service account using environment variables
- The service account using a JSON file
- The machine account

The first two approaches are the suggested ones in the majority of cases since the third applies only to circumstances where Ansible is run directly within the GCP environment.

The first approach is, once you have created the service account, set the following environmental variables:

- `GCP_AUTH_KIND`
- `GCP_SERVICE_ACCOUNT_EMAIL`

- • GCP_SERVICE_ACCOUNT_FILE
- • GCP_SCOPES

Now, Ansible can use the proper service account.

If you prefer not to use environment variables, you can download a service account file from the GCP interface directly. For convenience's sake, we are going to do this and we are going to save the file as ~/sa.json.

The third approach is by far the easiest since Ansible will be able to auto-detect the machine account if you are running it in a GCP instance.

Creating your first machine

Now that Ansible is able to connect to your GCP environment, you can proceed with the actual Playbook:

1. Create the gce.yaml Playbook with the following content:

```
---
- hosts: localhost
  tasks:
  - name: create a instance
    google.cloud.gcp_compute_instance:
      name: TestMachine
      machine_type: n1-standard-1
      disks:
      - auto_delete: 'true'
        boot: 'true'
        initialize_params:
          source_image: family/centos-stream-9
          disk_size_gb: 10
      zone: eu-west1-c
      auth_kind: serviceaccount
      service_account_file: "~/sa.json"
      state: present
```

2. Execute it with the following command:

```
$ ansible-playbook gce.yaml
```

This will create an output like the following one:

```
PLAY [localhost] ********************************************
***********************************

TASK [Gathering Facts] *************************************
***********************************
```

```
ok: [localhost]

TASK [create a instance] ***************************************
***********************************
changed: [localhost]

PLAY RECAP *********************************************************
***********************************
localhost : ok=2 changed=1 unreachable=0 failed=0 skipped=0
rescued=0 ignored=0
```

As for the AWS example, running a machine in the cloud is very easy with Ansible.

In the case of GCE, you don't need to set up the networks beforehand since the GCE defaults will kick in and provide a functional machine either way.

As for AWS, the list of modules you can use is huge. You can find the full list at `https://docs.ansible.com/ansible/latest/collections/google/cloud/index.html`.

Now that you have learned how to complement GCP with automation, you will learn how to seamlessly perform automation integration with Azure.

Seamless automation integration with Azure

Another global cloud that Ansible can manage is Microsoft Azure.

Azure integration, like AWS integration, requires quite a few steps to be performed in Playbooks.

The first thing you will need to do is set up the authentication so that Ansible is allowed to control your Azure account.

Installation

To let Ansible manage the Azure cloud, you need to install the Azure SDK for Python. Do this by executing the following command:

```
$ pip install -r ~/.ansible/collections/ansible_collections/azure/
azcollection/requirements-azure.txt
```

We can now proceed to install the Azure collection:

```
$ ansible-galaxy collection install azure.azcollection
```

Now that you have all the dependencies present, you can start the authentication process.

Authentication

There are different ways to ensure that Ansible is able to manage Azure for you, based on the way your Azure account is set up, but they can all be configured in the ~/.azure/credentials file.

If you want Ansible to use the principal credentials for the Azure account, you will need to create a file that resembles the following:

```
[default]
subscription_id = [YOUR_SUBSCIRPTION_ID_HERE]
client_id = [YOUR_CLIENT_ID_HERE]
secret = [YOUR_SECRET_HERE]
tenant = [YOUR_TENANT_HERE]
```

If you prefer to use Active Directory with a username and password, you can do something like this:

```
[default]
ad_user = [YOUR_AD_USER_HERE]
password = [YOUR_AD_PASSWORD_HERE]
```

Lastly, you can opt for an Active Directory login with ADFS. In this case, you'll need to set some additional parameters. You'll end up with something like this:

```
[default]
ad_user = [YOUR_AD_USER_HERE]
password = [YOUR_AD_PASSWORD_HERE]
client_id = [YOUR_CLIENT_ID_HERE]
tenant = [YOUR_TENANT_HERE]
adfs_authority_url = [YOUR_ADFS_AUTHORITY_URL_HERE]
```

The same parameters can be passed as parameters or as environmental variables if it makes more sense.

Creating your first machine

Now that Ansible is able to connect to your Azure environment, you can proceed with the actual Playbook:

1. Create the azure.yaml Playbook with the following content:

    ```
    ---
    - hosts: localhost
      tasks:
      - name: Ensure the Storage Account is present
        azure.azcollection.azure_rm_storageaccount:
          resource_group: Testing
          name: mysa
          account_type: Standard_LRS
    ```

```
- name: Ensure the Virtual Network is present
  azure.azcollection.azure_rm_virtualnetwork:
    resource_group: Testing
    name: myvn
    address_prefixes: "10.10.0.0/16"
- name: Ensure the Subnet is present
  azure.azcollection.azure_rm_subnet:
    resource_group: Testing
    name: mysn
    address_prefix: "10.10.0.0/24"
    virtual_network: myvn
- name: Ensure that the Public IP is set
  azure.azcollection.azure_rm_publicipaddress:
    resource_group: Testing
    allocation_method: Static
    name: myip
- name: Ensure a Security Group allowing SSH is present
  azure.azcollection.azure_rm_securitygroup:
    resource_group: Testing
    name: mysg
    rules:
    - name: SSH
      protocol: Tcp
      destination_port_range: 22
      access: Allow
      priority: 101
      direction: Inbound
- name: Ensure the NIC is present
  azure.azcollection.azure_rm_networkinterface:
    resource_group: Testing
    name: mynic
    virtual_network: myvn
    subnet: mysn
    public_ip_name: myip
    security_group: mysg
- name: Ensure the Virtual Machine is present
  azure.azcollection.azure_rm_virtualmachine:
    resource_group: Testing
    name: myvm01
    vm_size: Standard_D1
    storage_account: mysa
    storage_container: myvm01
    storage_blob: myvm01.vhd
```

```
admin_username: admin
admin_password: Password!
network_interfaces: mynic
image:
  offer: CentOS
  publisher: OpenLogic
  sku: '8.4'
  version: latest
```

2. We can run it with the following command:

```
$ ansible-playbook azure.yaml
```

This will return something like the following:

```
PLAY [localhost] *******************************************
*********************************

TASK [Gathering Facts] *************************************
*********************************
ok: [localhost]

TASK [Ensure the Storage Account is present] ***************
*********************************
changed: [localhost]

TASK [Ensure the Virtual Network is present] ***************
*********************************
changed: [localhost]

TASK [Ensure the Subnet is present] ************************
*********************************
changed: [localhost]

TASK [Ensure that the Public IP is set] ********************
*********************************
changed: [localhost]

TASK [Ensure a Security Group allowing SSH is present] *****
*********************************
changed: [localhost]

TASK [Ensure the NIC is present] ***************************
*********************************
changed: [localhost]
```

```
TASK [Ensure the Virtual Machine is present] *******************
***********************************
changed: [localhost]


PLAY RECAP ****************************************************
***********************************
localhost : ok=8 changed=7 unreachable=0 failed=0 skipped=0
rescued=0 ignored=0
```

You now have your machine running in the Azure cloud!

As you can see, in Azure, you will need all the resources to be ready before you can issue the machine creation command. This is the reason you create the storage account, the virtual network, the subnet, the public IP, the security group, and the NIC first, and only at that point, the machine itself.

Outside the three major players in the market, there are many additional cloud options. Many of which, including many private clouds, leverage OpenStack.

Using Ansible to orchestrate OpenStack

As opposed to the various cloud services we just discussed, all of which are public clouds, OpenStack allows you to create your own (private) cloud.

Private clouds have the disadvantage that they expose more complexity to the administrator and the user, but this is the reason they can be customized to suit an organization perfectly.

Installation

The first step to being able to control an OpenStack cluster with Ansible is to ensure that openstacksdk is installed.

To install openstacksdk, you need to execute the following command:

```
$ pip install openstacksdk
```

We can now proceed to install the OpenStack collection:

```
$ ansible-galaxy collection install openstack.cloud
```

Now that you have installed openstacksdk, you can start the authentication process.

Authentication

Since Ansible will use openstacksdk as its backend, you will need to ensure that openstacksdk is able to connect to the OpenStack cluster.

To do this, you can change the `~/.config/openstack/clouds.yaml` file, ensuring that there is a configuration for the cloud you want to use it for.

An example of what a correct OpenStack credentials set could look like is as follows:

```
clouds:
 test_cloud:
 region_name: MyRegion
 auth:
 auth_url: http://[YOUR_AUTH_URL_HERE]:5000/v2.0/
 username: [YOUR_USERNAME_HERE]
 password: [YOUR_PASSWORD_HERE]
 project_name: myProject
```

It's also possible to set a different config file location if you are willing to export the `OS_CLIENT_CONFIG_FILE` variable as an environment variable.

Now that you have set up the required security so that Ansible can manage your cluster, you can create your first Playbook.

Creating your first machine

Since OpenStack is very flexible, many of its components can have many different implementations, which means they may differ slightly in terms of their behavior. To be able to accommodate all the various cases, the Ansible modules that manage OpenStack tend to have a lower level of abstraction compared to the ones for many public clouds.

So, to create a machine, you will need to ensure that the public SSH key is known to OpenStack and ensure that the OS image is present as well. After doing this, you can set up networks, subnetworks, and routers to ensure that the machine we are going to create can communicate via the network. Then, you can create the security group and its rules so that the machine can receive connections (pings and SSH traffic, in this case). Finally, you can create a machine instance.

To complete all the steps just described, you need to create a file called `openstack.yaml` with the following content:

```
---
- hosts: localhost
  tasks:
  - name: Ensure the SSH key is present on OpenStack
    openstack.cloud.keypair:
      state: present
      name: ansible_key
      public_key_file: "{{ '~' | expanduser }}/.ssh/id_rsa.pub"
  - name: Ensure we have a CentOS image
```

```
    ansible.builtin.get_url:
      url: http://cloud.centos.org/centos/9-stream/x86_64/images/
CentOS-Stream-GenericCloud-9-20230424.0.x86_64.qcow2
      dest: /tmp/CentOS-Stream-GenericCloud-9-20230424.0.x86_64.qcow2
  - name: Ensure the CentOS image is in OpenStack
    openstack.cloud.image:
      name: centos
      container_format: bare
      disk_format: qcow2
      state: present
      filename: /tmp/CentOS-Stream-GenericCloud-9-20230424.0.x86_64.
qcow2
  - name: Ensure the Network is present
    openstack.cloud.network:
      state: present
      name: mynet
      external: False
      shared: False
      register: net_out
  - name: Ensure the Subnetwork is present
    openstack.cloud.subnet:
      state: present
      network_name: "{{ net_out.id }}"
      name: mysubnet
      ip_version: 4
      cidr: 192.168.0.0/24
      gateway_ip: 192.168.0.1
      enable_dhcp: yes
      dns_nameservers:
      - 8.8.8.8
  - name: Ensure the Router is present
    openstack.cloud.router:
      state: present
      name: myrouter
      network: nova
      external_fixed_ips:
      - subnet: nova
      interfaces:
      - mysubnet
  - name: Ensure the Security Group is present
    openstack.cloud.security_group:
      state: present
      name: mysg
  - name: Ensure the Security Group allows ICMP traffic
```

```
    openstack.cloud.security_group_rule:
      security_group: mysg
      protocol: icmp
      remote_ip_prefix: 0.0.0.0/0
  - name: Ensure the Security Group allows SSH traffic
    openstack.cloud.security_group_rule:
      security_group: mysg
      protocol: tcp
      port_range_min: 22
      port_range_max: 22
      remote_ip_prefix: 0.0.0.0/0
  - name: Ensure the Instance exists
    openstack.cloud.server:
      state: present
      name: myInstance
      image: centos
      flavor: m1.small
      security_groups: mysg
      key_name: ansible_key
      nics:
      - net-id: "{{ net_out.id }}"
```

Now, you can run it as follows:

```
$ ansible-playbook openstack.yaml
```

The output should be as follows:

```
PLAY [localhost] ************************************************
*****************************

TASK [Gathering Facts] ****************************************
*****************************
ok: [localhost]

TASK [Ensure the SSH key is present on OpenStack] *******************
*****************************
changed: [localhost]

TASK [Ensure we have a CentOS image] *******************************
*****************************
changed: [localhost]

TASK [Ensure the CentOS image is in OpenStack] *********************
*****************************
```

```
changed: [localhost]

TASK [Ensure the Network is present] ********************************
****************************
changed: [localhost]

TASK [Ensure the Subnetwork is present] ****************************
****************************
changed: [localhost]

TASK [Ensure the Router is present] ********************************
****************************
changed: [localhost]

TASK [Ensure the Security Group is present] ************************
****************************
changed: [localhost]

TASK [Ensure the Security Group allows ICMP traffic] ***************
****************************
changed: [localhost]

TASK [Ensure the Security Group allows SSH traffic] ***************
****************************
changed: [localhost]

TASK [Ensure the Instance exists] **********************************
****************************
changed: [localhost]

PLAY RECAP ********************************************************
****************************
localhost : ok=11 changed=10 unreachable=0 failed=0 skipped=0
rescued=0 ignored=0
```

As you can see, this process was longer than the public cloud ones we covered. However, you did get to upload the image that you wanted to run, which is something many clouds do not allow (or allow with very complex processes).

Summary

In this chapter, you learned how to automate tasks, such as managing Docker and Podman containers and managing Kubernetes objects. You also explored the modules that can help you automate cloud environments, such as AWS, GCP, Azure, and OpenStack. You also learned about the different approaches various cloud providers use, including their defaults and the parameters that you will always need to add.

Now that you have an understanding of how Ansible interacts with the cloud, you can immediately start to automate your cloud workflows. Also, remember to check the documentation in the *Further reading* section to take a look at all the cloud modules that Ansible supports and their options.

In the next chapter, you will learn how to troubleshoot and create testing strategies.

Questions

1. Which of the following is NOT a GKE Ansible module?

    A. `google.cloud.gcp_container_cluster`

    B. `google.cloud.gcp_container_node_pool`

    C. `google.cloud.gcp_container_node_pool_info`

    D. `google.cloud.gcp_container_node_pool_count`

    E. `google.cloud.gcp_container_cluster_info`

2. True or false: In order to manage containers in Kubernetes, you need to add `k8s_namespace` in the settings section.

    A. True

    B. False

3. True or false: When working with Azure, instances require a **Network Interface Controller (NIC)** to be able to connect to the network.

    A. True

    B. False

4. True or false: When working with AWS, it's necessary to create a Security Group before creating an EC2 instance.

    A. True

    B. False

Further reading

- More Docker containers: `https://docs.ansible.com/ansible/latest/ collections/community/docker/index.html`

- More Podman modules: `https://docs.ansible.com/ansible/latest/ collections/containers/podman/index.html`

- More Kubernetes modules: `https://docs.ansible.com/ansible/latest/ collections/kubernetes/core/index.html`

- More AWS modules:

  - `https://docs.ansible.com/ansible/latest/collections/amazon/ aws/index.html`

  - `https://docs.ansible.com/ansible/latest/collections/community/ aws/index.html`

- More GCP modules: `https://docs.ansible.com/ansible/latest/collections/ google/cloud/index.html`

- More Azure modules: `https://docs.ansible.com/ansible/latest/collections/ azure/azcollection/index.html`

- More OpenStack modules: `https://docs.ansible.com/ansible/latest/ collections/openstack/cloud/index.html`

12
Troubleshooting and Testing Strategies

In a similar way to any other kind of code, Ansible code can contain issues and bugs. Ansible tries to make it as safe as possible by checking the task syntax before the task is executed. This check, however, only saves you from a small number of possible types of errors, such as incorrect task parameters, but it will not protect you from others.

It's also important to remember that, due to its nature, we describe the desired state in Ansible code rather than stating a sequence of steps to obtain the desired state. This difference means that the system is less prone to logical errors.

Nevertheless, a bug in a playbook could mean a potential misconfiguration on all your machines. This should be taken very seriously. It is even more critical when critical parts of the system are changed, such as SSH daemon or sudo configuration, since the risk is you locking yourself out of the system.

There are many ways to prevent or mitigate a bug in Ansible playbooks. In this chapter, we will cover the following topics:

- Digging into playbook execution problems
- Using host facts to diagnose failures
- Testing with a playbook
- Using check mode
- Solving host connection issues
- Passing working variables via the CLI
- Limiting the host's execution
- Flushing the code cache
- Checking for bad syntax

Technical requirements

This chapter assumes that you have set up your control host with Ansible, as detailed in *Chapter 1, Getting Started with Ansible*, and are using the most recent version available – the examples in this chapter were tested with Ansible 2.9. Although we will give specific examples of hostnames in this chapter, you are free to substitute them with your hostnames and/or IP addresses. Details of how to do this will be provided at the appropriate places.

The examples in this chapter can be found in this book's GitHub repository at `https://github.com/PacktPublishing/Practical-Ansible-Second-Edition/tree/main/Chapter%2012`.

Digging into playbook execution problems

There are cases where an Ansible execution will interrupt. Many things can cause these situations.

The network is the most frequent cause of problems I've found while executing Ansible playbooks. Since the machine issuing the commands and the one performing them are usually linked through the network, a problem in the network will immediately show itself as an Ansible execution problem.

You can tell Ansible to repeat the execution of a task by registering a variable and using the `until` keyword.

Sometimes, and this is particularly true for some modules, such as `ansible.builtin.shell` or `ansible.builtin.command`, the return code is non-zero, even though the execution was successful. In those cases, you can ignore the error by using the following line in your module:

```
ignore_errors: yes
```

For instance, if you run the `/bin/false` command, it will always return 1. To execute this in a playbook so that you can avoid it blocking there, you can write something like the following:

```
- name: Run a command that will return 1
  ansible.builtin.command: /bin/false
  ignore_errors: yes
```

As we have seen, `/bin/false` will always return 1 as the return code, but we still managed to proceed with the execution. Be aware that this is a particular case. Often, the best approach is to fix your application so that you follow UNIX standards and return 0 if the application runs appropriately instead of putting a workaround in your playbooks.

Next, we will talk more about the methods we can use to diagnose Ansible execution problems.

Using host facts to diagnose failures

Some execution failures derive from the state of the target machine. The most common problem of this kind is the case where Ansible expects a file or variable to be present, but it's not there.

Sometimes, it can be enough to print the machine facts to find the problem.

To do so, we need to create a simple playbook called `print_facts.yaml`, which contains the following content:

```
---
- hosts: all
  tasks:
  - name: Display all variables/facts known for a host
    ansible.builtin.debug:
      var: hostvars[inventory_hostname]
```

This technique will give you a lot of information about the state of the target machine during Ansible execution.

Testing with a playbook

One of the most complex things in the IT field is not creating software and systems but debugging them when they have problems. Ansible is no exception. No matter how good you are at creating Ansible playbooks, sooner or later, you'll find yourself debugging a playbook that is not behaving as you thought it would.

The simplest way of performing basic tests is to print out the values of variables during execution. Let's learn how to do this with Ansible:

1. First of all, we need a playbook called `debug.yaml` with the following content:

   ```
   ---
   - hosts: localhost
     tasks:
     - ansible.builtin.shell: /usr/bin/uptime
       register: result
     - ansible.builtin.debug:
         var: result
   ```

2. Run it with the following command:

   ```
   $ ansible-playbook debug.yaml
   ```

   You will receive an output similar to the following:

   ```
   PLAY [localhost] ***********************************************
   **********************************

   TASK [Gathering Facts] *****************************************
   **********************************
   ok: [localhost]
   ```

```
TASK [shell] *********************************************
*********************************
changed: [localhost]

TASK [debug] *********************************************
*********************************
ok: [localhost] => {
    "result": {
        "changed": true,
        "cmd": "/usr/bin/uptime",
        "delta": "0:00:00.003461",
        "end": "2019-06-16 11:30:51.087322",
        "failed": false,
        "rc": 0,
        "start": "2019-06-16 11:30:51.083861",
        "stderr": "",
        "stderr_lines": [],
        "stdout": " 11:30:51 up 40 min, 1 user, load average:
1.11, 0.73, 0.53",
        "stdout_lines": [
            " 11:30:51 up 40 min, 1 user, load average: 1.11,
0.73, 0.53"
        ]
    }
}


PLAY RECAP *********************************************
*********************************
localhost : ok=3 changed=1 unreachable=0 failed=0 skipped=0
rescued=0 ignored=0
```

In the first task, we used the `ansible.builtin.command` module to execute the `uptime` command and saved its output in the `result` variable. Then, in the second task, we used the `ansible.builtin.debug` module to print the content of the `result` variable.

The `ansible.builtin.debug` module is the module that allows you to print the value of a variable (by using the `var` option) or a fixed string (by using the `msg` option) during Ansible's execution.

The `ansible.builtin.debug` module also provides the `verbosity` option. Let's say you change the playbook in the following way:

```
---
- hosts: localhost
  tasks:
```

```
- ansible.builtin.shell: /usr/bin/uptime
  register: result
- ansible.builtin.debug:
    var: result
    verbosity: 2
```

Now, if you try to execute it in the same way you did previously, you will notice that the debug step won't be executed and that the following line will appear in the output instead:

```
TASK [debug] ********************************************************
*****************************
skipping: [localhost]
```

This is because we set the minimum required `verbosity` to 2, and by default, Ansible runs with `verbosity` set to 0.

To see the result of using the debug module with this new playbook, we will need to run a slightly different command:

```
$ ansible-playbook debug2.yaml -vv
```

By putting two `-v` options in the command line, we will be running Ansible with `verbosity` set to 2. This will not only affect this specific module but all the modules (or Ansible itself) that are set to behave differently at different debug levels.

Now that you have learned how to test with a playbook, let's learn how to use check mode.

Using check mode

Although you might be confident in the code you have written, it still pays to test it before running it for real in a production environment. In such cases, it is a good idea to be able to run your code, but with a safety net in place. This is what check mode is for. Follow these steps:

1. First of all, we need to create an easy playbook to test this feature. Let's create a playbook called `check-mode.yaml` that contains the following content:

    ```
    ---
    - hosts: localhost
      tasks:
      - name: Touch a file
        ansible.builtin.file:
          path: /tmp/myfile
          state: touch
    ```

2. Now, we can run the playbook in check mode by specifying the `--check` option in the invocation:

    ```
    $ ansible-playbook check-mode.yaml --check
    ```

    This will output everything as if it were really performing the operation, as follows:

    ```
    PLAY [localhost] ************************************************
    *********************************

    TASK [Gathering Facts] ******************************************
    *********************************
    ok: [localhost]

    TASK [Touch a file] *********************************************
    *********************************
    ok: [localhost]

    PLAY RECAP ******************************************************
    *********************************
    localhost : ok=2 changed=0 unreachable=0 failed=0 skipped=0
    rescued=0 ignored=0
    ```

    However, if you look in `/tmp`, you won't find `myfile`.

Ansible check mode is usually called a dry run. The idea is that the run won't change the state of the machine and will only highlight the differences between the current status and the status declared in the Playbook.

Not all modules support check mode, but all major modules do, and more and more modules are being added at every release. In particular, note that the `ansible.builtin.command` and `ansible.builtin.shell` modules do not support it because the module can't tell what commands will result in a change, and what won't. Therefore, these modules will always return changed when they're run outside of check mode because they assume a change has been made. It is possible to find out whether a specific module supports check mode by looking in the module's documentation, in the *Attributes* section. A similar feature to check mode is the `--diff` flag. A big difference between those two options is that, while check mode will not make changes to the systems, `--diff` will perform the changes on the system! What the `--diff` flag allows us to do is track what exactly changed during an Ansible execution. So, let's say we run the same playbook with the following command:

```
$ ansible-playbook check-mode.yaml --diff
```

This will return something like the following:

```
PLAY [localhost] ************************************************
****************************

TASK [Gathering Facts] ******************************************
****************************
```

```
ok: [localhost]

TASK [Touch a file] *********************************************
****************************
--- before
+++ after
@@ -1,6 +1,6 @@
 {
- "atime": 1560693571.3594637,
- "mtime": 1560693571.3594637,
+ "atime": 1560693571.3620908,
+ "mtime": 1560693571.3620908,
 "path": "/tmp/myfile",
- "state": "absent"
+ "state": "touch"
 }

changed: [localhost]

PLAY RECAP *****************************************************
****************************
localhost : ok=2 changed=1 unreachable=0 failed=0 skipped=0 rescued=0
ignored=0
```

As you can see, the output says `changed`, which means that something was changed (more specifically, the file was created), and in the output, we can see a diff-like output that tells us that the state moved from `absent` to `touch`, which means the file was created. `mtime` and `atime` also changed, but this is probably due to how files are created and checked.

Now that you have learned how to use check mode, let's learn how to solve host connection issues.

Solving host connection issues

Ansible is often used to manage remote hosts or systems. To do this, Ansible will need to be able to connect to the remote host, and only after that will it be able to issue commands. Sometimes, the problem is that Ansible is unable to connect to the remote host. A typical example of this is when you try to manage a machine that hasn't booted yet. Being able to quickly recognize these kinds of problems and fix them promptly will help you save a lot of time.

Follow these steps to get started:

1. Let's create a playbook called `remote.yaml` with the following content:

    ```
    ---
    - hosts: all
    ```

```
        tasks:
      - name: Touch a file
        ansible.builtin.file:
          path: /tmp/myfile
          state: touch
```

2. We can try to run the `remote.yaml` playbook against a non-existent FQDN, as follows:

```
$ ansible-playbook -i host.example.com, remote.yaml
```

In this case, the output will inform us that the SSH service did not reply in time:

```
PLAY [all] *****************************************************
**********************************

TASK [Gathering Facts] *****************************************
**********************************
fatal: [host.example.com]: UNREACHABLE! => {"changed": false,
"msg": "Failed to connect to the host via ssh: ssh: Could not
resolve hostname host.example.com: Name or service not known",
"unreachable": true}

PLAY RECAP ****************************************************
**********************************
host.example.com : ok=0 changed=0 unreachable=1 failed=0
skipped=0 rescued=0 ignored=0
There is also the possibility that we'll receive a different
error:
PLAY [all] ****************************************************
**********************************

TASK [Gathering Facts] *****************************************
**********************************
fatal: [host.example.com]: UNREACHABLE! => {"changed": false,
"msg": "Failed to connect to the host via ssh: fale@host.
example.com: Permission denied (publickey,gssapi-keyex,gssapi-
with-mic).", "unreachable": true}

PLAY RECAP ****************************************************
**********************************
host.example.com : ok=0 changed=0 unreachable=1 failed=0
skipped=0 rescued=0 ignored=0
```

In this case, the host did reply, but we don't have enough access to be able to SSH into it.

SSH connections usually fail for one of two reasons:

- The SSH client is unable to establish a connection with the SSH server
- The SSH server refuses the credentials provided by the SSH client

Due to OpenSSH's very high stability and backward compatibility, when the first issue occurs, it's very probable that the IP address or the port is wrong, so the TCP connection isn't feasible. Very rarely, this kind of error occurs in SSH-specific problems. Usually, double-checking the IP and the hostname (if it's DNS, check that it resolves to the right IP) solves the problem. To investigate this further, you can try performing an SSH connection from the same machine to check whether there are problems. For instance, I would do this like so:

```
$ ssh host.example.com -vvv
```

I've taken the hostname from the error itself to ensure that I'm simulating exactly what Ansible is doing. I'm doing this to ensure that I can see all possible logging messages that SSH can give me to troubleshoot the problem.

The second problem might be a little bit more complex to debug since it can happen for multiple reasons. One of those is that you are trying to connect to the wrong host and you don't have the credentials for that machine. Another common case is that the username is wrong. To debug it, you can take the `user@host` address that is shown in the error (in my case, `fale@host.example.com`) and use the same command you used previously:

```
$ ssh fale@host.example.com -vvv
```

This should raise the same error that Ansible reported to you but with much more detail.

Now that you have learned how to solve host connection issues, let's learn how to pass working variables via the CLI.

Passing working variables via the CLI

One thing that can help during debugging, and definitely helps for code reusability, is passing variables to playbooks via the command line. Every time your application – either an Ansible playbook or any kind of application – receives input from a third party (a human, in this case), it should ensure that the value is reasonable. An example of this would be to check that the variable has been set and therefore is not an empty string. This is a security golden rule, but it should also be applied when the user is trusted since the user might mistype the variable's name. The application should identify this and protect the whole system by protecting itself. Follow these steps:

1. The first thing we want to have is a simple playbook that prints the content of a variable. Let's create a playbook called `printvar.yaml` that contains the following content:

    ```
    ---
    - hosts: localhost
      tasks:
      - ansible.builtin.debug:
          var: variable
    ```

2. Now that we have an Ansible playbook that allows us to see whether a variable has been set to what we were expecting, let's run it with `variable`, which is declared in the execution statement:

```
$ ansible-playbook printvar.yaml --extra-vars='{"variable":
"Hello, World!"}'
```

By running this, we will receive an output similar to the following:

```
PLAY [localhost] ***********************************************
**********************************

TASK [Gathering Facts] *****************************************
**********************************
ok: [localhost]

TASK [debug] ***************************************************
**********************************
ok: [localhost] => {
  "variable": "Hello, World!"
}

PLAY RECAP *****************************************************
**********************************
localhost : ok=2 changed=0 unreachable=0 failed=0 skipped=0
rescued=0 ignored=0
```

Ansible allows variables to be set in various modes and with different priorities. More specifically, you can set them with the following:

- System configuration settings in `/etc/ansible/ansible.cfg` (lowest priority)

- User configuration settings in `~/.ansible.cfg`

- Project configuration in `ansible.cfg` in the current directory

- The `ANSIBLE_CONFIG` environment variable

- Command-line options

- Role defaults

- Inventory files or the `vars` script group

- The `group_vars/all` inventory

- The `group_vars/all` playbook

- The `group_vars/*` inventory

- The `group_vars/*` playbook

- Inventory files or the `vars` script host

- The `host_vars/*` inventory
- The `host_vars/*` playbook
- Host facts/cached `set_facts`
- Play `vars`
- Play `vars_prompt`
- Play `vars_files`
- The `vars` role (defined in `role/vars/main.yml`)
- The `vars` block (only for tasks in the block)
- The `vars` task (only for the task)
- `include_vars`
- `set_facts`/registered vars
- Role (and `include_role`) params
- `include` params
- Command-line extra `vars` (highest priority)

As you can see, the last option (and the highest priority of them all) is using `--extra-vars` (or `-e`) in the execution command.

Now that you have learned how to pass working variables via the CLI, let's learn how to limit the host's execution.

Limiting the host's execution

While testing a playbook, it might make sense to test on a restricted number of machines; for instance, just one. Let's get started:

1. To use the limitation of target hosts on Ansible, we will need a playbook. Create a playbook called `helloworld.yaml` that contains the following content:

    ```
    ---
    - hosts: all
      tasks:
      - ansible.builtin.debug:
          msg: "Hello, World!"
    ```

2. We also need to create an inventory with at least two hosts. In my case, I created a file called `inventory` that contains the following content:

```
[hosts]
host1.example.com
host2.example.com
host3.example.com
```

Let's run the playbook in the usual way with the following command:

```
$ ansible-playbook -i inventory helloworld.yaml
```

By doing this, we will receive the following output:

```
PLAY [all] ***************************************************
***********************************

TASK [Gathering Facts] **************************************
***********************************
ok: [host1.example.com]
ok: [host3.example.com]
ok: [host2.example.com]

TASK [debug] ************************************************
***********************************
ok: [host1.example.com] => {
  "msg": "Hello, World!"
}
ok: [host2.example.com] => {
  "msg": "Hello, World!"
}
ok: [host3.example.com] => {
  "msg": "Hello, World!"
}

PLAY RECAP **************************************************
***********************************
host1.example.com : ok=2 changed=0 unreachable=0 failed=0
skipped=0 rescued=0 ignored=0
host2.example.com : ok=2 changed=0 unreachable=0 failed=0
skipped=0 rescued=0 ignored=0
host3.example.com : ok=2 changed=0 unreachable=0 failed=0
skipped=0 rescued=0 ignored=0
```

This means that the playbook was executed on all the machines in the inventory. If we just want to run it against `host3.example.com`, we will need to specify this on the command line, as follows:

```
$ ansible-playbook -i inventory helloworld.yaml --limit=host3.
example.com
```

To prove that this works as expected, we can run it. By doing this, we will receive the following output:

```
PLAY [all] *********************************************************
***********************************

TASK [Gathering Facts] *********************************************
***********************************
ok: [host3.example.com]

TASK [debug] *******************************************************
***********************************
ok: [host3.example.com] => {
  "msg": "Hello, World!"
}

PLAY RECAP *********************************************************
***********************************
host3.example.com : ok=2 changed=0 unreachable=0 failed=0
skipped=0 rescued=0 ignored=0
```

Before Ansible executes the playbook we mentioned in the command line, it analyzes the inventory to detect which targets are in scope and which are not. By using the `--limit` keyword, we can force Ansible to ignore all the hosts that are outside what is specified in the `limit` parameter.

It's possible to specify multiple hosts as a list or with patterns, so both of the following commands will execute the playbook against `host2.example.com` and `host3.example.com`:

```
$ ansible-playbook -i inventory helloworld.yaml --limit=host2.example.
com,host3.example.com
```

```
$ ansible-playbook -i inventory helloworld.yaml --limit=host[2-3].
example.com
```

The limit will not override the inventory but will add restrictions to it. So, let's say we limit to a host that is not part of the inventory, as follows:

```
$ ansible-playbook -i inventory helloworld.yaml --limit=host4.example.
com
```

Here, we will receive the following error, and nothing will be done:

```
[WARNING]: Could not match supplied host pattern, ignoring: host4.
example.com

ERROR! Specified hosts and/or --limit does not match any hosts
```

Now that you have learned how to limit the host's execution, let's learn how to flush the code cache.

Flushing the code cache

Everywhere in IT, caches are used to speed up operations, and Ansible is no exception.

Usually, caches are good, and for this reason, they are heavily used ubiquitously. However, they might create some problems if they cache a value that should not have been cached or if they are not flushed, even if the value has changed.

Flushing caches in Ansible is very straightforward, and it's enough to run `ansible-playbook`, which we are already running, with the addition of the `--flush-cache` option, as follows:

```
ansible-playbook -i inventory helloworld.yaml --flush-cache
```

Ansible can use multiple cache plugins to save host variables, as well as execution variables. Sometimes, those variables might be left behind and influence the following executions. When Ansible finds a variable that should be set in the step it just started, Ansible might assume that the step has already been completed, and therefore pick up that old variable as if it has just been created. By using the `--flush-cache` option, we can avoid this since it will ensure that Ansible flushes the Ansible facts cache during its execution.

Now that you have learned how to flush the code cache, let's learn how to check for bad syntax.

Checking for bad syntax

Defining whether a file has the right syntax or not is fairly easy for a machine, but this might be more complex for humans. This does not mean that machines can fix the code for you, but they can quickly identify whether a problem is present or not. To use Ansible's built-in syntax checker, we need a playbook with a syntax error. Let's get started:

1. Let's create a `syntaxcheck.yaml` file with the following content:

```
---
- hosts: all
  tasks:
  - ansible.builtin.debug:
    msg: "Hello, World!"
```

2. Now, we can use the `--syntax-check` command:

    ```
    $ ansible-playbook syntaxcheck.yaml --syntax-check
    ```

    By doing this, we will receive the following output:

    ```
    ERROR! 'msg' is not a valid attribute for a Task

    The error appears to be in '/home/fale/ansible/Ansible2Cookbook/
    Ch11/syntaxcheck.yaml': line 4, column 7, but may
    be elsewhere in the file depending on the exact syntax problem.

    The offending line appears to be:

     tasks:
     - debug:
     ^ here

    This error can be suppressed as a warning using the "invalid_
    task_attribute_failed" configuration
    ```

3. We can now proceed to fix the indentation problem on line 4:

    ```
    ---
    - hosts: all
      tasks:
      - ansible.builtin.debug:
          msg: "Hello, World!"
    ```

    When we recheck the syntax, we will see that it now returns no errors:

    ```
    $ ansible-playbook syntaxcheck-fixed.yaml --syntax-check

    playbook: syntaxcheck.yaml
    ```

When the syntax check doesn't find any errors, the output will resemble the previous one, where it listed the files that were analyzed without listing any errors.

Since Ansible knows all the supported options in all the supported modules, it can quickly read your code and validate whether the YAML you provided contains all the required fields and that it does not contain any unsupported fields.

Summary

In this chapter, you learned about the various options that Ansible provides so that you can look for problems in your Ansible code. More specifically, you learned how to use host facts to diagnose failures, how to include testing within a playbook, how to use check mode, how to solve host connection issues, how to pass variables from the CLI, how to limit the execution to a subset of hosts, how to flush the code cache, and how to check for bad syntax.

In the next chapter, you will learn how to get started with Ansible Automation Controller.

Questions

Answer the following questions to test your knowledge of this chapter:

1. True or False: The `ansible.builtin.debug` module allows you to print the value of a variable or a fixed string during Ansible's execution.

   A. True

   B. False

2. Which keyword allows Ansible to force limit the host's execution?

   A. `--limit`

   B. `--max`

   C. `--restrict`

   D. `--force`

   E. `--except`

Further reading

Ansible's official documentation about error handling can be found at `https://docs.ansible.com/ansible/latest/playbook_guide/playbooks_error_handling.html`.

13
Getting Started with Ansible Automation Controller

Ansible is very powerful, but it does require the user to use the CLI. In some situations, this is not the best option, such as in cases where you need to trigger an Ansible job from another job (where APIs would be better) or in cases where the person that should trigger a job should only be able to trigger that specific job. For these cases, AWX and Ansible Automation Controller are the best options to use.

The only differences between AWX and Ansible Automation Controller are that AWX is the upstream and open source version, while Ansible Automation Controller is the Red Hat and downstream component that is officially supported as part of the Ansible Automation Platform but for a price, and also the delivery method. AWX is available as a Kubernetes Operator that can run on any Kubernetes cluster, while Ansible Automation Controller is either installable via the Kubernetes Operator on a Red Hat OpenShift installation or on an RHEL 8.2+ machine, at the time of writing. In this chapter, we will use AWX and talk about AWX, but everything we will discuss also applies to Ansible Automation Controller.

The following topics will be covered in this chapter:

- Installing AWX
- Running your first playbook from AWX:
    - Creating an AWX project
    - Creating an inventory
    - Creating a job template
    - Running a job
- Controlling access to AWX:
    - Creating a user
    - Creating a team

- Creating an organization
- Assigning permissions in AWX

Technical requirements

Although there are a couple of ways to install AWX, we are going to use the suggested AWX installation, which is the operator-based one. For this reason, you will need to have a Kubernetes cluster available.

The easiest way to have one on your machine is to use minikube.

On Linux machines, it is enough to download it from GitHub (`https://github.com/kubernetes/minikube`) and run it with the following command:

```
minikube start --cpus=4 --memory=6g --addons=ingress
```

In the next section, we will use the `kubectl` command. To have it available using minikube, you will need to execute the following:

```
alias kubectl="minikube kubectl --"
```

On other operating systems, the process might be different, and I suggest checking minikube's official documentation (`https://minikube.sigs.k8s.io/docs/start/`) to see which installation method better suits your platform and needs.

Although we will give specific examples of hostnames in this chapter, you are free to substitute them with your own hostname and/or IP address; details of how to do this will be provided at the appropriate places.

Installing AWX

Before we discuss AWX, it is best if you have it installed on your machine so that you can follow the explanations and immediately start to use AWX.

The easiest way to install AWX Operator is using Kustomize.

We will need to create a file called `kustomization.yaml` with the following content:

```yaml
---
apiVersion: kustomize.config.k8s.io/v1beta1
kind: Kustomization
resources:
  - github.com/ansible/awx-operator/config/default?ref=2.3.0
images:
  - name: quay.io/ansible/awx-operator
    newTag: 2.3.0
namespace: awx
```

Note that version 2.3.0 is the most current at the time of writing. To find out which is the latest available version, go to `https://github.com/ansible/awx-operator/releases`.

Now that we have the kustomization file ready, we can apply it with the following command:

```
kubectl apply -k .
```

Once the previous command has finished, we shall be able to see the AWX Operator controller manager pod running:

```
$ kubectl get pods -n awx
NAME                                                    READY    STATUS
RESTARTS      AGE
awx-operator-controller-manager-23f4d5a324-hdk2x        2/2      Running
0             7s
```

We can now create the `awx.yaml` file with the following content:

```
---
apiVersion: awx.ansible.com/v1beta1
kind: AWX
metadata:
  name: awx
spec:
  service_type: nodeport
```

We can now edit the `kustomization.yaml` file to add the reference to the `awx.yaml` file. By doing so, we will obtain the following result:

```
---
apiVersion: kustomize.config.k8s.io/v1beta1
kind: Kustomization
resources:
  - github.com/ansible/awx-operator/config/default?ref=2.3.0
  - awx.yaml
images:
  - name: quay.io/ansible/awx-operator
    newTag: 2.3.0
namespace: awx
```

We can now apply the new configuration file:

```
$ kubectl apply -k .
```

Now, run the following commands to see that everything worked properly:

```
$ kubectl get pods -n awx -l "app.kubernetes.io/managed-by=awx-
operator"
```

```
NAME                          READY     STATUS     RESTARTS   AGE
awx-43a2624db1-hjw3e          4/4       Running    0          4m01s
awx-postgres-0                1/1       Running    0          4m11s

$ kubectl get svc -n awx -l "app.kubernetes.io/managed-by=awx-
operator"
NAME              TYPE        CLUSTER-IP     EXTERNAL-IP    PORT(S)
       AGE
awx-postgres      ClusterIP   None           <none>         5432/TCP
       4m14s
awx-service       NodePort    10.100.81.35   <none>         80:32754/TCP
   4m04s
```

Be aware that you may need to wait a few minutes before AWX is completely deployed and all the pods are running.

Once AWX has been fully deployed, it is possible to open a browser and connect to the AWX service. To obtain the URL, you can execute the following command:

```
$ minikube service -n awx awx-service -url
```

The default administration username is admin. To find the password, you will need to execute the following command:

```
$ kubectl get secret -n awx awx-admin-password -o jsonpath="{.data.
password}" | base64 --decode ; echo
```

Now that you have learned the necessary steps to install AWX, let's take a look at how to create a project in AWX.

Running your first playbook from AWX

As in Ansible, in AWX, the goal is running an Ansible playbook. Each playbook that is run is called a **job**. Since AWX gives you more flexibility and automation than Ansible, it requires a little bit more configuration before you can run your first job, so let's dive into it, starting with creating an AWX project.

Creating an AWX project

AWX uses the term **project** to identify a repository of Ansible playbooks. AWX projects support the placement of playbooks in all major **Source Control Management** (**SCM**) systems, such as Git and SVN, but also support playbooks on the filesystem or playbooks provided by Red Hat Insights. To create a project, follow these steps:

1. First of all, you need to go to **Projects** from the left-hand side menu bar, then click the **Add** button in the top-left section of the screen. This will open a window, similar to the following:

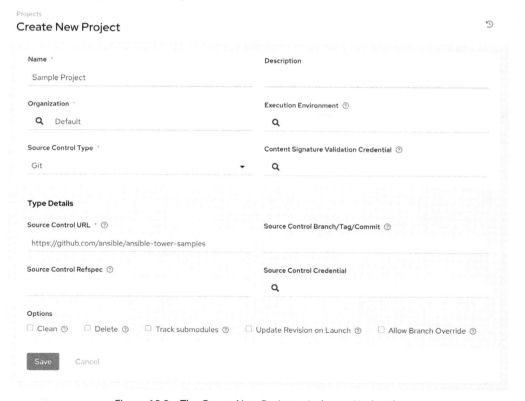

Figure 13.1 – The Create New Project window

2.   By filling in the name (`Sample Project`) and selecting **Git** for **Source Control Type**, the window will grow with new parameters:

Figure 13.2 – The Create New Project window – Git details

3. You can now add the SCM URL (`https://github.com/ansible/ansible-tower-samples`) and click the **Save** button, which should now be clickable.

As we mentioned at the beginning of this section, projects are used to store and use Playbooks in AWX. As you can imagine, there are many interesting additional configurations for AWX projects – the most interesting one, in my view, is `Update Revision on Launch`.

If flagged, this option instructs Ansible to always update the playbook's repository before running any playbook from that project. This ensures that it always executes the latest version of the playbook. This is an important feature to enable as, if you don't have it checked, there is the possibility (and sooner or later, this will happen in your environment) that someone notices that there is a problem in a playbook and fixes it, and then they run the playbook, feeling sure that they are running the latest version. They then forget to run the synchronization task before running the playbook, effectively running the older version of the playbook. This could lead to major problems if the previous version was fairly buggy.

The downside of using this option is that every time you execute a playbook, two playbooks are effectively run, adding time to your task execution. I think this is a very small downside and one that does not offset the benefits of using this option.

With that, you have learned the necessary steps to create a project in AWX (and Ansible Automation Controller). Now, let's learn how to create an inventory.

Creating an inventory

As with Ansible Core, to make AWX aware of the machines present in your environment, we can use inventories. Inventories, in the AWX world, are not that different from their equivalents in Ansible Core.

Let's learn how to create our first inventory in AWX by following these steps:

1. Click on the **Inventory** option in the left-hand side menu bar. You will be redirected to the **Inventory** window, where you can create your first inventory by clicking the **Add** button in the top-left section of the screen. This is different from when we created a new project as this button does not immediately open the creation form; first, it will ask you whether you want to create an inventory or a smart inventory.

2. After choosing the **Inventory** option, a box similar to the following will appear:

Inventories
Create new inventory

Name *
Sample Inventory

Description

Organization *
🔍 Default

Instance Groups
🔍

Labels ⓘ

Options
☐ Prevent Instance Group Fallback ⓘ

Variables ⓘ [YAML] [JSON]

1 - - -

[Save]   Cancel

Figure 13.3 – The Create new inventory window

3. In this window, you need to set a name and then save it. After you have clicked **Save**, the **Permissions**, **Groups**, **Hosts**, **Sources**, and **Completed Jobs** tabs will become clickable so that you can continue with the configuration.

Since an empty inventory is not useful in any way, we are going to add `localhost` to it.

4. To do this, select the **Hosts** tab, then click on the button with a white plus sign on a green background at the top left of the screen. This will open a window, as follows:

Inventories > Sample Inventory > Hosts
Create new host

Name *
localhost

Description

Variables [YAML] [JSON]

```
1  - - -
2  ansible_connection: local
3  ansible_python_interpreter: '{{ ansible_playbook_python }}'
```

[Save]   Cancel

Figure 13.4 – The Create new host window

5. We then need to add the hostname (`localhost`) and instruct Ansible to use the local connection by adding the following code to the **Variables** box:

```
---
ansible_connection: local
ansible_python_interpreter: '{{ ansible_playbook_python }}'
```

6. We can now click **Save**, saving our inventory.

In AWX, an inventory is something very similar to an Ansible Core inventory, but with additional features, such as built-in dynamic inventory support, which means you don't need to edit configuration files or install additional Python modules. To enable this, simply go to the **Sources** tab within an inventory to choose to auto-populate the inventory with information from a source of truth, such as a public cloud provider inventory (**Amazon Web Services (AWS)**, Azure, and **Google Cloud Platform (GCP)** are all supported), a private cloud inventory (such as VMware or OpenStack), or other systems, such as Red Hat Satellite or a custom script.

A special note about the inventory sources is that the **Sourced from a Project** option provides a form such as the following if chosen:

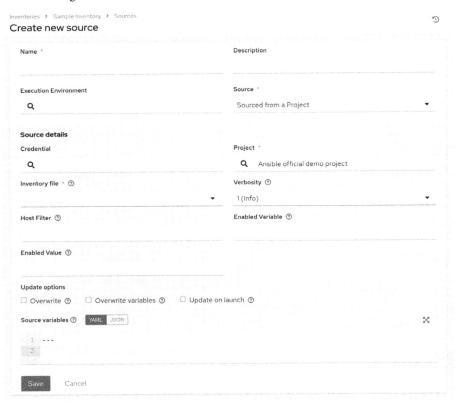

Figure 13.5 – The Create new source window

This is a very interesting feature, in my opinion, since it allows the user to check a dynamic inventory script of their design into a Git repository (either in its own repository or one where you also put in playbooks) and AWX pulls that information from the repository.

As for projects, when you add a source to your inventory, you might choose to select the **Update on launch** option, which behaves in the same way as the **Update on launch** option behaves for projects. For the same reasons that were discussed in the *Creating an AWX project* section, I strongly suggest that you use this option as well.

At the very beginning of the inventory creation process, we had the option to add an inventory or a smart inventory. What is a smart inventory? **Smart inventories** are inventories that are populated by AWX, starting from the hosts present in other inventories, and are filtered using the specific smart host filter that the user selected during creation. This can be incredibly useful for dynamically creating inventories with a specific type of host in them based on a filter and saves the need for manually creating lots of different groups – or worse, having to add the same host multiple times.

With that, you have learned the necessary steps to create an inventory in AWX. Now, let's learn how to create a job template.

Creating a job template

Now that we have the playbooks in our projects and the hosts in our inventories, we can start creating a **job template**.

A job template in AWX is a collection of the configurations that are needed to perform a job. This is very similar to the `ansible-playbook` command-line options. The reason why we need to create a job template is so that playbook runs can be launched with little or no user input, meaning they can be delegated to teams who might not know all the details of how a playbook works, or can even be run on a scheduled basis without anyone present. Let's take a look:

1. First of all, you need to click the **Templates** option from the left-hand side menu bar.

2. You can now create a new template by clicking the **Add** button at the top left of the screen. It will ask you whether you want to create a job template or a workflow template – you need to choose **Job template**. The following window will appear:

Templates
Create New Job Template

Name *

Hello World

Description

Job Type * ⑦   ☐ Prompt on launch

Run   ▾

Inventory * ⑦   ☐ Prompt on launch

Q   Sample Inventory

Project * ⑦

Q   Sample Project

Execution Environment ⑦   ☐ Prompt on launch

Q

Playbook * ⑦

hello_world.yml   ▾

Credentials ⑦   ☐ Prompt on launch

Q

Labels ⑦   ☐ Prompt on launch

▾

Variables ⑦   YAML JSON   ☐ Prompt on launch   ⤢

```
1  - - -
2
```

Forks ⑦   ☐ Prompt on launch

0

Limit ⑦   ☐ Prompt on launch

Verbosity ⑦   ☐ Prompt on launch

0 (Normal)   ▾

Job Slicing ⑦   ☐ Prompt on launch

1

Timeout ⑦   ☐ Prompt on launch

0

Show Changes ⑦   ☐ Prompt on launch

◯ Off

Instance Groups ⑦   ☐ Prompt on launch

Q

Job Tags ⑦   ☐ Prompt on launch

▾

Skip Tags ⑦   ☐ Prompt on launch

▾

Options

☐ Privilege Escalation ⑦   ☐ Provisioning Callbacks ⑦   ☐ Enable Webhook ⑦   ☐ Concurrent Jobs ⑦

☐ Enable Fact Storage ⑦   ☐ Prevent Instance Group Fallback ⑦

Save   Cancel

Figure 13.6 – The Create New Job Template window

As you can see, there are quite a few fields in this view. The only information needed to proceed is the name (we are going to use `Hello World`), the inventory (we are going to choose `Sample Inventory`, which we created in the *Creating an inventory* section), the project (we are going to choose the `Sample Project` project we created in the *Creating an AWX project* section), and the playbook (we are going to choose `hello_world.yml`, which is the only playbook available).

Then, we can click **Save**. Note that because we are running it using the local connection to `localhost`, we don't need to create or specify any credentials. However, if you were running a job template against one or more remote hosts, you would need to create a machine credential and associate it with your job template. A machine credential is, for example, an SSH username and password or an SSH username and a private key – these are stored securely in the backend database of AWX, meaning you can delegate playbook-related tasks to other teams without actually giving them passwords or SSH keys.

The first thing we had to choose was whether we were creating a job template or a workflow template. We chose **Job Template** since we want to be able to create simple jobs out of this template. It's also possible to create more complex jobs, which are the composition of multiple job templates, with flow control features between one job and the next. This allows for more complex situations and scenarios where you might want to have multiple jobs (such as creating an instance, customizing a company, setting up Oracle Database, setting up a MySQL database, and so on), but you also want to have a one-click deployment that would, for instance, set up the machine, apply all the company customization, and install the MySQL database.

You might also have another deployment that uses the same components except the last one, and in its place, it uses the Oracle Database to create an Oracle Database machine. This allows you to have extreme flexibility and reuse a lot of components, creating multiple, nearly identical playbooks.

It's interesting to note that many fields in the **Job Template** creation window have an option with the **Prompt on launch** caption. This allows you to set this value optionally while creating the job template but also allows the user running the job to enter/override it at runtime. This can be incredibly valuable when you have a field that changes on each run (perhaps the `limit` field, which operates in the same way as `--limit` when used with the `ansible-playbook` command) or can also be used as a sanity check, as it prompts the user with the value (and gives them a chance to modify it) before the playbook is run. However, it could potentially block scheduled job runs, so exercise caution when enabling this feature.

Now that you have learned the necessary steps to create a job template in AWX, let's learn how to create a job.

Running a job

A job, as its name suggests, is an instance of a job template. This means that to perform any action on our machine, we have to create a job template instance – or, more simply, a job – by following these steps:

1. Now that we have set the job template, we can run the job itself. To do so, we need to go to **Templates** from the left-hand side of the page.

2.   Find the job template you want to run (in our case, this is going to be `Hello World`) and click on the little rocket on the right-hand side of the page that corresponds to the correct job template, as shown in the following screenshot:

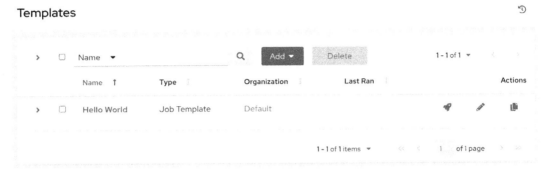

Figure 13.7 – Templates list window

When a job is running, AWX allows us to follow the job's execution in the job's output, as shown in the following screenshot:

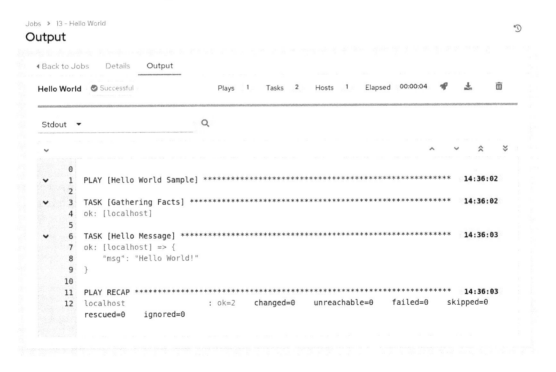

Figure 13.8 – Job output window

3. By clicking the **Details** tab, we can see additional details about the job:

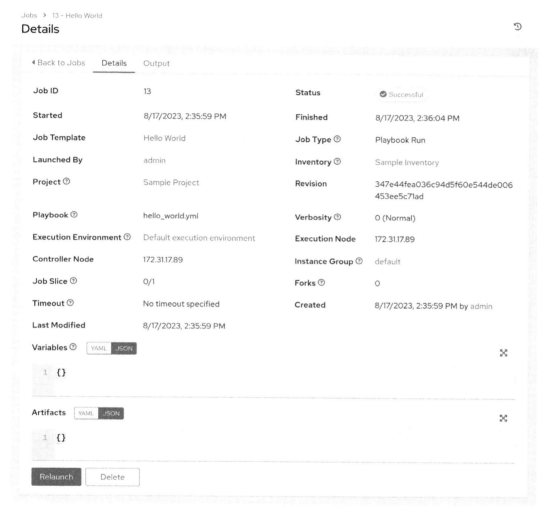

Figure 13.9 – The Details window

One of the great things about AWX and Ansible Automation Controller is that they archive this job's execution output in the backend database, meaning that, at any point in the future, you can come back and query a job run to see what changed and what happened. This is incredibly powerful and useful for occasions such as auditing and policy enforcement.

Now that you have learned the necessary steps to create a job in AWX, let's learn how to create a user.

Controlling access to AWX

In my opinion, one of the biggest advantages of AWX compared to Ansible is the fact that AWX allows multiple users to connect and control/perform actions. This allows a company to have a single AWX installation for different teams, a whole organization, or even multiple organizations.

A **role-based access control (RBAC)** system is in place to manage the users' permissions.

Both AWX and Ansible Automation Controller can link to central directories, such as **Lightweight Directory Access Protocol (LDAP)** and Azure Active Directory – however, we can also create user accounts locally on the AWX server itself. Let's start by creating our first user account locally!

Creating a user

One of the big advantages of AWX is the ability to manage multiple users. This allows us to create a user in AWX for each person that is using the AWX system so that we can ensure they are only granted the permissions that they need. Also, by using individual accounts, we can ensure that we can see who carried out what action by using the audit logs. To create a user, follow these steps:

1. Go to the left-hand side menu bar and select the **Users** option.

2. You will see the list of users and also create a new one by clicking on the button with a white plus sign on a green background at the top-left side of the screen. A form similar to the following will appear:

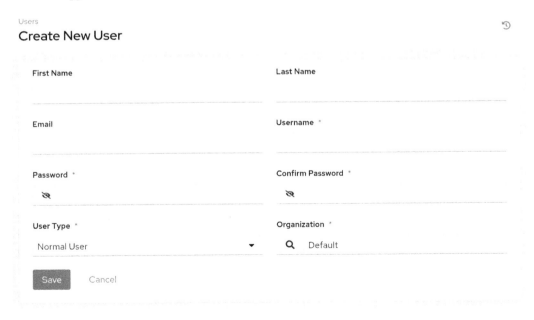

Figure 13.10 – The Create New User window

By adding an email address, username, and password (with confirmation), you can create a new user.

Users can be of three types:

- **A normal user**: Users of this type do not have any inherited permissions and they need to be awarded specific permissions to be able to do anything
- **A system auditor**: Users of this type have full read-only privileges on the whole AWX installation
- **A system administrator**: Users of this type have full privileges on the whole AWX installation

Now that you have learned the necessary steps to create a user in AWX, let's have a brief look at teams.

Creating a team

Although having individual user accounts is an incredibly powerful tool, especially for enterprise use cases, it would be extremely inconvenient and cumbersome to have to set permissions for each object (such as a job template or an inventory) on an individual basis. Every time someone joins a team, their user account has to be manually configured with the correct permissions against every object and, similarly, be removed if they leave.

AWX and Ansible Automation Controller have the same concept of user grouping that you would find in most other RBAC systems. The only slight difference is that in the user interface, they are referred to as **teams**, rather than groups. However, you can create teams simply and easily and then add and remove users as you need to. Doing this through the user interface is very straightforward and you will find the process similar to the way that most RBAC systems handle user groups, so we won't go into any more specific details here.

When you go to **Teams** and click the **Add** button, you will see an interface similar to the following, prompting you to provide some very basic information:

Teams

Create New Team

Name *

Description

Organization *

Q   Default

Save   Cancel

Figure 13.11 – The Create New Team window

Once you have your teams set up, I recommend that you assign your permissions to teams, rather than through individual users, as this will make managing AWX object permissions much easier as your organization grows. Speaking of organizations, let's take a look at the concept of organizations in AWX.

Creating an organization

Sometimes, you will have multiple independent groups of people that you need to manage independent machines. For those kinds of scenarios, the use of organizations can help you. An organization is a tenant of AWX, with its own unique user accounts, teams, projects, inventories, and job templates – it's almost like having a separate instance of AWX! To create an organization, you need to follow these steps:

1. To create a new organization, you need to go to the left-hand side of the screen and select the **Organizations** option.

2. You can then see the existing organizations and proceed to create a new one by clicking on the button with a white plus sign on a green background in the top-left section of the screen.

   A window similar to the following will appear:

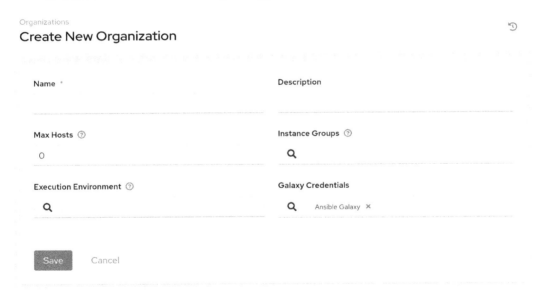

Figure 13.12 – The Create New Organization window

Since the only mandatory field is **Name**, you can just fill this in and click **Save**.

Once you've created the organization, you can assign any kind of resource to an organization, such as projects, templates, inventories, users, and so on. Organizations are a simple concept to grasp but also powerful in terms of segregating roles and responsibilities in AWX. Finally, before we complete this section, let's take a look at assigning permissions in AWX.

Assigning permissions in AWX

Through our journey of configuring our first project, inventory, and job template in AWX, you will have noticed that most of the screens we have navigated to have a button on them called **Access**. As we navigate the user interface with the administrator account, we get to see all the options – but of course, you would not want to give every single user administrator permission.

Individual users (or the teams that they belong to) can be granted permission on a per-object basis. So, for example, you could have a team of database administrators who only have access to see and execute playbooks on an inventory of database servers, using job templates that are specific to their role. Linux system administrators could then have access to the inventories, projects, and job templates that are specific to their role. AWX hides objects that users don't have privileges to access, which means the database administrators never see the Linux system administrator objects, and vice versa.

There are several different privilege levels that you can award to users (or teams), including the following:

- **Admin**: Users that have this permission can change all aspects of the resource
- **Execute** (only for job templates): Users that have this permission can run the job template
- **Use**: Users that have this permission can use the resource in a job template
- **Update**: Users that have this permission can update the resource
- **Read**: Users that have this permission can view the settings of the resource

That concludes our brief look at RBAC in AWX and our look at this powerful tool. AWX is a great addition to the power of Ansible in an enterprise setting and helps ensure that your users can run Ansible playbooks in a manner that is well-managed, secure, and auditable. We have only scratched the surface in this chapter, but hopefully, this chapter has given you a flavor of how AWX can help your team's or enterprise's automation journey.

Summary

AWX and Ansible Automation Controller are powerful, complementary tools that powerfully support the use of Ansible in an enterprise or team-based environment. They can help secure credentials that you would otherwise have to distribute widely, audit the history of playbook runs, and enforce the version control of playbooks. The web-based user interface of these tools creates a low barrier for entry for end users, meaning playbook runs can easily be delegated to teams who otherwise have little knowledge of Ansible (so long as suitable escalation paths are put in place should problems arise). In short, when implementing Ansible in a corporate setting, its usage should not be considered complete without the addition of Ansible Automation Controller or AWX.

In this chapter, you learned how to install AWX on your Linux host, as well as the necessary steps to run your very first playbook from AWX. You also learned about RBAC in AWX and how this can support large, multi-user environments in a corporate setting.

In the next chapter, we will deep dive into the concept of execution environments, which allow you to streamline your automation and keep it functioning even when you're updating Ansible, AWX, or Ansible Automation Controller.

Questions

Answer the following questions to test your knowledge of this chapter:

1. Which objects can you create in Ansible Automation Controller?

    A. Users

    B. Jobs

    C. Job templates

    D. Modules

    E. Projects

2. True or false? AWX is the upstream version of Red Hat Ansible Automation Controller:

    A. True

    B. False

14
Execution Environments

We have seen how Ansible Automation Controller enables you to scale your automation by leveraging an easy-to-use web interface, RBAC, and logging to allow other people to use the automation in a way that conforms to your company's rules.

In this chapter, we will discuss execution environments, a feature of Ansible that was released a few years ago, but it is critical to create automation that lasts. More specifically, we're going to cover the following main topics:

- The importance of execution environments
- Building an execution environment
- Running playbooks in an execution environment
- Uploading execution environments to a container registry
- Using execution environments in the automation controller

Technical requirements

To follow this chapter's examples, you will need `ansible-builder` version 3.0 or later.

Ansible Builder requires Python 3.8 or higher, which you probably have already installed on your system.

The easiest way to install `ansible-builder` is to use PyPi:

```
$ pip install ansible-builder
```

The importance of execution environments

The first question you might have is, why do we need an execution environment in the first place?

There are three reasons why execution environments can simplify your life:

- They allow better scalability by being distributed to multiple machines
- They allow you to freeze all dependencies to specific versions so that you can run the same playbook in five years, with the certainty that it will run exactly as you expect
- They allow you to use different ones for different playbooks so that you can decide when to upgrade each playbook runtime, independently from the others

So, how do execution environments achieve all this? They do so by leveraging containers. In fact, execution environments are containers that contain at least the Ansible runner and the required libraries to run. In addition, execution environments might also include an Ansible collection and many other components that are needed to run your automation.

Now that we have understood the importance of execution environments, let's look at how to build your first execution environment.

Building an execution environment

To create an execution environment, we will need a definition file. There are three versions of the definition file, and based on the version of `ansible-builder`, some versions might not be available to you. Let's be more specific:

- **Version 1**: Supported by all `ansible-builder` versions
- **Version 2**: Supported by `ansible-builder` versions 1.2 and higher
- **Version 3**: Supported by `ansible-builder` versions 3.0 and higher

Since version 3 of the definition is the easiest to learn and use, all examples will use this version.

We will start with a minimal example and then build on it.

Creating a minimal execution environment

To create an execution environment, we need to create a YAML file. By default, `ansible-builder` will be looking for the file named `execution-environment.yml`. Although different names can be used and `ansible-builder` can be informed using the `-f FILENAME` flag, we will stick with the default name in this book.

We will, therefore, create the `minimal/execution-environment.yml` file with the following content:

```
---
version: 3
```

```
images:
  base_image:
    name: quay.io/centos/centos:stream9

dependencies:
  ansible_core:
    package_pip: ansible-core==2.15.1
  ansible_runner:
    package_pip: ansible-runner==2.3.3
```

Before running it, I want to go through it so that it is clear what every line does.

The first line is the YAML file starter (- - -).

The second line (version: 3) declares that the file is written following the third version of the execution environment definition file. This is important to specify because if it is absent, the default is version 1, which is very different from version 3.

We then see the images block. In this block, we can define the base_image, using the name key to indicate the full container name and tag. Both the container's name and tag are required. In our case, we will use CentOS Stream 9 as a base image.

Lastly, we find the dependencies block. This block allows us to define what ansible-builder should add to the image. Even though we will see that we can use this section for much more than what we used it for in this example, we always need to define ansible_core and ansible_runner.

We are now ready to enter the minimal folder and run ansible-builder to build the image:

```
$ cd minimal
$ ansible-builder build --tag minimal-ee
```

We expect the following result if everything went as expected:

```
Running command:
  podman build -f context/Containerfile -t minimal-ee context
Complete! The build context can be found at: /home/fale/minimal/
context
$
```

Congratulations! You have just built your first Ansible execution environment!

Before starting to use the execution environment, we will see how to build more complex execution environments.

Creating an execution environment with a specific Python interpreter

We have seen how to create an execution environment based on CentOS Stream 9 with just Ansible and Ansible Runner.

As you surely know by now, Ansible is written in Python, as are the majority of Ansible modules. In our previous example, the default Python was installed (3.9), which is great for the majority of cases. However, some modules or libraries might require a specific version of Python, so in those cases, we will need to instruct `ansible-builder` to install the Python version we want forcefully.

To do so, we can create the `python/execution-environment.yml` file with the following content:

```
---
version: 3

images:
  base_image:
    name: quay.io/centos/centos:stream9

dependencies:
  python_interpreter:
    package_system: python3.11
    python_path: /usr/bin/python3.11
  ansible_core:
    package_pip: ansible-core==2.15.1
  ansible_runner:
    package_pip: ansible-runner==2.3.3
```

As you can see, we added a `python_interpreter` directive in the `dependencies` section, and we specified that we want the `python3.11` package installed from the system's package manager (`dnf`, in our case). We also specified what the path of the installed binary will be to ensure that Ansible will use this version and not other versions that might be present in the image.

We are now ready to enter the `python` folder and run `ansible-builder` to build the image:

```
$ cd python
$ ansible-builder build --tag python-ee
```

We expect the following result if everything went as expected:

```
Running command:
  podman build -f context/Containerfile -t python-ee context
Complete! The build context can be found at: /home/fale/python/context
$
```

Congratulations! You have just created your first execution environment with Python 3.11! Let's now explore how we can add additional dependencies.

Creating an execution environment with additional dependencies

There are many different ways to add a dependency on a regular system. In the same way, we will be able to add different kinds of dependencies in execution environments.

The three ways we can install dependencies in the execution environments are as follows:

- `python`: This option allows you to install Python dependencies from PyPi
- `system`: This option allows you to install dependencies from an operating system
- `galaxy`: This option allows you to install Ansible dependency from Ansible Galaxy

Although it is possible to pass dependencies files, it is usually preferable to put them directly inline so that the whole description of the execution environment is in a single file and is easier to follow.

Let's suppose we want to create an execution environment that has a couple of collections (`ansible.utils` and `community.windows`) and the `ping` command. In this case, we can create a `dependencies/execution-environment.yml` file with the following content:

```yaml
---
version: 3
images:
  base_image:
    name: quay.io/centos/centos:stream9

dependencies:
  ansible_core:
    package_pip: ansible-core==2.15.1
  ansible_runner:
    package_pip: ansible-runner==2.3.3
  python:
    - pywinrm
  system:
    - iputils [platform:rpm]
  galaxy:
    collections:
      - community.windows
      - ansible.utils
```

As you can see, we added the following:

- The Python `pywinrm` package, which is required by `community.windows`
- The `iputils` package via RPM, which provides the `ping` command
- The `community.windows` collection that we wanted
- The `ansible.utils` collection that we wanted

We can now proceed to enter the `dependencies` folder and build the execution environments as we did previously:

```
$ cd dependencies
$ ansible-builder build --tag dependencies-ee
```

We expect the following result if everything went as expected:

```
Running command:
  podman build -f context/Containerfile -t dependencies-ee context
Complete! The build context can be found at: /home/fale/ dependencies/
context
$
```

You have now built an execution environment that can be used for more complex playbooks!

Our exploration of the execution environments descriptor file ends here, but you can refer to the official documentation to discover all available options.

Running playbooks in an execution environment

Now that we have explored how to create execution environments, we can start using them. The first thing we will do is check the Ansible and Python versions.

To execute commands and Playbooks in execution environments, we can use `ansible-navigator`. To install it, we can execute `$ pip install ansible-navigator`.

The equivalent of the `ansible --version` command in the `minimal-ee` is the following:

```
$ ansible-navigator exec --eei minimal-ee -- ansible --version
```

As you can see, the biggest difference is the addition of `--eei minimal-ee`, which tells `ansible-navigator` which execution environment image to use, and running it will return the following:

```
ansible [core 2.15.1]
  config file = /etc/ansible/ansible.cfg
  configured module search path = ['/tmp/.ansible/plugins/modules', '/
usr/share/ansible/plugins/modules']
```

```
  ansible python module location = /usr/local/lib/python3.9/site-
packages/ansible
  ansible collection location = /tmp/.ansible/collections:/usr/share/
ansible/collections
  executable location = /usr/local/bin/ansible
  python version = 3.9.16 (main, Mar  7 2023, 00:00:00) [GCC 11.3.1
20221121 (Red Hat 11.3.1-4)] (/usr/bin/python3)
  jinja version = 3.1.2
  libyaml = True
```

Now, we can run the same command for the Python execution environment:

```
$ ansible-navigator exec --eei python-ee -- ansible --version
```

This will result in the following:

```
ansible [core 2.15.1]
  config file = /etc/ansible/ansible.cfg
  configured module search path = ['/tmp/.ansible/plugins/modules', '/
usr/share/ansible/plugins/modules']
  ansible python module location = /usr/local/lib/python3.11/site-
packages/ansible
  ansible collection location = /tmp/.ansible/collections:/usr/share/
ansible/collections
  executable location = /usr/local/bin/ansible
  python version = 3.11.2 (main, Feb 16 2023, 00:00:00) [GCC 11.3.1
20221121 (Red Hat 11.3.1-4)] (/usr/bin/python3.11)
  jinja version = 3.1.2
  libyaml = True
```

As you can see, the Ansible version is the same, since we required the same version while creating the two images. Conversely, the Python version differs, since in the Python execution environment, we force version 3.11, while in the minimal one, we used the default one (3.9).

Similarly, we can execute Ansible playbooks as well. Firstly, we will need a playbook, and for this example, we will create a very simple ping one:

```
---
- name: Test connection
  hosts: all
  tasks:
    - name: Test connection
      ansible.builtin.ping:
```

We will also need a straightforward `inventory` file with just `localhost`:

```
localhost ansible_connection=local
```

We can now proceed with the execution command:

```
$ ansible-navigator run ping.yml -i inventory --eei minimal-ee -m
stdout
```

As you have probably already predicted, the result is very similar to what we would have if the command was executed outside execution environments:

```
PLAY [Test connection] **********************************************
*********

TASK [Gathering Facts] **********************************************
***********
ok: [localhost]

TASK [Test connection] **********************************************
***********
ok: [localhost]

PLAY RECAP ******************************************************************
***********
localhost                  :
ok=2     changed=0    unreachable=0    failed=0     skipped=0
rescued=0     ignored=0
```

Although it is possible to use execution environments in this way, they are usually uploaded to a container registry and used from AWX or Ansible Controller.

In the next section, we will see how to upload those execution environments to a container registry.

Uploading execution environments to a container registry

As discussed, execution environments are packaged in the container image format to allow more flexibility. This means that we can upload an execution environment to any container registry. In enterprise settings, Ansible Automation Hub is usually used, since it is a tool very similar to Ansible Galaxy that can be installed in the private company network, and it hosts Ansible collections and execution environments. Companies often prefer Ansible Automation Hub, since it integrates a lot of nice features, such as synchronization with Ansible Galaxy. If you have an Ansible Automation Hub available, you can use it to follow the following steps. Otherwise, you can use any other container registry.

I will use `quay.io`, but the same steps apply to any other container registry.

Ensure your Podman is properly logged into your container registry of choice. You can use `podman login` to perform the login if you are not logged in yet.

The first thing to do is to find the image ID of the image we want to push. To do so, we can run this:

```
$ podman images | grep python-ee
```

The output will be something like the following:

```
localhost/python-ee 1.0 66b2c181df45 21 hours ago 292 MB
```

The third column is the image ID, so we can instruct Podman to push it to our container registry:

```
$ podman push 66b2c181df45 quay.io/$USERNAME/python-ee
```

Once the execution has finished, you can go to the container registry and check that the image arrived as expected.

We are now ready to use this execution environment image in our AWX or Ansible Automation Controller.

Using execution environments in Ansible Automation Controller

Using Ansible execution environments in Ansible Automation Controller is very straightforward, since it always uses an execution environment while executing Playbooks. The only difference is whether it is the default execution environment or the one that you built and specified.

The first thing we will need to do is add a new execution environment to Ansible Automation Controller or AWX. To do so, you need to go to execution environments in the navigation bar in the **Administration** section, and then click on the **Add** button. You can now fill in the name and the image URL and select **Always pull container before running.** as the **Pull** option, as follows:

Execution Environments
Create new execution environment

Name *

Python-EE

Image * ⑦

quay.io/fale/python-ee:latest

Pull

Always pull container before running.   ▼

Description

Organization

🔍

Leave this field blank to make the execution environment
globally available

Registry credential ⑦

🔍

Save   Cancel

Figure 14.1 – Creating a new execution environment window

After saving the execution environment by pressing **Save**, you can go to **Templates** in the navigation bar under **Resources** and create a new job template, or modify the one you already have. Once you are on the **Job Template** edit or create page, you can set the execution environment as follows:

Figure 14.2 – The field to choose an execution environment in the job template

You can now save the job template and execute it. This time, it was executed in the execution environment we created!

Summary

We started this chapter by seeing why execution environments can help you to create a more resilient automation solution in your environment. We then moved on to a more practical section in which you created multiple execution environments, firstly a minimal one, then one with a customized version of Python, and finally, one with some collections and other dependencies embedded. We then used those execution environments locally using `ansible-navigator`. We then uploaded them to a container registry and used them from Ansible Automation Controller or AWX.

We have now reached the end of this book, since this is the last chapter, and I would like to thank you for reading the entire book. I hope that it has taught you what you initially hoped to learn about Ansible, and more!

Questions

1. Ansible uses the standard container image format for execution environments:

    A. True

    B. False

2. Which of the following is an advantage of Ansible execution environments?

    A. They run Ansible playbooks without Ansible

    B. They guarantee the exact versions of Ansible, the dependencies, and the collections on every run

    C. They increase performance

3. What is the latest execution environment definition version?

    A. 1

    B. 2

    C. 3

    D. 4

Further reading

*   Ansible Builder documentation: `https://ansible.readthedocs.io/projects/builder/en/stable/usage/`

*   Ansible Navigator documentation: `https://ansible.readthedocs.io/projects/navigator/`

*   Execution environment version 3 specification: `https://ansible.readthedocs.io/projects/builder/en/stable/definition/#version-3-format`

Assessments

Chapter 1

1. A, B
2. C
3. A

Chapter 2

1. C
2. B
3. A

Chapter 3

1. E
2. C
3. A

Chapter 4

1. C
2. A
3. B

Chapter 5

1. D
2. E
3. A

Chapter 6

1. B
2. C
3. A

Chapter 7

1. D
2. A
3. A

Chapter 8

1. D
2. A
3. B

Chapter 9

1. C
2. A
3. A

Chapter 10

1. D
2. A
3. A

Chapter 11

1. D
2. B
3. A
4. B

Chapter 12

1. A
2. A

Chapter 13

1. A,B,C,E
2. A

Chapter 14

1. A
2. B
3. C

Index

www.packtpub.com

Subscribe to our online digital library for full access to over 7,000 books and videos, as well as industry leading tools to help you plan your personal development and advance your career. For more information, please visit our website.

Why subscribe?

- Spend less time learning and more time coding with practical eBooks and Videos from over 4,000 industry professionals

- Improve your learning with Skill Plans built especially for you

- Get a free eBook or video every month

- Fully searchable for easy access to vital information

- Copy and paste, print, and bookmark content

Did you know that Packt offers eBook versions of every book published, with PDF and ePub files available? You can upgrade to the eBook version at www.packtpub.com and as a print book customer, you are entitled to a discount on the eBook copy. Get in touch with us at customercare@packtpub.com for more details.

At www.packtpub.com, you can also read a collection of free technical articles, sign up for a range of free newsletters, and receive exclusive discounts and offers on Packt books and eBooks.

Other Books You May Enjoy

If you enjoyed this book, you may be interested in these other books by Packt:

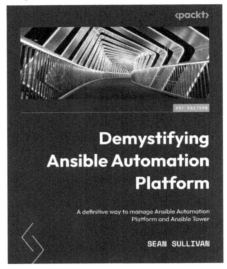

Demystifying Ansible Automation Platform

Sean Sullivan

ISBN: 978-1-80324-488-4

- Get the hang of different parts of Ansible Automation Platform and their maintenance
- Back up and restore an installation of Ansible Automation Platform
- Launch and configure basic and advanced workflows and jobs
- Create your own execution environment using CI/CD pipelines
- Interact with Git, Red Hat Authentication Server, and logging services
- Integrate the Automation controller with services catalog
- Use Automation Mesh to scale Automation Controller

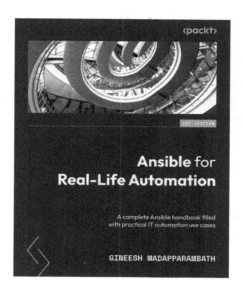

Ansible for Real-Life Automation

Gineesh Madapparambath

ISBN: 978-1-80323-541-7

- Explore real-life IT automation use cases and employ Ansible for automation
- Develop playbooks with best practices for production environments
- Approach different automation use cases with the most suitable methods
- Use Ansible for infrastructure management and automate VMWare, AWS, and GCP
- Integrate Ansible with Terraform, Jenkins, OpenShift, and Kubernetes
- Manage container platforms such as Kubernetes and OpenShift with Ansible
- Get to know the Red Hat Ansible Automation Platform and its capabilities

Packt is searching for authors like you

If you're interested in becoming an author for Packt, please visit authors.packtpub.com and apply today. We have worked with thousands of developers and tech professionals, just like you, to help them share their insight with the global tech community. You can make a general application, apply for a specific hot topic that we are recruiting an author for, or submit your own idea.

Share your thoughts

Now you've finished *Practical Ansible - Second Edition*, we'd love to hear your thoughts! Scan the QR code below to go straight to the Amazon review page for this book and share your feedback or leave a review on the site that you purchased it from.

https://packt.link/r/180512997X

Your review is important to us and the tech community and will help us make sure we're delivering excellent quality content.

Download a free PDF copy of this book

Thanks for purchasing this book!

Do you like to read on the go but are unable to carry your print books everywhere?

Is your eBook purchase not compatible with the device of your choice?

Don't worry, now with every Packt book you get a DRM-free PDF version of that book at no cost.

Read anywhere, any place, on any device. Search, copy, and paste code from your favorite technical books directly into your application.

The perks don't stop there, you can get exclusive access to discounts, newsletters, and great free content in your inbox daily

Follow these simple steps to get the benefits:

1. Scan the QR code or visit the link below

https://packt.link/free-ebook/9781805129974

2. Submit your proof of purchase
3. That's it! We'll send your free PDF and other benefits to your email directly

www.ingramcontent.com/pod-product-compliance
Lightning Source LLC
Chambersburg PA
CBHW060650060326
40690CB00020B/4579